Children's Writer
Guide to 2001

Editor: Susan M. Tierney

Contributing writers:
Marilyn D. Anderson
Myrtle Archer
Marnie Brooks
Toni Buzzeo
Pat Conway
Vicki Hambleton
Lisa Harkrader
Mark Haverstock
Jean Lewis
Suzanne Lieurance
Catherine Frey Murphy
Mary C. Northrup
Darcy Pattison
Ruth Sachs
Pegi Deitz Shea
Katherine Swarts
Carolyn P. Yoder

Cover art: Carole Marchese
Profile portraits: Joanna Horvath

Copy editor: Cheryl de la Guéronnière

Editorial and research assistants:
Pat Conway
Joanna Horvath
Marni McNiff

Publisher: Prescott V. Kelly

Copyright © Institute of Children's Literature® 2001. All rights reserved. The material contained herein is protected by copyright. Quotations up to 40 words are permitted when *Children's Writer Guide to 2001* is clearly identified as the source. Otherwise, no part of *Children's Writer Guide to 2001* may be republished, copied, reproduced, or adapted without the express written permission of the Institute of Children's Literature, 93 Long Ridge Road, West Redding, CT 06896-0811.

1-800-443-6078. www.writersbookstore.com
e-mail: services@writersbookstore.com

Printed and bound in Canada.

Table of Contents

Publishing 2001

Book Publishing, A Year for the Books	7
New Ventures, New Editor for Carus: Marc Aronson	15
Expansion at The Millbrook Press: Simon Boughton	17
Something Old, Something New: Justin Rood	26
A Life in Nonfiction: Frank Sloan	29
A Record Year in Magazines, Something for Everyone	33
A Living Past: Charles & Rosalie Baker	47
The Big Picture: Keith Garton	51
Online Markets, Go Internet, Young Writers	55
Regional Markets, In Your Own Backyard	65
Book Markets, A Rich Stock of Early Readers	77
Publishing News, A Banner Year	87

Submissions & Style

Dramatic Writing, Study Plays & Write Better Fiction	99
Publishing Awards, In Recognition of Tradition & Exploration	111
Speak Up: Laurie Halse Anderson	123
Judging YA: Frances B. Bradburn	126
Taking His Time: Christopher Paul Curtis	128
A Cinderella Moment: Kimberly Willis Holt	131
A Work of Art: Simms Taback	134
Style Check, Quantify Your Writing	137

Business & Career

Book Proposals, A Crack in the Door	151
Market Research, Scope Out the Competition	159
Contracts, Keeping Your Fair Share	165
Payment, Business Partners at Work	173
Promotion, Author Visits: Hope, Expect, Ensure	187

Reference & Research

Researching People, The Power of Our Family Stories	201
Researching Place, Location, Location, Location	209
Researching Cultures, A Kaleidoscopic Voyage Around the World	217
Reference Sites, Museums Online	229
Sources, References: In Print & Online	237

Idea Generation
Moving Ideas, Stuck in the Middle Again — 259
Surefire Ideas, How to Find More Topics Than You Can Write About — 265
Ideas, A Start with Statistics — 269
Competitive Ideas, What's Out There? — 283

Agent, Contest, & Conference Listings
Agents — 293
Writers' Contests & Awards — 305
Writers' Conferences — 347
  Conferences Devoted to Writing for Children — 347
    General Conferences — 347
    Society of Children's Book Writers & Illustrators — 350
  Conferences with Sessions on Writing for Children — 355
    University or Regional Conferences — 355
    Religious Writing Conferences — 364

Indexes
Subject Index — 369
Name Index — 384
Title Index — 390

Publishing 2001

Book Publishing
A Year for the Books
By Vicki Hambleton

"It was the summer children's books gained respectability," says Jean Reynolds, Editorial Director of Millbrook Press. Respectability, oddly enough, marked by midnight parties where wizards (alias costumed salespeople) entertained hordes of eager book buyers.

It was the year business boomed.

Hundreds of people across the country, many under the age of 10, lined up in the middle of a July night to buy a book. Parents brought cameras to record the moment their little Harry or Hermione appeared at the front of the store beaming, if staggering, under the weight of a newly released 734-page *Harry Potter and the Goblet of Fire*, the fourth book in the J.K. Rowling series. The book broke all sales records in its first weekend and immediately went back to press for another three million copies. "It was a true breakthrough for the industry," says Reynolds.

Four children's books—the four Potter books—held spots on best-seller lists simultaneously, when it is rare to have even one make the list. On July 23, 15 days after *Goblet of Fire*'s debut, the *New York Times* published its first ever list of children's best-sellers. The list combines fiction, nonfiction, chapter, and picture books.

Children's editors at houses large and small are smiling at sales figures. "We're feeling very bullish," says Susan Katz, President and Publisher of HarperCollins Children's Books, "and we just hope it keeps up!"

1 + 1 = 3

"My sense," says Katz, "is that when the economy is good, as it is now, people have money to spend. Harry Potter has been great for all of us in that it has gotten more people into bookstores and in the children's section. People who have other children in their lives bought Harry Potter and something for the other kids as well." Katz reports that HarperCollins's sales are up 12 percent over the preceding year. "With the exception of Scholastic, we have the largest growth of any children's publisher."

Katz notes in particular that sales figures for many classic backlist books are much higher than their usual numbers. "*Goodnight Moon, Charlotte's Web, Stuart Little*, and the *Chronicles of Narnia* all did extremely well for us," she says.

Scholastic made big news not just in what it sold, but in what it bought:

The Numbers

Numbers from booksellers were certainly up, even before the latest chapter in the Harry Potter phenomenon. The four largest bookstore chains, Barnes & Noble, Borders Group, Books-a-Million, and Crown Books reported sales increases of 8.4 percent. Amazon.com reported quarterly sales of $1.3 billion, as compared to $588 million in the previous year. Total revenues for the book publishing industry rose 4.3 percent to just over $24 billion in sales, according to a report from the Association of American Publishers. The best performing category was children's books, with revenues over $1 billion. Hardcover sales were up 11.1 percent and paperbacks, 23.5 percent.

Grolier. Everyone in the children's publishing world sat up and took notice when the two giants in the school and library market combined forces. Scholastic purchased Grolier from the French company Lagardére S.C.A. for $400 million in cash.

Hugh Roome, Executive Vice President at Scholastic, thinks the acquisition makes both companies stronger. "Our thought is that sometimes when you put two companies together, one and one equals three," he explains. "We think this is one of those rare moments." The two seem a well-matched pair. Grolier is the leading direct mail-to-home and e-commerce book club for children up to the age of six. It is also a leading trade publisher, through the Franklin Watts, Children's Press, and Orchard Books imprints, and it is the leading publisher of online reference materials for the young.

Scholastic's Chairman and CEO, Richard Robinson, says, "Grolier's direct-to-the-home business provides access to millions of parents of children under the age of six who Scholastic can transition to our products for the 6-to-12-year-old market."

"Despite the fact that they are our competition, we cheer them on," says Millbrook's Reynolds, "but at the same time, anyone has to be a little intimidated by the thought of Scholastic's wonderful marketing machine being applied to a list like Franklin Watts."

In another massive deal, the world's largest educational publisher, Pearson, purchased DK Publishing (Dorling Kindersley) for $500 million. The Pearson umbrella covers the Penguin Group and Pearson Education, as well as large holdings in Europe. The Penguin imprints include Avery, Berkley Books, Dutton, Plume, Putnam, Riverhead, and Viking in the U.S. and in the UK, Allen Lane, Frederick Warne, Hamish Hamilton, Ladybird, Michael Joseph, Puffin, and Viking. Pearson Education includes Addison Wesley Longman, Allyn & Bacon, Scott Foresman and Prentice Hall School, and Macmillan USA, among others.

McGraw-Hill Company also announced an agreement to acquire Tribune Education from the Tribune Company for $634 million. The units included in the deal are The Wright Group, NTC/Contemporary Publishing, Everyday Learning/Creative Publications, Instructional Fair Group, and Londoll, Inc. All produce materials for

Just Spinning

Along with the Harry Potter steamroller, another media machine helped Scholastic's sales enormously: Leading the paperback frontlist were Pokémon tie-ins from Scholastic and Golden Books. Seven of the top ten spots on the best-seller list went to Pokémon. Sales for the books exceeded $7 million.

"Our biggest revenue producer at Scholastic paper has been Pokémon," says Craig Walker, Vice President and Editorial Director of Scholastic Paperbacks. "We continue to make our biggest impact on the market with our digest novelizations. That is the part of the Pokémon license that we have and that is what we do best." Walker adds that the company is moving into other areas of licensing for book tie-ins because, he explains, "We personally don't believe in movies so much anymore." Still, Scholastic is banking on success from a spin-off series from the movie *The Sixth Sense*. "We realized how popular the movie was with kids: I mean it is a great ghost story and kids love ghost stories. Our books will all have original story lines."

Another spin-off is a series based on the popular television show *Malcolm in the Middle*. "We have always wanted to do good humorous stuff," says Walker, "and good humor is hard to find."

One company learned the hard way that movie tie-ins are not a guarantee. Dorling Kindersley (DK) bet the farm on the latest *Star Wars* movie, which as one insider puts it "was here today and gone today." The movie was a disappointment despite all the hype surrounding it and when it fizzled, DK suffered a 50 percent plunge in the price of its stock and put itself on the auction block.

the education and consumer markets.

Other publishing unions included a deal between Random House and Disney for Random House to publish books in a variety of formats for young readers based on Disney properties and characters. Random House has plans for publishing hundreds of Disney titles annually, including novelty books, early reader books, and storybooks. The new publishing program went into effect in January 2001.

Simon & Schuster's imprint Simon Spotlight is launching a new line of children's books in association with the Public Broadcasting Service (PBS). The first books are based on the animated television series for preschoolers called *Zoboomafoo*.

Simon & Schuster also has a new leader at the helm of its Children's Books division. Kristina Petersen was named President of the Children's Publishing Division. The announcement was made by President and CEO of Simon & Schuster, Jack Romanos. Romanos describes Petersen as "one of the most savvy and experienced executives in any precinct of our industry. She joins a division that has in the last five years doubled its sales." Petersen had been President of the Random

Books with the Year's Top Honors

For a close look at the award winners of the past year, see "Publishing Awards, In Recognition of Tradition & Exploration," page 111, but here is a brief look at the kinds of books receiving accolades today.

"It's funny, how ideas are, in a lot of ways, they're just like seeds. Both of them start real, real small and then . . . they've gone and grown a lot bigger than you ever imagined."

So says the main character, a 10-year-old orphan boy, in Christopher Paul Curtis's Newbery Medal 2000 book, *Bud, Not Buddy* (Delacorte Press). It is the story of a boy in Depression-era Michigan who sets out on a journey to find a man he thinks might be the father that he has never met. Along the way he meets many wonderful characters who tell the story of a time long ago, and who also become the family Bud is looking for.

Other books that won or were nominated for awards this year echo Bud's words. They are all books about individuals who learn something about their lives, but these books that caught the eyes of reviewers and publishers tell rich stories about many cultures, both past and present. All depict strong emotions that transcend time and nationality.

The Caldecott Medal for this year went to illustrator Simms Taback for *Joseph Had a Little Overcoat* (Viking Children's Books). The book uses an old Yiddish song to look at a way of life that has almost disappeared, and a time when clothing was so precious that it would be used again and again until it fell apart. Transferring the moral of the story to life, the author illustrates how "you can always make something out of nothing."

Stories from different parts of the world also took top honors in the National Book Award's Young People's Literature category. Contemporary India is the setting for the award winner, *Homeless Bird*. Gloria Whelan's book is the

---

House Media Group since 1998.

Many well-known children's publishers have entered into new agreements that will lead them into new territories and broaden their audience share. All agree that given favorable sales numbers and with the foundation of a strong economy, the time is right to try something new.

Pleasant Company, publisher of books and American Girl magazine, has added a new character to its American Girls Collection: Kit, a girl growing up in the Great Depression. The company has also added new books to its History Mysteries, AG Fiction, and Wild at Heart lines. Pleasant Company Editorial Director Judith Woodburn said last year, "Our future publishing agenda includes entering the world of acquisitions," and enter it they did. The company re-introduced *Angelina Ballerina*, star of a series of picture books for three-to-seven-year-old read-

Books with the Year's Top Honors

story of a young girl wed and widowed at 13. Koly learns to deal with her country's traditions and expectations, and to make her own future anyway.

Adam Bagdasarian's *Forgotten Fire* (Melanie Kroupa Books), a first novel, is based on the experience of the author's great uncle during the Armenian Genocide in Turkey in 1915.

In *Many Stones* (Front Street), author Carolyn Coman tells of a 16-year-old who learns of her sister's brutal death while volunteering at a school in Capetown, South Africa, and travels with her estranged father to her sister's memorial. The story is about that painful journey, and the journey of a country trying to become whole.

The Book of the Lion, by Michael Cadnum and published by Viking Children's Books, transports readers to the harsh world of the Crusades of the twelfth century. The nominated book follows the adventures of a 17-year-old apprentice who learns about compassion and courage.

The final nominee for the National Book Award is based on the real-life stories of African Americans who went to California during the Gold Rush. *Hurry Freedom!*, by Jerry Stanley (Crown Books), is the first book for young readers that explores the lives of these black pioneers, who sought not only riches, but freedom, on the journey West.

If the themes of these National Book Award nominees seem harsh, they are, in that they take on the struggles of the real world. But the books are also full of humor, excitement, and simple human experience. They are quite simply good stories. And if Taback's and Curtis's titles are any indication, they will also sell well. *Bud, Not Buddy* sold out in Borders the week after it won the Newbery. Three months after the Caldecott was announced, the number of copies of *Joseph Had a Little Overcoat* increased its copies from 30,000 to 170,000.

ers. In a licensing deal with HIT Entertainment PLC, American Girl will re-release five of nine existing Angelina titles as well as a brand new title and two activity books.

The company known to millions of girls also went after an audience of boys this year. Pleasant Company launched Matchbox Books for boys age three and up, tied to the classic Matchbox car brand. Each 12-page board book comes with a car or truck attached to it. Eight titles were launched with an initial printing of 1.2 million.

Nonfiction Upturn

The Millbrook Press also had a phenomenal year, with the company's Snappy Pop-up books reaching the million copy mark in sales, and because, "Nonfiction seemed to be the hot trend at the International Reading Association (IRA) meeting this year," says Reynolds. "We have been in a down-

The Latest Titles from Best-Selling Authors

Picture Books:

■ Fans of Laura Numeroff's *If You Give a Mouse a Cookie* were thrilled with the release of *If You Take a Mouse to the Movies* (HarperCollins). Numeroff's books, illustrated by Felicia Bond, have sold more than 4 million copies.

■ From Houghton Mifflin Books for Children, comes a newly discovered story by H.A. Rey and Margaret Rey, authors of the beloved Curious George books, called *Whiteblack the Penguin Sees the World*.

■ Rosemary Wells is back with another story about the rabbit Max, *Max Cleans Up* (Viking).

■ Babar is back in a new adventure in *Babar and the Succotash Bird* (Abrams), by Laurent de Brunhoff, whose father was the author of the original Babar books.

Middle-grade Fiction

■ The eagerly awaited next book in the Golden Compass series from Philip Pullman was *The Amber Spyglass* (Knopf).

■ Laurence Yep published *Dream Soul* (HarperCollins).

■ Little, Brown published two posthumous novels from Matt Christopher, the king of sports stories, *Wheel Wizards*, co-authored by Robert Hirschfeld, and *Skateboard Renegade*, co-authored by Paul Mantell.

■ From Phyllis Naylor Reynolds came *A Spy Among the Girls* (Delacorte).

■ Delacorte also published a new book by Katherine Ayers, *Silver Dollar*.

■ Patricia Reilly Giff's *Nory Ryan's Song* tells a story set in the nineteenth-century Irish Famine, also called the Great Hunger (Delacorte).

■ Karen Cushman's latest story about a medieval girl is *Matilda Bone* (Houghton Mifflin).

Young Adult Fiction

■ Francesca Lia Block's *The Rose and the Beast* offers fairy tales in contemporary Los Angeles (HarperCollins).

■ *The Beet Fields: A Sixteenth Summer* (Bantam Doubleday Dell) is Gary Paulsen's powerful new autobiographical novel.

■ An allegory about high school, *Stargirl* (Knopf) is Jerry Spinelli's latest.

■ M.E. Kerr's newest novel is a small-town saga, *What Became of Her*, (HarperCollins).

■ *Give a Boy a Gun* (Simon & Schuster), by Todd Strasser, is immediately reminiscent of stories in the news and encourages thought and action on school violence.

ward trend, I'd say, for the last 10 years, really the longest trough we have ever been in. The fact that we are pulling out of such a dive is very heartening. I think this last year was a good one for every publisher in the nonfiction market in particular."

Frank Sloan, until recently the Publishing Director of Raintree/Steck-Vaughn, agrees. "This is a great time for nonfiction publishers. The economy is strong and libraries seem to have more money to spend on books." (See the profile of Frank Sloan, page 29.)

"After some years of steady buying, librarians are now actively looking to enhance their collections beyond the core collection," says John Selfridge of Grolier Press. "I would also venture to say that in an age where truth often gives way to spin, readers are increasingly interested to get to the bottom of what really happened and understand that truth can only be got to by comparing multiple sources that take diverse approaches to historical detail."

That desire to get to the bottom of things is reflected in the growing popularity of books that rely on original source material. Marcia Marshall at Atheneum notes that young readers have what she describes as a hunger for detail. "It's the minute details that make history become real—that history is real people and it's also about what ordinary people have done." Marshall cites Betsy Kuhn's *Angels of Mercy: The Army Nurses of World War II*.

Another area growing in popularity is geography and maps. "Geography is coming back," notes Stephen Reginald, Editor in Chief at Chelsea House Publishers. "Geography and map skills are big right now and getting more attention in school curriculums."

Geography was a big topic at the book fair last spring in Bologna, and that interest has come to fruition in titles from a variety of publishers. Atheneum published its *Mapping the World*, by Sylvia A. Johnson. At Blackbirch, a fall offering was *The Blackbirch Kid's Almanac of Geography*, by Alice Siegel and Margo McLoone. Scholastic published *The Scholastic Atlas of the United States*, by David Rubel. The most unusual slant, perhaps, was in Simon & Schuster's *My America: A Poetry Atlas of the United States*, edited by Lee Bennett Hopkins and featuring poems that pay tribute to American landmarks and history.

Art books were also in the picture. "We do a series called Masters of Art," notes Peter Bedrick, Publisher of Peter Bedrick Books. "The books are basically about art, but they also delve deeply into the settings of the times, and the culture that is reflected in a given period's art and artists." A new Bedrick title is *The Sistine Chapel: Its History and Masterpieces,* by Vittorio Giuduci, for ages 10 and up. For a slightly younger artist-to-be, eight-to-nine-year-olds, Children's Press listed *Giotto* and *Marc Chagall* in the Getting to Know the World's Greatest Artists series. From HarperCollins Children's Books, author Diane Stanley has two books for age seven and up: *Leonardo da Vinci*, and *Michelangelo*.

While for many years Millbrook exclusively published nonfiction, it is expanding in many directions now. Thanks in part to its strong showing last year, the company announced plans to launch a new imprint. Millbrook currently publishes young adult material under its Twenty-First Century imprint and prekindergarten to grade six titles under the Millbrook name. The as yet unnamed imprint will have a separate staff.

"Our future plans call for the establishment of a major fiction and picture book line—very, very upscale picture books and fiction for the elementary through young adult readers," explains Reynolds. "We are a nonfiction publisher and yet fiction and picture books represent a huge percentage of the children's market. We thought, 'Why are we restricting ourselves this way?' If we do it as well as we do nonfiction we should be able to do very well."

Adventures in Fiction

Another company looking to spread its wings is Candlewick, the U.S. imprint of British publisher Walker and Company. Candlewick publishes fiction and nonfiction for children and adults. Walker announced that it plans to invest $7 million in growing and expanding Candlewick. The company opened a satellite office in Manhattan that, among other things, will produce novelty and character books. Candlewick has plans to publish between 90 and 100 U.S.-originated titles each year.

If the fictional character Harry Potter was the name on every child's lips last July, his popularity has had a ripple effect on books for middle-grade readers. Young readers anxious for more bought up adventure and fantasy titles in record numbers too. Two titles that did particularly well were by British author Eva Ibbotson. *The Secret of Platform 13* had a respectable printing in hardcover when it was released, but the paperback edition went back for eight printings and sold more than 90,000 copies. The paperback edition of *Which Witch?* sold more than 36,000 copies in its first year.

"The success of Rowling's books has, I think, made all children's books more credible," says Sloan. "With the creation of the *New York Times* bestseller list, I think children's books will get a lot more attention than ever before." Craig Walker, Vice President and Editorial Director of Scholastic Paperbacks, agrees: "The overall interest in Harry Potter and the traffic that it has brought to all of us in the industry is wonderful."

Middle-graders all, perhaps as parents hold their collective breath, become teenagers, and the size of the current middle-grade population is causing interest in the young adult category. "We are thinking that YA is a strong area for the future," says Katz. "Our books are doing very, very well and, in fact, we are expanding our YA list this year. The books we are publishing seem to be exceeding our sales projections and our sales projections are based on what would make a book profitable and successful."

In fiction, tough, edgy stories are still selling well. Gary Paulsen, Todd Strasser, Jerry Spinelli, and Francesca Lia Block and others have such books on the latest lists (see sidebar, "The Latest Titles from Best-Selling Authors," page 12), as does first-time novelist Patricia McCormick, whose *Cut* (Front Street Books) is about a girl being treated for self-mutilation. Nonfiction

New Ventures, New Editor for Carus: Marc Aronson

2000 was a landmark year for Carus Publishing: the purchase of Cobblestone Publishing, a new imprint, and plans for two or more new magazines. To coordinate the new nonfiction ventures, Carus hired editor and author Marc Aronson. His official title is Vice President for Content Development and Editorial Director. Aronson had been Senior Editor at Henry Holt and Company's Books for Young Readers, where he directed the Edge Books, a young adult imprint.

"The heart of the list I am going to be creating," at Carus, says Aronson, "is the same kind of books I acquired and edited for Edge Books. Many of the books will be geared towards the older teen, but not all. The list will follow my own sensibility. The single keynote that I look for is great writing backed by exceptional thinking." He will not accept "standard books that meet standard needs." It is also apparent that Aronson wants the imprint to be unlike any other. "The list will feature everything from picture books to books written by college professors, like the one I did at Holt on mixed race in America. I am looking for exceptional books, for a fresh voice for nonfiction that goes places people have not talked about."

Aronson will divide his time between New York and the Carus offices in Chicago, where he will oversee the nonfiction magazines *Muse* and *Click*. On the drawing board is a nonfiction magazine for 7-to-11-year-olds to be edited by Judy O'Malley, who joined Carus from *Book Links*. Aronson also hopes to expand the role of nonfiction magazines through the Cobblestone publications. "As our relationship with Cobblestone grows I imagine doing nonfiction books that coordinate with the magazines. If we develop a relationship with a writer on one of the magazines, we'll be in a position to go from magazine to book easily." Aronson cautions writers: "The bar is very high. I do publish some first authors, but their work must be truly exceptional."

Aronson will continue to write his own essays and books. His published titles include *Art Attack: A Short Cultural History of the Avant-Garde* (Clarion), which *Booklist* called passionate and ambitious, and *Sir Walter Ralegh and the Quest for El Dorado*. Published by Houghton Mifflin, the book has been lauded for its research, wit, and, once again, passion. Aronson's knowledge and fervor for good writing are much welcomed by the Carus group. Marianne Carus describes the new Editorial Director as " an exciting man, full of enthusiasm. We look forward to working with him."

authors and publishers are eager to satisfy the teen's every need with books on topics as varied as yoga for teens, to *It's My Life! A Power Journal for Teens: A Workout for Your Mind*.

In a joint venture with Parachute Press and *Seventeen* magazine, HarperCollins Children's Books launched its *Seventeen* publishing program with three nonfiction titles and four novels. Alloy Online, the parent of the popular teen website alloy.com, acquired the book packager 17th Street Productions and announced a deal with Penguin Putnam Books for Young Readers to publish teen titles. The initial plan calls for 12 books on teen issues, with topics drawn from the most popular areas of the Alloy website.

On Alloy's side, the venture affords them a new market for their core audience. For Penguin, it means access to eager consumers—teens—with money to spend. "Alloy's ability to provide us with real and fascinating material from teens is innovative for the publishing industry," explains Doug Whiteman, President of Penguin Putnam Books for Young Readers.

Publishers everywhere are eyeing the YA market with new interest. A number of publishers and booksellers attended a panel discussion called "Targeting Teens" at last year's Book Expo. Both sides are eager to find a way to tap into a potentially lucrative market. Booksellers look for ways to reposition YA material within bookstores to make it more appealing while publishers look to the Internet to help them reach teens.

Teen People and Book-of-the-Month Club have launched a new book club that will offer 100 titles each month selected from picks by a group of teens known as the Review Crew. The club will also have interactive elements that include chat rooms and live events for members only.

The year was marked by many publishers looking for new places to sell their books. In addition to the Internet, which has certainly changed the way millions of customers buy books, houses looked for new outlets. Mass-merchandisers like Wal-Mart, Target, and K-Mart now carry children's books and they are even starting to appear in places like the clothing retailer T.J. Maxx. Many companies have licenses with food manufacturers, like M&Ms candy and Kellogg's cereal and are exploring ways to market their books in grocery stores as well as on the labels of the manufacturers' goods. Books in turn sometimes come with discount coupons for a grocery product. Many of the larger grocery stores now have their own book sections as well, right down the aisle from snacks more often than not!

What to Expect in Parenting

Another realm that is getting a nod from many publishers is the market for parenting titles. A healthy birthrate, a strong economy, and a growing number of teens all have helped fuel the desire for more books for parents.

Gryphon House launched an imprint that is devoted solely to parenting titles, Robins Lane Press. But the new books are reaching out to a new kind of parent, according to Robins Lane Publisher Justin Rood (See the profile of Justin Rood, page 26.) "For one thing,

Expansion at The Millbrook Press: Simon Boughton

"My title is Publisher of something that is as yet unnamed," says Simon Boughton, with a sense of humor. At the time of this interview, he had been on the job exactly three days as Publisher of a new, high-quality children's trade imprint for The Millbrook Press.

Millbrook is a well-known name in the school and library market for children's books, but the new imprint will mark the company's first venture into trade publishing. "The imprint will be author-focused rather than curriculum focused," says Boughton, and will feature a mix of picture books, fiction, and some nonfiction, for children of all ages. Boughton stresses that the list will be not only author-driven, but author friendly. The new imprint will represent both new and established authors. "Certainly I hope to keep up some relationships with authors I have published before, but I am also anxious to have a good mix of established and new writers. I think if we can offer a small, family-like environment, we'll do quite well."

Boughton spent more than 10 years at Knopf and Crown Books for Young Readers and brings to Millbrook an intimate knowledge of the trade market. Before becoming Publishing Director of Knopf and Crown Books, Boughton was with Simon & Schuster for four years, and began his publishing career at Kingfisher Books in London before moving to the U.S. in 1986. "My publishing philosophy has always been that you publish good, distinctive work with original voices, and publish to an audience that can use, understand, and appreciate those books. It will be the same here at Millbrook."

As *Children's Writer Guide* went to press, the timing for the first list of Millbrook's new imprint was unclear. The original target was fall 2001, but that date depended on a deal in which Millbrook would purchase DK Ink; at press time, it appeared that the deal was falling apart. If the purchase is not made, "I would have had to hit the ground running," says Boughton. "We may still have a list in 2001; it may be the following year."

"This is a good time to be in children's publishing," Boughton says, "but it is also a challenging one. The retail environment has changed so much, and that has had an impact on our industry." But the combination of Boughton's knowledge of the trade market and Millbrook's established presence in the school and library markets seem the perfect mix to meet the challenges of a new era in publishing.

Small Presses & Imprints: Young Adult

The following companies do not publish YA books exclusively unless noted. For purposes of this chart, "small" means 20 or fewer titles published for any age.

Company	Fiction	Nonfiction	Titles last year
Absey and Company	General interest, in a list ranging from age 6 to YA.	Biographies, history, religion, education, poetry, educational activities.	6
Africa World Press	YA novels for niche audience. Folktales.	African, African-American, Caribbean, Latin-American issues.	2
Alloy Books (Penguin Putnam imprint)	Joint venture with website Alloy Online. Contemporary YA fiction.	Health, social issues, spirituality, current events, culture, teen issues.	8
ATL Press	None.	Science, technology, astronomy, geography, health, fitness, nature.	12
Avisson Press	Literary novels for adults.	History, ethnic, biography.	8
Bick Publishing House	None.	Psychology, meditation, disabilities, special needs of teens.	5
Blue Sky Press (Scholastic imprint)	Fiction for all ages, including YA.	Middle-grade only.	14
Branden Publishing	No YA.	Biography and reference on law, ethics, social issues, health, sports.	8
Chaosium	Fantasy, horror, Arthurian legends.	Role-playing game resource books.	6
I.E. Clark Publications	Plays.	None.	5
Coteau Books (Canadian authors only)	Many genres, but no romance or horror.	None.	16
Creative Editions	High-quality; original and classic stories.	Animals, nature, environment, biography, poetry.	6

Small Presses & Imprints: Young Adult

Company	Fiction	Nonfiction	Titles last year
Cricket Books	Mostly middle-grade; some YA. Realistic fiction, humor, fantasy.	None	7
Critical Thinking Books & Software	No YA.	Thinking skills, language arts, science, math, social studies.	8
May Davenport	Currently only wants YA. Adventure, mystery, humor, historical fiction.	None.	4
Dawn Publications	None.	Nature education.	8
Different Books	Protagonists with disabilities, but active roles.	None.	3
Discovery Enterprises	Historical fiction, plays. Must use primary source materials.	History, biography. Must use primary source materials.	20
Eerdmans Books for Young Readers	Religious, inspirational.	Religious, biography, educational.	14
Element Books	No YA.	Body, mind, & spirit. Hobbies, health, religion, sports, social issues.	15
Encore Performance Publishing	Plays; educational, bilingual, religious, ethnic, humorous dramas.	Theater arts.	20
Frances Foster Books (Farrar, Straus & Giroux)	Literary fiction.	Very little.	15
Free Spirit	None.	Self-help. Family, social issues, stress, creativity, self-esteem, self-awareness.	18
Front Street Books	Adventure, humor, historical fiction, science fiction.	YA primarily; some educational and novelty books for other ages.	14
Laura Geringer Books (Harper-Collins)	Fantasy, historical fiction, nature stories.	None.	15

Publishing 2001

Small Presses & Imprints: Young Adult

Company	Fiction	Nonfiction	Titles last year
Girl Press	None.	Books that empower YA girls. Entertainment, humor, career, culture, social issues.	2
Hampton Roads Publishing	Spiritual & metaphysical themes.	Spiritual & metaphysical themes.	3
Hendrick-Long Publishing	Regional & historical fiction on Texas & the Southwest.	Texas, the Southwest. History, geography, biography, nature.	8
Heuer Publishing	Plays. Musicals, comedy, drama, mystery, suspense, satire.	None.	15
Holloway House Publishing	None.	African-American biographies.	14
Impact Publishers	None.	Self-help. Psychology, social issues, self-esteem, individuality, creativity.	10
Jewish Publication Society	Religious fiction.	Judaism, Jewish values.	3
Journey Books (Bob Jones University)	Christian, historical, contemporary.	Biographies of well-known Christians & missionaries.	12
Judaica Press	Inspirational, religious, mystery, & suspense.	No YA.	20
Lillenas Publishing	Christian plays, dramatic resources.	Drama ministry, play production, scenery.	10
Lobster Press (Canada)	Adventure, contemporary, fantasy, humor, poetry.	No YA.	14
Mayhaven Publishing	Adventure, humor, science fiction, Westerns, poetry.	History, the West, travel, nature, cooking.	10
Meriwether Publishing	Theater scripts. Needs Christmas & Easter plays.	Theater reference books.	9

Small Presses & Imprints: Young Adult

Company	Fiction	Nonfiction	Titles last year
Naturegraph Publishers	Retellings of ancient Native American myths & legends.	Native Americans, nature, the outdoors, environment.	2
Peachtree Publishers	Humor, regional (the South), multicultural.	Regional (the South), nature, self-help.	20
Pitspopany Press	Jewish themes. Adventure, mystery, humor, ethnic, religious, historical.	Jewish themes. Health, sports, history, self-help, humor, religion, ethnic.	12
The Place in the Woods	Folktales, mystery, suspense, inspirational, humor, multicultural.	No YA.	3
Rainbow Books	None.	Self-help, nature, social issues.	18
Red Deer Press (Canadian authors only)	Adventure, fantasy, mystery, suspense, drama, contemporary, regional, ethnic.	No YA.	8
Rocky River Publishers	Inspirational, contemporary. Topics such as self-esteem, stress, substance abuse.	Drug education, self-esteem, stress, youth safety.	10
Running Press Book Publishers	None.	Learning & discovery kits. Science, geography, art, architecture, animals.	5
Saint Mary's Press	Drama, fantasy, historical, contemporary, religious fiction. Catholic.	Religion, spirituality.	20
SeaStar Books	Literary. Adventure, fantasy, humor, contemporary, historical.	No YA.	20
Silver Whistle (Harcourt, Inc.)	Inspirational, contemporary, adventure.	No YA.	13
Third World Press	African, African-American, Caribbean life.	Ethnic, multicultural, African-centered.	10
Megan Tingley Books (Little, Brown)	Contemporary, multicultural, humor, stories about music.	No YA.	20

Publishing 2001

-21-

Small Presses & Imprints: Young Adult

Company	Fiction	Nonfiction	Titles last year
UAHC Press	Judaism, historical, religious fiction.	Jewish education, bar/bat mitzvah preparation, the Holocaust, Hebrew.	18
What's Inside Press	Contemporary.	None.	9
Wiley Children's Books	None.	Nature, science, history, math, arts & crafts, multicultural, sports.	18
Winslow Press	Adventure, fantasy, humor, regional, contemporary, historical, folklore.	No YA.	17
Woodbine House	Children with disabilities.	ADD, cerebral palsy, Down syndrome, epilepsy, craniofacial anomaly.	12
World Book	None.	Reference, animals, arts, careers, hobbies, geography, health, nature, science.	15

Generation X is all grown up and starting families, and they are looking for a different kind of parenting title than their parents did," says Rood.

Add to that the changing face of the American family, in which new parents are just as likely to be 50 as 25, and in which stepchildren and ex-spouses figure. A favorable economy has helped this category, as has the large number of parents having children later in life. Older parents have established their careers and have extra money to spend when it comes to baby.

Traditional topics like pregnancy and birth still are at the top of the sales list, but books for parents (and there were more than 1,300 published in 2000, according to Amazon.com) cover an ever broader array of topics. Sample new titles include *The Mozart Effect for Children: Awakening Your Child's Mind, Health, and Creativity with Music*, by Don G. Campbell (William Morrow); *Learning Outside the Lines*, by Jonathan Mooney and David Cole (Simon & Schuster), about how to succeed despite learning disabilities and ADHD; among Amazon.com best-sellers were *How to Behave So Your Children Will, Too!*, by Sal Severe, and *Games Girls Play: Understanding and Guiding Young Female Athletes*, by Caroline Silbey and Shelley Smith (St. Martin's Press).

The dot.com in Publishing

It's impossible to open a newspaper or a magazine these days without reading something about e-publishing or e-books. All the talk was fueled in part by the leap into the new realm of e-publishing by Stephen King when he published his short story, "Riding the Bullet" on the Internet. The project was done with his publisher, Simon & Schuster. Next, King announced he would self-publish his next work as a serial e-book. *The Plant* costs readers a dollar per installment, to be paid on an honor system. The catch is that if the payments don't arrive, King will stop the installments and leave the audience hanging.

Three electronic publishing announcements were made on the same day last year, within 30 minutes of each other: Time Warner announced plans for a major new electronic publishing initiative; Microsoft announced it would join forces with Random House and Simon & Schuster; and Barnesand-Noble.com said it would make 15 *Star Trek* titles and Michael Crichton's latest book, *Timeline*, available on the Internet for free.

Early this year, Random House will launch a new imprint, AtRandom, that will publish 20 original books in e-form. Modern Library has plans to release 100 classic titles as e-books. The books will be available online or in the print-on-demand (POD) format at retail outlets. The company iPublish.com also announced plans for original e-books.

While the Internet is clearly on everyone's radar, most in the children's end of the market think it is still a distant beep for them. Certainly, the Internet has dramatically changed how books are sold and it has also become a must for every publisher to have a website. "We have a website, and it has a shopping cart," says Reynolds. "Do we sell a lot of books that way? Absolutely not. But could we do without a Web presence? Absolutely not."

For writers, the Internet has made access to publishers so much easier. Most publishers offer writers' guidelines, as well as previews of soon-to-be released titles, on their websites. In the future, Walker says he likes the idea of e-books for serials for young readers. "We are looking at series and the way we publish them very seriously," he says. "I think the days of a series like the Baby-sitters Club with 180 or more titles are over. The Internet may be a way to bring series to kids. We know, for example, that kids like to read in smaller chunks, but they won't buy shorter books. It's something I am sure we will look into."

Whatever new technology brings, publishers agree its impact on the industry will be a positive one. The good news for all is that more books for children are being published than ever before. "I've been in this business a long time," says Reynolds. "When I started, the filmstrip was going to make books obsolete. Then it was television, then the computer. We have survived a lot of extinctions, so I'm not quaking in my boots yet!"

Walker tells a story of being asked to give a speech on the history of children's books. "I realized as I thought about it, how far we have come since the start of the last millennium. It was quite a struggle for those individuals who fought to make children's books legitimate in the big houses in the 20s and 30s. Back then, salespeople would only sell children's books in the winter. Now we have our own best-seller list in the *New York Times*."

Selected Middle-Grade Fiction Publishers

The following smaller, lesser known, or niche publishers all include middle-grade fiction on their lists. The totals indicated are for all queries and submissions the company reports receiving and total list size last year.

Company	Address	Submissions	Titles last year
ABDO Publishing (hi-lo books)	4940 Viking Drive, Suite 622, Edina, MN 55435	300	120
Absey and Company	23011 Northcrest Drive, Spring TX 77389	1,000	6
Academic Therapy Pub. (ESL & special education)	20 Commercial Boulevard, Novato, CA 94949	25	18
The Bess Press (Pacific rim)	3565 Harding Avenue, Honolulu, HI 96816	215	4
Branden Publishing	P.O. Box 843, 17 Station Street, Brookline Village, MA 02147	1,000	8
Colonial Williamsburg Foundation	Publications Dept., P.O. Box 1776, Williamsburg, VA 23187	50	5
Creative With Words (anthologies)	P.O. Box 223226, Carmel, CA 93922	500	12
Cricket Books	332 South Michigan, Suite 1100, Chicago, IL 60604	1,800	7
DawnSign Press (deaf community)	6130 Nancy Ridge Drive, San Diego, CA 92121	50	6
Different Books (disabilities)	3900 Glenwood Avenue, Golden Valley, MN 55422	1,000	3
Discovery Enterprises (historical)	31 Laurelwood Drive, Carlisle, MA 01741	100	20
Down East Books (New England)	P.O. Box 679, Camden, ME 04843	400	22
The Feminist Press	The Graduate Center, 365 Fifth Avenue, New York, NY 10016	800	19
Front Street Books	20 Battery Park Avenue, Suite 403, Asheville, NC 28801	2,000	14
Graphic Arts Center Pub. (regional)	P.O. Box 10306, Portland, OR 97296	350	21
Hampton Roads Pub. (spiritual/metaphysical)	134 Burgess Lane, Charlottesville, VA 22902	not available	3
Hendrick-Long Pub. (Texas, the Southwest)	P.O. Box 25123, Dallas, TX 75225	500	8

Selected Middle-Grade Fiction Publishers

Company	Address	Submissions	Titles last year
Imperial International (supplementary education)	30 Montauk Boulevard, Oakdale, NY 11769	not available	6
Just Us Books (African American)	365 Glenwood Avenue, East Orange, NJ 07017	not available	6
Lee & Low Books (multicultural)	95 Madison Avenue, New York, NY 10016	2,500	20
Mayhaven Publishing	P.O. Box 557, Mahomet, IL 61853	2,000	10
Meadowbrook Press	5451 Smetana Drive, Minnetonka, MN 55343	600	18
Midwest Traditions (regional)	3710 North Morris Boulevard, Shorewood, WI 53211	60	3
Milkweed Editions (nonprofit)	1011 Washington Avenue South, Suite 300, Minneapolis, MN 55415	5,000	18
Moon Mountain Publishing	80 Peachtree Road, North Kingstown, RI 02852	800	2
National Geographic Society	1145 17th Street NW, Washington, DC 20036	400	25
Naturegraph Publishers (natural history)	P.O. Box 1047, 3453 Indian Creek Road, Happy Camp, CA 96039	not available	2
Overmountain Press (regional)	P.O. Box 1261, Johnson City, TN 37605	300	30
Peachtree Publishers (regional)	494 Armour Circle, NE, Atlanta, GA 30324	9,000	20
Phoenix Learning Resources (ESL, hi/lo)	12 West 31st Street, New York, NY 10001	110	25
The Place in the Woods	3900 Glenwood Avenue, Golden Valley, MN 55422	1,000	3
Rocky River Publishers (coping with problems)	P.O. Box 1679, Sheperdstown, WV 25443	1,000	10
Sandcastle Publishing (performing arts)	1723 Hill Drive, P.O. Box 3070, South Pasadena, CA 91031	not available	2
SeaStar Books	1123 Broadway, Suite 800, New York, NY 10010	1,200	21
Silver Moon Press	160 Fifth Avenue, New York, NY 10010	180	6
Tor Books (science fiction & fantasy)	175 Fifth Avenue, New York, NY 10010	1,200	35

Justin Rood: Something Old, Something New

Whatever you do, don't ask Justin Rood why, as a single 27-year-old, he has established a new imprint devoted to books for parents. "If my family business was a bakery, no one would ask me why I bake cakes. The answer is because I know how to bake well. In this business, I know what it takes to publish good books," he explains with a hint of amusement in his voice.

The Rood family business *is* publishing. "I grew up learning the family business," he says. His parents started Gryphon House more than 30 years ago. The small press has earned a reputation as a quality, niche educational publisher specializing in books on early childhood topics. "Over the years, after school and on summer vacations, I learned my way around and did a little bit of everything, starting with the warehouse, moving into customer service, and finally to the editorial side."

After high school, Rood left the East Coast and headed to California for college where he earned a degree in American Studies. He then worked in the media department of a small think tank. He took time off to travel, and then returned to the East and went to work at the family firm in suburban Maryland. That was five years ago. Two years ago, he came up with the idea for Robins Lane Press—an imprint of Gryphon House that focuses on parenting. The idea grew from the success of some of Gryphon House's educational books in the trade market. Rood explains: "We had done some books—notably *Games to Play with Babies,* by Jackie Silberg—that were very successful in the trade market. So, we started to look for more titles that could cross over from the education market to the trade market and be as successful at home as they were in the classroom."

True to the Mission

The idea was a good one, but with some drawbacks. "Our name and our reputation were in education," Rood explains. "The founding mission of Gryphon House was, and is, to publish books for early childhood teachers. It seemed that as we reached out to new areas, our mission was getting diluted a bit. My thought was to have a separate imprint with separate goals and a separate staff."

Rood thinks "there is a real advantage to creating a new venture in a family company, especially if you are creating a publishing company out of another

Justin Rood

publishing company. First of all, you have an entire staff whose expertise you can draw on, while having the freedom to create new books and new ideas."

But Robins Lane Press would primarily target the trade market, not an educational one. "I spent the first year trying to get as sophisticated as possible in understanding the trade market in general and the parenting market in particular," he says. Along the way, he talked to many parents about their needs and wants. "A lot of my friends are parents now—the Gen-Xers all grown up. When you think of my generation, people in their late twenties, what comes to mind is kids dressed all in black with lots of piercings and a fairly cynical attitude towards life. Somehow a few of us maintained our humanity enough to get married and have kids!"

But Rood discovered that this new generation of parents—from Generation Xers with babies to baby boomers with teenagers—were looking for a different kind of parenting book. They wanted real answers, he explains, "not fluffy parenting." He notes that in the last five years alone, parents have been faced with everything from increased violence in schools to a whole host of social problems. More often than not, when things happen, parents are blamed, rightly or wrongly, for their children's actions.

"I've had so many conversations with parents of kids of all ages who say they feel so much pressure as a parent to be more and more responsible and involved, and they are looking for books that will help." Rood says he is committed to publishing books that will make a difference in a parent's life.

The mission of Robins Lane Press, as explained in the catalogue and on the website, is to publish "timely, unique books on subjects of interest to today's parents. It takes a different kind of parent to raise children in today's world. New pressures, new technologies, new dangers, and new possibilities are changing what it means to be a kid, and what it means to raise one."

The Long Haul

Robins Lane Press published its first books in 2000. Asked where he found his authors, Rood describes the process as "a little bit like something old, something new, something borrowed, something blue." *The Business Traveling Parent*, by Dan Verdick, was a submission from a writer who is the marketing director of a small press distributed by Gryphon House. *The Child and the Machine*, by Alison Armstrong and Charles Casement, was originally published in Canada and brought to Rood's attention by one of his education contacts.

Being a small publisher in the trade market up against the big guns is a consideration that Rood admits can be "hard to get your mind around." "It is definitely hard, and this is a question I ask myself more than once: 'What in heaven's name do you think you are doing?' The truth is, as sappy as it sounds, that to be successful, you have to start with really good books."

Justin Rood

Rood lists the requirements for a book for Robins Lane Press: "The book has to be very carefully focused; it has to be very clear exactly who the audience for the book is; and the idea has to be new and have an edge to it." He says that "most of the big houses really focus on their superstar celebrity authors, and parenting is not a field where you find too many million-dollar advance authors."

The advantage of a small press too is that it can and does spend considerable time and energy in promoting each title on its list. A small house must look for books that will sell well on the backlist as well as on the frontlist, explains Rood. "I think you succeed by being as careful as possible in choosing what you publish and looking at its value in the long haul."

Robins Lane Press published five titles in 2000. Rood hopes to double that output every year until they are publishing about 20 titles a year. "I think for now, 20 is a good target for us. As a small publisher, you have to be conscious of how big is big enough and at what point, by getting too big, you lose all the good things about being small."

Whatever the fate of this new publishing house, its publisher is clearly driven to publish the best books on the market. He has a good foundation in a successful family publishing business; when the time is right, he will also have all the information he needs to be a great parent! Justin Rood's vision is new and fresh and Robins Lane Press is already becoming a familiar name among parents and booksellers alike.

Frank Sloan: A Life in Nonfiction

You could say that Frank Sloan, most recently Publishing Director at the school and library publisher Raintree/Steck-Vaughn, has publishing in his blood—or at the very least, printer's ink. When he was growing up in a small town in Western Pennsylvania, his father worked as a book designer for Harcourt Brace, which incidentally now owns Raintree/Steck-Vaughn.

"I've always been in publishing," he says. "I guess you really could say I was born into it. I don't mean to be arrogant when I say that, but my father worked in the business 50 years ago, for the company I am now part of, so I guess you could say I have come full circle. I've always loved the business and it never occurred to me to do anything else."

In a career that has spanned 35 years, most of it in children's publishing, Sloan has done a little bit of everything. Today he brings these varied experiences into play in his position as Publishing Director, a position he held for five years. While Sloan admits he just "sort of fell into" the children's end of the business—his first job was in the children's department of Random House—he has loved it from the start and has never looked back. He says with a laugh that his mother always used to ask him when he was going to grow up and get into adult publishing. "She never quite got it."

Career Turns

Sloan started out in the production department at Random House but was soon tapped to be an art director at Dutton. Dutton was one of Sloan's few ventures into the adult market, but the experience led him back to children's books before long. Like so many working today in the school and library market, Sloan spent time at the venerable Franklin Watts, part of Grolier. "Everybody who does nonfiction worked for Watts during one time of their career," he says.

For five years, Sloan worked in production at Franklin Watts and then for personal reasons decided it was time for a change. "I wanted to live abroad. It was one of those things I'd always felt I wanted to experience, and I knew that if I didn't do it when I was young, I never would."

He was lured back to the United States by a job at, you guessed it, Franklin Watts, and went to work for Jeanne Vestal who was, says Sloan, to become a mentor. He was hired primarily for his background in production because at the time, Watts was considering a line of picture books, but that never materialized.

-29-

Frank Sloan

Instead, he found himself working closely with Franklin Watts's U.K. division to acquire and develop titles for the American market.

In 1989, Judy Wilson, then head of Macmillan Children's Books, called Sloan and asked him to come work for her. "Macmillan had just acquired an imprint called Crestwood House," a line for reluctant readers, recalls Sloan, "and she asked me if I would run it. I didn't have to think twice; it was a natural next move for me." During his stint at Macmillan, Sloan worked in children's nonfiction. During Sloan's time there, Macmillan also launched an imprint called New Discovery Books, which Sloan describes as "an older age level line of single titles and series that really broadened Macmillan's base in nonfiction."

Simon & Schuster then acquired Macmillan and, says Sloan, "That was the end of my time there." He moved to Thomson Learning, which published nonfiction library materials. Before long, the parent company decided to sell, and Raintree/Steck Vaughn bought the contract for the company's books. Sloan was asked to come on board and head up the line.

Fresh Takes

At Raintree/Steck-Vaughn, Sloan and Walter Kossmann jointly shared responsibilities for the books produced as Publishing Directors. Half of Sloan's time was spent on the Raintree list and the other half on a new line for reluctant readers called Steadwell Books. "With the new line, we published for two reading levels: third grade and grades four to six. The books are 32 and 48 pages respectively. We know there are reluctant readers at both these levels," explains Sloan. "We tried to keep the list broad because I think some adult readers will be using the books as well, in ESL classes, for example. We tried to make them as 'non-babyish,' if you will, as possible so they would appeal to this broader base of reluctant readers. It was a real challenge, finding subjects that appeal to both child and adult readers." Sloan's job also involved working with an English publisher to acquire foreign titles for the American market.

The process he and Kossmann used to put together their lists, says Sloan, was part research and part instinct. "Of course, we considered what the states are doing at the various grade levels in terms of curriculum, but sometimes we used our instincts and experience in the field to come up with new ideas for books," he says. "For example, we found that ancient civilization, which has traditionally been taught in grades four to six, is now being introduced in younger grades. Sometimes these shifts are strictly curriculum-based and at other times, I think popular culture comes into play."

Sloan, Kossmann, and an editorial staff of 10 were responsible for turning out 200 new titles a year. "I love the idea of creating new material for kids," Sloan says. "I think it's very exciting. One thing that constantly amazes me is that we were able to keep coming up with something new. Just when you think

Frank Sloan

you can't possibly find another way to do a book on endangered species, someone comes along with a fresh take on the topic. I read a manuscript over one weekend on teen pregnancy, a topic that has certainly been visited more than once! And yet, the author found a way to make the topic come alive. It is, I think, the best book I have ever read on the subject."

During his spare time, Sloan says he often reads children's fiction. "I was teaching a course for a while at New York University on children's publishing, so I had to stay current with what was being published. I really enjoy reading children's fiction, even though I no longer teach the course!" Asked what he had read most recently, Sloan answers, "What else? *Harry Potter.* I think it's dynamite and it makes everyone aware of the power children's books can have."

As to the future, Sloan is optimistic. "Nonfiction is a good place to be right now. It certainly has been a strong year for us and I imagine for others as well." The challenge of finding "anything new and different that will appeal to kids" never gets old for him. "I really am lucky that I enjoy what I do and can't imagine being in any other business, even after 35 years."

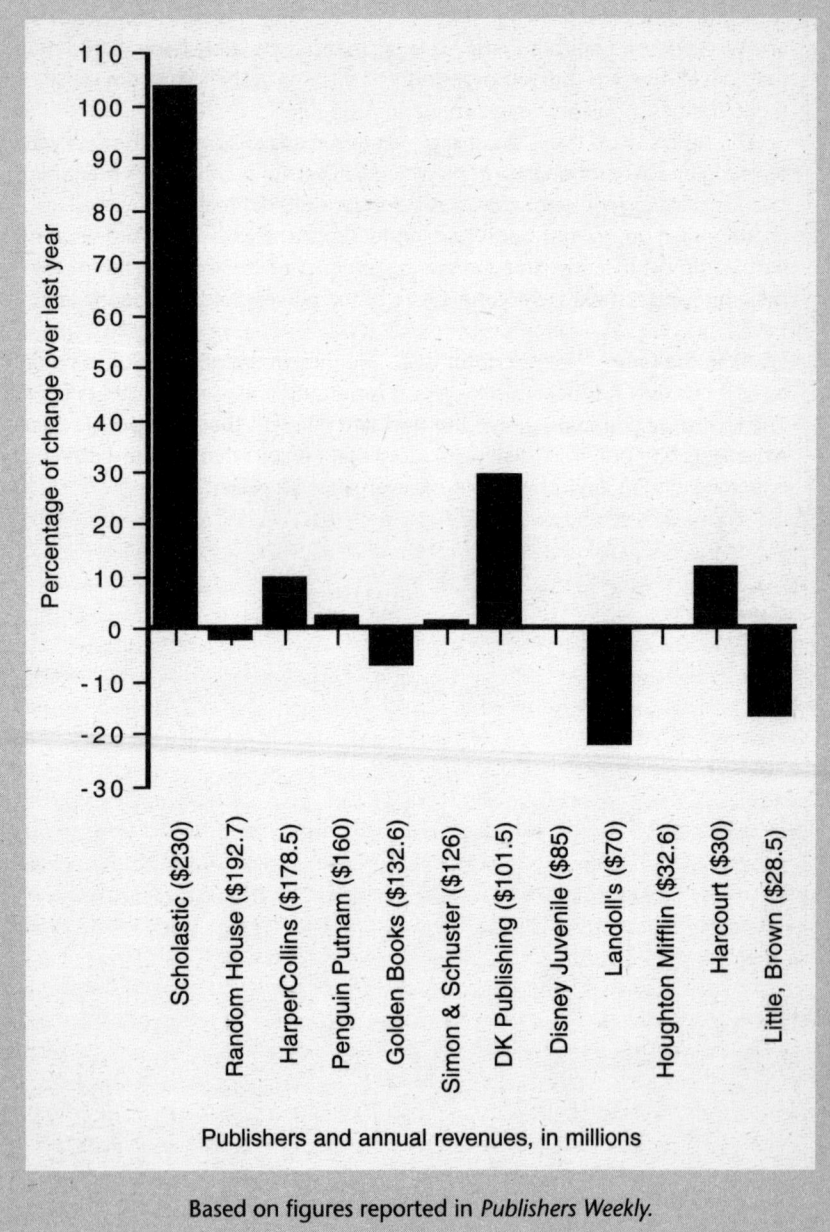

A Record Year in Magazines

Something for Everyone

By Vicki Hambleton

Paper and ink are to be trusted. In an era of almost immeasurable technological change, people remain more trustful of print technologies than of other. We may be enamored of e-mail and e-books and e-commerce, but consumers still turn first to paper, and our children may follow in our traditional footsteps:

- A Magazine Publishers of America survey found that consumers think magazines provide them with better information than either the Internet or television. The average U.S. household reads 4.9 magazines a month.
- Launches of magazines at the beginning of last year were the highest in 15 years.
- The number of consumer magazines has almost tripled over two decades, according to a report in the *Christian Science Monitor*.
- Spending on magazine advertising easily surpassed the $10 billion mark last year, with revenues increasing 16.4 percent and ad pages increasing 13.8 percent, according to figures from the Publishers Information Bureau.

These figures embrace our children: Teen magazines scream out on grocery lines and newsstands and magazines for the younger end of the teen decade—the 'tweens of 10, 11, and 12—are right by their side. Publications for younger readers are strong as well. More accept ads each year, an ideological hurdle for some writers and readers but a sign of market strength for others. The new magazines also cross a wide range of subjects, from music to movies to fathers to teenage boys to single parents to beginning readers.

A Very Good Place to Start

Let's start at the very beginning: magazines for the youngest audience. While *Crayola Kids* closed, the gap it left was already being filled by the bimonthly *Nick Jr.*, designed for two-to-six-year-olds and parents to use together. Its tagline is "where kids play to learn and parents learn to play." Each *Nick Jr.* includes a section featuring a story from the creators of the wildly popular *Blue's Clues* television program, giving the magazine instant appeal to advertisers.

The Meredith Corporation had startled everyone, including the *Crayola Kids* staff, when it announced that the magazine would close its doors. Meredith's official public relations explanation said that, although "*Crayola Kids* is a well-respected franchise,

Meredith and the licensor of the *Crayola Kids* name—Binney & Smith—have major strategic differences about how it should be managed."

Time Inc. apparently has no hesitations about the vision behind its franchise. Its newest magazine targets kindergartners and first-graders. *The Big Picture*, which launched in September with a 500,000 circulation, is the newest edition of *Time For Kids* and makes the company an even stronger competitor in the school and library market. Time, Inc. now has magazines targeting kindergarten to grade five, key for selling to schools that traditionally put these grades together in a single building.

"We felt it was important to do something for the younger kids," explains *Time For Kids* Publisher Keith Garton, "because in a K-5 building, we had this very obvious gap. Now we can go into K-5 schools and talk about it being a *Time For Kids* school and be able to offer this common reading experience across all the grades." Garton reports that the *Time For Kids World Report* edition, which targets grades four, five, and six, is currently the market leader. (See the profile of Keith Garton, page 51.)

Scholastic continues to be the leader in the kindergarten through third-grade classroom market and is the overwhelming leader in grades 7 to 12. Hugh Roome, Executive Vice President of Scholastic, is confident of continued growth for them. "I'm not sure how *The Big Picture* will affect us in the future," says Roome. "We are very powerful at these age levels: We have a big stake in schools and at those levels we are selling millions of subscriptions and tens of millions of books. Time, Inc. may open the market up a little bit because they do things differently—and that is good for the classroom magazine world in general."

Sports Platforms

Scholastic's magazine purchase of the year was *Soccer Jr.*, the highly successful sports magazine for young players and their parents. Editor and founder Joe Provey says the deal was good for both parties. "We have been one of those little start-up magazines with a small amount of money. We have been at it for eight years and done very well. But we felt we needed a partner to really grow to the next level. Scholastic stepped up to us and said, 'Here's what we can do for you,' and we thought the move was the best way to go forward."

"The reason for the acquisition of *Soccer Jr.*," explains Roome, "is we think it is a platform for sports publishing for kids. We already reach coaches with *Coach* magazine. When we looked at *Soccer Jr.*, we saw that they had a stake not only in soccer, but that there was a potential to be a platform for baseball, hockey, basketball, football." *Soccer Jr.* already owns the URLs for websites with comparable names, such as *Basketball Jr.* "We hope we can, down the road, expand into these other sports with magazines as well," Roome says.

The union between Scholastic and *Soccer Jr.* was big certainly, but even bigger news perhaps was that the Carus Publishing Company had purchased Cobblestone Publishing. The union brings together some of the very best in children's magazines in both fiction and nonfiction. "We've been interested in the Cobblestone magazines for a long time," says Mariane Carus, founder of Carus Publishing. "We always hoped that some day we could get together because we have the same commitment to quality."

The Cobblestone group, which includes *Calliope, Faces, Odyssey, Footsteps, Cobblestone,* and *AppleSeeds*, had been owned by the educational giant, Pearson. But last year, the company put the magazines on the block. According to Lou Waryncia, Cobblestone Managing Editor, the magazines will remain in New Hampshire and operate as they always have. But for both the Carus Group— at times known as the Cricket Group, for its flagship magazine—and Cobblestone Group, the new union will mean exposure to previously untapped markets. Says Waryncia, "Cricket does a lot of direct mail that we don't do and is more consumer-oriented. That will help us grow in the marketplace. At the same time, we will bring them entry into our primary market, the school and library market."

Surprise Endings

The folding of two other magazines surprised many in the industry. Parade Publications announced that it would close down its news and entertainment magazine for teens, *react*, and Guideposts announced that *Guideposts for Kids* is no longer in print.

Launched in 1995, *react* was distributed through national newspapers during the school year. Chairman and Publisher of *Parade*, Walter Anderson, said of *react*, "It was an editorial success: It was inserted into 225 papers with a circulation of 4 million. But we were not able to reach the same success with the advertising community. I wrestled with this for months, but it just did not work."

In early fall, word came that *Guideposts for Kids* would be folding its print version, on the tails of the announcement by the adult *Guideposts* that it would begin to accept advertising for the first time in its 55-year history. *Guideposts for Kids* and *Guideposts for Teens* began taking advertising last year. At that time, *Guideposts for Kids* Editor in Chief Mary Lou Carney said, "We have been riding the horse of philanthropy for 10 years now—*Guideposts for Kids* is not a moneymaker. The most *Guideposts* can hope for us is that we break even because we have such a big budget. Now we are going to ride the horse of advertising, but we are still going to carry the same message."

Carney has said that the movement online is a transition. "We'll still be buying manuscripts and we'll still be reaching kids," she said. "It will just be with a click of the mouse instead of the click of the mailbox lid." The already existing website Wally's World (www.gp4k.com), is incorporating many of the magazine's popular departments, including trivia, fiction, kid profiles, Dear Wally, and Tips From the Top.

The Boy's-Eye View

When it comes to the teen market, recent years have been marked by considerable activity among new titles for preteen and teen girls. The past year was no exception in growth in the teen market, but with a new wrinkle:

Educational & Classroom Magazines

This following list of educational publications identifies focus and audience, the percentage of material not written by staff, and payment rates for articles. Not included are publications not currently accepting submissions.

For Students
Career World: students 12-18 looking ahead to careers; 85%; $150+.
College Bound Magazine: young adults heading for college; 75%; $50-$100.
Current Health 1: health students in grades 4-7; 90%; $150+.
Current Health 2: health students in grades 7-12; 90%; $150+.
Keynoter: Key Club members, 14–18, on community service in high school; 65%; $150-$350.
Leadership for Student Activities: middle and high school student leaders and advisors; 67%; no payment.
Quantum: gifted high school and college students studying math and science; 50%; $200.
Read: grades 6-10, for classroom discussions; 80%; payment rate varies.
Scholastic Choices: teens studying health issues; 20%; payment rate varies.
Scholastic DynaMath: math students, grades 3-6; 20%; $250-$400.
Scholastic Scope: literature and language arts students, 12-18; 20%; $100+.
Science Weekly: K-8 science students; 100%; payment rate varies.
Science World: junior and senior high school science and health students, and teachers; 50%; $200-$650.
SuperScience: K-3 science students; 40%; $75-$600.

For Educators
Acorn: librarians, teachers, caregivers for K-3; 5%; no payment.
The ALAN Review: teachers, librarians of adolescent literature; 90%; no payment.
American School Board Journal: school board members and administrators; 60%; $500+.
American String Teacher: teachers of string instruments; 95%; no payment.
Art Education: K-12 art teachers; 100%; no payment.
Arts & Activities: K-12 art teachers; 95%; payment rate varies.
Book Links: teachers, librarians, media specialists, booksellers, parents interested in children's books; 90%; $100.
The Book Report: library and media specialists; 100%; payment rate varies.
Canadian Children's Literature: educators interested in children's books; 97%; no payment.
Challenge: parents and educators of the gifted; 100%; payment rate varies.
Child Care Information Exchange: early education professionals; 60%; $300.

Educational & Classroom Magazines

Class Act: English teachers, grades 6-12; 40%; $10-40.
College Outlook: young adults heading for college; 70%; payment rate varies.
College PreView: Black & Hispanic young adults planning for college or career; 90%; 10¢-15¢ a word.
Connect: K-8 science, technology, math teachers; 90%; honorarium.
Creative Classroom: elementary educators; 80%; payment rate varies.
Dimensions of Early Childhood: child development professionals; 100%; no payment.
Early Childhood Education Journal: child care and educational professionals working with children from birth to 8; 50%; no payment.
Early Childhood News: early childhood professionals; 90%; $75-$200.
Early Childhood Today: child care and educational professionals working with children from birth to 6; 75%; payment rate varies.
Educational Leadership: curriculum publication for elementary and secondary school educators; 90%; no payment.
Educational Oasis: middle-school teachers; 100%; payment rate varies.
Education Forum: Canadian elementary and secondary school educators; 90%; no payment.
Education Week: K-12 educators; 8% (125 pieces); $200 for Commentary.
English Journal: secondary school English teachers; 95%; no payment.
Gifted Education Press: educators and parents of gifted children; 75%; no payment.
Good Apple Newspaper: teachers, grades 2-5; 100%; payment rate varies.
Green Teacher: Canadian K-12 educators promoting environmental awareness; 80%; no payment.
The High School Journal: secondary school and college educators and administrators, focusing on adolescent learning and development; 80%; no payment.
The High School Magazine: high school administrators; 95%; no payment.
Holidays & Seasonal Celebrations: two editions, activity-based, for preschool, and for grades 1-3; 100%; payment rate varies.
Home Education Magazine: for home schoolers; 75%; $25-$50.
Home Schooling Today: for home schoolers; 60%; 8¢ a word.
The Horn Book Magazine: parents, teachers, librarians interested in children's literature; 70%; payment rate varies.
Instructor: preK-grade 8 teachers; 85%; $500-$750.
Journal of Adolescent & Adult Literacy: reading education professionals on literacy education; 80%; no payment.
Journal of Children's Literature: reading specialists, English and language arts teachers, librarians; 75%; no payment.
Journal of Health Education: health educators; 100%; no payment.

Educational & Classroom Magazines

Journal of School Health: health educators; 90%; no payment.
Kansas School Naturalist: teachers, librarians, conservationists on Kansas science, nature, biology; 75%; no payment.
Language Arts: Canadian reading and languages arts K-8 teachers; 100%; no payment.
Learning and Leading with Technology: educators using technology in the classroom; 90%; no payment.
The Learning Edge: home schoolers; 40%; no payment.
Library Talk: elementary school librarians; 100%; honorarium.
Lollipops: preschool-grade one education professionals and parents; 95%; $10-$25,
THE MAILBOX: preK- grade 6 teachers; all articles by assignment; payment rate varies.
Middle School Journal: middle-school teachers and administrators; 75%; no payment.
Momentum: K-12 Catholic and private school educators; 95%; $75.
Montessori LIFE: Montessori school educators; 90%; $100 a published page.
MultiCultural Review: librarians and teachers concerned with multiculturalism and diversity; 95%; payment rate varies.
NASSP Bulletin: middle and high school administrators and staff; 100%; no payment.
The New Advocate: educators, librarians, teaching writing and literature; 90%; no payment.
Our Children: PTA publication for parents, teachers, administrators; 25%; no payment.
Our Gifted Children: educators, parents of gifted children; 45%; no payment.
Read, America!: reading program leaders, educators, librarians; 20%; $50.
The Reading Teacher: educators in literacy learning; 80%; no payment.
Reading Today: International Reading Association members, preK-adult educators; 25%; no payment.
r*w*t: K-12 teachers developing student reading, writing, thinking skills; 50%; no payment.
SchoolArts: K-12 school art teachers; 90%; $25-$150.
Schooldays: K-3 teachers; 90%; $200.
The School Librarian's Workshop: K-12 school librarians; 25%; no payment.
School Library Journal: school librarians and media specialists; 80%; $300.
School Library Media Activities Monthly: school library media specialists; 80%; payment rate varies.
Science Activities: K-12 science teachers; 100%; no payment.

Educational & Classroom Magazines

Science and Children: preK-8 science teachers; 99%; no payment.
The Science Teacher: science educators, grades 7-12; 100%; $100-$200.
Social Studies and the Young Learner: K-6 social studies teachers; 80%; no payment.
Teacher Librarian: public and school librarians and educators; 100%; $50.
Teacher Magazine: K-12 teachers; 10% (commentary/opinion); $75-$100.
Teachers & Writers: language arts and English teachers, on teaching writing; 80%; $10 per 250 words.
Teachers in Focus: K-12 Christian teachers; 80%; $250.
Teaching Elementary Physical Education: K-8 physical education teachers; 90%; no payment.
TEACHING Exceptional Children: special education teachers and administrators; 90%; no payment.
Teaching PreK-8: elementary and middle school teachers; 90%; $20-$50.
Teaching Theatre: middle and high school theater teachers; 50% freelance; payment rate varies.
Tech Directions: vocational and technical teachers and administrators; 95%; $50 for first page, $25 per additional page.
Techniques: secondary school technical and vocational teachers; 50%; payment rate varies.
Technology & Learning: junior and senior high school educators and technology coordinators, on technology use in the classroom; 85%; $400-$600.
Today's Catholic Teacher: Catholic school educators; 90%; $100-$250.
VISION: Christian educators in public schools; 30%; $20-$40.
Voices from the Middle: middle school teachers of English and language arts; 100%; no payment.

lifestyle magazines for boys.

The first to announce a magazine for teen boys was TransWorld Media, a division of Times Mirror Magazines. *Stance* premiered as "the first general interest magazine for male teens." The company already knows the market well, as publishers of such titles as *TransWorld Skateboarding* and *TransWorld Snowboarding*. Editor Kevin Imamura describes *Stance* as "somewhere between *Teen People* and *Maxim*, but written from a skateboarder's point of view." Despite being first out of the gate with their announcement, however, the launch of *Stance* was postponed and there is, at press time, no word from the company as to when it will make its much heralded arrival.

The delays allowed Rodale Press's *MH-18* to reach its audience first. Rodale, publishers of *Men's Health*, has targeted the new magazine to ages 13 to 17. It published two issues in 2000, hopes to turn bimonthly first, and monthly by 2002. Rodale launched *MH-18* with 300,000 newsstand copies. A footnote: The magazine was originally dubbed *MH-17*, but Rodale changed the name after Primedia threatened a lawsuit, claiming *MH-17* was too similar to its own *Seventeen* for teen girls.

MH-18 Editor Jeff Csatari admits that the challenge will be in convincing a teenage boy to pick up the publication. He noted that "most titles aimed at guys are vertical sports titles" and describes the magazine's target reader as "the healthy active teenage guy who is looking for answers." Fitness, dating, relationships, sports, and grooming are among the topics covered in *MH-18*.

Yet another publication for young men, *Boys Illustrated*, from the publishers of the successful *Girls' Life*, is also on its way. "We always dreamed about publishing a boys' magazine, although the way we are evolving now, we are kind of becoming a boys-becoming-men magazine and we may target readers as old as 30," explains Jack Dott, President of Monarch Publications. *Boys Illustrated* will be similar to *Girls' Life* in that "it will be wholesome," says Dott. "We want the magazine to be something a parent will feel good about. We will certainly be competitive, but I think the approach we will take is going to be very different from, say, *MH-18*. For one thing, we won't have any sex." The first issue has a scheduled launch date of summer 2001 and an initial circulation of 100,000.

A year ago, who would ever have predicted fashion magazines for boys? In the category of least likely subjects for children's magazines, however, *FF* deserves special mention. The magazine hopes to appeal to a broad range of teens, all with one thing in common—a serious and active love of music. *FF* was launched by two owners of a small Minneapolis advertising agency. "This is a magazine for musicians, not music fans," explains one owner, Tom Whitney. The magazine, still to debut, will be less about celebrities than about the young musicians themselves. Editor Martin Keller says the cover story of the first issue will feature a 13-year-old jazz prodigy.

Girls Still Rule!

Have no fear. The ever popular teen girl category had its share of growth spurts

Girls' and Boys' Magazines: Freelance Percentages

The graph indicates the percentage of each magazine written by nonstaff writers.

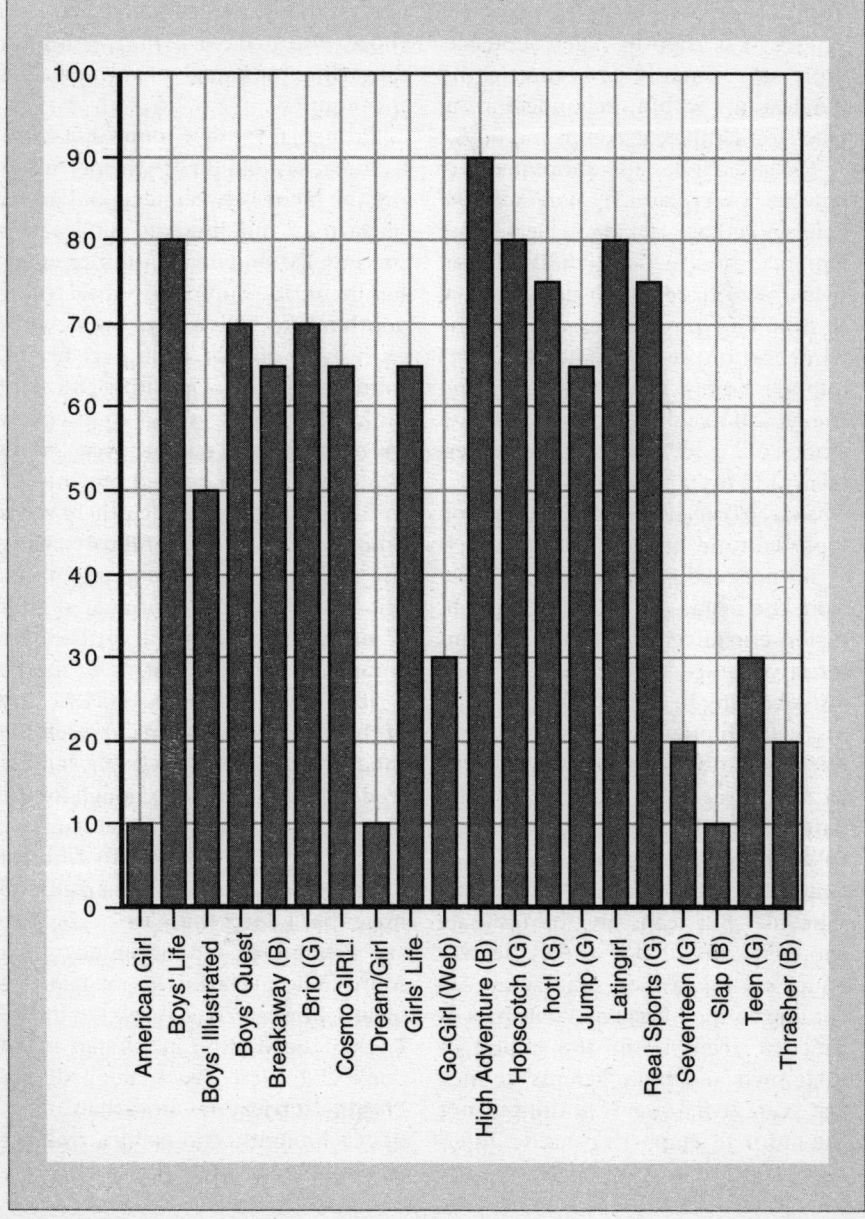

Publishing 2001

Magazine	Percentage
American Girl	10
Boys' Life	80
Boys' Illustrated	50
Boys' Quest	70
Breakaway (B)	65
Brio (G)	70
Cosmo GIRL!	65
Dream/Girl	10
Girls' Life	65
Go-Girl (Web)	30
High Adventure (B)	90
Hopscotch (G)	80
hot! (G)	75
Jump (G)	65
Latingirl	80
Real Sports (G)	75
Seventeen (G)	20
Slap (B)	10
Teen (G)	30
Thrasher (B)	20

this year. New additions included *Teen-Style* and *Hot!*, both from H&S Media; *Sweet16.com; Entertainmenteen,* from Primedia; *Teen Movieline;* and *Teen Vogue.*

Hot! targets the 'tween girl, between 8 and 12, while *TeenStyle* is designed to appeal to a slightly older audience. Both are primarily fashion/celebrity publications with a preponderance of pieces on clothes, makeup, and boys.

H&S Media has also announced yet another 'tween launch, *Mary-Kate and Ashley*. Perhaps taking a leaf from Oprah, the media-friendly Olson twins, who have grown up on television and in the movies, will be the name behind a magazine that H&S public relations says will "go beyond the typical teen magazines . . . to offer stories on education, health, self-esteem, and even electronics."

Sweet16.com is all about how you look. Editor Cheryl Schwartz calls it "your personal guide to looking great from the inside out." This new publication encourages readers to "get interactive" and read the magazine while also checking in at the website.

The high priestess of women's fashion magazines, *Vogue*, has given birth to *Teen Vogue*. Editor Amy Astley says parent company Condé Nast is waiting to see how the magazine sells before committing to a regular publishing schedule. But teens are the ultimate shoppers, and that's where the revenues are for fashion magazines. According to the Magazine Publishers of America, teens spent $98 billion of their own and their parents' money last year. *Teen Vogue* is nothing if not the ultimate shopper's paradise. Interviewed by the *New York Times* on the eve of the magazine's debut, *Vogue* Publisher Richard Beckman noted that he "was astonished by the level of sophistication" of teens today. Whether such sophistication is welcome news to parents and society, for advertisers and those who make a living writing for magazines the launch of any new titles is of interest.

Primedia Youth Group's *Entertainmenteen*, says Editor Hedy End, is filling the niche between teen idol poster magazines and lifestyle publications such as *YM* and *Teen*. Another entertainment title hoping to appeal to the youth market is *Teen Movieline*, devoted exclusively to hot young celebrities. John Evans, Chief Operating Officer of Line Publications, said in an interview in *Folio*, "The success of the teen books is obviously what piqued our interest in this market, and we felt there was a unique niche we could fill by tackling the subjects of movies and celebrities. Those are part of the formula at a lot of other titles, but none of them are completely devoted to it, as we are."

It will be nearly impossible for any of these new publications to catch the runaway success of *Teen People*, but the teen population is large enough for the race to accommodate several winners. Denise Keegan, Public Affairs Director of *Teen People,* says, "The market is so huge that I don't think we're going to see a point of saturation any time soon." The magazine is not taking a breath, however. *Teen People* has joined Book of the Month Club to start a teen book club. *Teen People* Book of the Month Club features more than 100 titles each month, chosen by a group of teenagers from across the country.

In another joint venture by a top teen magazine, *Seventeen* joined forces with HarperCollins to produce a line of fiction and nonfiction books for teen girls. *Seventeen* promises that its nonfiction "will be the first place teens turn to for guidance." The first three titles were *How to be Gorgeous, The Boyfriend Clinic,* and *Total Astrology.* The publishing program launched with a six-figure marketing campaign that included national advertising, online advertising, and distribution through mall and retail events.

Seventeen continues to lead the lucrative field of teen magazines and was the only children's magazine to make *Folio*'s list of the top 500 magazines. With a circulation of more than 2 million it ranked number 40 of all magazines in terms of advertising revenue.

While some teen magazines looked for new ways to expand, *Girl* changed its position in the market. Created by the publishers of *Mode*, a fashion magazine for large women, *Girl* started as a teen book for "the multi-sized and multi-ethnic." It has announced that it now intends to "expand its editorial coverage to specifically reflect and respond to the interests and needs of African-American girls, ages 12 to 19." In changing its target market, Editorial Director Corynne Corbett says, the new *Girl* will appeal to a vastly underserved market, and "speak to the teen in me who never got a magazine." The magazine has a new look and will expand from quarterly to six issues a year.

Parent Growth

Teen magazines are rivaled by parenting publications in numbers and niches. One magazine is targeting fathers exclusively, while another for moms and dads is already getting major media attention.

Launched as a bimonthly, *dads* started with a circulation of 200,000 and hopes to be a monthly with 500,000 readers by year three. "Our magazine is called *dads*, and our mission is to help fathers be better dads," explains Editor and Managing Partner Eric Garland. "Our target audience is professional men who have reached a certain level in their professional careers and want to have the same kind of success at home with their families. Today's dad is not the same as the father of 20 years ago."

The first issue of *dads* appealed directly to fathers who are also sports fans, with the venerable Cal Ripkin of the Baltimore Orioles on the cover. The next cover featured Chris Berman and Dan Patrick of ESPN with the tag line, "How ESPN's stars stay on top of their game at home and on air."

One problem that could influence sales of publications such as *dads* and *MH-18* is position on the average newsstand. They do not belong to a clear-cut category and so are planted in a variety of places. In some stores, for example, *dads* is shelved with the parenting magazines; in others it is with men's magazines. *MH-18* suffers the same identity crisis, with no firm place to call its own on newsstands: It can be found at different times and places in the men's section, the sports section, or the children's section with the teen girl magazines.

Identity is an obstacle that *Offspring*, a joint venture between Hearst

Magazines and *SmartMoney*, is ready to hurdle. The quarterly has already been represented on the major morning news programs and one issue sported a sticker claiming, "New from the editors of the *Wall Street Journal*." While *Offspring* will cover education, technology, health care, and finance, its editors say it is not anything like *SmartMoney*. "We are a different kind of parenting magazine," says *Offspring* Editor Steve Swartz. Still, the magazine is clearly going after the same professional audience; a representative lead story reported on the 100 best school districts in the country.

Other new parenting titles include *Single Parents*, a quarterly that launched with a circulation of 500,000. It describes its target audience as "single parents striving to provide their children with a nurturing, stable environment." African-American parents also got a title dedicated to them with the launch of the quarterly *Today's Child*.

Primedia, which publishes *American Baby*, *Healthy Kids*, and *Childbirth*, announced the acquisition of Baby Faire Inc., a trade show for young families. Of the purchase, Tom Rogers, CEO of Primedia said, "the acquisition of Baby Faire is another example of how at Primedia we are continuing to create exciting and innovative access for our advertisers to their key consumers."

Still in the expectant stage: Reports say that Martha Stewart is considering launching *Martha Stewart Baby* as a full-fledged publication. The magazine appeared last year as a single issue, sponsored entirely by Baby Gap. The chief financial editor and administrative officer of *Martha Stewart Living* Omnimedia admits that the company is "in the early stages of growing a potential magazine."

(See "Regional Markets, In Your Own Backyard," page 65, for information on regional parenting publications.)

What's Coming Up?

Just when it seems that everything is new, the old faithfuls in the children's magazine market remind us of their importance the reasons behind their success.

National Geographic World has celebrated its twenty-fifth anniversary, which it kicked off with a national tour of the worldmobile—a bus that travels to schools around the country and features contests on the National Geographic website. The magazine also started the millennium with a new editor, Melina Grosa Bellows. Bellows plans a total redesign of the magazine in the coming year. She intends to take the high quality of the content and make it even more current and relevant to kids. *World* will also become less like a textbook and more sophisticated in appearance.

Zillions, published by *Consumer Reports*, celebrated its twentieth anniversary by announcing that the magazine for 8-to-14-year-olds would leave print behind to become an e-zine exclusively, at www.zillions.org. Peter Chidsey, Vice President of Marketing and Circulation, has explained that the company wanted to make *Consumer Reports Online* a family site and that the rising costs of producing a kids' magazine contributed to the decision.

Production costs have driven changes at other children's magazines, particularly those strictly subscriber-based. In the past year, many companies have looked for ways to expand their presence without having to take advertisements. Two magazines making changes that will put them in closer touch with their primary audiences are *Highlights for Children* and *Ranger Rick.*

"We have something quite exciting going on here," announces Gerald Bishop, Editor of *Ranger Rick.* "*Ranger Rick, Your Big Backyard,* and our newest magazine, *Wild Animal Baby,* have all been incorporated into the National Wildlife Federation's education division. We are looking for better ways to use the magazine's resources."

While the new union is still in its infancy, Bishop admits that one possible scenario would have the magazines moving into the school market. "At this time, we are not exactly sure what our role in that market could or should be, but there may be something there."

The other big news from the group is the success of its newest magazine, *Wild Animal Baby.* At a year old, says Bishop, the magazine has already doubled its projected circulation. The magazine, which appears 10 times a year and is directed at an audience six months to two-years-old, is the brainchild of Donna Johnson, Editor of *Your Big Backyard* and now Senior Director for Education Publications.

The venerable *Highlights for Children* is about to launch its website, a project that has been a year in the making. "The challenge we set ourselves," explains Managing Editor Christine Clark, "was to build a website for kids that is more than bells and whistles. We know we are not the first out there, but that was by design." The site will have a wealth of material, including archives of stories, crafts, and science questions; a virtual classroom visit with the illustrator of each of the magazine's covers that will include questtions and answers; an extensive games section; and a place where kids can hear poetry read aloud and guess at a mystery sound.

Clark also says, "We are conducting some editorial research into the print version of the magazine. I can't say yet where that will lead us, but we are putting a lot of resources behind it, so next year I should be able to say more about the results. We are always looking for ways to improve the magazine, and I think we are closer than ever to the pulse of kids these days."

Clark notes that *Highlights* is in the process of rewriting the writers' guidelines for the first time in a number of years. They will soon be available at www.highlights.com.

Whether at a children's magazine with a respected history, like *Highlights*, or a new launch, the magazine business has its surprises, but true success is never a surprise. The good magazines find a way to stick around by growing like the children who remain entranced by them. Most children's magazines are likely to stay on paper, even as others, like *Guideposts for Kids* and *Zillions* morph onto screens. But the health of the industry today is of a breadth that can support them all.

History and Historical Fiction: Magazine Publishers

The following are general or special interest magazines that publish history or historical fiction. The list indicates reader age, percentage of the magazine that is written by nonstaff writers, and pay rate.

American Girl: both history & historical fiction, 8-12, 10%, payment varies.
American History: history, 14-Adult, 80%, 20¢ a word.
AppleSeeds: history, 8-10, 85%, $50 a page.
Archaeology's dig: history, 8-13, 70%, 50¢ a word.
Calliope: both, 8-14, 80%, to 25¢ a word.
Click: both, 3-7, 90%, 25¢+ a word.
Clubhouse: historical fiction, 9-14, 85%, $25-35.
Cobblestone: both, 10-14, 85%, to 25¢ a word.
Cricket: both, 9-14, 100%, to 25¢ a word.
Crinkles: history, 8-14, freelance percentage not available, $150.
Discovery Trails: both, 10-12, 90%, to 10¢ a word.
Faces: history, 8-14, 75%, to 25¢ a word.
Footsteps: history, 8-14, 80%, to 25¢ a word.
High Adventure: historical fiction, 6-17, 90%, 5¢ a word.
Highlights for Children: both, 2-14, 98%, payment varies.
Hopscotch: historical fiction, 6-12, 80%, 5¢ a word.
Keynoter: history, 14-18, 65%, $150-350.
Kids Discover: history, 6-9, 100%, but currently not looking for new writers.
Kid's World: historical fiction, 2-18, 100%, no payment.
Muse: history, 8-14, 90%, 25¢ a word.
New York Times Upfront: history, 14-18, 55%, payment varies.
Odyssey: history, 8-14, 100%, to 25¢ a word.
Power and Light: history, 11-12, 90%, 5¢ a word.
Quantum: 14-21, science history, 50%, $200.
Read: both, 10-18, 80%, payment varies.
The Rock: historical fiction, 10-14, 25%, payment varies.
Stone Soup: historical fiction, 6-13, 100%, $25.
Synapse: history, 14-21, 85%, no payment.
U*S*Kids: historical fiction, 5-10, 30%, 20¢ a word.

Charles & Rosalie Baker: A Living Past

Charles and Rosalie Baker manage to do what few couples accomplish. They work and live together. While for many couples the idea of nearly 24 hours a day together is a nightmare, when you meet the Bakers, it's clear that the union is a perfect fit. What brings them together is a passion for world history and for teaching children. Together they edit two magazines, the award-winning *Calliope*, and the three-year-old *Footsteps*, a magazine devoted to African-American history and culture. 2001 marks the twentieth anniversary of *Calliope*.

Rosalie grew up in the same New England coastal city they live in today, and Charlie and his family summered there, but they never met as youngsters. Rosalie describes their meeting: "Friends urged us to go on a blind date and we both said no at first, but then we did and the rest, so they say, is history. We were married two years later."

Both had planned careers in education. Rosalie has an undergraduate and master's degree in classics and taught high school Greek and Latin. Charlie got a degree in political science, and a master's in English. He has, as he puts it, "taught just about every subject there is, mostly in middle school classrooms."

The idea of starting a magazine was never part of the plan, but the Fates stepped in. "I had a major operation," explains Rosalie, "and I had to spend a long time in bed." Picking up the story without missing a beat, Charlie says, "She was bored. I suggested she write a book, but she didn't want to write a book, so we came up with the idea of a magazine. Rosalie feels that ancient history and the classics are so important in a child's education and we wanted to find a way to get them to study the classics and like them. We called our magazine *Classical Calliope*."

Foundations

The first issue of *Classical Calliope* came out in January 1981. "It was black and white and 12 pages long," says Rosalie, "and we did everything—the writing,

Charles and Rosalie Baker

the layout, everything." Charlie adds, "I did all the artwork and a printer would come to our house and pick up the proofs, bring them to Fall River, and then print them up and deliver them back to us."

"Charlie had to hand-address every one of those early issues," says Rosalie. "Our first issue, we printed 500 copies. He kept addressing them all the way up to 2,400 subscriptions." The magazine was then a monthly. Rosalie and Charlie worked during the day as teachers and produced the magazine in their spare time. "It was crazy," recalls Rosalie, "but we didn't have children and we just spent all our spare time on *Calliope*."

The first subscriptions went to family and friends and then the Bakers decided they needed to advertise to get more subscribers. They put ads in the *Christian Science Monitor* and the *New York Times*. "Then, I started thinking that we needed to appeal to parents and grandparents who had taken the classics and wanted their children to learn about them," says Charlie. "I had always loved the *New Yorker* and thought it would be the perfect place for us to advertise." What he did not realize was the price. "We couldn't believe how much it cost—and remember in the beginning we were the only backers of *Calliope*. All we could afford was a tiny ad. So we wrote this small ad, and put a picture of the muse *Calliope* in it, along with a post office box. We didn't want people to know that it was just us working out of a spare room at our house; we thought a post office box would make us more official!"

Rosalie laughs and adds, "No one knew, but we did everything back in those days: We were president and secretary and the dog was chairman of the board!"

After the ad came out, Charlie recalls stopping every day after school to see if there was any mail. "Finally, I went one day and there was a subscription order, and we were so excited." Then, Rosalie adds, "All of a sudden, we had thousands of subscriptions and we thought, 'Oh my gosh, how are we going to do this all?'" Up until that point the couple did not even own a computer. Rosalie's brother convinced them to get one, at least to address the labels so Charlie wouldn't have to hand write them anymore. But Charlie says, " I still had to stick the labels on and separate and bundle the issues by state and zip code for the post office. We had them spread out in a room that didn't have much furniture in it. I remember that it was one of the Dakotas that was the fiftieth state where we had a subscription. We also had subscribers in 22 foreign countries."

Building

"I don't think people realize how much clerical work goes into a venture like this," says Rosalie. "It was a killer!" It became particularly difficult to maintain once the Bakers had a child.

Charles and Rosalie Baker

"Our son was born a year after we started *Classical Calliope*," recalls Rosalie. "For the first few months, it was fine, because he slept a lot, but then things got crazy and I found I was falling asleep at the dinner table." The Bakers decided that they couldn't keep up the hectic pace of producing a monthly and informed the subscribers the publication would become an annual. At the same time, a neighbor's daughter brought the Bakers a copy of *Cobblestone*, an American history magazine that had launched a year before *Classical Calliope*.

"We wrote to the head of *Cobblestone* and told him who we were and that we would like to freelance for his magazine," says Rosalie. "It was incredible: We got a call from Publisher Ted Dawes the day after he got the letter. He said he wanted to come and see us because he wanted to continue the magazine. The *Cobblestone* board met in January of 1983. In January, 1993, we became partners with *Cobblestone* and *Classical Calliope* became a bimonthly."

While the Bakers were still doing most of the work, at least the clerical end was handled in Peterborough, New Hampshire, where *Cobblestone* was based. The magazine continued to grow and change. "Charlie felt we should expand from classical culture and history to become a world history magazine," explains Rosalie. In 1990, we changed our name to *Calliope* and at that point we started to use freelancers. In 1996 we went to four-color."

Heritage

Today, *Calliope* is still produced largely from the Bakers' home, although each of them has an office. Rosalie does much of the initial research and together they plan each issue's outline. Charlie spends some of his time traveling around the country, going to conferences and talking to kids about *Calliope* and the other Cobblestone Publishing magazines, including *AppleSeeds, Faces, Footsteps,* and *Odyssey*. Over the summer he also ran a series of workshops for teachers on how to teach history. "The workshops are primarily for teachers in grades four to seven," explains Charlie, "and in the couple of hours I have these teachers, I try to make history come alive for them, so they are excited about it and can take that excitement back to the classroom. Children know if a teacher likes something and they are very sophisticated as far as what you do know and what you don't know."

When Rosalie and Charlie talk about history, their passion is contagious. That enthusiasm translates to the magazine and to the kids in the classrooms that Charlie visits. "All it takes is one adventure, one idea, to excite a child. That can change that child's life, really," says Charlie.

Calliope has gone on to win just about every award it is possible for a children's magazine to win, including the Golden Lamp Award. So when Cobblestone Publishing needed an editor for a new magazine it had developed, it came straight to the Bakers. Charlie agreed to become editor of *Footsteps*.

Charles and Rosalie Baker

"When they asked me to edit *Footsteps*, I found I really knew very little about African-American history, and I didn't think I really had an interest in it," recalls Charlie. "Boy, was I wrong! I have since become fascinated by the history of African Americans and their contributions to this country. We have so many scholars of African-American history who want to write for the magazine, the response has really been overwhelming," says Charlie. "I think they see it as a vehicle to tell the story of this rich, beautiful, diverse heritage."

"Each of us has a heritage," explains Charlie, "and I tell kids that your heritage is like the foundation of your house. You may have a fancy foundation, it may be very simple, it doesn't matter. What matters is what you decide to build on that foundation. You might build a castle, you might build a ranch house, you might build a cabin. It doesn't matter, but you need a foundation and you need to be proud of that foundation."

As *Footsteps* goes into its second full year of publication, the Bakers sit back and say that one of these days they are going to slow down. Almost simultaneously they mention possibly expanding *Footsteps* to nine issues a year.

The future is likely to hold other challenges: Cobblestone Publishing has been purchased by Carus Publishing, publishers of *Cricket, Spider, Ladybug, Babybug, Muse,* and *Cicada.* For the time being, no staff changes will occur at any of the Cobblestone magazines, but the union should open new doors. Carus magazines have strong visibility in the home market, while the Cobblestone magazines reach schools and libraries. Together, these magazines are a powerhouse in children's publishing in fiction and nonfiction.

One of these days, the Bakers may just slow down, but readers hope that day doesn't come too soon. "We were thinking about a magazine on archaeology for kids, but we just don't have time to do it right now," says Rosalie with a laugh. Past, present, and future—the Bakers live in them all.

Keith Garton: The Big Picture

When *Time For Kids* entered the school magazine market five years ago, it offered young readers something no news-based children's publication had ever done before: truly *timely* coverage of major events. It shook up the world previously owned by *Weekly Reader* and *Scholastic* and changed the market.

Now a proven success, Time, Inc. has given the magazine its own publisher, Keith Garton. Since he came to Time as Publisher of *Time For Kids,* he has demonstrated clearly his longstanding commitment to kids and education. The classroom editions of *Time For Kids* are read by 3 million kids. This past year, the company launched its newest edition, *The Big Picture,* for kindergarten and first grade.

For Garton, the big picture is looking pretty good. After five years in publication, *World Report,* the edition of *Time For Kids* directed to grades four, five, and six, is the leader in the classroom magazine market. *News Scoop,* for grades two and three, has just had its best year ever. All that pleases Garton, but if you want to see him light up, ask him to talk about the development of his baby, *The Big Picture*.

"Teachers asked us for something for emergent readers and we started thinking about this new magazine. We wanted to make sure we could really meet their needs in the classroom, so we asked the teachers to tell us what they wanted." Tell him they did. The concepts behind *The Big Picture* are the result of a joint effort and collaboration between those educators and Time, Inc. staff. "Our focus groups with teachers really helped us to define what the magazine would actually be," explains Garton. "They are some of the best focus groups I have ever been a part of."

First Direction

Listening to Garton talk, it is evident how dedicated he is to children's education, even though he says, laughing, "I sort of stumbled into educational publishing and have never been able to get out of it!"

Like many professionals, what he thought he'd do in life is a far cry from what he is actually doing. He attended Oklahoma State, where, he says, "I did my undergraduate degree in advertising and communications, and I have a graduate degree in statistical analysis. I always pictured myself working someplace like the Gallup Organization."

Keith Garton

Garton has always been interested in educating the mentally handicapped. In his first job out of school, he worked for a volunteer organization and "went around the state of Oklahoma talking to schools and communities about the educable retarded." His task was to get such students mainstreamed into classrooms and then find volunteers to act as in-class aides to teachers. In his travels, Garton got to know a number of sales representatives and consultants for various publishing companies. After a year and a half, one of them approached him saying, "You need to work with us." Garton agreed and hasn't stopped moving up the educational publishing ladder since.

Now settled in New York City, home of the Time, Inc. empire, Garton has worked for many of the biggest names in the school and library market, including Scholastic, McGraw-Hill, and most recently, Prentice Hall, where he was Senior Vice President of Marketing.

Signature

As the first publisher of *Time For Kids*, Garton is responsible for increasing the division's school sales and developing new products for Time's K-12 educational publishing. *The Big Picture* is only the first of the potential new products to have Garton's signature; meeting the needs of the market are a high priority for him.

"Teachers told us they loved the idea of being able to share news stories with their students. We have tried to make *The Big Picture* meatier than other products on the market and provide more content. Teachers love it because they can connect to science and social studies themes through the news." He cites an edition on money tied to the issuing of the new gold dollar coin. *The Big Picture* is delivered to teachers every two weeks, and also comes to teachers in an oversized edition called *The Bigger Picture* that allows for group reading sessions. Half of the issues are themed and the other half are devoted to age-appropriate news stories.

Garton explains that an important part of *The Big Picture* might be called the *cool factor*. "We try to present information in a way that is both colorful and dynamic and at the same time written in a voice that talks to our readers as peers who have points of view of their own. We never talk down to kids. I think this makes them feel important and we try to do that with all our magazines. Kids often tell me that they feel very grown up when they are reading *Time For Kids* and I think that is a compliment to our product."

Referring to the readers of *The Big Picture*, Garton says, "At this age, kindergarten and first grade, if you establish confidence in kids that reading is a great way to find out new things and new information, you are well on the way to establishing success in that child in all content areas," and, he says, instilling in those youngsters a lifelong passion for reading and learning—despite the fact that K-1 kids may not read fluently. *The Big Picture*, says Garton, differs from its competitors at Scholastic and Weekly Reader, because of its stress on text, even for a kindergartner. "We want kids to learn from *The Big Picture* the concept of print," he stresses, "and what a reader does with print."

The Big Picture also makes very good business sense for *Time For Kids* and Garton is quick to point that out. "We can now go into a K-5 school or a K-6 school and offer them something for every student in that school," he says. *The Big Picture* is very likely to boost sales of all of the company's school publications.

More to Come

While *Time For Kids* has focused all its energy on the younger grades, Scholastic and Weekly Reader Corporation have been looking upward. Last year, both companies launched newsmagazines for older students: *Teen Newsweek*, from Weekly Reader and *Newsweek*, and *UpFront* from Scholastic and the *New York Times*.

"We are definitely interested in doing something for older kids," Garton says, "but right now we are still trying to find out from teachers the kind of magazine that would best meet their needs and talking to them about the kind of product we should develop."

As he talks, Garton is busy pulling up an e-mail on his computer that he received earlier in the day. It is from the father of a third-grader, a man Garton met at a recent conference. He reads the message aloud: "My daughter's class was so moved by an article in *Time For Kids* on the famine in East Africa that they decided to hold a fund-raiser to support relief efforts. All the third-graders brought items from home that they sold to each other. The event raised $250 that has been sent to the Red Cross." Accompanying the message are pictures of the class effort. As he reads it, Garton sounds as proud as any father about his magazines.

Educational publishing is not only a vocation for Garton, it is also a passion. "I am really very lucky," he says laughing, "to have stumbled into this career. It is something I really enjoy."

Online Markets

Go Internet, Young Writers

By Mary C. Northrup

Pioneers in children's writing: Head to the expanding frontiers. The Internet is open territory for e-zines. Your audience is growing up with electronic media the way the mid-century generation grew up with the exploding paperback markets. Bookstore magazine racks and magazine sections at public libraries display an incredible variety of children's print magazines. The same wide assortment is found in e-zines or websites designed specifically to inform or entertain children and teens. If you've always wanted to be a pioneer, the Internet is the place to do it.

Since e-zines are so new, finding markets for your work is not as easy as picking up a market directory or studying sample copies. But if you enjoy surfing the Web and keeping up with what is out there, you can find opportunities to see your work in print and add publication credits to your résumé.

The Territory
E-zines have been around for less than a decade, many considerably less. The e-zine sites taking hold combine attributes of print publishing and stake their own territory as well. Some are educational, some pure fun. Some are by kids, some about kids but for parents, teachers, or other adults.

MidLink Magazine grew out of a classroom teacher's writing assignment. Caroline McCullen, Editor, believes it is the oldest website of its type. On this site (www.cs.ucf.edu/~ MidLink/), schools from all over the world share learning activities and projects. "I saw the motivation in students and was determined to share it with others," says McCullen, who began the site in 1994. Students can search current articles, archives, and a list of "cool schools" by continent, and link to related sites and search tools. As for freelance opportunities, writers with teaching experience may want to investigate sites such as *MidLink*. "We are looking for ways to involve teachers," says McCullen.

Another long time site, in Internet years, is *Parents and Children Together Online,* which has been on since late 1994. "Our print and website were comparable, but with distinct differences," reports Editor Christopher Essex. "The print came with a companion audiotape. We tried putting audio on the Web, but it was slow; the file sizes were too big back then. The print version also

Keep Current: Sources

Keeping up with children's e-zines is an obvious challenge. As with many websites, they come and go. Just as you would do to keep abreast of the print market, you will need to search several sources. Here are just a few, print and electronic:

Books
- *Magazines for Libraries,* 10th edition (Bowker, 2000), a standard print reference book in public and academic libraries. Arranged by subject, it contains hundreds of magazines with contact information, circulation, and annotations. After each subject, electronic journals are listed if they exist. Children's writers will want to look under "Children and Teenage."

Online
- **Yahoo!:** (www.yahoo.com) has lists of sites for children and teens. For children's sites, select Society and Culture, Magazines, and then Children. For teens, select Society and Culture, Magazines, and then Youth.
- **AskJeeves:** (www.askjeeves.com) has a special search, Ask Jeeves for Kids, that leads to websites and e-zines of all kinds for children, with a parents and teachers section.
- **Outer-Net Links for Kids: E-zines and Magazines:** http://www.outer-net.com/~software/kidsmags.htm
Outer-Net is an Internet access company that features a list of e-zines, magazines, and other children's links on its website.
- **Berit's Best Sites for Children:** www.beritsbest.com
A number of websites attempt to sort out the good sites from the inferior and evaluate them. On Berit's, e-zines and other children's websites are not only listed, but also described and rated.

Libraries
Many online libraries include lists of magazine sites among the other resources on their homepage. Check these out:
- **Michigan Electronic Library:** mel.lib.mi.us/children/magazine.html for children's magazines, or mel.lib.mi.us/children/ymags.html, for young adult magazines.
- **Colorado Alliance of Research Libraries:** www.coalliance.org
Click on E-Journals, then on Electronic Journals by LC Subject Headings, then on "C" for *children*.

More Children's E-zines and Websites

Just as print magazines cover a wide range of topics, so also do materials available on the Web. Take a look at some of these for children, teens, and parenting:

- **ABC News 4 Kids:** abcnews.go.com/abcnews4kids/kids/index.html
  News stories, both national and international.
- **Amazing Adventure Series: Stories of Imagination:** www.amazingadventure.com/index_fl.html
  Stories and activities.
- **Dodoland:** www.swifty.com/azatlan
  Stories, games, and art gallery; concentrates on the arts and the environment.
- **Fathering Magazine:** www.fathermag.com
  Articles on a wide range of topics pertaining to fathers. Includes writers' guidelines.
- **FutureScan:** www.futurescan.com
  Career information for teens and links to other career sites.
- **Girl Power!:** www.health.org/gpower
  Health and fitness, sponsored by the U.S. Department of Health and Human Services.
- **Kids' Castle:** www.kidscastle.si.edu
  Educational articles, games, and message boards; from Smithsonian magazine.
- **A Kid's Life:** www.kidslife.com
  Lessons and fun for boys and girls.
- **Kidtalk News Family Magazine:** www.kidtalknews.com
  Stories, surveys, games, jokes, recipes, homework help, links.
- **StoryPlace: The Children's Digital Library:** www.storyplace.org
  Stories and activities for the preschool and early elementary levels.
- **Yak's Corner:** www.yakscorner.com
  News, crafts, recipes, puzzles, jokes; by the Detroit Free Press.
- **Youthline USA:** www.youthline-usa.com
  Fun for kids, resources for teachers and parents.

Print Magazines with Websites

Most magazines that have a Web presence are there to provide information to entice people to subscribe. They generally provide subscription information, contact information, a photo of the cover, and (especially for younger children) a message to parents about content and safety. Look at these examples:

- **Boys' Life**: www.bsa.scouting.org/mags/boyslife/index.html
From the homepage, view the table of contents, e-mail *Boys' Life* about your troop's outing plans, enter contests, ask questions, read jokes and riddles, and see previous issues.
- **Children's Better Health Institute**: www.cbhi.org/magazines.htm
This site links to all seven of the Institute's magazines (*Turtle, Humpty Dumpty, Children's Playmate, Jack And Jill, Child Life, Children's Digest, U*S*Kids*). Visit individual titles, where you can see the cover of the current issue, view table of contents, order a subscription by e-mail, link to safe websites found in recent issues, read a message to parents, or e-mail the Institute.
- **Cricket Magazine Group**: www.cricketmag.com/
From this page, connect to *Babybug, Ladybug, Spider,* and *Cricket* (you can also get to *Muse* and *Click* from here). At the sites for younger audience magazines, stories and "play and sing" activities appear. *Spider* contains poems, stories, puzzles, activities, and the opportunity to send e-mail and jokes. *Cricket* shows this month's issue, a puzzle, recommended reading, contests, and an invitation to send e-mail.

   For *Muse* and *Click*, go to http://www.musemag.com/. From this site you can "Fly to *Click*" or "Beam to *Muse*." The *Click* site, for ages 3 to 7, consists of stories and activities. *Muse*, for ages 8 to 14, contains a variety of activities (poetry, Q & A, cool math stuff, contests), information about this month's issue, next month's previews, articles, news, and a list of books and links on one topic.
- **National Geographic World**: www.nationalgeographic.com/media/world/index.html
This site, which includes advertising, allows you to click on a feature story, view archives, send and read messages, and join a pen pal network. From this site you can also get to Kids@nationalgeographic.com, which is filled with activities related to the magazine.

Print Magazines with Websites

- **National Wildlife Federation,** *Ranger Rick* and *Your Big Backyard*: www. nwf.org/rrick/ and www.nwf.org/ybby/
  On the *Ranger Rick* site, you can read articles in English and Spanish; see a list of magazines, books, and videos; peruse the archives; and investigate the Q&A. You may also connect to Kids Zone to find out about National Wildlife Federation activities. At *Your Big Backyard*'s site, you can connect to a listing of activities from the current issue, look at past issues' table of contents, view information about the magazine, and read about the wildlife activities sponsored by the National Wildlife Federation.
- **Owl Kids Online:** www.owl.on.ca/
  From here, connect to chickaDEE Net, where you'll see puzzles, crafts, jokes, links to other sites, and where you can send in drawings for an online art gallery and e-mail. Or connect to Wired Owl, which features this month's cover of the magazine, polls, jokes, riddles, Mighty Mites cartoons, links, and the opportunity to send e-mail.
- *Seventeen* **Online:** www.seventeen.com/
  This site is full of entertainment and celebrity news, gossip, horoscopes, beauty and fashion advice, news, marketplace, daily polls, and much more.
- *Sports Illustrated For Kids*: www.sikids.com/
  SI For Kids is filled with articles, sports trivia, and answers to questions. You can also view videos, play fantasy sports, and find the birthdays of favorite athletes.
- *Time For Kids*: www.timeforkids.com/
  With its familiar red cover, this magazine's site includes *World Report,* for grades four to six; *News Scoop,* for grades two and three (both editions also available in Spanish); an opportunity to vote in a poll; messages for teachers and parents; and a special section on kids' environmental projects: Heroes for the Planet.
- *YES Mag*: www.yesmag.bc.ca/
  This magazine, from Canada, features on its site a variety of science news, a long list of projects to do at home, challenging questions, reports on what some kids are doing in science, and reviews of books and software.

Publishing 2001

had few features for parents. The website is more varied and has more content for parents, teachers, and older kids, three times as much content as the print."

Now, on *Parents and Children Together Online* (http://www.indiana.edu/~eric_rec/pcto.html), children can read new stories and poems, look at back issues, and link to other resources while parents can read articles, book reviews, and link to other websites. The site is part of ERIC, the Educational Resources Information Center, which is a "federally funded national information system" consisting of clearinghouses on specific subjects to serve educators, parents, and others. ERIC has provided educational materials and services to teachers and others interested in language arts for 40 years.

Parents and Children Together Online is very open to freelancers. Essex is looking for writers who have respect for children, who do not talk down to them or use clichéd subject matter. The ideal writer has a "connection to the child sensibility," he says, but is "not necessarily a teacher; it could be a parent or creative writer." Extensive writers' guidelines are available at the site.

Those who enjoy constructing puzzles may find a market for their work on the Web, too, at a unique site that is educational and fun, *Kid Crosswords* (www.kidcrosswords.com). Brian Goss, creator of the site and a puzzle constructor himself, says he "conceived the site to give teachers content." The audience—educators, children, homeschoolers, parents, and grandparents—can select a puzzle to fit a lesson or current holiday. Puzzle subjects for the start of the school year, for example, included *Charlotte's Web*, subtraction, famous hurricanes, the Summer Olympics, Pennsylvania, *Treasure Island*, World War II, and more. Originally, *Kid Crosswords* puzzles had to be printed out and worked on paper, but "the site has become more sophisticated," says Goss. "Kids can do the puzzles online, which broadens the audience. Besides providing educational activities or information for the kids, or sources and assistance for the adults, some sites are just a place to hang out.

FreeZone (www.freezone.com) began as the print magazine *Curiocity for Kids*, and now offers a variety of content and interactive areas. Members can play games, take part in polls, look for advice, and go into monitored chat situations. "*FreeZone* has been around for four and a half years. We're the first safe online community for kids," says Ali Pohn, Managing Director. "The mission of the site has always been to empower kids. Kids write 80 percent of the site and what they don't write, they suggest or request."

Getting girls into technology has inspired the creation of dedicated sites. *Club Girl Tech* (www.girltech.com) began on the Web on Take Your Daughter to Work Day in April 1996. "We created *Club Girl Tech* because at that time there were no sites for girls on the Internet," states Emily Keller, Webmaster. "Since our company's mission is to encourage girls in technology use, creating a website for them seemed an obvious first step." The site consists of eight areas: chat, sports, role models, female inventors, news, games, review sites, and the parents' and teachers'

> ## By Kids, for Kids
>
> Besides Cyberkids (www.cyberkids.com) and Cyberteens (www.cyberteens.com), here are just a few of the many sites that feature writing almost exclusively by young people:
> - **Electronic Elementary:** www. inform.umd.edu/EdRes/Topic/Education/K-12/ mdk-12/homepers/ emag
> - **FreshLimeSoda:** www.freshlimesoda.co
> - **A Girl's World:** www.agirlsworld.com
> - **KIDS Report:** kids.library.wisc.edu
> - **KidzMagazine:** www.thetemple.com/KidzMagazine
> - **Teenvoice.com:** www.teenvoice.com

areas. "We send a strong message throughout our site that girls are strong, capable, and valued," says Keller. "We have some freelance writers contributing to *Club Girl Tech* content. We look for writing that is educational and at the same time fun for kids."

Just 4 Girls (www.gsusa.org/girls) is part of the Girl Scouts of the USA website. Chris Bergerson, Director, Interactive Education, explains its origin almost three years ago: "We began the site as an offshoot of a science and technology grant that we had received. We created the initial *Just 4 Girls* using Post-Its on the wall, and then refined the organization from there." Girls can investigate trips and sports, read about crafts and careers, explore a variety of subjects, as well as explore Girl Talk and Girl Space, which consists of stories, art, poems submitted by girls.

At *Just 4 Girls*, the staff prefers to contact a writer rather than the other way around. "The reason we would go to an outside writer is that we do not have the staff within to do the project or we want a certain type of expertise," explains Bergerson. Writers who have the necessary qualifications—"kid-ability, knowledge of subject and ability to integrate it into our program, enthusiasm and sense of humor, creativity, and writing skills"—can send a résumé to Webteam@girlscouts.org.

Just like print magazines, e-zines offer age-related content. Sometimes a single e-zine site is divided into grade levels or age ranges. Other e-zines handle different ages at separate, tailored sites. *Cyberkids* (www.cyberkids.com) and *Cyberteens* (www.cyberteens.com) are run by Able Minds, whose President, Julie Richer, tells how the sites started: "While I was running my previous company, Mountain Lake Software, we sponsored a story contest for kids and teens. We were so impressed by the entries, we decided it would be great to publish them to a wider audience, so we decided to start kids and teens websites to showcase original creative work by young people." On the Able Minds sites, readers can play games, use chat rooms, display their writing or art, read the news, get homework help, link to other sites, and more. The company also oversees a site for young composers of music. *Cyberteens* offers a somewhat unique writing opportunity. "From time to time we publish a novel for our target audience serially (one chapter per week)," says Richer.

A Different Medium

Electronic formats are changing definitions of many products and mediums. Some sites that have the qualities of a magazine in print call themselves e-zines. Others call themselves websites.

"We consider *Club Girl Tech* an online community rather than an e-zine because girls are able to respond directly to the content and view their responses the following week," says Keller. "They are not merely reading the words, they are responding and sharing their views with each other."

"I don't really consider our pages an e-zine," says Bergerson, of *Just 4 Girls*. "We are doing it to complement our materials that are in print and to deliver programming activities and information through a different medium."

"Magazines come out in issues, which is how we used to do our website," reports *Cyberkids*' Richer. "Recently, we've changed our strategy. Now, we publish new stories, poems, and art in the appropriate categories, so that it's easy to find. Ability to navigate the site easily and find what you want is of prime importance to websites."

Still, whether it is an e-zine or a website, as with print submissions, be familiar with the market, target appropriate sites and areas within the site, and send only relevant material in a professional manner. To submit work, look for the e-mail address on the web-

> ### Books for Online Writers
>
> ■ *Online Markets for Writers: How to Make Money by Selling Your Writing on the Internet,* by Anthony Tedesco and Paul Tedesco (Henry Holt). Lots of good information for writers and an extensive list of online markets.
>
> ■ *Writing.com: Creative Internet Strategies to Advance Your Writing Career,* by Moira Anderson Allen (Allworth Press). How to use the Internet to research, communicate, and publish online. Includes a chapter on finding markets online.

site. It will connect you to the editor or someone who can answer your query.

The differences stem from the nature of the Web. An advantage of the medium is that you could see your work published more quickly than in print. "If something happens tonight, I can put it up tomorrow," says Goss of *Kid Crosswords*. Current events can translate into a story, article, or puzzle that will still be current when it appears.

Length is also affected when writing for a website or e-zine. Although technically there are no limits to possible length, as there might be in a print magazine, Keller points out, "Reading from a computer screen often isn't as comfortable as reading from a magazine or book, therefore articles need to be shorter." Richer agrees: "Kids don't like to scroll too much, so chapters need to be short."

Bergerson believes that writing for a website "requires a more global approach—right brain, if you want to put it that way. I think it has got to be catchy, have the potential for interaction or linking to resources and the needs of the audience, and utilize the medium that it is posted on."

The rapid expansion of these media frontiers means unlimited potential—for good and bad.

McCullen of *MidLink* is concerned about the trend toward commercialism in educational websites, but she's resisting such shifts. "You'll never see that on *MidLink*. We don't want advertising. Supported by a software company and two universities that provide space for sound, instructional content, *MidLink* provides an example of the best of what happens in classrooms around the world."

Goss of *Kid Crosswords* also sees more commercialism: "There will be a lot more people in it, but no trend toward more content."

"I think that delivery will be as important, if not more important than content, unfortunately, to capture audiences initially," says Bergerson. "However, I think that kids are also getting more sophisticated in their use of time on the Internet. I think that the sites that will survive will be those that have a specific purpose, rather than those that try to be everything to everyone."

Because of cost and accessibility, "e-zine publishing is certainly cheaper," says Keller. She also foresees more subscription e-zines.

Interestingly, some see the future still turning to the traditional: Richer predicts "more interaction between readers and authors." She entertains the idea that *Cyberkids* and *Cyberteens* may possibly go to print. At *FreeZone*, Pohn "looks forward to a time where *FreeZone* will have a newsstand/subscription-based magazine."

Whether print and electronic, or web-based only, children's e-zines will emerge, definitions will continue to change, ideas and formats will continue to expand. All to the good, if such changes continue to provide new learning opportunities for kids, interactive fun, and opportunities for freelancers to write and sell.

Regional Markets

In Your Own Backyard

By Suzanne Lieurance

Whether you live on the East Coast, the West Coast, or somewhere in between, you'll find a variety of regional publications in your own backyard. But, have you ever tried writing for these markets? If you're looking for a way to acquire some impressive clips, earn extra money, or maybe even gain a local following, these markets just might be the way to do it.

While many of these publications are written strictly for adults, others are aimed at parents, grandparents, and families. With a little refocusing, your articles for children can be written about children and may become just perfect for these publications.

I'm not talking about *Southern Living, Sunset,* or any of the big city magazines like *San Diego* or *Boston* here. Those glossies usually feature articles on more sophisticated topics, aimed for adults who may or may not be parents. Instead, look for the smaller, free tabloids that are usually placed in entryways to bookstores, libraries, and even some stores. If you've bypassed these publications, thinking they weren't worth your time or energy, it might be worth your while to take a closer look.

While some may pay nothing or next to nothing, you might be surprised at what others offer. Not all regional tabloids, magazines, and newpapers are created equal. True, some pay only in contributor's copies, but others pay quite handsomely for a feature article. The best part is, most of these publications don't receive the monthly deluge of submissions and queries that the glossy, national magazines do, so your chances of seeing your byline here are much better.

Near or Far

United Parenting Publications (UPP) has become the largest network of regional parenting publications in the United States. Every month, more than 1.3 million parenting magazines are distributed across the United States by UPP. According to the UPP online distribution map, each of their many parenting magazines features "a comprehensive local events calendar; articles; entertainment, education and school directories; baby, camp, and party guides and much, much more."

Even so, each of these publications is quite different when it comes to payment rates and rights purchased. Submitting to your local UPP publication

Regional Parenting Magazines

Take a look at regional family and parenting publications online when you can, to read current and past articles and see the kinds of topics they cover. Some websites include the writers' guidelines. Some publications without individual sites can be found through parenthoodweb.com or parenthood.com (both sites of United Parenting Publications) or family.com, which may provide the e-mail addresses to write and request guidelines.

- Alaska Parenting: editor@alaska.net
- Arizona Parenting: www.parenthood.com
- Atlanta Baby: www.atlantaparent.com
- Big Apple Parent/QueensParent/WestchesterParent: www.parentsknow.com
- Birmingham Family Times: www.parenthood.com
- The Boston Parents' Paper: www.parenthood.com
- Capital District Parent: publisher@cdparent.com (New York capital district)
- Central Florida Family Magazine: www.floridafamily.com
- Central Penn Parent: www.journalpub.com
- Charlotte Parent: www.family.com
- Chesapeake Family: www.chesapeakefamily.com
- Chicago Parent: www.chicagoparent@localmom.com
- Child Times: www.family.com
- City Parent: www.family.com (Canadian cities)
- Cleveland/Akron Family: www.clevelandakron.com (North Eastern Ohio)
- Colorado Parent: www.parenthood.com
- Connecticut Family: www.parenthood.com
- Connecticut Parent Magazine: www.ctparent.com
- Connecticut's County Kids: www.countykids.com
- Dallas Child: dchild@airmail.net
- Dallas Family: www.parenthood.com
- Eastside Parent: www.parenthood.com (the Northwest)
- Florida Baby Magazine: www.floridababy.com (Wisconsin)
- Genesee Valley Parent Magazine: www.family.com
- Georgia Family Magazine: www.georgiafamily.com
- Houston Family: www.parenthood.com
- Hudson Valley Parent: www.hudsonvalleyparent.com
- Indy's Child: www.indyschild.com
- Iowa Parent & Family: www.iowaparent.com

Regional Parenting Magazines

- **Island Parent Magazine:** www.coastnet.com/~iparentmag (British Columbia)
- **Kansas City Family:** www.kansascity.com
- **Kansas City Parent:** www.grapevine.com/kcparent
- **KIDS Magazine:** www.kidsmagazine.com
- **Kids VT:** www.kidsvt.com
- **L.A. Parent Magazine:** www.laparent.com
- **Lexington Family Magazine:** www.lexingtonfamily.com
- **Long Island Parenting News:** www.parenthood.com
- **Los Angeles Family Magazine:** www.childrenmagazine.com
- **Mahoning Valley Parent:** www.mvparentmagazine.com
- **MetroKids:** www.MetroKids.com (Pennsylvania, New Jersey, Delaware)
- **Metro Parent Magazine:** www.metropar.com (Michigan)
- **Minnesota Parent:** www.parenthood.com
- **Nashville Parent Magazine:** www.parentworld.com
- **N.E.W. Kids:** www.ericksonpublishing.com
- **New York Family:** www.parenthood.com
- **Northwest Baby & Child:** www.nwbaby.com
- **OC Family:** family.com (Orange County, CA)
- **Our Kids Austin:** www.parenthood.com
- **Our Kids San Antonio:** www.parenthood.com
- **PARENTGUIDE News:** www.parentguidenews.com (New York, NY)
- **Parenting Orange County:** www.parenthood.com (CA)
- **Parenting Bay Area Teens:** www.parenthood.com
- **Parents Express:** www.parents-express.com (Delaware Valley, PA)
- **Parents' Monthly:** www.parenthoodweb.com (Sacramento, CA)
- **Piedmont Parent:** piedmontparent@aol.com
- **Pittsburgh Parent:** www.pittsburghparent.com
- **Portland Parent:** www.parenthood.com
- **Puget Sound Parent:** www.parenthood.com
- **Sacramento/Sierra Parent:** www.sacramentosierra.com
- **San Diego Family Magazine:** www.sandiegofamily.com
- **San Diego Parent:** www.parenthood.com
- **San Francisco Bay Area Parent:** www.parenthood.com
- **San Francisco Peninsula Parent:** www.sfparent.com

Publishing 2001

Regional Parenting Magazines

- **Seattle's Child:** www.nwparent.com
- **South Florida Parenting:** www.sfparenting.com
- **Syracuse Parent:** www.syracuseparent.com
- **Tidewater Parent:** www.family.com
- **Today's Family:** www.family.com (Massachusetts and Connecticut)
- **Today's Family Magazine:** www.todaysfamilymagazine.com (Florida)
- **Toledo Area Parent News:** www.toledoparent.com
- **Valleykids PARENT NEWS:** www.valleykids.com (Illinois)
- **Washington Families Magazine:** www.washingtonfamilies.com (DC, Virginia)
- **Washington Parent:** www.washingtonparent.com (Washington, DC area)
- **Westchester Family:** www.parenthood.com
- **West Coast Families:** www.westcoastfamilies.com (British Columbia, Canada)
- **Western New York Family Magazine:** www.wnyfamilymagazine.com

is not always the wisest choice. Before you send out a query, do some careful study of several publications from UPP.

If you do, you'll find that *L.A. Parent* is aimed at parents and families in the Los Angeles, California, area. This publication is 50 percent written by nonstaff. It receives 42 queries a month and publishes 36 freelance submissions each year. Pay is 25 cents a word for First Rights, plus one contributor copy.

Colorado Parent, on the other hand, is only 10 percent written by nonstaff writers, receives only two queries and manuscripts each month, and publishes two freelance submissions a year. Pay is 10 cents a word, and contributor copies are provided upon request. This publication buys First North American serial and computer rights.

As you can see, even if you live in Colorado, it would be more profitable to submit a "general" parenting article to *L.A. Parent*, rather than *Colorado Parent*. If you're a Colorado resident and have an article with a local slant, however, *Colorado Parent* would be more likely to accept your article.

Eighty percent of *Minnesota Parent*, another UPP publication, is written by nonstaff writers. Editors there receive 17 to 21 queries and unsolicited manuscripts each month, and of these, 50 to 60 submissions are published each year. *Minnesota Parent* buys first and reprint rights. Payment for cover articles is $350, while payment for other articles is $150, and reprints earn just $25.

Seattle Child, San Diego Parent, Portland Parent, New York Family, and many

Regional Parenting Magazine Submissions

The graph indicates the number of freelance submissions each magazine publishes annually.

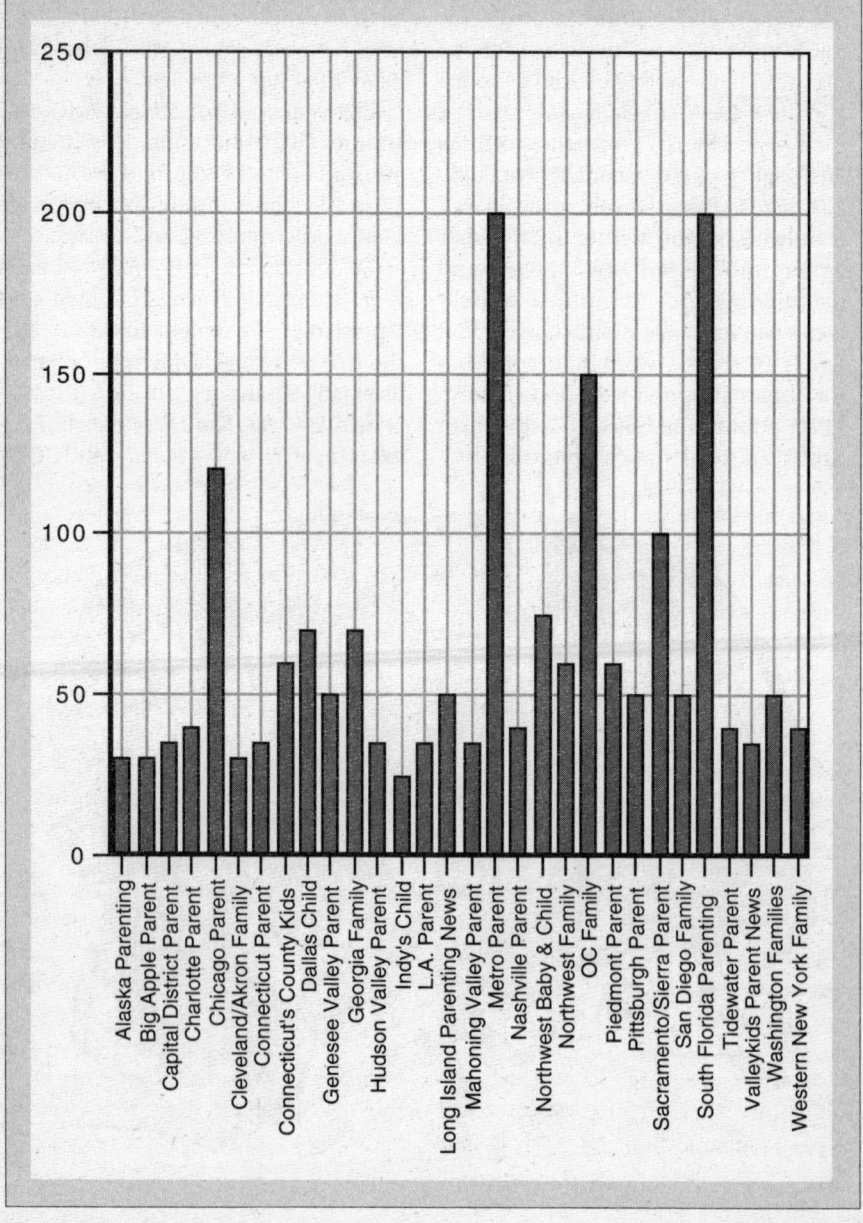

Alaska Parenting	30
Big Apple Parent	30
Capital District Parent	35
Charlotte Parent	40
Chicago Parent	120
Cleveland/Akron Family	30
Connecticut Parent	35
Connecticut's County Kids	60
Dallas Child	70
Genesee Valley Parent	50
Georgia Family	70
Hudson Valley Parent	35
Indy's Child	25
L.A. Parent	35
Long Island Parenting News	50
Mahoning Valley Parent	35
Metro Parent	200
Nashville Parent	40
Northwest Baby & Child	75
Northwest Family	60
OC Family	150
Piedmont Parent	60
Pittsburgh Parent	50
Sacramento/Sierra Parent	100
San Diego Family	50
South Florida Parenting	200
Tidewater Parent	40
Valleykids Parent News	35
Washington Families	50
Western New York Family	40

other parenting publications are all distributed by UPP, yet each has different guidelines, pay rates, and needs. Look for these guidelines in a current writers' market guide, or write for guidelines before submitting or querying to any of these regional tabloids.

Other Special Interest Publications

Several years ago, when I was just beginning to write for children, I had my share of rejection slips from the slick, glossy publications. Rather than get discouraged, I decided to submit articles and queries to local special interest publications. Since I enjoyed teaching crafts to kids, I sent several how-to articles to a local magazine for crafters.

Wow! Not only did the publication accept several of my articles, but soon I was asked to write a regular column. A few months later, the producer of a local cable television show called to ask me to appear on the show to demonstrate some of the crafts I had written about in the magazine.

I wasn't paid for the articles I wrote for the magazine, yet I was given free advertising for any crafts I wanted to sell. After appearing on the television show, I received phone calls for weeks about my crafts ideas and my column provided me some impressive clips, which I soon used to find writing assignments that did offer payment. All in all, I'd say it was worth my time and effort to write for this small, nonpaying regional market.

Joanne Keating, a writer in Nanaimo, British Columbia, Canada, had a similar experience with a local publication. "I wrote for a publication for women in the Vancouver Island area for a year, long enough to build up 12 clips, and then I moved on to writing features for a city newspaper," she says. Later, those clips helped Keating land an assignment with *Chatelaine*, a national Canadian women's magazine, which paid $500 for a one-page article.

Local special interest publications are available everywhere. *Houston Homeschooler* is a regional publication for homeschoolers and their parents in the Houston, Texas, area. Editor Cyndi Simmons, says, "We're always looking for articles on homeschooling, general education, family, child motivation, parenting related humor (nonsarcastic), college planning, family travel (taking education out on the road) that give you a good base. Pay rate begins at 20 cents a word. Interested parties should query HHQueries@aol.com."

Simmons points out that her company, Log Cabin Publishing, is preparing to launch a national magazine as well. Writing for *Houston Homeschooler* just might lead to bigger assignments with the national publication later.

Regional General Interest Publications

Children's writers should also consider writing for regional general interest publications. Pat McCarthy, who has written several biographies for children as well as a slew of articles for national magazines, enjoys writing for the *Darke County Profile*, a general interest publication for residents of Darke County, Ohio. At just $20 an article, McCarthy surely doesn't do this for the money, but she enjoys the work and has a comfortable relationship with the Editor, Diana J. Linder.

Publishing 2001

"I've been writing for Diana since January 1995," says McCarthy, who contributes word quizzes, as well as profiles of local people, and an occasional travel piece. Guidelines for the *Darke County Profile* are available online at www.darkecountyprofile.com and McCarthy says Linder does accept material, usually fiction, from writers who live outside Darke County.

Getting Your Foot in the Door

Even though regional markets often pay less than national publications, they still have high standards for writing. To get your foot in the door at any of these publications, don't think you can present sloppy work.

Linda Johns, who has written for *Seattle Child*, says that when writing an article for a local publication, "You need to treat the article as if you were writing for a national magazine. In other words, you still need the most current, in-depth research and quotes from top experts in the field. You can bring in the local angle with some quotes and examples from people in your community. With luck, you'll have some experts right in your backyard. It's critical, however, to have local community resources that support your article."

Johns also points out, "Although I'd queried a few times over the years, all my articles in parenting magazines were done on assignment. I think the queries helped keep my name in front of the editors, but it seemed like most of their articles are developed and conceptualized by the editorial staff."

Terri Jean, another writer who has had success with regional markets, offers a different way to get assignments with local publications. Jean is former editor and publisher of Turquoise Butterfly Press, her own publishing company. She says, "I have ADHD and so does my youngest child who is now seven. In 1995 I started publishing *Mama's Little Helper*, a national newsletter for parents of ADD/ADHD children. I became well known with my subject matter and soon I was the 'writer to call' when publications wanted a particular topic. I also kept sending queries to parenting publications, saying I could write an original article for them and then I'd list the topics that I covered most. After a few letters, they knew my name and would even call me at home to run over ideas with me."

With all the different regional publications available, there's sure to be a local market to fit every writer's tastes and interests. Sometimes, however, smaller publications have no formal editorial calendar or writers' guidelines available, so it's difficult to tell how to approach this particular market. If that's the case with a publication that interests you, don't be afraid to call and ask to speak to the editor. You won't want to pitch an article idea by phone, of course, but politely asking the editor if queries are acceptable is okay. Then, if the publication does work with freelancers, get a query in the mail right away, while the editor still remembers you.

Writing for regional markets can be the perfect way to obtain some impressive clips, make a little extra money, and maybe even develop a local following for your work.

Adult Regional Publications

For those ready to write for adult regionals as well as for children, here's a list of the abundant city, state, and regional publications to be found. Some are general interest, some very focused. Some are magazines and some newspapers. Some are news-oriented, others are lifestyle magazines, some not much more than vehicles for advertising. But opportunities for freelance writers abound in regional publications. Research their addresses, editors, websites, styles, stories, and their freelance writing needs through such print directories as Ulrich's International Periodical Directory (R.R. Bowker) and Standard Periodical Directory (Oxbridge Communications), or online at such sites as www.magazine-rack.com, www.magazineoutlet.com, or www.mediafinder.com, or www.newsdirectory.com.

Alabama
Southern Discoveries

Alaska
Alaska
Peninsula Clarion

Arizona
The Carefree Enterprise Magazine
Mountain Living
Phoenix Home & Garden

Arkansas
Arkansas Newsmagazine
Ozark Life

California
BRNTWD
California Seasons
Coast
Diablo
San Francisco Magazine
Los Angeles
Montecito
OC Metro
Orange Coast
Palm Springs Life
San Diego
San Francisco Downtown
San Francisco Focus
San Francisco Magazine
San Jose
South Bay
South Coast
SV 1
Westways

Colorado
5280, Denver's Mile-High Magazine
Aspen
Boulder
Colorado Homes & Lifestyles
Steamboat
Steppin' Out
Telluride
Telluride Style

Connecticut
Connecticut

Delaware
Delaware Today

District of Columbia
Washingtonian

Florida
Boca Raton

Adult Regional Publications

Florida Living
Halifax, The Journal of Florida's Fun Coast
Jacksonville Magazine
Miami Metro
Ocean Drive
Orlando
Sarasota
Water's Edge

Georgia
Atlanta
Atlanta Homes & Lifestyles
Atlanta Sports and Fitness Magazine
Cartersville Magazine
Southern Flair Magazine
The Newcomer Magazine

Hawaii
Hawaii
Hawaii Island Journal
Honolulu
Ohana
Waikiki News

Illinois
Chicago
Chicagoland Gardening
Springfield

Indiana
Arts Indiana
Indianapolis Monthly
The Indianapolis Recorder
Our Brown County

Iowa
The Iowan

Kentucky
Louisville

Louisiana
Louisiana Life
New Orleans
Offbeat
River Parish Pride
St. Charles Avenue

Maine
Down East
Maine Antique Digest
People, Places & Plants

Maryland
Annapolis
Baltimore
Community Life Montgomery County
Frederick

Massachusetts
Arts Around Boston
Booming
Boston
Cape Cod
Cape Cod Life

Michigan
Bay Area Times
Michigan
Traverse
West Michigan

Minnesota
Lake Country Journal
Lake Superior
Mpls.St.Paul
RipSaw

Adult Regional Publications

Missouri
Kansas City
St. Louis Homes & Lifestyles

Montana
Montana

Nebraska
Nebraska Life
Omaha

Nevada
Las Vegan
Las Vegas
Las Vegas Life
Nevada

New Hampshire
New Hampshire
Northern New Hampshire
Valley Fun

New Jersey
New Jersey Life
New Jersey Monthly

New Mexico
Desert Exposure
Gateway
New Mexico

New York
New York
Time Out New York

North Carolina
Charlotte's Best

North Dakota
North Dakota Horizons

Ohio
Cleveland
Ohio
Upper Arlington Magazine

Oklahoma
Oklahoma Today

Oregon
Jefferson Monthly

Pennsylvania
Central PA
CityBeat
Philadelphia
Pittsburgh Magazine
Susquehanna Life
Westsylvania

Rhode Island
Newport Life
Rhode Island Monthly

South Carolina
Charleston

South Dakota
South Dakota Magazine

Tennessee
Memphis

Texas
Austin Monthly
Brazos Valley Insite
Country Line

Publishing 2001

Adult Regional Publications

El Paso Inc.
Lubbock
Texas Monthly

Utah
Salt Lake City

Vermont
Vermont Life
Vermont Weathervane

Virginia
Blue Ridge Country
Charlottesville Arts & Entertainment
Roanoaker

West Virginia
Huntington Quarterly
Wonderful West Virginia

Washington
Seattle
Seattle Homes & Lifestyles

Wisconsin
Madison
Milwaukee
Wisconsin Outdoor Journal

Wyoming
Yellowstone Journal

Other Regional Publications
American Cowboy
Baja Life
Coastal Living
Midwest Living
Midwest Today
Mountain Sports & Living
Pacific
Paper
Range
Southern Living
Sunset
Yankee

Book Markets

A Rich Stock of Early Readers

By Catherine Frey Murphy

"It is cold.
See the snow.
See the snow come down.
Little Bear said, "Mother Bear, I am cold.
See the snow.
I want something to put on."

These words begin Else Homelund Minarik's *Little Bear*, illustrated by Maurice Sendak and first published in 1957 by Harper & Row. Minarik chose simple words and short sentences for *Little Bear* because she wanted to write a book that would be easy for children to read on their own. She and her editor, Susan Hirschman, probably weren't planning to establish an entirely new genre of children's literature. But today, decades after the publication of Minarik's pioneering classic, children's bookshelves everywhere are richly stocked with easy readers in the tradition first established by *Little Bear:* short, carefully structured books whose simple language and appealing stories are designed to help kids learn to read by themselves.

"We have 200 titles now, from that auspicious beginning," says Anne Hoppe, Editor at HarperCollins, the corporate descendant of Harper & Row. Hoppe is primary editor of the I Can Read series that began with *Little Bear,* moved on to Syd Hoff's *Danny and the Dinosaur,* and eventually included books about characters like Russell Hoban's *Frances*, Gene Zion's *Harry the Dirty Dog*, and Arnold Lobel's *Frog and Toad*. The Frog and Toad books, Hoppe says, are the only books for beginning readers to have won both Caldecott Honor and Newbery Honor medals. "Working from the core of these really great characters and stories, we do poetry collections, historical fiction, mysteries, and a little bit of nonfiction," says Hoppe.

Many other publishers have easy reader lists. Just a few of these are Random House's Stepping Stone Books and Step into Reading series, Simon & Schuster's Ready to Read, Dial's Easy To Read and Cartwheel's Hello Reader! Educational publishers such as Kaeden Books, the Wright Group, and Mondo (which also publishes trade titles) also publish easy readers in a slightly different form, often called "emergent readers," and designed specifically for use in the classroom.

The Field

Dial's Easy to Read list includes the Fox books, by Jim Marshall, the Amanda and Oliver tales of Jean Van Leeuwen, and other titles. As the list continues to grow, Editor Toby Sherry says, "We're still looking at the same thing: interesting characters, very good writing following the easy reader format," and stories that will leave children "entranced." The success of this approach is apparent in comments like this one, posted by a reader-reviewer on Amazon.com's webpage for Van Leeuwen's *Amanda Pig and Her Big Brother Oliver:* "My four-year-old fell in love with this book and others in the series. Short, repetitive sentences, humorous stories, and appealing animal characters made it a hit; it's also helping her learn to read."

Most easy readers are aimed at children between the ages of four and eight, or from prekindergarten to second or third grade—a span that covers a broad range of reading abilities. As Sherry points out, "A four-year-old is normally being read to," but many eight-year-olds are reading on their own. "Some books are geared toward the younger age and some of them are a little more sophisticated. Maybe the words are a little harder, or the concept is a little older."

In easy readers, the stories themselves are usually quite short. "When kids are beginning to read, it's hard for them. Just going over a five-page, self-contained story is a lot," says Sherry. Easy readers often include 4 or 5 brief stories in a 48- or 64-page book, allowing inexperienced readers what Sherry calls a "pause place" between stories.

Within the stories, the text is carefully arranged. In Dial's books, Sherry says, "No line is more than 37 characters long. Subjects and predicates are always together on the same line. Phrases are always together, too, to make it easier for children to understand." Illustration is important as a cue to the meaning of the words and also as a means to make the books "more fun," Sherry adds, with pictures appearing on every double-page spread or sometimes on every page.

Distinct from Picture Books

Although art is important in easy readers, writers should understand that picture books and easy readers are entirely different.

Jane Gerver, an Executive Editor of Cartwheel Books, an imprint of Scholastic, explains, "Any successful children's book writer does need to know the difference between, say, a picture book and an easy reader. A picture book can have much more difficult text, even though it's aimed at a younger audience, and that's because a picture book is intended to be read to a young child."

Ronne Kaufman, Editorial Director at Mondo, adds, "Traditionally, most picture books were created to be read to the child. Mondo balances its picture book list with some that are appropriate for beginning readers."

Sherry says the difference is evident in vocabulary and sentence structure. "Picture books tend to run in sentences and have paragraphs," she says. In easy readers, on the other hand, "most of the words are much shorter. The sentences are very short, very easy, and there's a rhythm to them."

Some rhythm is typical of easy readers, whether it takes the form of rhyme, repetition, or a repeating pattern in the

Publishers Report: Early Reader Books

The graph indicates the number of new easy-to-read books the publishers reported on their lists for the last year.

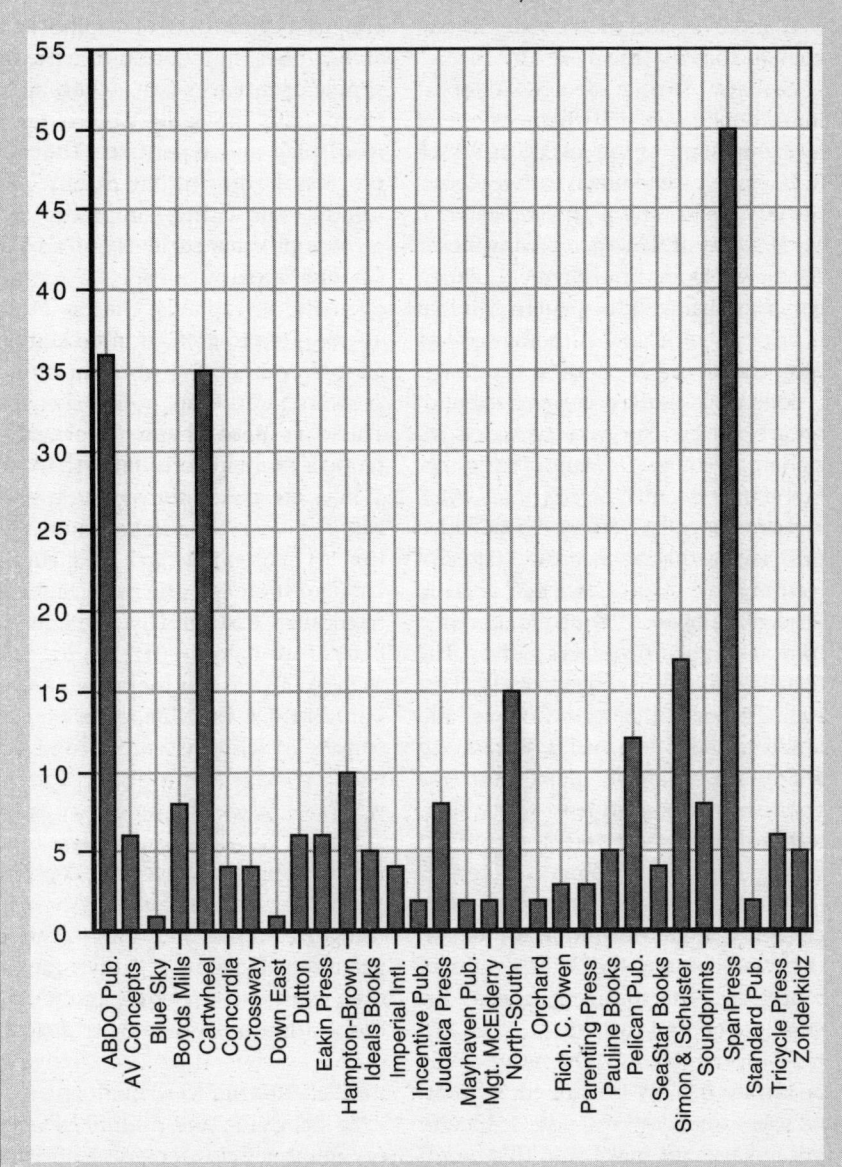

Publishing 2001

ABDO Pub.	36
AV Concepts	6
Blue Sky	1
Boyds Mills	8
Cartwheel	35
Concordia	4
Crossway	4
Down East	1
Dutton	6
Eakin Press	6
Hampton-Brown	10
Ideals Books	5
Imperial Intl.	4
Incentive Pub.	2
Judaica Press	8
Mayhaven Pub.	2
Mgt. McElderry	2
North-South	15
Orchard	2
Rich. C. Owen	3
Parenting Press	3
Pauline Books	5
Pelican Pub.	12
SeaStar Books	4
Simon & Schuster	17
Soundprints	8
SpanPress	50
Standard Pub.	2
Tricycle Press	6
Zonderkidz	5

sentence structure. Rhythm is so important to Sherry's concept of the easy reader that she says, "When I'm about to sit down and write the flap copy for an easy reader, I read the manuscript over and over, and then I write the flap copy in that rhythm."

Bethany Snyder, Senior Editor at Ideals Books, says that rhyme is one of several reasons for the success of Patrick K. Hallinan's well-known easy-reader series (*My Mother and I, My Brother and I, My First Day of School,* and many more): "These books are all in rhyme. Children get so familiar with the pattern of it that it helps them learn." Although editors agree that rhyme does not work unless it is done well, it's the secret ingredient of some of the best-known easy readers, including, of course, Dr. Seuss's classics *The Cat in the Hat* and *Green Eggs and Ham.*

Easy reader lists are often subdivided into levels that reflect the stages of learning to read. Cartwheel's Hello Reader! Books are intended for children to read on their own, says Gerver. The five different levels range from My First Hello Readers (for preschoolers and kindergartners) to Level 4 (for second and third graders). Books for the youngest readers use large fonts, illustrations that closely correspond to the text, and only a few words on each page.

As the intended age group increases, so does the amount of text on the page, the length of words and sentences and the sophistication of the concepts behind the stories. At all levels, Gerver explains, "Our easy-to-read books are heavily illustrated, with art on every spread. We do not use specific vocabulary, but make sure that words are not too difficult for the intended audience. In addition, we try to use complete, albeit short, sentences in our lower level books."

HarperCollins's I Can Read series begins with My First I Can Read, for readers just beginning to decipher words and phrases. In addition to extremely simple sentences and vocabulary, Hoppe says the earliest books feature word play and repetition. The series progresses through three subsequent levels of increasing complexity to its most sophisticated level: I Can Read Chapter Books.

As Hoppe explains, "Just as it's a really big step to go from not reading at all to decoding, it's just as big a step to go from 'I Can Read' books to novels." The I Can Read Chapter Books are intended to help kids take that step. "These are not middle-grade novels," Hoppe notes. "We still pay close attention to sentence length and vocabulary, but there's a little more room and freedom." Text in the easy chapter books is arranged in paragraphs, rather than in lines as it is for younger levels, but full-color art still appears on every spread, to lend eye appeal and offer clues to the meaning behind the words.

Simon & Schuster's Ready to Read list includes four levels: Recognizing Words, for children just beginning to recognize words; Starting to Read, for beginners; Reading Together, for children gaining confidence; and Reading Alone, for those whose skills are taking off.

Ellen Krieger, Vice President, Associate Publisher, and Editorial Director of Simon & Schuster's Aladdin Paperbacks, says that the company is about to add another level with the new series, Ready for Chapters. "It is conceived as a first chapter book program that's a logical step up from our Ready to Read books," she explains. Aimed at "kids who have outgrown the beginning reader," Ready for Chapters books will be more accessible than novels, says Krieger, but more sophisticated than easy readers. Illustrations will be in black and white, not color, because to older children, "that's babyish," she says. The books will be short, running 64 to 80 pages, with large type, simple sentences, and one full page of black-and-white line art or half-tone illustration per chapter. Some books will be reprinted from other lists, while others will be original paperbacks created expressly for the series. On the first lists, authors will include Cynthia Rylant, Daniel Pinkwater, and other well-known writers.

Emergent Readers

Another type of easy reader is the *emergent reader*, designed for beginning readers to use as a supplement to basal reading texts in the classroom. Marketed directly to schools, these books share many features in common with trade-list easy readers: limited text, simple vocabulary and syntax, and levels of difficulty that correspond to reading ability.

"The text is accessible to the child," explains Kaufman. At the earliest levels, especially, "there's a close picture-text match, so a child gets a lot of clues from the picture." Patterned text for very young children may use a structure as basic as "This is a boat," on one page, and "This is a house" on the next.

For older readers, a more complicated pattern may be repeated on each double-page spread. "Through exposure to words over and over again, kids read more easily," Kaufman explains.

To keep this sort of repetitive structure from getting boring, Kaufman likes to see a twist at the end. As she explains, "Children need a payoff at the end of a story, something to make it worth reading." Sometimes that payoff is created by illustration. A recent title repeated the line "This is a mess," on each page, with illustrations showing a child taking items one at a time from an untidy heap on the floor. In the final illustration, the child has picked up all the items—and transferred them to a new, equally messy heap. Thus, the final repetition of "This is a mess!" becomes a joke.

One difference between emergent readers and trade easy readers is that the former often use specific, limited vocabularies, sometimes taken from vocabulary lists created by educators.

Like easy readers, emergent readers progress through levels of difficulty corresponding to the capability of the reader. "In the very easy ones, action is completed on the page itself," Kaufman says. "In more complex texts, it's ongoing. Our easy chapter books don't necessarily have a picture on every page. The story is more complex and the characters are more fully developed." In every story, Kaufman looks for something more than a fundamental reading text. "One of the things Mondo prides itself on is that we try to create literature," she says.

At the Wright Group, emergent readers begin with what Gloria Bancroft,

Manager of Curriculum Development, describes as "label books, for kids who don't even have the concept of print," and move on through increasing levels of difficulty. The books cover a wide range of topics, Bancroft says. "First of all, we have to spark an interest! That's a tough thing to do, because kids' interests vary so extremely, so we include a wide range of topics." Many of the Wright Group's books are used in guided reading programs in elementary schools, in which children are "grouped according to their skill needs and their developmental needs."

Although emergent readers are developed differently, they share a critical element with their trade-publishing cousins: the importance of story. "As with all good books, you have to start with a good story," explains Kaeden Books's President Craig Urmston. "The story is first. Whether it's a greeting card or a book, you pick it up because of the story." For his company's emergent readers, Urmston looks for stories that are "founded in the experience of the child." In *Dressed-Up Sammy*, a child puts various articles of clothing on a dog. "All kids have done this!" Urmston says. "Kids can identify with it."

Familiarity is the cornerstone of early reading, Urmston points out. "The language you use has to be current with the child's vocabulary," with a small edge of unfamiliarity to add challenge.

Market Demands

In general, editors say that the market for easy readers is steady, remaining fairly healthy year to year. "For a while we were being told that parents weren't buying as much in hardcover," Sherry says, "but now we're told they're clamoring for it. It seems to stay steady."

Some point out that increasing use of trade books in the classroom has led to a greater diversity of easy reader subjects. "We're finding that there's a great demand for nonfiction," says Kaufman, at Mondo, where easy readers have been published on nature subjects like frogs, insects, whales, and exploring habitats. Many editors note that series of easy readers featuring the same characters do especially well. As Kaufman notes, "Kids like to see what happens to the characters next!"

Market demands affect whether easy readers are published in hardcover or paperback. For school and library markets, hardcover is the most durable format. Paperbacks often work better for family buyers, Sherry notes. "I would think that most parents would buy easy-to-read books in paperback, because kids outgrow them very quickly." School book clubs, designed to appeal to kids who buy their own books with limited funds, also use paperback versions.

"Cartwheel's Hello Reader! Books are school book club-driven at the current time," Gerver says. "In other words, we acquire manuscripts specifically for easy-to-read books that will be offered for sale only through Scholastic's school book clubs, rather than sold in trade channels (i.e., retail stores). We do take some of the club titles and put them on our trade list in later seasons." Submissions to Cartwheel are reviewed both by the editorial staff and by book club managers, Gerver says, adding, "Because of the volume of manuscripts sent to Cartwheel Books, it can take quite a while to hear back from us."

At present, Krieger says she is not acquiring aggressively for the Ready for Chapters list from new authors. "Because it's a new program, we're trying to work with authors who have a track record," she explains, adding, however, that the ultimate goal is to "build the program so that new authors can be launched."

In the educational publishing world, most books are not developed from unsolicited submissions. Instead, books are often assigned to writers who have already proven their proficiency in writing for the educational market. At Mondo, for instance, Kaufman says, "We are not reviewing unsolicited submissions, although we receive hundreds and hundreds and hundreds of them." At the Wright Group, Bancroft says, "We don't solicit submissions." Writers who want to explore this market are most likely to find work by submitting résumés with clips of their publications, which may lead to assignments later.

Kaeden, on the other hand, does review manuscript submissions for emergent readers, but the competition is stiff. "We get 500 to 700 submissions a year, and we're printing 15 to 17 a year," says Urmston. Send a full manuscript, he recommends, warning that because of the high volume of submissions, "it may take us up to a year to review what we have and make our selections for the coming year."

The good news is that the steady state of the market means that many publishers add new titles to their easy reader list each year—which means that writers who can handle the form well are in demand. "As these books are extremely difficult to do, we are always looking for more," says Hoppe.

Straight Talk

What does it take to handle easy readers well? Hoppe answers, "A lot of talent and a lot of hard work!" To appeal to young readers, stories need "great characters and a strong plot that will pull kids along," she says, adding that it's particularly challenging to accomplish this within the easy-reader format. "Writers must be able to work with a relatively limited vocabulary and short sentence structure, but still make the story not boring, not flat," she says. Even more important is a willingness to take young readers seriously. "Often lacking is respect, for the characters, for the story, for the readers. Kids really want substantial stories!"

Although many easy readers feature animal characters, like Little Bear or Frog and Toad, Hoppe suggests that among today's readers, there's a need for "more stories about contemporary kids. Kids are, at increasingly young ages, wanting to read about other kids. If you want to read about animals, we have that covered!"

Krieger says that, while good characterization is essential, action is also particularly important in easy readers. With chapter books, for example, "A manuscript that will page out to the size we're looking for will only be 40 or 50 pages. You can't go in for a lot of mood setting or back-story," she notes. Instead, writers need to get right to the action and keep the story moving. "I hate to say we want plot-driven stories,

Early Reader Series and Standalones

Early Reader Series
- **Barron's:** Get Ready...Get Set...Read!; Petsitters Club
- **Candlewick Press:** Brand New Readers
- **Carolrhoda:** On My Own
- **Children's Press:** Rookie Readers
- **Dial Books:** Dial Easy-to-Read
- **Dorling Kindersley:** DK Readers
- **Dutton:** Dutton Easy Readers
- **Golden Books:** Road to Reading
- **Grosset & Dunlap:** All Aboard Reading
- **Harcourt Children's Books:** Green Light Readers
- **HarperCollins Children's Books:** My First I Can Read; I Can Read; I Can Read Chapter Books
- **Holiday House:** Holiday House Readers
- **Kingfisher:** I Am Reading
- **Little Brown:** Arthur Chapter Books
- **The Millbrook Press:** Real Kids Readers
- **Puffin:** Puffin Easy-to-Read, Puffin Chapters
- **Random House:** Junie B. Jones; Magic Tree House; Marvin Redpost; Step into Reading; Stepping Stones
- **Scholastic:** Hello Reader (Cartwheel Books); JumpStart, with Knowledge Adventure's educational software
- **Simon & Schuster:** Recognizing Words; Starting to Read; Reading Together; Reading Alone; Ready for Chapters
- **Viking:** Viking Easy-to-Read

Other Early Reader Publishers

A&B Publishers Group
ABDO Publishing
Bantam Doubleday Dell Books for Young Readers
Boyds Mills Press
Charlesbridge Publishing
Children's Nature Institute
Clarion Books
Clear Light Publishers
Concordia Publishing
Creative Teaching Press
Critical Thinking Books & Software
Eakin Press
Educators Publishing Service
Eerdmans Books for Young Readers
ERIC/EDINFO Press
Falcon Publishing
Farrar, Straus & Giroux
Feminist Press
Forest House
Formac Publishing
Good Year Books
Greene Bark Press
Greenwillow Books

Early Reader Series and Standalones

Gulf Publishing
Hachai Publishing
Hampton-Brown Books
Harcourt Religion Publishers
Heian International
Houghton Mifflin Children's Books
Ideals Children's Books
Jonathan David Publishers
Journey Books
Kaeden Books
Learning Resources
Learning Triangle Press
Lee & Low Books
Arthur A. Levine Books
Magination Press
McGraw-Hill School Division
Modern Publishing
Mondo Publishing
Moody Press
North-South Books
NorthWord Press
Orca Book Publishers
Richard C. Owen Publishers
Owl Books
Parenting Press
Pauline Books & Media
Pelican Publishing
Phoenix Learning Resources
Pitspopany Press
Rainbow Publishers
Raintree/Steck-Vaughn Publishers
Rocky River Publishers
St. Anthony Messenger Press
Sandlapper Publishing
Sandpiper Paperbacks
Seedling Publications
Silver Whistle
Small Horizons
Somerville House Books
Span Press
Sports Illustrated For Kids Books
Starry Puddle Publishing
Stemmer House
Sterling Publishing
Sundance Publishing
Teacher Created Materials
Third World Press
Through the Bible Publishing
J.N. Townsend Publishing
Transworld Children's Books
Tricycle Press
Tyndale House
Walker and Company
WaterBrook Press
The Wright Group

because obviously, characterization is important. But story is really important! You have to keep kids turning pages. This is a very good age for mysteries," she suggests, adding that the wild popularity of J.K. Rowling's Harry Potter books among slightly older readers also makes fantasy appealing to children who want to feel that they are reading "big kid books."

"The most important thing is to read," recommends Krieger. "I would tell writers to read some of the best in the genre," agrees Sherry. Often mentioned examples include Lobel's Frog and Toad books, Jim Marshall's Fox books, Mary Pope Osborne's Magic Tree House series, and Barbara Park's books about Junie B. Jones. Urmston adds a final bit of particularly good writing advice: concentrate on story. "It's hard to write a good story for a particular educational level. Instead, just write for a good story."

In the end, writers should remember the fundamental goal of the easy reader: to make children want to read on their own. While parents, teachers, or librarians often choose picture books for children, children often choose easy readers for themselves. That means that writers in this genre have an opportunity to speak directly to kids.

An easy reader must have what Krieger calls kid appeal. She says, "When I read an easy reader manuscript I try to regress to the child's level. If it doesn't work that way, nothing can save it!" Gerver adds, "Keep in mind that our Hello Reader! Books are not intended to be instructional textbooks, but are fun, easy-to-read paperback books that kids can pick up and read on their own." As Sherry explains it, "The main thing is to make kids love reading—to entertain them and to capture their imaginations."

Publishing News

A Banner Year

By Pat Conway

Anniversaries in Children's Publishing

Books

■ David Adler's ace detective Cam Jansen, the girl with the photographic memory, celebrated her twentieth anniversary with Viking Children's Books.

■ Celebrating a milestone fiftieth anniversary, the series of books in The Chronicles of Narnia, by C.S. Lewis, are being reissued by HarperCollins with full-color illustrations by Narnia's original artist, Pauline Baynes.

■ First published 25 years ago by Farrar, Straus & Giroux, *Tuck Everlasting*, by Natalie Babbitt, was published in an anniversary edition in 2000 that included an interview with the author.

■ Henry Holt and Company issued *The Wizard of Oz Centennial Edition* to mark the hundredth anniversary of the publication of L. Frank Baum's classic.

■ The creator of *The Little Prince*, Antoine de Saint-Exupéry, celebrated his hundredth birthday. To mark the occasion, Harcourt released a new translation of the book by poet Richard Howard.

■ Eric Hill's curious pooch, Spot, turned 20 this year. To celebrate, Putnam released an anniversary, lift-the-flap board book of Hill's original adventure, *Where's Spot?* The Spot titles have sold more than 28,000,000 copies in 65 languages since Spot's debut in 1980.

■ To celebrate Raggedy Ann's eighty-fifth birthday, Little Simon, an imprint of Simon & Schuster Children's Publishing, launched a Raggedy Ann and Andy publishing program with a line of six new books in various formats.

■ Arthur, the aardvark created by Marc Brown, turns 25 in 2001. Little, Brown is celebrating his birthday by issuing an anniversary edition of *Arthur's Nose*.

■ *Strega Nona*, by Tomie dePaola, celebrated a twenty-fifth anniversary. A brand new title, *Strega Nona Takes a Vacation*, was issued by G.P. Putnam's Sons in honor of this silver anniversary.

Magazines

■ *Sports Illustrated For Kids* celebrated its tenth anniversary.

Awards

- The American Library Association (ALA) presented its John Newbery Award to Christopher Paul Curtis for *Bud, Not Buddy* (Delacorte). The ALA's Randolph Caldecott Medal was awarded to *Joseph Had A Little Overcoat* by Simms Taback (Viking).

- The ALA's Coretta Scott King Awards honor African-American authors and illustrators of outstanding children's and young adult books. Winners were Christopher Paul Curtis for *Bud, Not Buddy* (Delacorte); and illustrator Brian Pinkney for *In the Time of the Drums* (Jump at the Sun/Hyperion Books for Children).

- The Margaret A. Edwards Award, which honors lifetime contribution in writing for teens, was awarded to young adult author Chris Crutcher.

- The Michael Printz Award for excellence in young adult literature was awarded to Walter Dean Myers for *Monster* (HarperCollins).

- The Aesop Prize, conferred by the American Folklore Society, was awarded to *King Solomon and His Magic Ring*, by Elie Wiesel (Greenwillow); and *Trickster and the Fainting Birds*, by Howard Norman (Harcourt).

- The Jane Addams Peace Award was given to *Bat 6*, by Virginia Euwer Wolff (Scholastic) and *Painted Words/Spoken Memories: Marianthe's Story*, by Aliki (Greenwillow).

- The New England Book Award, which honors authors and publishers whose body of work is a "significant contribution to the region's literature," was given to Marcia Sewall.

- The National Jewish Book Award was won by Sandy Asher for her book *With All My Heart, With All My Mind: Thirteen Stories About Growing Up Jewish* (Simon & Schuster), which she edited.

- The Hans Christian Andersen Author Award was given to Ana Maria Machada, of Brazil, who has written more than 100 books for children. British author Anthony Browne won for illustration.

- The SCBWI Golden Kite Award for fiction went to Laurie Halse Anderson for *Speak* (Farrar, Straus & Giroux). For nonfiction, Marianne Dyson won for *Space Station Science: Life in Free Fall* (Scholastic); and for picture book text, Deborah Hopkinson won for *A Band of Angels* (Atheneum).

- The *Los Angeles Times* Book Prize for young adult fiction went to Robert Cormier for *Frenchtown Summer*.

- The Library of Congress awarded medals to 78 "living legends," including artists, entertainers, and activists as part of its bicentennial celebration. Katherine Paterson, Beverly Cleary, Ursula LeGuin, Fred Rogers, and Judy Blume were among the children's book authors honored.

Mergers & Acquisitions

- Pearson has purchased Dorling Kindersley for $522 million, making DK part of Pearson's Penguin Group. DK's illustrated reference publishing program will complement Penguin's fiction and nonfiction businesses.

- Scholastic acquired Grolier for $400 million. The acquisition will help Scholastic expand its presence internationally; give the company greater access to school and library markets and Internet business; and—given Grolier's direct marketing to parents—increase Scholastic's access to home customers. The sale makes Scholastic one of the five largest publishers in the U.S., with revenues of about $1.8 billion.

- Scholastic has acquired *Soccer Jr.* magazine and other assets of Triplepoint, Inc., including *Soccer for Parents* magazine. The acquisition included the soccerjr.com website, and rights to the names for similar sites, including footballjr.com, baseballjr.com, hockeyjr.com, and basketballjr.com.

- Nelvana Ltd., a Toronto-based children's entertainment company, acquired children's publisher Klutz for $74 million. Nelvana will expand the Klutz products and help them in the preschool market.

- Zany Brainy purchased Noodle Kidoodle for more than $40 million. Both stores sell toys, games, books, videos, and other products, but Zany Brainy has put more emphasis on books. It stocks 7,000 to 10,000 titles in each store.

- Alloy Online acquired book packager 17th Street Productions. Alloy operates a website (www.alloy.com) and direct-marketing operations aimed at the Generation Y market—the most important demographic for 17th Street.

- Torstar Corporation's Children's Supplemental Education Publishing Division acquired Cambridge Physics Outlet (CPO), a publisher and distributor of science equipment and science and math curriculum materials for middle and secondary schools.

- Electronic publisher Thomson Corporation bought the Prometric testing division of Sylvan Learning Systems for $775 million. Prometric delivered standardized tests and exams at 2,900 testing sites in 141 countries. The acquisition helps to make Thomson's Learning division a leading provider of computer-based testing administration, delivery, and certification.

- Dover Publications has been acquired by Courier Corporation, a customized education and specialized publisher and full-service book manufacturer. Courier paid $39 million in cash to acquire Dover, which specializes in children's activity books, crafts, and literature classics for juvenile markets.

- IDG acquired online learning/training company HungryMinds.com, based in San Francisco. Founded in early 1999, Hungry Minds.com features a customized database of online learning courses for college and professional development markets.

- After a settlement of a $1 million libel suit, most of the assets of Roberts Rinehart Publishers have been bought by Court Wayne Press, of Boulder, Colorado. The new owner plans to continue publishing children's fiction and nonfiction on nature and the environment.

- Guideposts Publishing has acquired Ideals Books, publisher of the children's imprint Candy Cane Press.

- The McGraw-Hill Companies purchased the Tribune Company's educational publishing unit for $634.7 million plus estimated adjustments of $45 million for working capital and sharing of income.

Book Launches & Expansions

- Megan Tingley, Executive Editor of Little, Brown and Company, now has her own imprint, Megan Tingley Books. The imprint publishes picture books, middle-grade titles, and young adult novels.

- Michael diCapua has moved his children's imprint, Michael diCapua Books, from HarperCollins to Hyperion Books for Children.

- Random House signed a deal with Disney Publishing Worldwide for the rights to publish English-language books in the U.S. and Canada based on Disney properties and characters. Terms of the deal allow Random House to publish books in an array of format, including activity books, storybooks, novelty books, and early readers. Craig Virden, President and Publisher of Random House Children's Books, will oversee the Disney publishing program.

- Katharine Holabird's popular Angelina Ballerina books for ages three to seven have been re-released by Pleasant Company, which is owned by Mattel. A new hardcover and a merchandise line will follow.

Pleasant Company has launched a line of eight Matchbox board books for boys three to five. Each 12-page book comes with a Matchbox toy.

The newest addition to Pleasant Company's American Girl Collection of historical dolls, fiction, and activity books is Kit Kittredge, who grows up during the Great Depression.

- Candlewick Press, an affiliate of the U.K.'s Walker and Company, is doubling its staff and doubling its titles to more than 100 annually. It is also opening an office in New York City, in addition to its Boston location.

- Pegasus, Canada's largest book wholesaler, launched a new division, Pegasus Library and Education Services (PLES), to penetrate the library and education market. The new division will serve Canadian schools and libraries exclusively, and makes Pegasus Canada's first full-service library wholesaler.

- PBS Kids Books is a new line of children's titles from Simon Spotlight and the Public Broadcasting Service. The books complement the PBS Kids Ready to Learn Service, a weekday line-up of award-winning television programming.

- *Seventeen* magazine, in partnership with HarperCollins and Parachute Press, has introduced a line of fiction and nonfiction for teen girls. The titles deal with beauty, fashion, school, sexuality, and other teen interests.

- Marc Aronson, formerly of Henry Holt, will oversee a new young adult imprint at Carus Publishing, where he has become Vice President for Content Development, Nonfiction. He will also oversee the development of new nonfiction magazines.

- The Millbrook Press is launching a new imprint of quality fiction and picture books for elementary through young adult readers. Simon Boughton, former Publishing Director at Crown Books, is Publisher of the new imprint.

- The *New York Times* launched a children's best-seller list in its Sunday Book Review section. The list features three categories—picture books, paperbacks, and chapter books—that rotate weekly.

- Richard Jackson Books moved to Simon & Schuster's Atheneum Books for Young Readers.

- Sterling Books launched a preschool imprint, Pinwheel Publishing, that features innovative formats and colorful art.

- Christopher Franceschelli, former publisher of Dutton Books, started his own children's publishing company, Handprint Books. His initial offerings included picture books, board books, and lift-the-flap titles aimed at young children. Middle-grade and young adult fiction will be added to the next list.

- SeaStar Books, a division of North-South Books, debuted. David Reuther, President and Publisher, plans on publishing 25 to 30 titles annually.

- Sierra Club Books for Children and Gibbs Smith Publishers agreed to co-publish Sierra Club Books for Young Children. Sierra Club is handling editorial development, while Gibbs Smith is responsible for marketing and manufacturing the titles.

- AskJeeves, the Internet search company based in Emeryville, California, launched its own book imprint, releasing two children's titles in 2000.

- McGraw-Hill teamed with *Ladybug* to publish two new picture book series featuring characters from comics that appear monthly in the magazine. The first series is based on the sheepdog Mop; the second is based on the characters Molly and her cat Emmett.

- Two inaugural books, *The Two Brothers* and *Daisy and the Doll,* are the first two in the Family Heritage series for children, published by the Vermont Folklife Center in Middlebury.

- Two-Can Publishing, a division of London-based Zenith Entertainment, set up its own children's publishing company with children's titles and book/CD-ROM packages. Previously, it had licensed its products to other publishers, including World Book.

Magazine Launches & Expansions

■ The Cricket Magazine Group purchased Cobblestone Publishing from Pearson Education Group. Cobblestone's stable of magazines include *Faces*, *Odyssey*, *Footsteps*, *Cobblestone*, *AppleSeeds*, and *Calliope*. Cobblestone will continue its publishing operations from New Hampshire.

■ *FF*, a national magazine devoted to young musicians 14 to 24, has launched. Martin Keller is Editor and Marti Buscaglia is Publisher.

■ H&S Media launched *TeenStyle* magazine, for fashion-conscious young women 12 to 18, and a website, www.teenstylemag.com. Sara Fiedelholtz is Publisher. *Hot!*, also from H&S Media, labels itself for the 'tween girl between 8 and 12.

■ Carus Publishing plans a new nonfiction magazine for ages 7 to 11. Former *Book Links* Editor Judy O'Malley will head this new publication. Plans call for O'Malley and the new Carus Vice President for Content Development, Nonfiction, Marc Aronson, to launch a number of new nonfiction theme magazines for Carus.

■ *Zillions*, the *Consumer Reports* magazine for children, ended its print publication. It is now available free online.

■ *Kids Post*, a new page in the Style section of the *Washington Post*, was launched. Targeted to 9-to-13-year-olds, this page includes sports, entertainment, news, politics, and stories of interest for young readers.

■ Rodale, the Emmaus, Pennsylvania, publisher of *Prevention* and other health and lifestyle publications, began a magazine for teenage boys, *MH-18*. A spin-off of *Men's Health*, the new title includes features on health, fitness, dating, and relationships.

■ Time Inc. launched *The Big Picture*, its latest addition to the *Time For Kids* editions. Targeted to schools, this new publication is geared to emergent readers.

■ The publishers of *Girls' Life* are bringing out a brother publication. *Boys Illustrated*, a bimonthly with an initial circulation of 100,000, offers a wholesome approach to male readers.

■ Exclusively for fathers, *dads* magazine states that its mission is to help fathers be better dads. Published by Dads Media LLC, the publication started off with a rate base of 200,000.

■ A new quarterly, *Single Parents* covers topics such as relationships, family ties, single fathers, spirituality, and dating.

■ Condé Nast, publisher of *Vogue*, issued the first *Teen Vogue*. Editor Amy Astley said everyone is taking a cautious stance in deciding on a regular publication schedule.

■ Kalmbach Publishing of Waukesha, Wisconsin, bought two magazines, *The Writer* and *Plays*, formerly published by Sylvia K. Burack in Boston. Operations have moved to Wisconsin.

■ *Kirkus Reviews*, known throughout the book industry for its coverage of new titles, appointed a new Senior Editor of Children's Books, Karen Breen. Breen's aim is to provide 60 reviews in each of the biweekly issues.

Multimedia News

■ *Between the Lions*, a new children's literacy series, debuted on PBS. The daily half-hour program stars a family of lion puppets who oversee a magical library where books come to life.

■ A new public radio series, *The Loose Leaf Book Company*, was launched to help parents choose among the thousands of new books published yearly. Each weekly hour-long show features a theme and includes interviews with authors, editors, librarians, and those involved in children's literature.

■ Clifford the Big Red Dog, created by Norman Bridwell nearly 40 years ago, got his own TV series on the Public Broadcasting System (PBS).

■ Pearson has launched the K-12 feature of its online education Learning Network, a three-year alliance with America Online. Learning Network features resources on a Parent Channel, Teacher Channel, and Student Channel. Each uses the content and tools of traditional and online educational publishers with the Network's own resources.

■ Cable network Nickelodeon has decided to produce six to eight original television movies each year. Some of the movies will be adapted from books considered contemporary classics for children, including the Newbery Medal winner *Maniac McGee* by Jerry Spinelli about a 12-year-old homeless youth.

■ The unabridged audio version of *Harry Potter and the Goblet of Fire*, on 12 audiocassettes, was proclaimed the fastest selling audiobook in history.

■ Scholastic is establishing boutiques in 1,215 Toys 'R' Us and Imaginarium stores worldwide. The boutiques will feature Scholastic arts and crafts, activity toys, puzzles, games, school supplies, and electronic learning aids. Initially, there will be 40 products with a goal of 150 in the next few years. All the products will be developed exclusively for their Toys 'R' Us shops, although the publisher will retain the right to distribute them through selected distribution outlets.

■ Houghton Mifflin's Great Source supplemental division and JL Hammett Company, an independent school supplier, agreed to offer the online technology of Chapbooks.com, a K-12 classroom publication service in which students write, edit, proof, and order print versions of their work in paperback. Students enter or paste in text, upload digital images, choose layouts online, view proofs, and receive their finished printed book in several days. Rights are retained by the authors.

■ The Learning Company, an educational software company geared to teachers, was sold by its owner, Mattel Toys, to an affiliate of Gores Technology Group of Los Angeles. The deal called for no cash to be exchanged. Instead, Mattel will share in the future profits of the Learning Company.

■ Golden Books signed a five-year publishing and distribution agreement with Encore Software, which will produce and sell CD-ROMs based on Golden Books. The CD-ROMs feature storytelling paired with educational activities and for ages three to six.

■ Dr. Seuss's *How the Grinch Stole Christmas*, a movie starring Jim Carrey, is being followed by plans to bring *The Cat in the Hat* to the silver screen with Tim Allen as the cat.

■ CNN Interactive launched a news and education site for teachers, CNN-fyi.com. It features student-oriented world news, classroom content by educators, and resources from education content providers.

■ A new website, TheDrama.com, from the Syndicate Media Group, promotes new print books for young urban hip-hop audiences and offers original multimedia content. The books are shaped like CD cases and packaged with CD soundtracks, featuring songs that will not be released commercially. Initially sold at record stores and clothing boutiques before becoming available in conventional outlets, the books are receiving support from various artists, who are reading excerpts from them during performance tours.

■ Parachute Press and HarperCollins Children's Books joined forces to present the first new series in six years from children's author, R. L. Stine. The Nightmare Room is both a book series and online website (www.harpercollins.com) where each week readers can view a new installment of an exclusive online story. Young readers can also play games, and write and post their own work on the website.

People

Books

■ Marc Aronson is now Vice President for Content Development, Nonfiction, and Editorial Director for Carus Publishing.

■ Liz Bicknell was promoted to Associate Publisher and Editorial Director at Candlewick Press.

■ Simon Boughton, former Publishing Director at Crown Books, is Publisher of a new imprint, yet to be named, at The Millbrook Press.

■ David Gale was promoted to Editorial Director, Books for Young Readers, at Simon & Schuster.

■ Kate Nunn was promoted to Editorial Director at Benchmark Books.

■ Christy Ottaviano was promoted to Executive Editor at Henry Holt Books for Young Readers.

■ Michelle Poploff, former Editorial Director at Random House Children's Books, was named Vice President.

■ Pleasant Rowland, who founded Pleasant Company in 1985, has retired as President and Vice Chairwoman of Mattel, the company that bought Pleasant Company in 1998. Her successor is Ellen Brothers, who was Senior Vice President of Operations at Pleasant Company.

■ Andrea Schneeman was promoted from Executive Editor to Editor in Chief of SeaStar Books, the American imprint of North-South Books.

■ Garen Thomas has been named Editor at Gulliver Books, an imprint of Harcourt, Inc.

■ Tim Travaglini was named Editor in the children's books department of Walker and Company.

Magazines

■ Larry Becker was named the new Editor of *Listen*.

■ Lisa Benenson has been named Editor in Chief of *Working Mother*.

■ Kelly Carr was named Editor of *Encounter* magazine.

■ Ron Givens was appointed Editorial Director of the the *New York Times* national teen newsmagazine, *Upfront*.

■ Annemarie Iverson was named Editor in Chief of *YM*.

■ Linda Platzner was named Publisher of *Seventeen*. She had been Group Publisher of Primedia Youth Entertainment.

■ Richard Spencer was named Editor of *Twist*.

Deaths

■ Verna Aardema, author of the Caldecott Medal winner *Why Mosquitoes Buzz in People's Ears: An African Tale*, died in Florida at the age of 88. Her publishing career spanned more than 40 years and 30 children's books.

■ Author/artist Barbara Cooney, winner of two Caldecott medals and a National Book Award, died at the age of 83.

■ Robert Cormier died at 75, after a career writing 18 books for young adults that uniformly drew critical acclaim and criticism. His books included *The Chocolate War, I Am the Cheese, Heroes*, and *Frenchtown Summer*.

■ Beatrice Schenk de Regniers, author of more than 40 books for children, died in March at the age of 86.

■ Jean Karl, who founded Atheneum Books for Young Readers in 1961, and was an author as well, died in Lancaster, Pennsylvania, at the age of 72. Karl wrote a column for *Children's Writer*.

■ Charles Schulz, the creator of *Peanuts*, died on February 12, the same night that hundreds of newspapers were printing the last cartoon of his 50-year career.

■ Illustrator Leonard Weisgard, who wrote and illustrated his first book, *Suki, the Siamese Puppy* in 1937, died at the age of 84.

Closings

■ *California Chronicles*, from Cobblestone Publishing, has ceased publication

- *Crayola Kids* stopped publishing when Meredith Corporation and the makers of Crayola crayons, Binney & Smith, had a parting of the ways on editorial development.

- *Marion Zimmer Bradley's Fantasy Magazine* has ceased publication.

- Parade Publications closed down *react*, a weekly aimed at teens.

- *The Drinking Gourd* is defunct.

- *Black Belt for Kids* has suspended publication.

- *The Goldfinch*, published by the State Historical Society of Iowa, ceased publication.

- *Sport*, from the Petersen Publishing Company, has ceased publishing.

- *Guideposts for Kids* has ceased publishing its print edition, but continues online.

Submissions & Style

Dramatic Writing

Study Plays & Write Better Fiction

By Marilyn D. Anderson

Writers of drama face unique limitations and freedoms. Whether it's stage or film, the artfulness and practical approaches of these disciplines hold lessons that other writers of fiction might well explore for their own uses.

John Allen, Editor of the teen magazine *Cicada*, believes studying dramatic structure can help novices in particular. "Beginner writers might profit by thinking of fiction as if it were a play. It might help beginning writers learn how to 'space out' a story."

"If people would think of a story like a play," says *Young Explorers* Editor Lisa Lyons, "they might eliminate unnecessary fluff and maybe not have kids sounding too knowledgeable for their ages." *Young Explorers* is a children's church curriculum for grades one to five.

"If you get muddled with a piece of fiction," young adult novelist Barbara Shoup advises her writing classes, "write a treatment of the story for a movie or TV because it helps you see the scene. Otherwise, you may get a plot that happens mostly in the head, and that just isn't very interesting."

Playwrights approach structure, conflict, character, dialogue, and setting from a slightly different angle than novelists and short story writers, and sometimes a fresh viewpoint is just what's needed to bring new life to a story that doesn't quite work.

Act by Act

Gary Blackwood had considerable experience writing fiction and drama, but a book called *Screenplay*, by Syd Field, completely changed his perception of the way he structures his fiction. Blackwood explains Field's method this way: "If you're writing a two-hour play with two acts, the *turning point* of the story should come at the end of the first act. This turning point is where everything changes for the main character and can never be the same again."

That moment in the action, he says, is like "a see-saw. If you walk up a see-saw and get to the fulcrum, it's in balance. When you pass that point, everything comes crashing down and you've got a whole new situation."

All fiction starts with a conflict, external or internal, that shows the status quo and the challenge to it. But "about halfway through the first act (or the one-quarter mark in a novel) is the point where the real conflict begins—

Submissions & Style

A Closer Look at <u>The Shakespeare Stealer</u>

Gary Blackwood, author of the middle-grade novel The Shakespeare Stealer, *has been influenced by Sid Field's book* Screenplay, *which discusses play structures. Let's examine how Blackwood's novel illustrates Field's formula for dramatic structure—literally by where events occur in the book.*

The Shakespeare Stealer is a 216-page historical novel set in Elizabethan England.

On page 50, about one-quarter of the way through the novel: The main character, Widge, gets so caught up in watching the production of *Hamlet* that he forgets to copy parts of its text, which he is under great pressure to steal. This event clearly defines Widge's main goal, and the consequences he will face if he fails are indicated. The problem, or conflict, is established.

On page 102, about halfway through: After a fellow player has rescued Widge from some ruffians and another player has offered him friendship, Widge begins to feel a certain loyalty to the company. If he steals their play, he will be betraying the only people he has ever really cared about. This is a whole new level of conflict.

On page 160, about two-thirds through: An amazing discovery sets the wheels in motion for Widge to take a starring role in a play to be performed for the queen herself. This chance opportunity causes Widge to begin to dream of a career as an actor.

the one that has to be resolved," says Blackwood. "Halfway through the second act of the play (about the three-quarter point in a novel) is what I call *the clincher*. It is something that takes place that determines the outcome, the dénouement, of the story."

Blackwood wasn't aware of this method of structuring when he wrote his early plays or middle-grade novels, but when he checked his work, he found that he had instinctively followed Field's formula. It's an approach many writers could use to plan out their story or novel, or they might use it in their revising to test the power and pacing of the action.

The conflict, also known as the *problem*, is the heart of the structure for play or prose. "Most important for any story," says writer Elsa Marston, "is to find the right problem. Make it as big as you can and have it still be something the main character can work with realistically. Something unexpected is also needed to achieve drama."

Although best known for her short stories, Marston also writes novels and picture books. Just like a playwright, she strives to make her material fit within limitations and keep her audience guessing. When Marston wrote "The Olive Tree," a short story that appeared in *Highlights for Children* and won several awards, she "first thought of how an olive tree grows. It twists and turns back on itself in unexpected directions, and that's dramatic. I wondered what would happen if such a tree grew on one person's property but dropped its fruit on somebody else's." She used this simple conflict between two neighbors to explore a very complicated civil war in Lebanon.

This *personification* of conflicts that are too big for the mind to grasp is standard technique for dramatists because of stage limitations. In Marston's story, the olive tree personified the conflict. The well-known play *Fiddler on the Roof*, for example, used a main character who was a composite of many men's experiences to explore the effect of centuries of tradition and persecution for Russian Jews. Personification of the problem or creating composite characters works equally well in fiction.

Opening Act

Once you have determined the overall structure of your story and the conflict—the core of the dramatic action—it's time to write the specifics of beginning, middle, and end.

"The opening material is the DNA of fiction, carrying all the genetic material for what is to come," says Jane Yolen, the highly acclaimed author of more than 200 children's books.

Consider Shakespearean openings: Hamlet's ghost at Elsinore castle, a shipwreck in a tempest near a magical island, a headstrong woman's encounter with a man determined to tame her spirit. Each of these introduces characters, sets up

The Elements of Drama

Drama is comprised of a cast of characters, dialogue, action, sets, costumes, and props. Let's hear what editors and writers have to say about how each of these elements might best be handled by the fiction writer.

Cast

- "Fiction writers might do better if they would block out certain scenes as if they were writing a play. It might keep them from crowding the stage with bit players and keep the scenes focused on the important action." ***John Allen**, Cicada*
- "In fiction you can have the whole Russian army do a left flank with a few words, but you must decide how well-defined each of your characters needs to be. In fiction, some people are just cannon fodder." ***Jane Yolen**, author*
- "I get stories about a pony club, and the authors think they need to describe everybody there. If a character doesn't have anything directly to do with the story, he should only be mentioned briefly." ***Susan Stafford**, Horsepower*
- Character names can be important. "In high school, Hermia and Helena, the two main characters in Shakespeare's *A Midsummer Night's Dream*, drove me nuts because I could not keep them straight. I try to give my characters in fiction distinctive names." ***Pamela Service**, author*

Dialogue

- "In a play (or a story), everything that a person says has to reveal something about them or the conflict or the conflict ahead. I compare a play to a boxing match. One person gives a few punches and the other person punches back, even though the first person isn't done punching." ***Gary Blackwood**, author*

Action

- "I picture scenes when I'm writing them. I see where everyone is and when they need to come on to speak their piece." ***Sandy Asher**, author*
- "In fiction you are the actors, the director, and the scene setter. Fiction is for control freaks, and plays are for people who will let others into their playground." ***Jane Yolen**, author*
- "People are not just voices. Even though they're talking on the telephone, they may be doodling on paper or nervously tapping a pen while they talk. If I were writing a book, I might say 'she nervously tapped her pen' to break up the floating unconnected voices." ***Pamela Service**, author*
- "In a play writers have a schedule to keep, so they're not going to be rambling on. Every word counts. They know that less is more." ***Susan Stafford**, Horsepower*

The Elements of Drama

Sets
■ When writing, "See what each scene looks like. I try to make sure the audience is picturing the same scene that I am." *Sandy Asher, author*
■ Many poorer stories lack a sense of setting. "Sometimes I can't get a setting in my head. I'm not sure if they're in a hot climate or a cold climate or if the scene is taking place inside or outside." *Susan Stafford, Horsepower*
■ "The number of sets in a piece of fiction can vary greatly, depending on whether you're writing about a sick boy who never gets out of the house or if you're writing *War and Peace*, which goes all over Russia and France." *Jane Yolen, author*

Costumes
■ Many beginning writers feel they must describe what each character is wearing, but "if your character is noticing what someone is wearing because it's important to move the story forward, then you include it. If she's noticing it because you want to describe this dress, that's not good enough." *Sandy Asher, author*

Props
■ Although the details of a room or an outdoor scene can add authenticity to a play or a piece of fiction, "if you have too many props on stage, they tend to take over. If you have too many details in fiction, the reader loses track of what's important." *Pamela Service, author*

Dramatic Magazine Needs

Cicada
Cricket Publishing
John Allen, Editor
P.O. Box 300, Peru, IL 61354
"About a year ago," says Allen, "we printed 'The Problem with Linnie,' by Lauren Myracle. This was something different for us in that it was panel-fiction, which is sort of like a comic strip or comic book. It's really very similar to playwriting because things are carried on with dialogue and minimal narration, and the artist blocks this out with sets and scenes and action. It's something that we're continuing to look for."

Horsepower Magazine
Susan Stafford, Editor
P.O. Box 670, Aurora, Ontario L4G 4J9 Canada
"*Horsepower*'s current needs are primarily how-to, educational articles," says Stafford. "We get a lot of fiction, and I try to run one story per issue, but generally, the kids want to learn more about how to take care of their horses, not that Janie won the big race! We have a six-page cartoon series in every issue, called 'Penny Stables.' It's about the adventures of a bunch of kids at a riding stable, and it always has a moral of sorts." Other fiction should be horse-related, although the genre may be sports, adventure, or humor.

Young Explorers
Lisa Lyons, Editor
General Council of the Assemblies of God
1445 Boonville Avenue, Springfield, MO 65802-1894
http://ag.org
Lyons says of her current needs: "I'm accepting skits. We try to write them so they can be used by either two actors or two puppets. The players are grade school age children. We have four characters and a dog. They have certain personalities, so the writer must write accordingly and stick the dog in there once in a while. That's the format, and we give the writer the theme."

conflict, and folds the audience into the play's style within minutes. A short story can do the same. While a novel has more room to set up and develop (and should take advantage of the possibilities), the principle remains the same. The beginning must create a foundation that can carry the reader through the story like a suspension bridge carries people to the other side of a chasm.

"The book has to grab the reader," declares Sandy Asher, who writes award-winning plays and fiction, and puts together short story collections, as in her recent book, *With All My Heart, With All My Mind: Thirteen Stories About Growing Up Jewish*. "You often do that by dropping the character into trouble immediately. Playwrights have an advantage over authors here in that the audience can't just put down the play and walk away, as a reader might."

Horsepower's Editor Susan Stafford uses the terms of another writing category: "I have a journalism background, so I want to see the 'who, what, when, where, and why' in the first two paragraphs. You also need to get the reader's attention and develop your character." You need a character who grabs the stage, steals the limelight.

Allen believes that *Cicada*'s readers need to know the main character's goals in short order. "In children's writing, it's very important to get out the desire early on, to get down the motivations of the character. What's he going to be doing? What's he up against? It helps the reader unconsciously figure out: 'What's the standard for a happy ending?'"

But Shoup points out that quiet openings can work well for young adults. To teach this approach, she has her writing students watch the opening scenes of the movie *Witness*. "You see these people come over the hill. You look at their clothes and they go into a house and you start to put all this stuff together. I ask my students, 'How do you know what you know in that movie? What visual details gave you this information? How would you write that?' This helps them to not just tell the story."

When Sinda S. Zinn, who edits *Discovery Trails*, a Sunday school paper for ages 10 to 12, gets a short story that begins with abundant description, she knows that beginning is not going to work for her readers. But the submission won't necessarily be rejected, either. "If the opening doesn't get right into the story, we make it do that. We will help the story with dialogue and action if the story has a good message."

Speak Easy

Dialogue is the principal material the dramatist uses to build his creation. This was something Pamela Service had to learn when she turned her book *Wizard of Wind and Rock* into a children's play called *Merlin, Wizard Boy*.

"In my first version of the play," Service says, "I used the same scenes, and I even had a narrator to introduce things and give the historical background needed. When a real playwright read my play, he quickly pointed out that this is not how you do a play. The audience must learn what they have to know through dialogue and interaction between the characters. Drama is *show, don't tell* in its purest form." That *show, don't tell* is a concept all fiction writers

Drama Markets

Authors interested in trying their hand at plays might look into the following publishers. The market for drama is strong.

Anchorage Press
Orlin Corey, Editor
P.O. Box 8067, New Orleans, LA 70182
Anchorage Press publishes 10 plays annually for children of all ages. It also produces dramatic arts titles for teachers working with preschool through high school students.

Baker's Plays
Ray Pape, Associate Editor
100 Chancy Street, Boston, MA 02111
www.bakersplays.com
This company publishes about 20 titles a year for all ages. Their materials include classic, musical, one-act, operatic, holiday, religious, and other plays, as well as books on theater.

Contemporary Drama Service
Meriwether Publishing
Theodore Zapel & Rhonda Wray, Assistant Editors
885 Elkton Drive, Colorado Springs, CO 80907
www.contemporarydrama.com
Contemporary Drama publishes about 60 "theatricals" annually for school, community, and church groups. Middle-grade and high school materials are specialties. They also publish books and videotapes. Guidelines are available at the website.

Dramatic Publishing
Linda Habjan, Acquisitions Editor
311 Washington Street, Woodstock, IL 60098
www.dramaticpublishing.com
Founded in 1885, this company publishes about 60 titles a year for all ages. It prefers that children's plays are constructed so that they can be expanded to use more actors.

Drama Markets

Eldridge Publishing Company
Susan Shore, Editor
P.O. Box 1595, Venice, FL 34284
www.histage.com
Another well-established company, Eldridge was founded in 1906. It publishes about 70 titles a year for children and adults, including holiday plays, musicals, religious plays, melodramas, and more. Skits for youth groups and plays that adults can put on for children are of special interest. Writers' guidelines are available at the website; separate guidelines are available for Christian plays.

Encore Performance Publishing
Michael Perry, President
P.O. Box 692, Orem, UT 84059
www.encoreplay.com
Since 1979, this publisher has offered full-length and one-act plays, musicals, skits, and monologues. Encore publishes around 20 titles each year for professional and community groups to perform for children, adults, and families.

Pioneer Drama Service
Beth Somers, Assistant Editor
P.O. Box 4267, Englewood, CO 80155
www.pioneerdrama.com
Pioneer publishes about 25 titles a year for all ages and in all categories, but with an emphasis on comedy and musicals. It calls itself the "top-grossing publisher" of plays for middle-graders, young adults, and community theaters. Guidelines are on the website.

Plays, The Drama Magazine for Young People
Kalmbach Publishing Company
Elizabeth Preston, Managing Editor
120 Boylston Street, Boston, MA 02116
www.playsmag.com
Plays has been publishing for 60 years. It buys about 75 one-act plays each year. Content must be "wholesome" and suitable for children in grades 1 to 12. Humor is a specialty, but musicals are excluded except for new songs with new words to well-known tunes.

must learn to strengthen their writing, even if the demands are not quite as absolute as in drama.

Studying what the dramatist chooses to include and exclude in dialogue can also be of value to the fiction writer. Blackwood explains, "I used to have my students listen to an actual taped conversation between my wife and another lady. Then I had them make this into play dialogue. It was soon obvious how many unfinished sentences there were and how much overlapping, how much repetition. Characters in plays can't speak the way people in real life do or the audience would be bored out of their skulls. This also applies to writing fiction."

"Personally, my training in theater is tremendously useful in writing fiction," Asher comments, "because I tend to act out all the characters' parts and think about 'What would they say in this situation?'"

Young readers want to see an abundance of direct quotes on the page, but Allen cautions fiction writers not to rely on dialogue to the extent that dramatists do, "or it will end up reading like one long conversation. Dialogue is like good red wine. A little of it is excellent, but a lot of it sends you reeling. In fiction it is more appropriate to get exposition out in expository (non-dialogue) writing."

The Construct

A strong lead brings the reader on stage, but what happens in the middle of a play, novel, or short story keeps him in the playhouse. "You have to ask yourself if this is the right place in the book for this to happen," says Allen. "I've read plenty of book manuscripts in which nothing happens for 100 pages, and on the last five, a whole bunch of stuff happens. A playwright would never do that because you want the audience to come back after the intermission."

"Variety in pacing is very important," Marston warns. "If everything goes along in rapid action, that rapid action loses its effectiveness. You have to have quiet places in between so that, when the action does pick up, there's dramatic contrast." In her picture book *Cynthia and the Runaway Gazebo,* which has been developed into a musical play by Lenny Hort, Marston contrasts the restrained atmosphere of a tea party with an attack by pirates on the high seas.

In plays and in fiction, each subplot must be given proper attention. "The development of a plot is like braiding hair," Shoup says. "You start out with certain elements, like characters and ideas, and you keep pulling them through the story. If you let any go, it would be like leaving a hunk of hair out. If you don't braid in the right rhythm, that wouldn't look good either." Consider what the play *Arsenic and Old Lace* would have been like if brother Teddy, who thinks he's Teddy Roosevelt, left the play after the first act.

Dramatists work on the principle that each action in the play should be caused by the action that came before it and should, in turn, cause the next bit of action to come. Asher suggests that approach also can be applied to fiction. "In each chapter, a catalyst starts the action, and by the end of the chapter, there's been a new turn. Something has been changed, learned, settled, but then there's the next chapter in which to deal with what was new."

Karen Grove, Consulting Editor at Harcourt, Inc., observes, "Certain books are written more as flashbacks or glimpses of the character. Although a scene doesn't build on the scene before it, it does build on what the total person is." This approach would probably not work as well in a play.

The Climax

No matter how you structure your fiction, it must lead up to a climactic scene that allows the *star of the show*—the protagonist—to prove his mettle and that produces a satisfying ending. You don't need a pile of bodies lying around stage for this to happen, but you do need suspense and high stakes for the characters, right up to the point where your main conflict is resolved, even in comedy.

Remember how the policemen and the crooks kept dodging each other at the end of *Arsenic and Old Lace*? Didn't you wonder whether the lovable old aunts would end up in the hands of Mr. Witherspoon from Happy Dale or be hauled off by the police?

"You have to risk everything to get a good ending," says Yolen. "If there's no promise of total disaster, then anything that happens is sort of flat. If the opening line is the promise, the ending is the payoff on that promise."

It's almost easier to say what an ending should not be. Asher agrees and cautions writers of both disciplines to avoid endings in which "a magical element suddenly comes in. The main character cannot suddenly become powerful in a way he never was before and never showed any signs of being."

Sermons by adults, even at the end of religious stories, are also to be avoided. "The lesson should be part of the story itself and be part of the person's character," says Zinn.

Allen warns against the truly theatrical ending. "You don't want to crowd the whole cast out on the stage again just so you can see them one more time."

Overwritten endings also bother Grove: "It's not the big crash scene that will stay with you. Some of the best books are the ones that leave you heading in a certain direction, but you're not quite sure where. It allows the reader to personalize the story more."

Grove gives author Elaine Marie Alphin high marks for the ending of her book *Counterfeit Son*. A boy is rescued from the home of a man who preys upon boys and is taken in by a family who believes the boy is their missing son. The book deals with the boy's struggle to make the family continue in this belief. We learn things about him that make us think he'll survive in this new home and other things that make us question his chances. Then, in the same way the Russian Jews' existence was still threatened at the end of *Fiddler on the Roof*, Alphin ends with her main character's future still in doubt. "Elaine left off at a critical point where things can turn in several ways," Grove reports. "That's what makes it powerful. If she were to add an extra chapter at the end of the book showing him happy and now part of the family, it would take all that emotional power away."

The Actors

Structuring and finding the best way to tell your story are important, but Grove believes that knowing the *protagonist*—in classical Greek the word means *actor*—well is the real key to writing a good novel. "You can have a great dramatic structure, but without the character and the voice there, you really don't have much. You need the actor to bring life to it."

Hamlet, for instance, takes on his perceived enemies, and handles the ghost's demand for revenge, differently than Henry V. Hamlet is young, lacking in political power, and he's crafty, so he comes up with an unusual way to outsmart enemies. Henry V is young, trying to win political power, and while crafty, his personality and purpose are more motivated by a desire to prove his capability and demonstrate leadership. Hamlet, it may be argued, learns little of himself, while Prince Hal—the new king Henry V—has learned much.

Fiction writers, too, must give their characters this chance at a life on their own terms. Asher finds that, just as actors make suggestions that are often incorporated into the final script, her characters sometimes write her story for her. Much of her novel *Summer Begins* was written in this "blissful" way. When her main character's editorial in the school paper caused such a ruckus that the character's teacher was asked to resign, Asher thought she knew what came next. "But when I sat at the typewriter the next day, one of the other characters announced that the kids were going to stage a protest. That day I just typed what the characters dictated."

Asher recommends the USA Plays For Kids website, usaplays4kids.cjb.net, which provides links to playwrights, plays, and useful organizations.

Also a firm believer in the character-driven novel, Yolen says that even the style of the story's telling must be dictated by the character of the protagonist. "You don't force the style on the story. It rises up organically out of what the story is that you're going to tell." One can't imagine her historical novel *The Gift of Sarah Barker* told in the same style as her *Wizard's Hall* because these characters are as different as day and night. Similarly, Thornton Wilder's play *Our Town* would lose much of its power if its characters sounded too highly educated or appeared on a stage full of furniture.

Drama and fiction are different mediums, created to entertain and be thought-provoking in different ways. A novelist cannot adopt every stage technique. But an understanding of dramatic structure in its truest form can raise the curtain on stronger fiction.

Grove sums up when she says, "Plays are a great way to learn structure, pacing, and plot, but there is a gap between that and having a book that is ready to be published. You have to make an extra leap to get that character right. If the structure of a book needs work, it's relatively easy to fix. If the character needs work, it's tough going. In terms of a play, you can have a brilliantly written classic performed with poor actors and the whole thing flops. Characters can make or break your story."

Whether or not your novel or short story works depends in large part on your success in getting fascinating characters on stage to say their lines in a believable way. The best stories are those in which we identify with the actors and imagine ourselves as players.

Publishing Awards

In Recognition of Tradition & Exploration

By Marnie Brooks

Questions about the effects of technological and social change on children's books loom large on the publishing horizon. Will printed books disappear? Never! Of course! Is children's literature too shallow, too controversial? Yes! No!

One traditional factor in children's literature may be a surprising bellwether. Venerable awards such as the Newbery, Caldecott, Coretta Scott King Award, Golden Kite, and National Book Award, and new honors, like the Michael L. Printz Award, are acknowledgements of excellence. They also encourage writers, promote literacy, and may be harbingers of the future.

Picture Book Magic

Picture books are the essence of children's literature for many readers. When language and image harmonize, storytelling is magical. Those images can explore vast new horizons today with the explosion in graphics software, printing technology, and electronic formats. Are these changes reflected in the Caldecott Medal—the highest honor a children's book illustrator can receive?

Artist Simms Taback, recipient of the 2000 medal for *Joseph Had a Little Overcoat* and a 1997 Caldecott Honor for *There Was an Old Lady Who Swallowed A Fly*, says, "Electronics broaden the whole entertainment field, and that's what books are. By itself, a book is a special experience—a tactile one."

A 1998 Caldecott Honor winner for *Harlem*, Christopher Myers thinks new technologies are interesting because they continue to depend on the same principles as traditional media. "Storytelling is a skill that will never go out of style. Growing up in the beginnings of the computer age, I realize how much all the flash-and-bang of digital technologies doesn't make up for solid storytelling and visual sophistication. Even with 3-D graphical interfaces and surround-sound on CD-ROM, if the characters and pictures are flat, no child will be interested."

Myers likes working with digital video and children's media but says, "What makes a piece interactive is the level of involvement with story and character. Bound books made with printing presses are remarkably interactive. I'm all for sophisticated work for children on all levels, as long as it's committed and honest."

The Caldecott

Named in honor of the nineteenth-century English illustrator Randolph J. Caldecott, the Caldecott was established in 1937 to honor picture book artists. It is awarded annually by the Association for Library Service to Children (ALSC), a division of the American Library Association (ALA). While the Caldecott Committee is given specific criteria to consider—artistic technique, pictorial interpretation of the story, theme, concept—each of the 15 expert committee members is touched by personal perceptions of illustrative expression.

Barbara Kiefer, Chair of the 2000 Caldecott Award Selection Committee, says the experience "was one of the highlights of my career. When we came together in January, I was thankful I had 14 others to help make a choice. The fact that the award is chosen by consensus represents a model of group process." Kiefer is a painter and a professor at Teacher's College, Columbia University. She also served on the 1987 Caldecott committee.

In *Joseph Had a Little Overcoat*, the 2000 Caldecott Medal winner, Kiefer says, author/illustrator Simms Taback's painting and photographs recall Polish klezmer music in his lively retelling of this Yiddish folktale. Vivid colors, clean-edged figures, and loads of pleasing details contribute to the book's raucous merriment and take the story far beyond simple words. The patchwork layout of the pages, two-dimensionality of the paintings, and the exaggerated perspective are reminiscent of folk art and the very fabric of the overcoat that becomes a story."

Of one of the Caldecott Honor books, Molly Bang's *When Sophie Gets Angry*, Kiefer says, "With the vivid colors and close-up face on the cover of *Sophie*, a wonderful book for preschoolers, we have no doubt that she is furious. Bang has captured all the emotional volatility of the young child thwarted in her desires. The story line is simple, in keeping with the book's audience. The pictures carry the message in a way that is much more satisfying to a young child than words alone could ever be."

Molly Bang, who wrote and illustrated the 2000 Caldecott Honor book *When Sophie Gets Angry,* finds "it fun to explore all ways of making pictures. The new trends keep me on my toes, keep me exploring."

Freedom of Ideas

Over the last three-quarters of a century since the ALA's Newbery Medal was created, children's literature has embraced a wider scope of subject, genre, and format. The Newbery is a mirror on the state of children's books—as literature and the business of publishing.

"The greatest gift a writer can receive is to be granted the freedom to pursue any idea, no matter how impractical or eccentric, without financial pressures and constraints. That is one favor, among many, the Newbery Medal bestowed on me," says Russell Freedman,

The Newbery

Awarded by the American Library Association (ALA) to an author whose book is "a distinguished contribution to American literature for children," the Newbery Medal was established in 1922 and honors eighteenth-century British bookseller John Newbery.

A committee of 15 is chosen annually to select the medal winner and honor books. 1999 Newbery judge Teresa Young is a former middle school teacher and current youth services manager at the Eva H. Perry Library in Apex, North Carolina. "It was a great honor to be part of the selection committee, but there are demographics involved, too," Young says. The ALA tries "to balance the committee in every possible way—gender, profession, etc. We come from all walks of life: editors, librarians, teachers, professors and, of course, writers, all people who are considered qualified to evaluate children's literature."

The committee reviews each book for plot development, theme, characters, style, and more, but various aspects touch individual judges. "No subject is restricted, but books must be considered appropriate for children up to and through age 14. That leaves room for many themes, mature ones. Nothing is ruled out," says Young. Personally, she thinks, "Plot is great, but I'm more interested in characterization. I like books that don't always proceed in a linear fashion—more of a complex telling of a story in that it's not until the end that you fully realize what happened."

---

a two-time Newbery honoree and 1988 winner for *Lincoln: A Photobiography*.

Christopher Paul Curtis, winner of the 2000 Newbery Medal for *Bud, Not Buddy*, says, "The Newbery does wonders for your career. Many people have asked if winning these awards puts pressure on me. Actually, it's given me a sense of freedom. It encourages me to try different things, to be myself. When I write, I try to be honest with readers and treat them as I'd like to be treated." Curtis is the only black man to win a Newbery. His first novel, *The Watsons Go to Birmingham—1963*, was a 1996 Honor Book. (See the profile of Christopher Paul Curtis, page 128.)

Wendy Lamb, Executive Editor at Delacorte Press, edited Curtis's books. "Everyone here loved *The Watsons* and worked hard for it," she says. "We were all rooting for something to happen for *Bud*. I felt it was a real saga, a story that left you feeling satisfied and moved that you'd had a true experience, away from your own life."

Winning the Newbery boosts not just author, but publisher. "Publishing is such a team effort and lots of people here contributed to the book—marketing, sales, art direction, copy editing, and fellow editors," says Lamb. "Delacorte, and our larger group, Random House, has never had the Newbery, so it was thrilling to break that barrier."

Louis Sachar, 1999 Newbery Medal-

A New Award: The Printz

Introduced by the ALA and its division of Young Adult Library Services Association (YALSA) in 2000, the award honors the late Michael Printz, a Kansas school librarian and long-time active member of YALSA.

The Printz considers all genres of YA books: fiction, nonfiction, poetry, or anthologies for ages 12 to 18. It has one winner and up to four honor books. The first Printz Committee was given guidelines covering elements such as story, voice, setting, characters, illustration, and design, but as with all literature awards, individual selection committee members have personal requirements. The first winner of the award is Walter Dean Myers, for *Monster*, illustrated by Christopher Myers.

Even for authors who have moved beyond award expectations, the Newbery is gratifying. Richard Peck received a 1999 Newbery Honor for *A Long Way from Chicago: A Novel of Stories*. "Seeing how it was my twenty-eighth book, I had learned to live without such an honor. However, I was very pleased. I don't write for awards; I write for the readers, even if they don't know what a Newbery is. But it was wonderful to have recognition from librarians." The Newbery also raises an author's stock with publishers. Peck's editor asked for a sequel. *A Year Down Yonder* is the result.

A former high school teacher, Peck says the Newbery isn't promoted enough. "I'm sorry this country isn't more interested in what its children read, enough to know what the award is. It isn't widely known outside our field. More and more high school librarians buy books only for reference and not light reading. Some stock the classics because they please parents and funding is limited. This is a terrible shame. We need books that follow young people through high school. Kids aren't relating the classics to their own lives. They need books that are metaphors for them today."

Take Notice of Teens

The ALA's new Michael L. Printz Award, cosponsored by *Booklist*, should encourage books that do provide those metaphors. The award is the first given specifically for excellence in books for young adults.

"We hope the Printz Award will change the way high schools look at YA literature," said Frances B. Bradburn, Chair of the 2000 Printz Award.

---

ist for *Holes*, believes the award helped his writing. "I feel like winning has made it easier. It was a challenge to write *Holes*. The fact that I succeeded at it has given me confidence for future challenges." One such endeavor is a screenplay for the book.

"Children's publishing has a bright future," says Sachar. "Some of the best children's books have been written over the last 10 or 20 years and I see no reason why the trend shouldn't continue. Writers are willing to tackle difficult subjects, and we respect the intelligence of our young readers."

"The Newbery wasn't enough. Books can cross back and forth between middle-grade and YA, depending on the development of each child. Although there are truly wonderful books for young adults that are Newberys, they are not YA by any stretch of the imagination." They do not deal with subjects, or have styles, directed to the issues and growing sophistication of teens, rather than preteens. (See the profile of Frances B. Bradburn, page 126.)

Walter Dean Myers won the first Printz Award for his uniquely formatted book, *Monster*, illustrated by his son, Christopher Myers. The book was also a National Book Award finalist and a Coretta Scott King Honor Book. *Monster* has a double narrative structure that combines a screenplay format and handwritten journal with visuals that include photographs, graphics, and different print styles.

"You couldn't read *Monster* without immediately attaching yourself to the format," says Bradburn. "The distinct narrative and graphics showed the risks Walter was willing to take in his career. He has pushed himself to reach what he has become over the years.

"Every one of us on the committee worked hard to choose extraordinary books. It haunted us because we realized how people would look at the first committee and we wanted to make sure the books we chose were truly of literary merit."

Editors, often the unsung heroes of award-winning books, are as deeply affected by these honors as the writers.

Monster's Editorial Director, HarperCollins Executive Editor Phoebe Yeh, says, "Naturally, award recognition for a book that you've acquired and edited gives you a sense of accomplishment, pride, and terror. How can you maintain this standard in the author's next novel, or the books on the rest of your list? The priority is to try and stay focused on making sure books on your backlist, frontlist, and upcoming lists get the attention they need."

The first year of the award, three Printz Honor books were also chosen: *Skellig*, by David Almond (originally published in Great Britain), *Speak*, by Laurie Halse Anderson, and *Hard Love*, by Ellen Wittlinger.

Speak is Anderson's first novel. "What excites me most about the Printz Award is that it lets the world know that teenage readers exist—lots of teenage readers. It promotes people who think teenagers are important and try to write for them." (See the profile of Laurie Halse Anderson, page 123.)

Wittlinger, a former children's librarian and author of two YA novels in addition to *Hard Love*, agrees. "I'm so pleased the ALA is now honoring YA authors in this way. Books for teenagers, especially for older teens, have gotten lost in the shuffle in past years, often overlooked by critics as well as award presenters. I hope the inauguration of the Printz Award will bring more notice to terrific YA books."

"For me, winning the Printz Honor was overwhelming," Wittlinger says. "The fact that this was the first year the award was given made it that much more special. As I was writing *Hard Love*, I sometimes wondered if I was on the wrong path. Was I going too far afield to please kids, publishers, and what of reviewers? Winning the award validated my belief that if I write what I feel strongly about, somebody else will love it, too."

Skellig, David Almond's debut work for young people, also received the coveted 1998 Great Britain Whitbread Children's Book of the Year Award. Almond is British, but Printz Award criteria allow a foreign author to receive the award as long as an American edition has been published during the period of eligibility. In contrast, the Newbery is only awarded to citizens or residents of the U.S.

Within All People

Among the more cutting-edge issues children's publishing sporadically took on in the later years of the century, were ethnic and multicultural subjects.

The Coretta Scott King Award

Presented each year by the Coretta Scott King Task Force of the ALA's Social Responsibilities Round Table, the Coretta Scott King Award commemorates the life and work of Dr. Martin Luther King. It also honors his widow for her courage and determination in continuing the work for peace and world brotherhood.

The seven-member Coretta Scott King Award Jury also chooses The Coretta Scott King New Talent Award (created in 1974). This award honors books showing talent and excellence in writing or illustration at the beginning of a career.

Were minorities truly represented in children's literature? How might cultural differences be depicted, and who should write about them? How do books appeal to all children and their divergent realities?

For 30 years, the ALA's Coretta Scott King Award has been given in recognition of work by authors and illustrators of African descent. It encourages artistic expression of the African-American experience through literature and graphic arts.

In recent years, many of the same authors recognized by this award have also received Newbery and Caldecott honors. Curtis won the 2000 Coretta Scott King Award for *Bud, Not Buddy* and the 1996 Honor for *The Watsons*. Christopher Myers, 2000 Coretta Scott King Illustrator Award winner as author/illustrator of *Black Cat*, won a 1998

SCBWI Golden Kite

Two major children's literature awards from another source are the Golden Kite Award and the Magazine Merit Award from the Society of Children's Book Writers and Illustrators (SCBWI). Both are chosen annually by a jury of SCBWI members, all illustrators or authors themselves and all recipients are SCBWI members.

It annually honors outstanding children's books illustrated or written by an SCBWI member. Award categories include nonfiction, fiction, picture book text, and illustration.

According to SCBWI founder and President Stephen Mooser, the Golden Kite was established in 1973 because "of the desire to honor those who, we as authors and illustrators, felt were striving toward excellence in children's literature."

Caldecott Honor for *Harlem*.

"What made winning this award for *Bud* especially touching," says Curtis, "was that the call came on Dr. King's birthday. I'm honored that my books were chosen by the Coretta Scott King Committee. Both honors were surprises—really beautiful ones."

"Getting an award for a book is so special because it means people are hearing you out there in the world," Myers says. "You sit in your house and make up stories and pictures and sometimes you don't know if those stories exist anywhere outside your head. When enough people recognize my story as one that's inside them, too, it means I am sharing part of some larger story that's within all people."

Sharon Draper won the 1995 Coretta Scott King New Talent Award for *Tears of a Tiger* and the 1998 Coretta Scott King Award for *Forged by Fire*. "I felt proud and humbled to receive recognition from such a well-honored and highly respected source. As a writer, the awards gave me affirmation as well as recognition." Draper, a teacher, says, "When I write I find myself teaching a much larger audience, affecting the lives of young people I've never met. My *classroom* has been expanded tremendously because of these two books and the honors they received. Those who write must do so because of the love of language and story and the need to transport that love into magic and onto paper. I hope the King Award will encourage young people to read and dream of their own visions of magic."

Peer Appreciation

The awards of the Society of Children's Book Writers and Illustrators (SCBWI) are representative of quality, but also give the working writer direct, process-driven, hands-on support and recognition. The Golden Kite is the only award presented to children's book authors and artists by their peers.

"The Golden Kite is extremely meaningful, in a different way than other awards," says 1999 Golden Kite winner Laurie Halse Anderson, author of *Speak*, "because I owe so much to SCBWI for my career and because it was chosen by my peers."

Once again, Curtis's *Bud, Not Buddy* took an award, a Golden Kite Honor.

Honoring Magazine Writing

Awards are few and far between for children's magazine writing. The Society of Children's Book Writers and Illustrators (SCBWI) is the exception. Its annual Magazine Merit Award (MMA) brings recognition to writers whose work appears in shorter form.

Three-time winner Lisa Harkrader (1999 and 1995 Fiction, 1998 Poetry) found magazine writing helped her toward her goal to publish children's books. She also discovered that she loved writing short stories. "I started out wanting to write books, but decided to give magazines a try," she says. "Within a couple of months I'd sold my first story. It's a great way to gain quicker publication, income, and writing credits. It's a great stepping stone to book publishing, but it's also rewarding and valuable in its own right." Harkrader's stories have appeared in magazines such as *Cricket* and *Guideposts for Kids*, and in anthologies, including *Newfangled Fairy Tales*. She now ghost-writes for the Animorphs series and has published two books under her own name.

Children's nonfiction writer Sneed Collard III is a two-time winner of the Nonfiction MMA (1997 and 1998) and also served as a judge. "Not only has it been an honor to win two years in a row," he says, "but I think it's great that there is an avenue through which magazine writers can receive recognition. That is due entirely to the efforts of Dorothy Leon, the Award Coordinator, who almost single-handedly created this honor."

Collard has some strong opinions on the value of magazine writing: "It's clear that magazine writers still receive far less respect than book writers, even within SCBWI. Golden Kite winners are invited to the annual conference to speak, MMA winners are not. The point is, magazine writers still have a long way to go in the respect department. As a past judge, I loved seeing the ways writers crafted their articles and stories. I'd like to see librarians and organizations do more to raise the profile of this body of work."

Collard has written about 25 articles and a dozen fiction pieces for magazines including *Cricket, Spider,* and *Highlights for Children*. He has also published more than 25 nonfiction books, including *1,000 Years Ago on Planet Earth, Animal Dads,* and *Making Animal Babies*.

1998 MMA Fiction winner for "Shlemiel Crooks," Anna Olswanger found it an advantage to have her name listed on the SCBWI home page as a winner. It gave her name recognition when she contacted a literary agent. She has published many articles via the Web and in magazines, including *Hearing Health* and *Cricket*.

He won the 1995 Golden Kite for *The Watsons*. In his recent onslaught of honors, Curtis notes that the SCBWI awards "are so gratifying because they come from people who have been through the same struggles you have. Writers are often insecure and solitary," Curtis says. "Other writers have a deep understanding of what's involved. For them to say your work is among the best, that's an extremely good feeling."

Recognition is even better when accompanied by contracts. Susan Campbell Bartoletti, whose photoessay *Growing Up in Coal Country* landed the 1996 Golden Kite Honor for nonfiction, believes it helped launch her career. "I joined SCBWI in 1988, attended its functions, and read its publications. SCBWI taught me how to be a professional. I sold my first children's book in 1992 and two more by 1995, including *Coal Country*. When it won the Honor, it was validation of the greatest kind." Bartoletti went on to sell 10 more novels, photoessays, and picture books.

"SCBWI's goal is to help our membership further their careers by providing information, conferences, and networking opportunities," says the organization's founder and President, Stephen Mooser. "We are expanding our online services and adding critique groups, classes, and back-in-print options for members' books. We also continue to press for authors' rights, and fight against censorship through alliances with the National Censorship Coalition, the Authors Guild, and other associations." SCBWI also offers yearly grants for fiction/nonfiction, picture books, and illustration.

A Public Life

The nation's premier literary prize, the National Book Award (NBA) has been presented annually since 1950. It recognizes merit in fiction, nonfiction, poetry, and young people's literature.

Winners receive $10,000; five finalists receive $1,000. For a children's writer, that's a rich piece of recognition. The NBA also garners substantial media attention, with a celebrity-hosted dinner/awards ceremony in New York, and a tour of speaking engagements, public readings, and television appearances.

Kimberly Willis Holt, 1999 Young People's Literature Award winner for *When Zachary Beaver Came to Town*, describes the experience: "It felt like the Oscars. You have no idea until you get the call that you're a finalist, or even being considered. Just to be a finalist—that sounds so cliché—was enough. It was confirmation that someone likes my writing—people I respect." (See the profile of Kimberly Willis Holt, page 131.)

Awards also affect a writer's personal life with demands for travel and loss of anonymity. Sachar's *Holes* won the 1998 NBA. "I've always kept my personal life separate from my writing life. I'm an avid bridge player and have been playing at the Austin Bridge Studio for the past seven years. Most of the other players knew nothing of my professional life and that suited me fine. Of those who did know I wrote children's books, most barely gave it a thought, imagining children's books to be 'See Spot run.' When I won the awards, I lost my anonymity. I found it very disconcerting."

Speak was a 1999 National Book

The National Book Award

The National Book Foundation sponsors the National Book Awards through funding by a variety of corporate, foundation, and private philanthropic entities. The budget includes the $10,000 cash prize for the four winners and $1,000 for finalists in each category.

"The National Book Awards Gala Ceremony & Dinner is our major fundraiser of the year, providing much of our annual general operating support," explains Meg Kearney, Associate Director of the National Book Foundation. "The Gala is underwritten by several major leadership sponsors."

The first prize for Children's Literature was awarded in 1969 to Meindert DeJong for *Journey to Peppermint Street,* 19 years after the inauguration of the National Book Award.

"Unfortunately, there is not much information in our archives to tell why a children's category was not added sooner. Perhaps prior to 1969 the administrators of the National Book Award believed this category was properly represented by the Newbery and Caldecott," says Kearney.

Five judges are chosen to select winners and finalists for fiction, nonfiction, poetry, and young people's literature. "All judges are highly respected writers, and sometimes writers/critics in their field; they change each year," says Kearney. "We ensure no judge has a book coming out during the award year."

Hazel Rochman, Editor for Young Adult Books for *Booklist,* the reviewing journal for the American Library Association, was a judge for the 1999 Young People's Award. "The National Book Award is for quality and literary distinction, but I believe there can be no fixed criteria for judging, absolutely none," says Rochman. "Just when you try to define what you mean by literary quality, a great new book comes along that makes you rethink everything. We know what quality is not."

When speaking of the 1999 winner, *When Zachary Beaver Came to Town,* by Kimberly Willis Holt, Rochman says, "In my job as a book reviewer, I have to be open to the world of that one book, even as I bring with me my experience. In the case of *Zachary Beaver,* I loved the way you get to know the small Texas town in all its neon particulars and its gentleness, the way those particulars are universal. Holt also reveals the freak in all of us, and the power of redemption."

2000 National Book Award

The National Book Award's winners were named as *Children's Writer Guide to 2001* went to press. The winner of the Young People's Literature award was Gloria Whelan's *Homeless Bird* (HarperCollins), a novel about a 13-year-old girl in contemporary India. The protagonist is married off, widowed, and begins to create a life despite the ostracism of society.

The other nominees for the young people's award were:

- Adam Bagdasarian, *Forgotten Fire* (Melanie Kroupa). Set in the Armenian Holocaust of 1915, *Forgotten Fire* tells of a 12-year-old from a wealthy family who sees his family destroyed but learns to survive.
- Michael Cadnum, *The Book of the Lion* (Viking Children's Books). A young squire journeys to the Holy Land during the Crusades.
- Carolyn Coman, *Many Stones* (Front Street). An American girl in South Africa faces her sister's murder and a breach with her father.
- Jerry Stanley, *Hurry Freedom* (Crown Publishers). A novel about the lives of African Americans during the California gold rush focuses on the true story of Mifflin Gibbs.

Award finalist and Anderson says, "All the attention has taken a lot of time away from my personal life. I've had to learn to be deliberate about balancing time for my family, writing, and publicity. It's a problem, but a very pleasant one."

Han Nolan, two-time finalist and 1997 NBA winner for *Dancing on the Edge*, found the award momentous. "I was so thrilled that it won, although the experience was quite humbling. The other writers were all excellent and any of their books could just as easily have won. *Dancing on the Edge* was tough for me to write. Being a part of the main character's life for three years was also difficult. Winning the award made me more aware that the book belonged to the public and was no longer just my little story. The award gave the book lots of exposure, which meant more young adults and adults read it. I received many letters from people saying how my story affected them and that was the most gratifying of all."

Tomorrow's Winners

Awards mark excellence in the current literary environment, but they have enough clout to shape the future of publishing.

Bradburn hopes awards like the Printz can generate funding and support for YA literature. "Unfortunately, funding is truly politically charged. Having an award touting literary merit will make it easier for teachers of high school English and the librarians that support them. One of the problems with YA literature in the past was this moniker of dirty book"—witness *Catcher in the Rye*. "I see the possibility that the Printz will allow teachers to use some of these titles with more legitimacy."

Barbara Kiefer, Chair of the 2000 Caldecott Award Selection Committee, believes awards can help smaller publishers in a time of mergers forming huge companies. "I was so happy that a small publisher like Holiday House had a winner with *A Child's Calendar*," although size is never a consideration in awarding the Caldecott. "There are wonderful editors in new conglomerates and I believe they will fight for quality. I also believe there are enough of us in the profession—editors, librarians, and teachers—who will continue to demand high quality. Awards like the Caldecott can only help, since publishers interested in the bottom line know there will be profits in award-winning books."

> ### *Websites*
>
> **American Library Association:** www.ala.org
> **National Book Award:** www.publishersweekly.com/nbf/docs/about.html
> **Society of Children's Book Writers & Illustrators:** www.scbwi.org

Speak Up: Laurie Halse Anderson

Laurie Halse Anderson, author of the honor-laden young adult novel *Speak,* hopes that teens will find something familiar in her characters or their conflicts and see they are not alone.

"Watching my children grow up helps me re-experience the emotions of childhood and adolescence in a way that's impossible if you don't live with it day by day. I think the most painful aspect of being young is the feeling of isolation. Teens often feel no one understands who they are or what they go through."

Anderson, the mother of two teenage daughters, Stephanie and Meredith, believes her children keep her current on language, music, and fashion. While she acknowledges that her daughters and their friends influence her writing, "I am very careful not to steal things from their lives. That's an invasion. I listen to their dialogue and pay attention to what they care about. I may have to borrow my neighbor's kids when mine go to college!"

Make that Ten

As a child of the campus minister for Syracuse University, Anderson grew up in a house filled with college students. "I had countless brothers and sisters. We ran an open house. We never knew who was going to be there for dinner. I lived in a wonderful neighborhood where every house was filled with kids. We came home from school, put on old clothes and sneakers, and went outside to play for hours until somebody called us for dinner."

When Anderson graduated from Georgetown University with a degree in language and linguistics, she decided to overcome her aversion to math and took a job that would force her to use it. She became a stockbroker. "It was clearly the stupidest thing I've ever done in my life. I was the worst stockbroker in Washington, DC. Because I was a minister's daughter, I felt so bad hitting people up. Actually, I was good at talking them into investing until I'd find out it was their life savings. Then I'd turn around and convince them that investing in the stock market was too risky. Although I didn't make it as a stockbroker, I did learn to deal with math."

Anderson married while still in college. After her youngest daughter was born, she started looking into the writing world. With two babies at home, she went a bit stir crazy and sought "some kind of intellectual stimulation." She took courses in creative writing, English literature, and Greek plays at a

Laurie Halse Anderson

community college. She wrote adult short stories and did all sorts of writing, including a short stint as a reporter.

"On September 7, 1992, at about 9:10 AM, when my daughter went off to first grade, I had my bus stop epiphany., my Scarlett O'Hara moment. I gave myself five years to get a children's book published and if I didn't make it, I was going to get a normal, practical job," Anderson says. "Once I got into writing for children, I realized I was totally naive. I should've given myself 10 years because 5 is definitely not enough. The fact that I was published so soon was a stroke of good fortune. Many talented writers take at least 10 years to break into publishing."

Perspective

Anderson suggests trying magazines first because they're more open to new writers and offer the chance to establish publishing credentials. She sold her first stories to *Highlights for Children.* Another hint for new writers is to attend conferences to meet editors. Anderson cautions, "When you meet one, be professional. Don't shove your manuscript in an editor's face!"

Having written picture books, nonfiction, middle-grade, and young adult novels, Anderson feels open to writing everything. "Some stories are YA, some are obviously picture books. That's one of the exciting things about writing for children—a flexibility of storytelling voice that you don't have in the adult genre."

Although writing styles for picture books and novels are canyons apart, Anderson says perspective is the key to creating different kinds of stories. "You have to understand the perspective of your readers, where they are in their development and what they can understand, and understand the perspective of what a child brings to the book. A 5-year-old needs visual input as well as the rhythm of the words, while a 15-year-old operates from a very different context. To me, that's part of the challenge and what makes it fun and interesting."

Anderson thinks the only down side of writing for children is dealing with "arrogant assumptions that children's writing is for beginners, and that children's literature is inferior to books written for older people."

When Anderson hits a writing wall, she heads for the gym. She also believes that when she faces a writing block, "It's a sure sign I've started too early. I need to think about my piece more. One of my first mistakes when I started writing was to act on an idea and rush it out too fast. It would come back in a week. Now I make notes, start a file, and dedicate a notebook to it. Then the story builds momentum to the point where I have to write it or I'll explode."

Her solution for rejection blues is warm milk. For those who are "lactose intolerant, try chamomile tea."

Laurie Halse Anderson

What Anderson loves best about writing is exercising her brain and having control over her life. She says, "an ideal writing day happens about every three months because real life happens to get in the way."

With 13 published books, Anderson has had a few good days. Currently, she's involved with a middle-grade series she developed with Pleasant Company called Wild at Heart, based on the adventures of kids at a veterinary clinic. She has another YA novel in the works and feels enthusiastic about that genre. "There have been some good changes recently. Bookstores are looking at YA and saying, 'How do we sell to young adults and promote reading? We have great books, kids who want to read, and who are willing to buy them, so let's see how we can bring them together.'"

The most important tip Anderson can pass along, and one she heeds herself, is to take time to understand whatever market you want to write for so you'll know where to target the stories you've taken such care to craft.

Judging YA: Frances B. Bradburn

Champions come in all sizes and genders and defend many causes. Children's literature has a champion in Frances Bryant Bradburn, the first Chair of the new Michael L. Printz Award for young adult literature.

"The Printz Award has been a long time in coming," Bradburn says. "There's been a lot of work behind the scenes for a long time to get the Printz Award. I was in the background, hoping this would take place, but there were so many people who worked far harder than I ever thought possible, to move this forward. We're already able to see it bearing fruit." She names Michael Cart, Chair of the Printz Award Creation Committee, and committee members such as Roger Sutton, Editor of the *Horn Book;* Hazel Rochman, from *Booklist;* and several librarians, school media specialists, and college professors as the true champions. "Without their dedication, there wouldn't be an award."

Bradburn says that being selected for the chair position during the inaugural year of the award was "one of the most flattering professional acknowledgments I've ever had. Although I was on the creation committee, I'm still not sure how I got on as chair. It's also been an incredibly exciting year in young adult literature."

Cornerstone

"Reading is the cornerstone of all that we teach and do. It allows us to move forward in any direction we want to go, at any age. It has become the foundation of everything we work with in the field of education," Bradburn firmly believes.

A native of North Carolina, Bradburn is Director of Educational Technologies in the North Carolina Department of Public Instruction in Raleigh. Before becoming director, her position as head of evaluation services kept her busy assessing print, nonprint resources, and technology for North Carolina schools.

Bradburn graduated from Wake Forest University with a B.A. in English. She taught for several years before pursuing a library science degree at the University of North Carolina, where she became interested in children's and YA literature. She worked as a bibliographer for the Elementary School Library Collection, which focused on K-8 resources. That experience moved her into the middle and high school environment, sharpening her focus on young adult writing. In 1988, she became a member of the Young Adult Library Services Association (YALSA) and later joined the Best Books for Young Adults Committee, serving as chair for one year.

Her avid reading of the genre led Bradburn to book reviews. She currently

Frances B. Bradburn

reviews for *Booklist* and spent seven years writing the middle books column for the *Wilson Library Bulletin*. "Writing that column gave me the opportunity to see almost everything that was published for the middle-school range, a sort of catbird seat."

From her well-earned perspective overlooking the range of middle-grade and YA books, Bradburn can say, "I honestly believe children's and YA authors have to be better than adult writers. Children's writers *have* to synthesize the story and bring it down to a certain number of pages. Within this framework, they must also create memorable characters, plots that talk to kids, and settings that kids can identify with, whether it's science fiction or nonfiction."

Bradburn expands on her view: "A really good young adult or children's book is greater than anything an adult author can publish because it's held up in many ways to much higher standards. These authors have a moral responsibility when they write for children and young adults—a sense of honesty and ethical nature to their work that we don't require of adult authors."

When given a choice, Bradburn still prefers to read young adult and children's literature over adult books. It helps her keep a frame of reference for her job and for her work as a reviewer. "Even my adult kids come home and ask me what's good to read."

Diversity & Quality

The Printz Award is exciting, Bradburn says, because "we have the chance to increase the actual number of YA books that come into publication. We focused carefully on the young adult definition, which is any book that is targeted for age levels 12 to 18. This gave us a good range to hit, and huge diversity in subject. Each of us was thrilled with the responsibility and determined to make the best possible choice."

Even with the pressure of selecting the best books for this new award, Bradburn says, "we had a fabulous committee of nine dedicated members. Everybody read and everyone shared. I didn't see anyone with a hidden agenda or not willing to listen. There was really good young adult material this first year and I'm hoping that each year there will be more. We had high-quality titles to choose from and everybody respected each other for where we've been. Many of us had worked together before."

Bradburn felt humbled by the honor of participating and says, "The really wonderful part of the final process was making the phone call to the authors on the Monday morning before the winners were announced at the press conference." She adds, "It felt great to be able to say, 'You've won the award, or the honor, for your superior work.'"

Taking His Time: Christopher Paul Curtis

You can't rush a masterpiece or a Newbery winner. Living proof is Christopher Paul Curtis, who received a Newbery Honor for his first book *The Watsons Go to Birmingham—1963* and four years later won the 2000 Newbery Medal for his second, *Bud, Not Buddy.*

Curtis takes his time when writing. He composes in long hand and then transfers it to the computer. "This slows me down, but helps me take the time to make my work ready. I keep working till I feel it's right. I'm my own harshest critic."

Some publishers recognize that nurturing talent also takes time. Curtis has high praise for the people who took a chance on him. "In all my dealings with Delacorte/Random House, there is a real concern for quality. I'm extremely fortunate to have the editor I do, Wendy Lamb. She's wonderful. I'm grateful she's taking care of my books and me. They expect quality and are willing to wait. And I want to give it to them."

Both of Curtis's books have won other prestigious awards including the Coretta Scott King Honor and the Award itself, the Gold Award, and both the Society of Children's Book Writers and Illustrators' Golden Kite Award and Honor. Awards haven't changed his outlook on life or writing, however. "I cope with life by having low expectations. That way I'm protected from ever thinking things like this [awards] are going to happen. If they come they're a total surprise, a beautiful one—overwhelming. After *The Watsons,* I was asked how I would top it. I made a conscious effort when writing *Bud* not to think about that. I had a story to tell and a good time telling it."

Family is an important part of Curtis's life. He grew up in Flint, Michigan, as the second of five children. "I had a happy childhood. My parents were strict, but we were allowed to be children. I'm grateful for that, especially when I see what kids go through now. It's important that you have a chance to be a child. I felt protected and secure."

Curtis dreamed of being a professional athlete, a doctor, a lawyer, and even a hermit. In reality, he studied political science at the University of Michigan and worked on a senatorial campaign when he had political aspirations. "Working for the senator took care of that. Politics wasn't for me!" He also mowed lawns, worked for the Detroit Power Company, took census information, loaded trucks, and hung car doors for 13 years.

Although he admits he never had the drive to be a writer when he was

Christopher Paul Curtis

growing up, Curtis did love to write. "I remember writing an article about Roman times in school. When I brought it home to finish it, my mother read it and said, 'I wish you hadn't brought this home, because now they're going to think an adult did it.' That was a great feeling."

A strong sense of family permeates Curtis's books too. In *Bud*, Lefty Lewis and Herman Calloway are based on family members. Curtis's grandfather, Herman Curtis, was a band leader classically trained in violin who also played bass fiddle, accordion, and piano. His other grandfather, nicknamed Lefty, played baseball. Musical talent continues in the Curtis family with the author's eight-year-old daughter, Cydney. "She's becoming a wonderful pianist. She's really amazing. It does my heart good to hear her play. We started piano lessons at the same time and then she just blew me away. I travel a lot and don't get the chance to practice as much as I'd like to, but I keep trying."

Curtis lives in Windsor, Ontario, where his wife Kay is an intensive care unit nurse. Originally from Trinidad, Kay worked in Canada while Curtis was in the U.S. "After we married, we chose to live in Windsor, which allowed Kay to keep her practice and me to commute over the bridge to work in Detroit."

The Audience He Was

Dreaming is something Curtis encourages kids to do. "I'm fortunate to be living my dream. I worked at jobs I hated for most of my life, and that's nothing special. Many people do, but I'm lucky to be able to be doing something now that I absolutely love and make a living at it." He hopes his books reach children for generations to come. "The main thing I want them to know, on the nonliterary level, is that they should follow their hearts. I never imagined that what has happened to me was possible. But I followed my dream and my wife's dream and wonderful things resulted."

Curtis didn't read many books as a child. "I read *Mad Magazine* and comic books. My parents bought me the Hardy Boys and Tom Swift, but I never got into them. They sat on my shelf. There weren't many books that dealt with African-American kids or kids I identified with. That was one of the great impediments of my getting into reading. So now I write for the audience that I was."

Curtis hopes teachers will continue to introduce subjects like the Depression and the civil rights movement through fiction. "Books personalize history and help children view an era. While my books weren't exactly about the Depression or civil rights, they were about people during that time. Kids can get involved with characters and have a better understanding of what it was like to live through something like that."

Curtis's next book is a young adult novel called *Bucking the Sarge,* about a 15-year-old whose mother is a con artist. "This is a change," he says. "It's set in modern times. I've found the switch to YA wasn't hard. I made a conscious effort

Submissions & Style

Christopher Paul Curtis

to have fun and tell the story. I didn't think about an age group when I was writing *The Watsons* or *Bud*, and I'm not now."

While Curtis's favorite piece of writing advice is to ignore advice, he does offer something that worked for him. "I entered the Delacorte contest and didn't win, but they published the book anyway. Contests are a great way to get noticed. You have little chance at being read if you're new. A lot of it is luck and whose desk your manuscript lands on. When *The Watsons* went to another contest, it received a rejection with something like, 'Nice try, but when the last page is turned, the novel will not resonate with someone.'"

Obviously, *The Watsons Go to Birmingham—1963* resonated with someone beyond the award committees: It sold more than 400,000 copies.

A Cinderella Moment: Kimberly Willis Holt

What's your encore after garnering 10 awards for a first novel, including an American Library Association Notable Children's Book and a Boston Globe-Horn Book Honor? You could win a National Book Award.

It was "surreal" and "a Cinderella moment" when Kimberly Willis Holt did just that by winning the 1999 National Book Award for Young People's Literature with her third novel, *When Zachary Beaver Came to Town*.

Her mastery of character and coming-of-age books spring from a place deep within, where she recalls what it's like to be the new kid standing in the gym and the last picked for volleyball. "Those moments, that fear of failure, keep me writing about that time and reliving the coming-of-age stories in my heart."

Rooted and Independent

Born in Pensacola, Florida, Holt, her husband, and teenage daughter now call Amarillo, Texas, home, but also has strong ties to Louisiana, where her ancestors planted roots seven generations ago. She didn't grow up in the small town atmosphere prevalent in her novels, however. Her father was in the Navy, so she lived around the world and across the U.S.

The oldest of three girls, Holt found it hard to be uprooted repeatedly and even now feels shy, especially when it comes to being in the limelight. Since winning so many awards, shyness is something she's learning to overcome, but still finds hard to do. While it was tough to move every few years, a mobile life had advantages. She learned to speak French in Paris, explored caves in Guam, and rode ferries across Puget Sound in Washington state.

Always an avid reader, Holt devoured the Nancy Drew books, *Little Women*, and the Little House on the Prairie books as a child, and remembers *The Heart is a Lonely Hunter*, by Carson McCullers, as a "life-changing" book. "That's when I knew I wanted to write." Holt also appreciates history, which was her minor at the University of Louisiana. She's fascinated with the twentieth century because it's still possible to talk with people who lived at its beginnings. Her mother-in-law is 93 and remembers what it was like to grow up as a farm girl in Texas in the early 1900s.

Holt cherishes being a writer for many reasons, including the option of working in her pajamas, but mostly she loves the independence. "Although it

Kimberly Willis Holt

really is teamwork because there are so many people behind a book, ultimately I'm the one who writes it. I can't imagine not being a writer. It's my dream."

Like most authors, Holt has had other jobs outside writing. She studied broadcast journalism in college, worked at radio stations in Baton Rouge and Texas, and then went into radio sales. She liked meeting people and the freedom a sales job offered; she also worked in advertising and did marketing for a water park. After settling at home with the birth of her daughter, Holt had so much fun decorating the nursery that she did other nurseries on the side. While she liked it, she "wasn't great at it and there's probably a whole bunch of people out there whose drapes don't hang right!"

Promise and Paralysis

Holt has learned how to make a page "hang" right, since her first published piece, a gardening essay that paid with a byline and copies.

She says her sales work taught her how to handle rejections as "part of the job." Holt has had her share of returned manuscripts and thinks the most valuable part of rejection is what you can learn from each "no, thank you." If you get only form letters, then your work isn't ready yet, she says. When a personal letter arrives, "Pay attention. Editors won't take time to respond if they don't see promise in your writing."

Writers should take care not to send their work out too soon, Holt says, "When it comes down to it, good books *do* sell. Being patient with a manuscript means reworking it over and over until you get it right."

Holt heeded this advice while writing *When Zachary Beaver Came to Town*. During the period two years ago when *My Louisiana Sky* came out, she was deep into *Zachary*'s first draft. All the acclaim for *My Louisiana Sky* made her "terrified to put words on the page. I had a difficult time; in fact, it was one of my worst first drafts. It was scary. I thought 'What have I done? This book will never be like *My Louisiana Sky*,' which of course was fine!"

One afternoon she sat in her kitchen with that "terrible" first draft, scattering chapters around the table looking for a start. None of them worked. She felt like "the biggest failure." She pushed through, and winning the National Book Award restored her faith in herself. She now knows "I can get through that type of crisis. It's not that I don't struggle and that writing became any easier, it's just because I went through such a paralyzing situation, I know what *can* happen if you just keep chugging along."

When Holt's not on the road, she keeps a faithful writing schedule starting around 7:30 AM, after her daughter leaves for school. She doesn't spend too many hours on first drafts because they can get stale, so she works on rewrites to sharpen her focus. The first and second draft pushes are "so intense," but she could rewrite "all day. I love to polish." Even prolific writers become blocked, so

Kimberly Willis Holt

when this dreaded condition happens to Holt, she gets in her car and takes a drive to Happy, Texas, about 30 miles from her home. The wide-open spaces relax her and free her mind.

Currently hard at work on a novel titled *Dancing in Cadillac Light,* Holt says the idea came from a short story she wrote with adult characters. She liked them so much that she turned the story into a children's novel. She thinks it's great fun that the characters were adults before they were kids. But that's part of Holt's joy in being a writer for young people. "I get to pretend and have an extended childhood, like sitting in my favorite treehouse in Guam, where I daydreamed and made up stories. Now I can still do that and get paid for it."

A Work of Art: Simms Taback

What makes a great picture book? One answer is an illustrator with a gift for blending art and words, who also loves children's literature. Caldecott Medalist Simms Taback is an artist with that gift.

Taback has illustrated more than 30 children's books, but his mainstay has been commercial art. He also owned a greeting card business. When his commercial prospects slowed a few years ago, he wondered how he would make a living. "I did a dummy for a book called *There Was an Old Lady Who Swallowed a Fly* and hoped something might happen," he says. "It turned out to be well received."

"Well received" is an understatement. Taback won the 1998 Caldecott Honor for it. Two years later, he won the 2000 Medal for *Joseph Had a Little Overcoat*. "I felt lucky because I knew I could now work exclusively on children's books—something I love."

Happy in Mediums

Winning the Caldecott Honor and Medal opened doors for Taback that 40 years in commercial art couldn't. "All of a sudden, it puts you in a special place and gives you a certain amount of respect from the business. Things open up as you become sort of a bankable commodity."

Commercial art can take a toll on a creative soul. Taback wanted to move on from the field. "I did a lot of commercial work that didn't please me. It wasn't easy. Children's books have been a wonderful area for me. I have a lot of creative control from beginning to end. I even hand-letter some of my books and design them, too. By having this kind of input, I discover different directions. I never know how it's going to turn out which makes it really interesting."

Commenting on style he says, "We all develop our own. It may not look too much different to the layperson, but I've tried many mediums. I like to experiment." Variety makes art fun for Taback. "I don't get bored. I was lucky to start out as a graphic designer and later become an art director. Now I look at a piece and the director in me says, 'It should look this way.' I don't always use the technique I'm known for. When I approach it as a designer, many ideas come up."

Taback's next book is a version of *This Is the House that Jack Built*. "Through my art, I find out interesting things. While researching the story, I discovered it was originally a Hebrew folktale or poem from the sixteenth century."

Simms Taback

Art & Science

Born and raised in "a great neighborhood in the Bronx," Taback started drawing almost as soon as he could walk. Guided by his mother, who had great respect for the arts and education, he took special art classes even before he went to grammar school.

While Taback advises illustrators as well as writers to read as much as possible, he wasn't much of a reader as a child. "We didn't have any kids' books when I was growing up. My father was interested in current events, so there were newspapers and magazines around. That's what I read most of the time." Taback's artistic talents replaced a lack of books in an unusual way. "I put on puppet shows and made my own puppets, which was an extension of my art. I wrote scripts and created my own theater stage. That took the place of kids' books for me."

"I was fortunate to get into the High School of Music and Art when I was a teenager. That experience changed me. It was a wonderful school. I met lots of talented artists and musicians." Gifted as he was, Taback felt drawn to another career. "There was a time when I was graduating in music and art that I didn't want to be an artist. I wanted to be an engineer."

Fate intervened. "For some reason, I wasn't able to get into City College and my parents didn't have money to send me anywhere else. The only possibility open to me was free college. I got into Cooper Union, which specializes in sciences and fine arts. I was good with math and loved the sciences. Art started out as a second choice. Obviously, now I'm quite happy with it!"

Taback now lives in the Catskill Mountains with his wife and two mixed Labradors, Rosie and Hooch. "I'm happy here. My studio is 75 feet from the house. Who could ask for anything better than that?" With three grown children, Taback is also a soon-to-be four-time grandfather. He loves having his grandchildren join him in his studio. "My grandchildren are completely unimpressed with what I do, but Rachel, who's 15, surprised me about winning the Caldecott. Actually, what impressed her was that I was on TV. She said, 'Oh Grandpa, that's so cool, you were on the *Today Show*.'"

Create "Leave-Behinds"

But even Caldecott-winning artists face creative blocks like writers. "I have hot and cold days. I can work for 14 hours at a stretch and sometimes I can't get anywhere. I don't know what it is. As a commercial artist, money was an equalizer for me. It kept me moving."

Taback laughed. "Deadlines work, too. I'm a terrific procrastinator. Doing commercial work for many years, I knew how long it took to do something. I was an expert at leaving exactly the right amount of time to finish. I don't

Simms Taback

suggest anyone use procrastination to break a block!"

Although it's hard for new artists to get noticed, nothing is impossible. "Put your best work together in a portfolio," Taback says. "Make the rounds of publishers and magazines. Never stop trying. Take work from wherever you can." He adds, "Beware of directories. Unfortunately, many art directors use these exclusively to find talent, but it's expensive to place ads in them. Fees can range from $3,000 to $6,000 per ad, per book. That's a lot of money to put out when you're starting."

Taback suggests an alternative. "Create 'leave-behinds' like postcards with a color illustration. You can have a couple of thousand printed up quite cheaply and leave them with directors you've met, or send them after they've seen your portfolio." Many publishers have what they call *drop-offs*, where you can leave your portfolio on a certain day, Taback also advises. "Even if you can't get to see an art director, you can leave a sample. Make sure somebody sees it. Our business is always looking for fresh talent. Don't give up. In this day, perseverance pays off."

Style Check
Quantify Your Writing
By Pegi Deitz Shea

Twelve hundred words divided by 60 sentences equals . . . trouble. No, this isn't the version of *Math Curse* for writers. At first, applying mathematical operations to your words may make you curse—especially if your sentences average 20 words! But in the long run, quantifying your writing will lead to a higher quality of writing.

How? You can't fix your writing if you can't see what's broken. Sometimes, you're so emotionally connected to your piece that you can't see its warts. By arranging your piece in equations and solving them, you can see your writing more objectively. You can *dis-solve* the warts. For instance, it may shock you that 31 of your 50 sentences use the verb *was*. You could invigorate at least 15 of those sentences with more precise action verbs. Do you really need each of those 40 dialogue tag adverbs, especially when your dialogue content is so revealing? Ax them all and you've bought yourself 40 new meaningful words for your 1,000-word teen story.

I wish I could take credit for this technique, but I've adapted it from a workshop given by Professor Pat Tobin at Rutgers University. Nearly 20 years ago, she taught us hot shot senior honors students how boring our A+ papers were. Thank you, Pat!

Now, writers, grab your calculators. (Nobody said you had to solve by hand, on scrap paper!)

Compare and Correct

To begin spotting weaknesses in your piece, simply compare numbers. You won't even have to calculate anything yet. Use the form on page 138.

Let's look at sentence types first. In nonfiction, you'll naturally have more declarative sentences. If you have nothing but declarative sentences, however, your article will be as dry as Aunt Sophie's pound cake. To correct this, add an exclamation to highlight a surprising fact; a quiz or rhetorical question; or an imperative for readers to do something proactive. In fiction, if your piece has nothing

Simple Addition

First, you'll need your story or article's basic numbers to compute. So, add up the following.

Number of:
- Pages _____
- Paragraphs _____
- Total sentences _____
    - Declarative _____
    - Interrogative _____
    - Exclamatory _____
    - Imperative _____
- Sentence structures
    - Simple _____

    (one independent clause)
    - Compound _____

    (two or more independent clauses)
    - Complex _____

    (one independent clause and at least one dependent clause)
- Total sentences _____
- Words required (if applicable) _____
- Words total _____
- Nouns _____
- Verbs, action _____
- Verbs, being (is, are, was, were) _____
- Adjectives _____
- Adverbs _____
- Active voice (a subject does the action) _____
- Passive voice (a subject is acted upon) _____
- Dependent clauses (a phrase that cannot stand alone) _____
- Number of clauses beginning in *which* or *that* _____
- Participle phrases _____
- Prepositional phrases _____
- Adverbs _____
- Metaphoric images (metaphors, similes, analogies) _____

but declarative sentences, you'll receive nothing but rejections! Diversifying sentence types is much easier in fiction. Dialogue and interior monologue can contain sentence fragments and exclamations. When two child characters converse, one is bound to ask a question. When an adult and child converse, the adult is bound to speak an imperative.

Once you have a better balance of sentence types, distribute them appropriately through your article or story. You don't want a snoozer of a page consisting of all declarative sentences. At the other extreme, not every sentence in a paragraph should end in an !. Too many exclamations make readers' blood pressure soar. Don't ask too many rhetorical questions, either. They can weaken writing, just as the passive voice does.

Compare the number of passive voice and active voice sentences. Your key indicator of passive voice is the combination of a verb of being and another verb. In the passive voice, your subject receives the action: *Pegi was bitten by a snake. She was taken to the ER.* In the active voice, your subject does the action: *A snake bit Pegi. Jim took her to the ER.* (I prefer *Pegi bit the snake,* but that would change the meaning.) Overusing the passive voice makes your main character into a dolt—a reactor, not one who acts.

While we're looking at voice, count how many words my example of passive voice sentences required. Compare that answer to the number of words in the active voice. A difference of two words may not seem like much, but those saved words over many sentences add up fast. With more active voice sentences, your story will pick up strength, speed, and verve.

Using the active voice doesn't guarantee you've chosen a precise action verb. *Eileen was sick* is an active voice sentence, but the verb of being, *was*, is a vague, lazy verb. *Eileen barfed* is more precise, not to mention messier—and you know how kids like messes. So, compare the number of verbs of being to your total number of verbs. If boring *was*'s and *were*'s account for more than a third of your total, get substituting more exciting verbs.

Average, to Make Your Writing Above Average

Averaging your piece's numbers will point out many weaknesses to fix. Figure the following averages and think about how to improve your quotients. (See the "On Average" form, page 140.)

Number of paragraphs to a page. Paragraphs in children's literature are shorter than in adult literature, no matter the age. If you average fewer than five paragraphs on a manuscript page for fiction, consider how to reconstruct or redesign your page. Do you need more dialogue? Can you pause in a long passage of description for your point-of-view character's interior monologue, or a specific action that involves elements of description?

If you average fewer than three paragraphs on a manuscript page for nonfiction, break them up to give readers some white space. Or, consider choosing a bullet format or a sidebar to deliver a list of facts.

Number of sentences to a paragraph. This averaging works well with nonfiction. For fiction, however, the answer

On Average

- Number of paragraphs to a page. _____
- Number of sentences in a paragraph. _____
- Number of words to a sentence. _____
- Number of prepositional phrases to a sentence. _____
- Number of adjectives to a sentence. _____
- Number of adverbs to a sentence. _____
- Number of verbs to a sentence. _____
- Number of participle phrases to a sentence. _____
- Number of words separating subject and verb. _____
- Number of letters in a word. _____
- Number of sneaky words to a sentence. _____

may not give you an accurate picture because one-line paragraphs of dialogue may compensate for way-long paragraphs of narration. If your characters are giving speeches instead of conversing, chop it up a bit. If their dialogue is too choppy, add some thinking aloud or a bit of action.

Number of words to a sentence and *number of prepositional phrases to a sentence.* Both of these averages will alert you to wordiness. I have heard or read of a good tip: *the magic two.* Try to delete two words automatically from every sentence in your first draft. Many prepositional phrases are simply unnecessary.

For instance, if characters are inside a cabin and they build a cozy fire, you don't have to specify that the fire is in the fireplace. Now, if it's an old wood stove, that might be a detail you would like to keep. If your characters sit down for dinner, you don't need to write that they are at the kitchen or dining room table. If they're climbing Mount Everest, you might want to specify that they have stopped to eat at a rest station or sat on fanny warmers.

Number of adjectives to a sentence. If you average more than two adjectives in a sentence, you're verging on flowery prose or overwriting. Shoot for the most specific noun possible or substitute a metaphor. Instead of writing *The really tall man stood almost seven feet,* try *He stood taller than Shaquille O'Neal.* If you have an average below one adjective per sentence, you might want to free up a bit and smell the roses. If you have no metaphors or similes (go back to your original counts), highlight every adjective in your draft and see if you can substitute more unique wording. *Minutes before the storm, the thrashing leaves sounded like whitewater.*

Number of adverbs to a sentence. I'd like to draw and quarter the person who made up adverbs and adverbial

These Words Are Numbered

Sneaky words can be those unneeded adverbs, or clichés or euphemisms, or redundant phrases. Here is a random listing of sneaky words to subtract from your writing.

absolutely nothing	just
all	look/looked
a lot	particular example
also	per (use *a* or *an*)
And, or, but , however, indeed at the beginning of a sentence	period of time
	personal friend
back	really
circle around	repeat back
continued to	respective(ly)
check up	start in
end up	thing
end product	to myself
even	total of nine (*nine* is enough)
firstly, secondly (first, second)	utilize (use *use*)
in order to	very
in size (large or small in size)	very unique
I thought/felt/decided/believed (when the point-of-view is clear)	visit with

phrases. In many cases, adverbs are unnecessary or redundant. So, if you average more than one adverb to a sentence, you may need to take two steps: (1) Make your verbs more precise and cut the adverbs. Don't say *walked slowly* when you can say *plodded* or *trudged*. (2) Work on your dialogue. The content in a dialogue set and its context should make it clear how something is said. I'm not promoting the use of *said* as a dialogue tag every time, but there's no reason (especially in fiction) you can't write *mumbled* instead of *said confusingly in a low voice*.

Number of verbs to a sentence and number of participle phrases to a sentence. A pet peeve with me. What's wrong with this sentence? *Buckling her shoes, Lisa ran down the stairs carrying her homework.* Lisa cannot possibly buckle her shoes and run and carry her homework. Participle phrases are tricky. Verbals ending in *ing* should indicate simultaneous action. You should make the first participle an adverbial one, showing a sequence of action: *After buckling her shoes, Lisa ran down the stairs with her homework.* You don't need the *carrying* of the first version, either.

Keep things simple, lean. One verb/one sentence. Or one compound verb/one sentence. *Sam sang and played the guitar.*

While we're discussing participle phrases, count how many times you begin a sentence with one. Also count how many times you begin a sentence with a dependent clause: *After Lisa buckled her shoes, she tripped down the stairs.*

Other dependent clause tip-off words include *while, because, when.* There is nothing wrong with dependent clauses. They are necessary to indicate time frame, for one. Five straight sentences beginning with a participle or dependent clause, however, will lull your reader to sleep. Even two or three start weakening your writing. You should have a good reason *not* to begin a sentence with its subject and main verb. Strings of dependent clauses resemble a freight train in slow motion.

Another very common problem with participle phrases, and other phrases and clauses, is misplacement. They become *misrelated modifiers* and often cause humor where none is intended: *Suddenly hugging the surprised Kaitlin, the ice cream cone flew from Harry's grasp.* The ice cream cone didn't hug Kaitlin, but that's what the sentence says. Try it this way: *Suddenly hugging the surprised Kaitlin, Harry dropped his ice cream cone.* The clause now modifies Harry.

What Else Counts?

You can benefit by counting many more examples of usage and other elements of your writing. The additional forms and exercises that accompany this article will help you self-evaluate and refine your writing.

Average words separating your subject from its verb. Hint: It better be somewhere between zero and one.

Average number of conjunctions in a sentence. Don't hook up anymore freight cars, or we'll be here all day.

Average number of letters in a word. The cliché fits. Don't use a dollar word when a dime one will do, especially with readers under 10.

Number of sneaky words. Sneaky words and phrases are those many writers misuse, but also includes words and phrases that are technically fine, but that you're prone to overuse. Avoid *even, really, very, but,* and my personal enemy, *just.* Find more of your own foes and terminate these infiltrators.

The sum total of counting over a piece in this way is to alert you to the structural and language choices you make. You may be a wordsmith first of all, but being a word-bookkeeper for a time will improve the quality of your bottom line.

Exercise: Passive to Active Constructions

Change these passive voice sentences to active voice and make further cuts if you wish. Write your new word count next to the original count.

■ Ferrying water back and forth from the well, Terry was laughed at by the villagers.

_____

_____

(15 words/   words)

■ Joyce was totally overcome by embarrassment when she was struck out by her best friend Christine for the last out of the softball championship.

_____

_____

(24 words/   words)

■ Tom said loudly to Rachel that no way was he going to be tricked again by her deceitful lies and behavior.

_____

_____

(21 words/   words)

■ Running away, the little gray mouse was captured by the big yellow and white cat and immediately devoured.

_____

_____

(18 words/   words)

■ Clavin was busy defending the space station when he was transported by the Ferenghi ambassador who was captivated by his looks and strength.

_____

_____

(23 words/   words)

Submissions & Style

Exercise: Two, Two, Two Sentences in One

Change each of the following long, wordy sentences into two crisp ones. Don't forget to get rid of any sneaky words.

- Petting her cat, Barbara made herself some Earl Grey tea in the kitchen and went to drink it on her sunporch outside.

_____
_____

- Ian, being an impulsive sort of guy, ran quickly into the fireworks area where he was burned on his leg by a Roman candle just about to shoot up into the sky.

_____
_____

- Carrying a bouquet of really pretty flowers, Joan opened the door for her Aunt Edna and went to fetch a vase to put some water in it.

_____
_____

- Just when I think I could not possibly eat another one of those chocolate cookies with the creme inside, my hand just reaches out and into the package and grabs one before I'm scolded by my mother.

_____
_____

- Jennifer, holding the jump rope handles in each hand, twirling the rope around and around, jumping each time the rope came down around her feet, said to Nancy in a singsong voice for her to jump in with her.

_____
_____

Exercise: They Said What?

Change these wordy dialogue sets into punchy speech with precise tags. See how many strong rewritings you can create with these examples.

Example: "We should definitely check the closet next," Jillian said excitedly.
"Check the closet!" Jillian suggested.

- "I think you're acting very impolitely," Grandma said sternly.

_____
_____
_____

- "Deirdre, you had better stop fooling around," Dad said in a hushed tone.

_____
_____
_____

- "Bill is definitely the best-dressed guy in school, everybody says," Kate said sarcastically.

_____
_____
_____

- "I don't want to visit that mean family the Calloways," Tommy said chokingly.

_____
_____
_____

- "That would make me very happy," Mom said in an excited voice.

_____
_____
_____

Exercise: Ax the Adverbs

Think of as many precise action verbs for the following phrases as you can:

- ran really fast
- went cautiously
- was quiet
- looked intently
- was seated noisily
- drove dangerously
- was embarrassed
- is fooling around
- laughed softly
- walked painfully
- is being sloppy
- let go carelessly
- read quickly
- cooked laboriously
- stopped abruptly
- yelled loudly
- asked snidely
- searched secretly
- ate messily
- watched wistfully
- acted shy

Exercise: To Your Specifications

In place of adjectives, specify a more precise noun or substitute a simile or metaphor.

- really messy desk
- head of curly hair
- short white dog
- scratchy voice
- difficult golf hazard
- angry teacher
- muddy lake
- wild horse
- crowded store
- lively song
- other kids on the team
- failing grade
- many neat toys
- 10-year-old crybaby
- awesome looking girl
- horribly off-key singer
- very stinky farm odors
- fast sports car
- noisy, pesty birds
- coolly colored wall

Business & Career

Book Proposals

A Crack in the Door

By Catherine Frey Murphy

"Submit proposal." This brief entry in writers' guidelines may seem clear to some writers and editors, but it can mystify others. Just what is a book proposal, anyway? What information has to be included, and how should it be organized? Is it really true that an editor would agree to publish a manuscript that hasn't even been written yet?

Yes, Virginia, this surprising fact is true—sometimes. It's also true that book proposals provide writers with an indispensable tool for organizing a book idea, planning its execution, and testing its marketability. In addition, proposals speed up the publication process by allowing overworked editors to evaluate many more book ideas than they could possibly consider in full manuscript form. There's an art to creating a well-executed proposal, but as many a successful author will attest, it's an art that any writer with skill, creativity, professionalism, and a true passion for ideas can master.

Proposal or Manuscript?

Editors agree that the first and most important step in preparing a proposal is also the step that is most often overlooked: researching publishers' needs before submitting. "Familiarize yourself with the publisher's list," recommends Jennifer Elliot, Publisher of Tilbury House. "I can't tell you how many times we get Fluffy the Dog stories, or Timmy the Turtle. It's a waste of money for the author and the publisher." Tilbury publishes books for grades three to six on the environment and cultural diversity.

Katrina Wentzel, Editorial Acquisitions Assistant at Free Spirit Publishing, agrees. "The number-one thing is that people do their research. We get so many manuscripts for great books that we can't publish, because the topics or genres aren't even close to being right for us." After all, as Frances Gilbert, Children's Acquisitions Editor at Sterling Publishing Company, points out, "You wouldn't go to a job interview without doing some research first about the company!"

In today's wired world, it's especially easy to acquire basic information about a publisher's needs. In addition to the traditional methods of writing to publishers for guidelines and consulting listings in market guides, modern writers can explore the Internet. "Many publishers have websites now," Elliot explains. Tilbury's webpage, for example,

Book Proposal Do's and Don'ts

Don't:
- *Allow proofreading errors.* "You would not believe the number of cover letters I see that include typos and misspellings," says Katrina Wentzel, Editorial Acquisitions Assistant at Free Spirit Publishing. "This makes it hard to have faith in the author's credentials."
- *Use friends and family as market research.* Statements like "My second-grade class thinks this is terrific" don't help editors evaluate proposals. As Frances Gilbert, Children's Acquisitions Editor at Sterling Publishing, says, "Of course they think it's terrific. You're their teacher!"
- *Send a proposal out before obtaining an objective critique.* "Give it to your writer friends," suggests Dawn Weinstock, Managing Editor, Children's and Family Resources, for Concordia Publishing. "It's as important to have your critique group review a proposal as it is to have them review a manuscript."
- *Put your energy into show-off tactics instead of the idea itself.* "Gimmicks or cutesy attention-getters are rarely effective and can actually be off-putting," says Jill Braithwaite, Managing Editor, Nonfiction for Lower Grades, at Lerner Publishing. "Save that creative energy for the manuscript."

Do:
- *Show enthusiasm.* "It's important that the summary shows the enthusiasm you have for the book," says Gilbert. "You're trying to win over an editor who sees a lot of these!"
- *Use a format that helps the editor.* "Some of my better proposals have a very professional quality," says Wentzel. "They may be in a binder or a folder, not just loose. They're organized within that folder so I can check back and forth between sections. If somebody has a sample chapter and an annotated table of contents, for instance, a format like this makes it easy to go back and forth between the two."
- *Describe relevant credentials.* Prior publication helps, but it's not the only information that counts. If you're proposing a book of birthday party ideas, the fact that you've been running successful children's parties in your neighborhood for years may be more relevant to an editor than a résumé full of unrelated publishing credits. As Gilbert notes, "Sterling publishes many new writers."
- *Include an SASE.* "I know it's basic," says Wentzel. "But having that envelope for return just makes everything easier."
- *Be patient.* "Staffing tends to guide how quickly we can get to these proposals," Weinstock says. Don't assume that your idea has been overlooked just because a few weeks have gone by.
- *Show your professionalism in every detail.* As Weinstock explains, "Despite the fact that it's really easier to say no, a truly professional submission is swaying." In the competitive world of children's publishing, give yourself that advantage!

provides general information about the publisher's list along with writers' guidelines and a complete catalogue.

The next step is to determine if your book idea is appropriate for submission by proposal, or if you should consider sending the full manuscript.

When evaluating a picture book, for instance, most editors agree that no proposal can adequately convey the voice, tone, and approach that set a fine manuscript apart from other submissions. "For shorter works, such as picture books and beginning readers, we need to see an entire manuscript to determine whether we're interested in pursuing the project," explains Jill Braithwaite, Managing Editor, Nonfiction for Lower Grades, at Lerner Publishing Group.

But Lerner specializes in the school and library market and publishes a wide range of titles from nonfiction on science, math, history, and geography to picture books, easy readers, and historical fiction. Braithwaite prefers to see proposals for "longer works, such as novels and biographies for middle and older readers."

For houses like Tilbury or Charlesbridge Publishing, whose lists consist primarily of picture books, then, the proposal inevitably is a less-favored form of submission.

"In almost all cases, we do not sign up a book on the basis of a proposal," says Charlesbridge Editorial Director Harold Underdown. "We've got to see the manuscript. Maybe it's a great idea, but how do we know you can finish it up?" Even when he is evaluating a longer work, Underdown says that unless an author has published several books with him personally, he generally prefers to see a complete manuscript. "Something might come in as a proposal or a query, and we'll say no, but the manuscript may have been better than it looked as a proposal. There could be a number of proposals that we say no to, where the author would have been better off sending us a complete manuscript instead!"

Generally, the proposal form is most appropriate for nonfiction, and for longer works of fiction. At Sterling, for instance, proposals are the preferred submission form for the company's nonfiction list, which emphasizes humor; activity books on subjects like card tricks, magic, and chess; science fair projects; math puzzles; and word puzzles.

At Concordia Publishing, with a list offering religious fiction and nonfiction for children, Managing Editor

> **Book Proposal Contents**
>
> Book proposals should contain material that conveys the contents, structure, and tone of the proposed book clearly enough to allow the editor to make an informed decision. Typically, they include:
> - summary or a synopsis
> - an outline, table of contents, or annotated table of contents
> - a brief market analysis
> - information on the author's research sources
> - a sample of the text itself
> - a résumé or biographical information, especially credentials directly relevant to the proposed book

Dawn Weinstock notes that while proposals for picture books generally incorporate the manuscript itself, ideas for longer works, such as collections of devotional prayers for children, should be presented in the form of a cover letter, an outline, and a sample chapter. "Include one or two of the devotions themselves, too, so that we know you can write for kids," Weinstock suggests.

A writer's publishing history can also affect the proposal-versus-full-manuscript decision. Publishers can be reluctant to make decisions based on proposals alone from unpublished writers without a track history.

"We are happy to look at proposals from unpublished writers," says Braithwaite, "but we would rarely if ever acquire a project without seeing a well-executed manuscript first. We are more likely to acquire a project based solely on a proposal if it's from a writer with whom we've worked before—and who has proven ability to conceptualize and complete a manuscript and work successfully with an editor. For a writer who has published, but not with us, we generally do like to see a complete manuscript. Still, for all writers, a solid, appealing proposal that demonstrates skill and hard work can be the first step toward getting a publisher interested in *seeing* an entire manuscript."

Informed Decision

What elements make a proposal "solid and appealing" enough to capture an editor's attention? First, write a strong cover letter. Keep it short and clear. "Write a cover letter that gets to the point, that succinctly outlines what the book is about," says Gilbert.

"We don't have a lot of time," Weinstock explains. At Concordia, "we get about 3,000 freelance manuscripts a year, not all of them children's books, and there are only two of us reviewing them." The importance of "a concise cover letter that gets right to the point" becomes very clear. An excellent cover letter, according to Weinstock, explains what the book is, its content, and the appropriate age group, "right up front!" The letter may also include a concise marketing survey and an author's credentials, although Weinstock suggests that a well-published author may prefer to enclose a résumé instead.

"About cover letters, I say the simpler, the better," says Braithwaite. "It should be clear and concise, and it should convey enthusiasm and professionalism. A cover letter can contain some essential explanation or context, but the work must stand on its own."

Editors also value a writer who takes a professional attitude towards working on a manuscript. "I appreciate cover letters that express willingness to revise," Braithwaite says, "if the author really is willing to revise, of course!"

As for the proposal itself, editors ask for different details, but all seek the same essential information: material that conveys the contents, structure, and tone of the proposed book clearly enough to allow the editor to make an informed decision. Writers can determine a publisher's specific requirements by consulting writers' guidelines and market listings. In general, most editors ask for a summary or a synopsis, an outline or table of contents, a brief market analysis, information on the author's research sources, and a sample of the text itself.

Passion: *Sell* Your Idea

A writer's passion for a subject is a potent secret weapon. Well-conveyed enthusiasm can infect an editor, inspiring so much interest and curiosity that a proposal almost sells itself. When Patricia Cronin Marcello developed her proposal for *Classically Human and All That Jazz*, a book on the human side of 12 great composers, she didn't confine her synopsis to dry historical data. Instead, she communicated her own interest in her subject with this appealing teaser:

> Consider the incredible power of Peter Ilyich Tchaikovsky's *1812 Overture*, complete with its grand finale of firing cannons. Would it surprise you to know that the composer was a little man, who always kept one hand supporting his chin while he conducted an orchestra, because he thought his head might fall off? Igor Stravinsky liked to hang upside down in the nude, and always wore a green beret, even to bed. And our esteemed Johann Sebastian Bach was a duelist who had immense trouble staying on the good side of his employers.

An author's passion for an idea can show, not just in the text itself, but also in the thoroughness and professionalism with which the proposal is developed. Dawn Weinstock, Managing Editor, Children's and Family Resources, for Concordia Publishing, describes a proposal she received from an author with whom she had already worked on previous titles. Ordinarily, she explains, with such an experienced author, the proposal process might begin with a telephone conversation or an e-mail. "But this author proposed a new fiction series with an outline and sample chapter for the first book, a cast analysis, story synopses for the first four titles, and 'Gee, I don't know' thinking for four more." Although he already knew the editor, he also sent a cover letter explaining the idea and why he believed Concordia was the best publisher for the series. The thoroughness and professionalism of his presentation was arresting, Weinstock says. "I was through it in five minutes and knew already that I wanted to consider it seriously!"

Put together, enthusiasm and professionalism can make a proposal almost irresistible. Confronted with especially well-presented proposals, Weinstock admits, "A couple of times I've really struggled to say no to something, even though I knew it wasn't right for Concordia's list!"

Business & Career

"Essential elements depend on the project," says Lerner's Braithwaite. "But the basic pieces I like to see are a simple, clear cover letter; an outline; a bibliography with sources used and any special research done; and sample text. Samples of illustrations, photos, or diagrams are generally not necessary, although providing information about potential photo sources can be helpful."

At Sterling, Gilbert looks for "a clear summary of what the book is about, and an outline." The summary is a brief synopsis to "flesh out what your plans for the book would be." Gilbert also wants to see a sample chapter—"enough to get a sense of your writing style"—as well as samples of artwork or photography you plan to include, and a stamped, self-addressed envelope.

A proposal submitted to Free Spirit should include a résumé or biography, an annotated table of contents, a simple market analysis, and a sample chapter or two, Wentzel says. The annotated table of contents is comparable to a simple outline, in which each chapter title is followed by a brief paragraph explaining what the chapter will be about.

A good proposal, Wentzel says, is exceptionally well written. The author shows familiarity with Free Spirit's line, along with credentials that demonstrate the writer's experience with the subject of the book. "Our authors need to be viewed as experts. They don't necessarily have to have a Ph.D. in the subject, just the experience that shows they're qualified to write about the subject."

Sample Text

Almost every editor needs to see sample text before making a decision on a proposal. In fact, sample text may be the single most important element of any proposal, because it offers writers a chance to demonstrate abilities, and editors the opportunity to evaluate them.

"A concept and outline can help us assess the marketability of a project," Braithwaite explains, "but the sample text is crucial for evaluating an author's skills. In nonfiction, we're looking for liveliness, clarity in the writing and organization, appropriate reading level, and simply whether or not the manuscript makes you want to keep reading."

Sample text also allows the author to show the editor the voice or tone in which the finished book will be written. As Gilbert says, "the purpose of the sample chapter is to give the editor a sense of how the book will sound." Braithwaite adds, "The style and voice of a manuscript are best left to the sample text. The cover letter and other parts of a proposal package should be in the author's professional voice."

Weinstock agrees that the individual *voice* of a manuscript is better demonstrated in the sample text than in the rest of the proposal. "It's too overbearing and salesman-like in the rest of the material," she explains. "But the voice had better be good in the sample text! It has to be authentic."

The amount of sample text to include depends in part on the length of the project, Braithwaite says. "The preferred length of a sample text depends on the length of the intended book. We need to see enough to get a good sense of the author's style and skill level. Speaking very generally, for a 6-chapter book I'd want to see 1 chapter. For a 20-chapter book, I'd want to see 3 or 4 chapters."

Unique to the Market

Few children's writers have M.B.A.s, and perhaps that's why market analysis is often the most puzzling part of preparing a book proposal. But market research doesn't have to be carried out at a business-school level. The essential purpose of market analysis in a book proposal is simple: to inform the editor what books, if any, already exist on your subject, and to explain what makes your approach uniquely interesting and marketable. (For more detailed information on market analyses, see "Market Research, Scope Out the Competition," page 159.)

Wentzel suggests, "Go to a good bookstore, to *Books in Print,* or to Amazon.com. Tell us what other books are similar to yours, and why your idea is different or superior." Braithwaite adds, "If market research is extensive, it should be included in a separate section. Short market analysis can be shared in a cover letter. Either way, a writer should let us know what sets the project apart, or how and why it can compete successfully in the marketplace."

Writers need to distinguish carefully between market research and market planning. Underdown says, "What I don't want to see in a proposal is a detailed marketing plan, or a lot of marketing suggestions. Some writers spend more time talking about marketing than about the idea itself! I have a marketing department, and they know how to market books. I am concerned with what's already out there. Is this yet another rain forest book? If so, how is this one different?" Underdown also cautions writers to make sure their market research is accurate and thorough. "I don't want writers to say, "I couldn't find another book in my bookstore, or in the local library. I can't tell you how often I get letters that blithely assert there are no other books on this topic, when there are five or six!"

Be aware, too, that the absence of books on a given topic doesn't necessarily mean that there's a need for a book on the subject. "Don't assume that there's a vast and undiscovered market for your idea," advises Underdown. "It may not be as vast as you think it is, or there may be no way to get books into that retail channel, especially in nonfiction."

Braithwaite concurs: "Market research is certainly helpful, but authors must also be mindful of the fact that just because there are no books about a certain topic doesn't mean that a book on that topic will be successful. There may be a very good reason that there are no books about that topic."

On the other hand, Underdown says that the mere fact that books already exist on a given topic will not necessarily bar him from publishing a new one, if it's good enough. "If I want to do a book, I'm not going to be deterred by others on the market. I just want to know what I'm getting into beforehand. It's nice to know that the author is professional enough to do the research."

Good Fits

As multiple submissions have led to a deluge of manuscripts, more and more publishers have had to close their doors to unsolicited submissions. The good news is that many publishing houses have left a crack in the door for well-crafted proposals.

At Sterling, for instance, Gilbert says, "I'd be happy to take a look at new proposals. Sterling is expanding its children's list right now." She is eager to review proposals for joke, activity, and science-project books.

Tilbury looks for picture books for children 8 to 12 on topics related to cultural diversity and the environment, along with related teachers' guide materials. Although she prefers to review full manuscripts, Elliot will respond to an intriguing picture book proposal by asking to see the story in full. "Our titles must have a duality," Elliot explains, appealing not only to children and parents, but also to teachers. To make Tilbury's books more useful to schools, teachers' guides are often published alongside each title, or informative material is added at the back of the book.

Shy Mama's Halloween, by Anne Broyles, is the story of an immigrant mother's first adventure in America, led by her children. Elliot explains that the story's usefulness in schools is enhanced by two pages at the back providing factual information about immigration and about Halloween. "That was an unsolicited manuscript, and a fit with our list in that we have done books on immigration," Elliot explains.

At Free Spirit, Wentzel looks for good submissions within the company's three primary areas: self-help for children and teens; enrichment activities for teachers; and books on successful teaching and parenting strategies. Wentzel says that writers should pay attention, not just to what a house has published in the past, but also to trends for the future. "We have published a few books that focus on girls only. Now there are a lot of books on the market for girls. We're still getting proposals for girls' books, but we need to be very select at this point."

Instead, proposals for Free Spirit should be "gender-balanced," Wentzel says, adding a word of encouragement for battle-scarred writers. "I would hope that authors would not be discouraged if they've gotten a rejection. Just because an author is rejected once doesn't mean they'll be rejected again. Submit to us again if you have a proposal you feel is viable for us!"

There's no one secret ingredient that makes a book proposal irresistible. Instead, editors look for a well-crafted package that includes a great idea, an original approach, solid research, sensible organization, and helpful market information. Then there's the indefinable quality Underdown calls the *x-factor*: "How professional is this person in the way they've presented the idea? Do they understand the market in that under-the-skin way?" For writers who can meet these tests, the proposal is an indispensable tool, both for developing ideas and for building a successful children's writing career.

Market Research

Scope Out the Competition

By Darcy Pattison

Consult a typical writing book about how to put together a nonfiction proposal, and you'll find a recommendation to include a market analysis. A proposal package typically includes a sample chapter, an outline or chapter breakdown, a biography or résumé, an indication of how the text will be illustrated, and a market analysis. Writers understand the first four, but many don't know what to do with the last, the pesky *market analysis*.

The importance and components of a market analysis are a matter of debate among writers and editors. Whatever your ultimate opinion of such a report as a writer, you may very well come upon a publisher that requires one. At the very least, the ability to put together information on markets can help you identify subjects, angles, and companies to target.

(See "Book Proposals, A Crack in the Door" page 151, for a discussion of the other elements in a nonfiction proposal package and "Competitive Ideas, What's Out There?" page 283, for examples of the process of market research.)

The Value of Market Analysis

For publishing houses that do want to see the writer's take on markets, the requested specifics may differ. All market analyses, however, are write-ups of research into competition in the marketplace or suggestions for where and how to target a project. Writers submit these research reports as part of the "sales package" they put together to sell the book to an editor or publisher.

Marc Aronson, Senior Editor for Henry Holt, says a market analysis can be valuable, but only if it contains specific and concrete information that is realistic for a publisher to pursue. For example, Holt will be publishing a *graphic novel* that is also a memoir—that is, an autobiography done as a comic book. The author makes his living as a comic book artist and knows how to distribute and appeal to this niche market. The specific suggestions in his market analysis were helpful in showing Holt how to target a market it doesn't normally reach. In other words, a market analysis should provide information to a publisher that makes it clear how the book can find the right readers.

Nicole Geiger, Publisher of Tricycle Press, also sees benefits in the analysis. A cover letter or a brief paragraph should show her that authors have

> ### Market Analysis Process
>
> It's an easy trip for an author to the library or bookstore, or online, to begin researching the competition for a book. Look for other titles on your topic. Check them out or buy them and then study them. Here's a checklist of questions to ask.
>
> ✔ Are they for the library, trade, or mass-market audience?
>
> ✔ What age level is this book aimed at?
>
> ✔ How is the book illustrated? What slant does the book take on the subject?
>
> ✔ How many competing titles are there?
>
> ✔ What is the publication date of the competing titles?
>
> ✔ Is this sold through any niche markets that have well-defined distribution channels?

that reflects a strong voice and likeable style, Pleasant Company may consider working with the author on another project or line. "What catches my attention," says Falligant, "is a piece that's well written and suitable for our audience."

With a strong negative opinion on the subject, Jill Davis, Senior Editor for Viking Children's Books, says, "The market analysis is just junk mail. Authors should be trying to sell their writing and everything else comes last. Editors have limited time to even look at the writing sample. The rest of the package is junk mail."

Davis looks first at the writing sample, then at the information on how the text will be illustrated. "More and more with nonfiction today, the focus is how text and illustrative material complement each other. I want to see photocopies of photographs (no originals), not just a list. If it is in the twentieth century, there are photos. Before that, you can find etchings, plates, lithographs, or items to photograph." If text and illustration grab her, Davis says, she will do her own market analysis.

done their homework. She wants to know what competing titles are already published, how those titles differ from the proposed book, and how the book will add to the field. These help her evaluate how well the book might do.

Most nonfiction proposals that Pleasant Company receives, says Submissions Editor Erin Falligant, do not include a market analysis. Although she agrees that such an analysis might be helpful to an author during the development of a project, enclosing a market analysis with a submission "is not as important as following the publisher's guidelines and sending a great sample chapter." If an author submits an idea that has already been done but

The Value for an Author

Positive or negative, underlying all these editors' comments is the assumption that writers have done market analyses for themselves, even if they don't share it with the publisher.

"Why would an author spend time doing a particular topic if it's been done before?" asks Geiger. "If it has been done, the author should aim to do it better or in a unique way. A pre-writing market analysis can save you from wasting your time doing something that doesn't need to be done again."

In the proposal for her book, *The Head Bone's Connected to the Neck Bone: The Weird, Wacky, and Wonderful X-Ray* (Farrar, Straus & Giroux), says Carla McClafferty, "I pointed out that the existing books about x-rays used artist illustrations and mine would use historical photographs."

Sneed B. Collard III, author of *Animal Dads, Our Wet World,* and more than 25 other nonfiction children's books, says, "Just because a publisher doesn't mention how great your market analysis is doesn't mean you shouldn't do it. But it suggests that it may be more valuable in helping you choose and shape a topic than it is in selling an idea to a publisher. As always, if your writing is strong and you focus on something you are genuinely passionate about, chances are that passion will come through to an editor and a sale will result.

"As far as targeting publishers, I don't consider the market analysis as much as the writer being familiar with what different publishers are publishing. This familiarity is important." Collard has that familiarity, with his extensive publishing experience working in his favor. Beginning writers need to work to gain this knowledge of various publishers. The best way to do that is to do market analyses of topics of interest and let the information build as the process is repeated for different manuscripts.

Davis also suggests researching specific editors. On the copyright page of *Restless Spirit: The Life and Works of Dorothea Lange* (Viking), by Elizabeth Partridge, there is an acknowledgment that reads, in part, "Grateful thanks to my editor, Jill Davis." Davis says, "Any

Publisher Needs

Henry Holt and Company
115 W. 18th Street, New York, NY 10011

Former Senior Editor Marc Aronson looks for a fresh take on popular topics, and fast-breaking books that move into territory that hasn't been explored and will reach a wide audience. Titles he has edited include *Remix: Conversations with Immigrant Teenagers*, by Marina Tamar Budhos; *The World According to Horses*, by Stephen Budiansky, which combines a love of horses with passion for science; and *Who Is Baseball's Greatest Hitter?*, by Jeff Kisseloff. Manuscripts must be very well written. He recently started working part-time for www.zooba.com, a Web service that researches designated topics for subscribers, so he personally will be acquiring fewer books.

Pleasant Company
8400 Fairway Place, Middleton WI 53562-0998

Submissions Editor Erin Falligant says that Pleasant Company's nonfiction needs include advice, activity, and craft books. All titles should be of interest to girls. Recent titles include *Paper Clip Jewelry*, *School Smarts*, and *Help! A Girl's Guide to Divorce and Stepfamilies*.

Tricycle Press
Imprint of Ten Speed Press, P.O. Box 7123, Berkeley, CA 94707

Publisher Nicole Geiger says that Tricycle Press is known for their unusual, offbeat titles. They publish no biography and extremely limited social history. Good titles for them include activity books such as *The Kids' Clay Ceramic Book*, by Kevin Nierman and Elaine Arima, a pottery book for kids. Also of interest are real life titles, such as books on issues kids need to cope with: *We Can Work it Out: Conflict Resolution for Children*, by Barbara K. Pollard. Tricycle does some science and nature titles, including *G Is for Googol: A Math Alphabet Book*, by David Schwartz and Marisa Moss.

Viking Children's Books
Division of Penguin Putnam, 375 Hudson Street, New York, NY 10014

Jill Davis, Senior Editor at Viking Children's Books, is not looking for unsolicited manuscripts and warns of long delays before you can expect an answer. She is only interested in biographies and social history issues. No science or natural history. You must have unique illustration possibilities for any serious consideration.

Online Book Publishing Sources

American Booksellers Association: www.bookweb.org
Book Publishing Reports: www.simbanet.com
R.R. Bowker: www.bowker.com
  Bowker publication sites include:
    Literary Market Place: www.literarymarketplace.com
    BookWire: www.bookwire.com
Children's Book Council: www.cbcbooks.org
Library of Congress: www.loc.gov
Media Central: www.mediacentral
  Media and marketing news, including book publishing.
Publishers Weekly: www.publishersweekly.com
Subtext: www.subtext.net
  A subscription service on the business news of book publishing.

---

nonfiction book that is fascinating requires an acknowledgment to the editor because the process is so long and involved. Look at the acknowledgments!"

Doing the Research

If taking a detailed scope of the market and competition is always advantageous in some way—whether in the prewriting or in submitting—optimizing market research resources should be an ongoing process for all writers.

"When considering a proposal, our editors often go to a library or bookstore that shelves books by topic to see what the competition is," says Falligant. Online, booksellers such as Amazon.com have a wealth of information made accessible by flexible search engines. You can search by topic, age range, and publisher.

Many publishers have their own websites that are gold mines of information. You can often guess at the URL, or web address, for a publisher by entering www.publisher'sname.com (insert the publisher's name where indicated). If that doesn't work, consult the Children's Book Council or the Library of Congress for a listing of publishers' websites. (See the sidebar above.)

Collard summarizes his market analysis process: "I include a simple market analysis in my proposal. I used to look up subjects and titles in *Books in Print*, but now I run a search by age on Amazon.com. This provides me not only with similar books on that subject, but advance warning on forthcoming books. I also try to pay attention to what's coming out by browsing through publishers' catalogues. As I look through competing titles, I especially note who the publishers are. It could be that there are 15 books on the Aztecs, for instance, but if 14 of them are from library or mass-market publishers, I don't consider that a threat to a high-quality trade book and I'll mention that in my proposal. If there is another trade book that seems to mimic mine, but is different, I use my investigation to determine how my pro-

Business & Career

posal is unique. If I can't draw a distinction, I occasionally shelve a project for a few years or recast it in some way."

Presentation

If you do include a market analysis, Aronson at Henry Holt emphasizes that you should be realistic. "Don't give me pie-in-the-sky comments like, 'Oprah will love it!'" Also unhelpful is a comment such as "There are a million fourth-grade teachers who will all love this book." It's not grounded in real research or reality.

Marina Tamar Budhos, author of *Remix: Conversations with Immigrant Teenagers* (Henry Holt), hired a research team to find teachers of English as a Second Language (ESL) and social workers who work with immigrants. Part of what she found was information about online list-servs for ESL teachers.

Aronson says, "That kind of very targeted marketing information does help. Publishers will evaluate information like this." He says it's always a trade-off of time and money whether or not publishers can follow up on the information aggressively, but they will always consider it and do what they can.

The actual analysis can be as short as a couple of sentences in a query letter or could be a separate section of a proposal entitled, "Marketing Analysis," or "Similar Titles," or "Titles on the Same Topic." First, list the competing titles, then add a brief notation of how your title differs. One crucial difference is to note if the title is for the mass-market, trade, or educational market. Look also at copyright dates. The more recent the title, the more it should factor in as competition. If competing titles were published more than three years before, include the titles anyway, says Davis.

Second, list any special markets that might be appropriate. Aronson warns, "The danger is being too broad. Think niche markets. Be specific, concrete and realistic."

Be thorough in what you present. McClafferty says, "I don't hold anything back from the editor that I find out because if I can find this information, the publisher can, too. I think it is better to be straightforward about all the facts and find a way for your project to fill a niche within what is already out there."

Length of a marketing analysis, Aronson says, is a matter of common sense. "If a book is self-evidently marketable, you can omit the analysis altogether, or keep it very short. If someone scratches their head and says, 'Why this book?,' then more is necessary."

Geiger has some cynicism about authors and market research, despite her belief that authors need to know the markets: "There seems to be an inverse relationship between the marketing analysis and the quality of writing: The longer the marketing analysis, the worse the actual writing." She has seen an eight-page marketing analysis accompanied by a two-page outline for the text. She emphasizes that good writing comes first, marketing second. A market analysis can be a valuable addition to a nonfiction proposal that helps the editor and publisher envision both the book and its market, but ultimately, good writing sells a book.

Contracts

Keeping Your Fair Share

By Mark Haverstock

Everyone wants a deal. We shop sales, bargain for cars, and travel to stores with fistfuls of coupons. Until the advertised company failed, we even put up with the off-key riffs of William Shatner long enough to get the scoop on how to save on everything from gasoline to groceries on the Web.

The same applies on both sides of the table when it comes to contracts. Author and publisher seek a win-win proposition whereby each can cut their best deal in rights and dollars. Today, three issues are becoming a major source of contract conflict: control of electronic rights; all rights versus work-for-hire; and duration of contract. All are linked around a common theme—electronic publishing.

E-Rights and E-Wrongs

Electronic rights were rarely, if ever, specifically mentioned in contracts before the mid-1990s, but now they're a hot topic for everyone in publishing and other media. "The top three concerns I see among writers are electronic rights, electronic rights, and electronic rights," says Brett Harvey, Executive Director of the American Society of Journalists and Authors (ASJA). "This is the major contract problem—it existed before the *Tasini* lawsuit and it's even more of an issue now."

In 1993, National Writer's Union (NWU) head Jonathan Tasini filed a suit on behalf of its members against the *New York Times* and other publishers, attempting to prevent them from using articles from their periodicals on websites, online databases, and CD-ROMs without express permission from the author. Furthermore, Tasini believed that authors should receive additional compensation if their work is to be extended to these new media formats. In 1997, the courts decided in favor of the publishers, and the NWU appealed the decision.

The most recent ruling in *Tasini* is good news for authors, at least in theory. In 1999, the federal appeals court overturned the earlier District Court ruling, reinforcing the writers' ownership of copyright and specifically e-rights. Publishers' response to *Tasini* has been to go on the defensive, developing new contracts that add work-for-hire or all rights clauses. "They're currently asking for rights to all media, those that exist as well as those to be developed in the future with no additional payment," explains Harvey. She

Exercising Your Rights

Your publisher secured rights to your manuscript for audio books, CD-ROMs, e-books, and foreign rights—and you've agreed to split the profits. But are they actively marketing your work in these areas?

"Rightscenter.com provides a marketplace where rights holders, the agents, or the subrights department of the publisher, can securely submit all their deal information up to and including full manuscripts to their potential buyers," says Kip Parent, CEO and founder. It's a business-to-business tool that your agent or publisher can use to get more exposure for their work and to help sell subsidiary rights.

How does it work? Buyers can come to rightscenter.com and arrange to purchase rights from works listed in the directory. Agents can deal new titles instantaneously without sending multiple paper copies of your manuscript, so copy and delivery costs are cut substantially. It's always up to date: Revisions are instantly available and information is electronically tracked.

Sales of an author's work can be more timely and get into more markets. "Many works don't even see emerging markets like Latin America, Eastern Europe, or Asia because the costs of getting the materials out are prohibitive," says Parent. "Our mission is more ideas to more places and in the end, the author benefits."

Rightscenter.com's major clients currently include: Bantam Doubleday Dell, HarperCollins Children's Books, Little Brown and Company, Jean V. Naggar Literary Agency, and Hyperion Books.

---

believes that it's only fair that authors should share in any proceeds.

According to the ASJA, the ideal way for writers to maintain control of their electronic rights is to retain those rights. Writers are then free to evaluate and act on specific electronic publishing opportunities that arise. In the event writers are unable to retain all or part their electronic rights, they should negotiate for safeguards in the grant of those rights. These would include, but not be limited to, unauthorized duplication, limiting formats, duration of rights, and approval of abridgement or anthologizing.

"The vast majority of U.S. publishers are still wrestling with the issue, so you should read very carefully any contract offered to see how electronic rights are worded, after checking for work-for-hire and the rights being purchased," says Gordon Burgett, author of *Sell and Resell Your Magazine Articles*. "If the publication agrees to compensate you for additional use of your article or book, and the rate seems reasonable, sign."

Hired Pen

The all rights and work-for-hire clauses are a result of publishers wanting to acquire electronic or other subsidiary rights automatically. The clauses have become hire is to offer first rights only, with either nonexclusive electronic rights or your right to approval of use. In this way, the publisher has first crack at the manuscript without worrying about market competition, and they can still post it on their website. You have a say in where your piece is published and could possibly profit from future sales.

Never-Ending Rights

Another concern brought about by the growing e-publishing and print-on-demand industry is the duration of contract and return of rights. (See the sidebar, "Do-It-Yourself Book Publishing," opposite.) "Book authors are more concerned about publishers holding onto rights forever—things like print-on-demand are becoming issues," says attorney Mary Flower. Books need never go out-of-print, given the possibilities of electronic media, and rights that in the past would have reverted automatically to the writer are no more. "It's a thorny issue," says Flower. "I don't like the idea of publishers being able to keep books in print because that possibility happens to be available electronically. It's fine if people are actually buying the book and generating some kind of realistic income."

Harvey agrees. "Until a few years ago, it was inconceivable that there would be any use for out-of-print titles," she says. "My hunch is that mainstream publishers will change their contracts so they don't release those books so readily to the author." One way to limit this practice is to set reasonable time limits or termination clauses. "Agree to give the publisher exclusive rights for a specific amount of time and then have them revert back to you," says Harvey.

Another way is to update the definition of *out-of-print*. The Authors Guild suggests that the ideal contract definition of *out-of-print* should be the work is not available in the U.S. through regular retail channels in an English language, book form edition, and is not listed in the publisher's catalogue. Availability through print-on-demand or other electronic or mechanical means alone doesn't make a book still in print.

Just Ask

One fact remains constant in any bargaining process: You've got to ask for what you want—otherwise you can't get it. But writers, especially inexperienced ones, often feel uncomfortable with negotiating. They fear that if they ask for better contract terms or better pay, they'll be passed up in favor of the next writer in line or anger an editor.

"They shouldn't be afraid to ask for changes in the contract," says Flower. "There are still items to negotiate, even in first contracts." Publishers routinely expect to do some negotiating, but Flower warns that economic differences are the toughest to deal with. "They have a line below which they can't go and still make a profit."

When the stakes are high in a lucrative book contract or complex negotiations, you may want to opt for the services of a literary agent or attorney. Good agents and attorneys know more about contracts than most writers can learn on their own, and having a third party can act as a buffer during a particularly difficult round of bargaining.

Ken Wachsberger, a book contract

> ## Do an E-Check
>
> Are your e-rights being used legally? Most websites and databases are careful to follow copyright laws and purchase rights, but you might be surprised where your articles are appearing on the Internet!
> - Try some of the major search engines, such as www.altavista.com, www.yahoo.com, www.lycos.com. Conduct a search for yourself, but be sure to put your name inside quotes ("Mark Haverstock") in the search box.
> - Perform your search at sites that specifically sell reprints of articles from periodicals: www.northernlight.com, www.contentville.com, and uncweb.carl.org are just a few examples.
> - If you find what you feel to be a discrepancy, contact the sites and your publisher too. I found 21 matches at one site—magazine article reprints selling at $2.95 each—some of which I found didn't have e-rights licensed in the original magazine contract.

advisor for the National Writer's Union, advises that writers who choose to negotiate for themselves should know their bottom line prior to making that phone call. Prepare a list in advance and don't be pressured to make a snap decision. "In negotiating, you seldom get everything you want. The idea is to improve your contract as much as possible through compromise but not be so rigid that you lose a potentially workable contract," he says. Not every contract is workable, however. "What are your line-in-the-sand issues, the ones for which you would rather walk than compromise?"

If you're established and have some clout in the market, you might take a more aggressive approach. From her personal experience as a contract advisor and negotiator, Harvey suggests an approach: "When you get a contract insisting on all rights, begin by calling your editor and saying 'I've received this contract and there must be some mistake—this is an all rights contract. I don't sign all rights contracts if I can possibly avoid it. What can we do?'" Explain that electronic rights are additional rights and you're happy to license them, but you need to be compensated in some way for these additional uses of your work.

Realize that the publisher's standard contract, or boilerplate, isn't engraved in stone and usually has some room for change. "Any contract provides the opportunity for an almost unlimited number of changes," says Richard Balkin, author of *A Writer's Guide to Contract Negotiations*. "But a line must be drawn somewhere, and in drawing it we are guided by three factors: common sense, the amount of leverage the writer has, and the writer's priorities."

It's Good to Be King

But the ultimate in keeping the maximum rights for your work may be to bypass the publishing establishment altogether to distribute your own work through publishing-on-demand ser-

An Unexpected Offer on E-books

Rumbling beneath all the predictions and experiments in electronic publishing is the longstanding author-publisher argument about rights and payment. Random House has made a move to quiet the debate by announcing that it would split electronic book sales revenues evenly with authors. That's in contrast to the standard 10 to 15 percent royalty on hardcovers and 7.5 percent on paperbacks. The Authors Guild has long recommended an even split, saying electronic publishing agreements are really licenses of intellectual content rather than a traditional arrangement for the traditional production of a paper product.

Random House, owned by the German conglomerate Bertelsmann, is the largest publisher in the English language. The impact of the Random House move is expected to be extensive. The company's impetus was to align publisher and author interests, reduce debate, and take steps to set industry standards for electronic publishing.

vices or e-publishing. Both offer opportunities for writers to showcase their work and pocket most of the profit for themselves.

Author Stephen King is one of the celebrity pioneers in the new game of mass-market e-publishing. His novella *Riding the Bullet,* published only as an e-book, was downloaded by more than 500,000 readers—impressive figures in any market. Although King's publisher, Simon & Schuster, was involved in this venture, they aren't a part of his new experiment, *The Plant,* an unfinished serial novel whose first installment appeared at www.stephenking.com on July 24, 2000.

With this new project, King has chosen instead to forge a contract with his reader. On the honor system, readers are asked to send him one dollar for each installment downloaded or printed out. He promises to complete the story only if at least 75 percent of the downloaders pay. Pay and the story continues, steal and it folds. The response after the first installment was strong enough for King to continue.

"We have a chance to become Big Publishing's worst nightmare," King has said. He also is quick to point out that he still loves his editors, publishers, and the traditional printed book. "But if I could break some trail for all the midlist writers, literary writers, and just plain marginalized writers who see a future outside the mainstream, that's great." Pointedly, *The Plant* is about a vampire vine that takes over the offices of a publishing house and offers financial success in exchange for human sacrifices.

Let's face it: Publishers require a black bottom line to stay in business, and writers need to make a living. For both to happen, any contract must serve both parties well in an ever-changing market. Writers need to hold onto subsidiary rights that they can reasonably use, or at least negotiate a reasonable split with the publisher.

Publishers need to let go of the notion that they have to stake a claim to all rights in the possible event they may be able to exercise them some time in the future.

"Always seek what's legitimately yours," says agent Jeff Herman, "but always do it in a way that might work for you as opposed to making yourself persona non grata until the end of time." Above all, be a professional.

Payment

Business Partners at Work

By Myrtle Archer

Writers are partners with publishers. Between us, we can entice children to read and read. Writers should also be partners with publishers concerning money, but that is too often not the case.

Writers are notoriously deficient in attention to the financial aspects of their profession. In addition to knowing simple bookkeeping, writers should be educated about copyrights and contracts, especially the new electronic rights laws, if they are to reap bigger rewards. Becoming informed, however, doesn't have to mean spending weeks reading dry business or law books or taking courses. We can learn from knowledgeable writers, publishers, books, and websites.

Lay the Groundwork

The first piece of advice experienced writers will give is to begin your common sense decisions about payment at the beginning of the writing and publishing process: Submit only suitable material to targeted magazines and you can forestall many money concerns.

Market research on magazine needs—and business—is the first step to selling an article and getting paid for it. You know what to do. Use market guides. Send for samples and guidelines. Check out publication websites. Jesse Florea, Editor of *Clubhouse Jr. Magazine* and *Clubhouse Magazine*, says, "The most serious error writers make is not being familiar with a magazine. Knowing the demographic, style, and tone before sending in a story will greatly increase a writer's chance of publication, save the writer money in postage, and the editor time."

In the midst of all that market research, take notes on payment rates and policies. Make comparisons. Ask yourself some questions about the material you want to write and how it will be compensated.

■ What are the payment policies? What kinds of rights are purchased?

■ What is the timing of payments—on acceptance, on publication, or some other?

■ What are the payment rates for the various rights?

■ Does a higher fee warrant selling all rights? How much higher than a rate another publication pays for first or one-time rights?

■ Is there a good way to sell this article for all rights, but rework the idea for another publication and increase the return on this subject or idea?

- What are the reprint policies and payments?
- What do you know of this editor, this publication, and their working arrangements? Do you know the editor and company's reputation for reasonable dealings and prompt payment, or have you heard of problems?
- Are the assignments relatively informal (by general correspondence or by conversation) or formal (contract or letter agreement)?
- What are the limitations, if any, the magazines set on reselling after first rights?

Your study and self-education on all of these questions can be strongly bolstered through professional organizations such as the Society of Children's Book Writers and Illustrators, Authors Guild, Writer's Guild of America, and organizations on the Internet, including the Children's Writing Resource Center and Children's Literature Web Guide.

Put It in Writing

Once you've done your research, selected the magazines you want to target with the properly crafted material, learned as much as you can about the best payments and about the magazines' business policies, you're ready to submit.

Mail off your manuscript? Sandy Huff, a writer with a total of 773 credits (and climbing) that include *Highlights for Children*, *Small Farmer's Journal, Saturday Evening Post, Girl Scout Leader*, and *Wildife & Nature*, tries "to have assignments or on spec agreements before I send in any manuscripts." But that's not always feasible; some publications want manuscripts, not queries. Most writers have manuscripts with no agreements out and about at the same time they are working with other editors to obtain assignments or contracts. (See "Contracts: Keeping Your Fair Share," on page 165.)

Whichever route a writer and editor take to negotiate over a particular piece, the business partnership must next begin in earnest. From an editor's standpoint, says Beula Postlewait, Editor of *Power and Light,* the job simply is "to acquire the rights necessary to publish," while "the most important clause for a writer to get into an agreement is date of publication." Florea thinks, "The most important clause a writer should look for in a contract is amount due and schedule of payment."

In agreements, heed the missing points—as in writing itself, what is not said is as important as what is. While beginning writers or writers new to a publication may not have as much leverage or confidence as those with more established business relationships, no writer needs to accept everything an editor offers at face value. Clarification, and sometimes negotiation, are possible if you believe something is missing or not quite right.

For instance, whenever you can, include a licensing clause. Although the situation doesn't arise much in sales to children's magazines, always reserve audio, movie, television, merchandising, and electronic rights, unless you have a very good reason for licensing them now. Carol Amen's short story "Last Testament," which was first sold to *St. Joseph's Magazine* for one-time rights, was made into a film. Nobody knows what wonders of publishing will

The Rights to Sell

- **All rights:** You sell your work to the publisher with no limitations. After making payment and fulfilling your contract, the publisher owns the work and can publish it as often and in any format it wishes. You cannot license use of the work again.
- **First rights:** The publisher has the right to publish your work for the first time, in book or periodical. The rights then revert to you.
- **First serial rights:** These are the rights to publish your work for the first time—in a periodical. They then revert to you.
- **First North American rights:** You sell first rights, but restrict publication to the North American continent. You could sell the rights again, for first-time publication in, say, Europe, Asia, or Australia.
- **One-time rights:** You sell the nonexclusive right to publish the work once, no matter that it has appeared elsewhere before.
- **Reprint rights:** A publisher may reserve reprint rights to a piece you have sold to them and they previously published. While the rights to the piece return to you after first publication and you may sell the piece to another magazine, if the original magazine wishes to reprint the piece, it may. The fee is usually a percentage of the original fee paid for the first appearance.
- **Second rights:** This is the right to publish a previously published work as a first reprint.
- **Other:** Rights and combinations of rights—audio, book, CD-ROM, dramatic, merchandising, motion picture, online, subsidiary, television—may be modified by agreement between publisher and author.

be invented, so never give up rights in undeveloped technology, unless you are positive you want to do so.

When you do have some leverage as a successful writer, or confidence (not bravado) that what you're asking is more than reasonable, you can try to obtain a better payment rate than the first offer a publication makes. Have a number in mind, but only after you're sure the amount is in line with what is being paid in the marketplace. While children's writers might well argue that it takes the same work to write a 1,000-word piece for young readers as it does a piece for an adult readership, a children's magazine may pay $100 for that length and an adult magazine might pay $1,000. Unfair? Maybe, but that is what the market will bear. Perhaps another children's magazine pays $250 for that length; you can work with that information, which is why you lay your groundwork.

Every writer would prefer to receive payment on acceptance rather than on publication, but some well-respected children's magazines have a strong policy of payment on publication. No harm in asking, however, if that policy has exceptions. For an offer to pay on publication, you might request a higher fee,

Sample Clauses

The phrasing of clauses that contract for purchase of a piece of writing can be simple and direct, or they can be tinged with legalese. Here are some samples.

- The author grants to (*Publication Name*) First North American serial rights to publish the work ("Title"). In return the author shall receive payment of $_____ plus two copies of the issue upon publication.
- (*Publication Name*) would like to feature ("Title") in the online journal (*Online Publication Name*). Payment for one-time rights will be $_____ upon publication. All rights transfer back to the author 90 days after publication. If the story is not published within 20 months of this contract date, all rights revert to the author.
- I am pleased to enclose our check (*Check #*) in the amount of $_____ as payment for our use of "Don't Expect Anything for Christmas" in (*Publication Name*)'s Best-Loved Stories 2001. This payment is for our edition and for a licensed edition to the trade only.
- We are offering $_____ for one-time publication rights to ("Title"). You will receive payment when it is published.

or for an offer to pay on acceptance, accept a lower rate.

Note other terms of the publication's purchase of rights as well. *Children's Writer*, for instance, allows writers to sell reprints of a manuscript one year after publication in the newsletter. Other publications may not specify, and it is a question you might ask your partner, the editor. You and your editor might agree that noncompeting magazines could reprint your work.

Whether your business negotiations take place by phone, in e-mails, or in other correspondence, when you've reached an understanding the editor may send a formal contract or letter of agreement. If not, when the publication has accepted a manuscript and you have accepted the terms, immediately write to the editor, repeating all conversation relevant to payment and rights issues.

When memories are fresh, any misunderstandings can be negotiated. If the editor does not dispute terms, the letter acts as an implied agreement.

When you don't like some wording in the written agreement, try crossing it off and initialing the change. The editor will initial the change as well, if it is acceptable. If the change is reasonable and your writing strong, publishers often accept variations in the wording of agreements. Huff says, "My modus operandi now is simply to know my editors, keep in constant touch, and if an assignment doesn't work out, shrug and forget it."

When the Check Comes, or Doesn't

Sometimes a piece is submitted and published and a check is sent to the writer even with no prior formal acceptance, negotiations, or written agreement and no indication in the writers' guidelines what rights are purchased. This is to be avoided if possible, but when it happens, it is reasonable to conclude that the magazine accepted only First Rights. Write "First Rights" on the back of the check you receive and make a copy of the check.

Keep good notes and copies of all stages in your business partnership with an editor or publication. In your computer or manual files, note when the manuscript is accepted and indicate all the terms—an acceptances file, which includes contracts. Keep a second file for sales that indicates the accounts payable, with amounts and dates. Highlight upcoming payments and periodically review the highlighting to see if any editors or accounting departments need gentle reminders on payment.

Manuscripts are sometimes accepted without a promised date of publication. Decide whether this is acceptable from a publisher who pays on publication; it very well may not be. Payment on acceptance may mean you receive a check, but the piece is sitting in a file and not in the mail for resale. Never-published manuscripts can lose writers money. You don't have to accept that situation. As Postlewait says, "Simply request the manuscript back. Maybe many writers are not aware they can do that."

If a publisher has paid for a manuscript but never published it, write to offer some minimal amount to buy back the rights. The manuscript may be languishing for reasons unrelated to its quality or topic. Florea says, "Date of publication may matter, but sometimes it is beyond the editor's control. A couple of last-minute ads could change a whole magazine's layout, which could mean a story gets bumped. As editors we try to be respectful of our writers and print their stories in a timely manner." With an offer to buy back the rights, most publishers may push to publish, sell back the rights for a small amount, or give them back.

After a manuscript has been published, thank the editor with a short, professional note. Busy editors deserve respect for their busy schedules and appreciation for working with you.

One More Time

The first-time publication of a manuscript can be the barest beginning of marketing and payment. Next, look into reprint marketing. Since waking up to reprints, I've been happily involved in reselling my stories, articles, poems, and novel. New markets for re-publishing manuscripts have opened up wide on the Internet.

Contracts and letter agreements should cover reprint rights. If reprint rights are in question or have never been addressed, write to the publisher and request them. Generally, periodicals are willing to return reprint rights, even if they state that they buy all rights. To date, I have never been turned down. Of course, keep letters and forms the publisher sends concerning these rights for legal proof you can remarket the manuscript.

In your original research into markets, note which magazines don't take reprints. Keep sending out all published manuscripts for which you have reprint rights to those that do, until all possibilities are exhausted or the manuscript

File-Keeping

Acceptances File
A file keeping you up to date on the work that has been accepted might include notations such as the following:
- "The Wastage," accepted (*date*) by *Aim*. First rights. To be published (*date*).
- "The Wonder of the Party," accepted by Short Story International (a book publisher) accepted (*date*) for reprint rights and publication in *Student Series* (*publication date*).
- "Plink, Plank, Plunk," licensed to Kendall/Hunt Publishing Company (a textbook publisher). All rights under a work-for-hire contract but: "If at a future date you have the opportunity to publish this piece, you must first write to Kendall/Hunt Publishing Company and request permission to publish. Kendall/Hunt will more than likely grant you permission to publish as long as it is determined that it does not compete with the Integrated Language Arts Program."
- "Wait Susan!" accepted by *Children's Friend* (*date*) for First rights and publication (*date*).
- "Pepito the Jailbird," accepted by *Journeys* (*date*) for First North American serial rights and publication (*date*).
- "The Good Deeder," accepted as a reprint (*date*) and publication (*date*).
- "Where Is Sarawak?" accepted by *Working for Boys* (*date*) all rights and publication (*date*).

Sales File
Similarly, a file tracking completed sales might have an entry such as the following:
- "The Wastage" published (*date*) by *Aim*. First rights. Payment received (*date*). Amount, $_____ . Check # _____ .
- (*Magazine Name*) accepted ("Title") on (*date*) for (*amount*) to be paid on (*schedule of payments*). Payments made on (*dates*); complete on (*date*).

is obsolete. Reprint payments often add up to many times the amount of an original sale. Amen's "Last Testament" made over a million dollars on reprint and film rights. A reprint payment seldom equals the payment for an original, but reprint payments can add up. Bylines on originals are delightful but fleeting. Reprint payments can continue until the work lives on into the public domain, and even then some publisher might be willing to pay you or your heirs for publication.

If you wish to check the copyright of any manuscript to help with establishing reprint rights, the United States Copyright Office charges no fees to connect to their Internet resources, but also offers no search assistance. Its records, in machine-readable form, are catalogued from January 1, 1978, to the present and they include COHM, which contains all original and renewal registrations except for serials.

When you are sure you may resubmit a published story, indicate Second Rights Offered at the top of the manuscript. Some rewriting may be required, since magazines differ in their styles, but on any revision indicate on the manuscript, "A version published originally in *Magazine Name*."

My story "Cocoon of Love" has been reprinted many times, as has my writing article, "The Use of Parallels," which is still on the market. I've also sold reprint rights to poems. It is particularly important for poets to keep reprint rights, since most poets wish eventually to bring out a poem collection. After a second sale of a piece, replace the Second Rights Offered with Reprint Rights Offered. One article of mine has been published more than 30 times, but I don't point that out unnecessarily, in case an editor might think, "Old hat." If asked, of course, I would say how many times the piece had been published.

Since amiability and professionalism settle most business matters between partners, I have only consulted a lawyer once in a long career, to review a contract. But if you should wish legal advice, try the websites of the American Bar Association, or *Martindale-Hubbell Law Directory*, the About the Law section.

"I figure that most editors begin their endeavors in good faith," says Huff. And most continue in their partnerships with writers in good faith. It's a good business that helps writers live and children read.

Sample Rates and Policies

Magazine Title	Rates	Policies
AppleSeeds	$50 a page.	All rights. Pays on publication.
Archaeology's dig	50¢ a word.	All rights. Pays on publication.
Babybug	$25, minimum.	Rights negotiable. Pays on publication.
Bounty SCA Worldwide	$100	All rights. Pays on acceptance.
Boys' Life	Articles, $400-1,500. Fiction, $750+.	First serial rights. Pays on acceptance.
Boys' Quest	5¢ a word.	First and second rights. Pays on acceptance.
Bread for God's Children	Articles, $25. Fiction, $40-50.	First rights. Pays on publication.
Breakaway	15¢ a word.	All rights. Pays on acceptance.
Calliope, Cobblestone, Faces, Footsteps, Odyssey	20-25¢ a word.	All rights. Pays on publication.
Chickadee	Fiction, $250. Other, rates vary.	All rights. Pays on acceptance.
Children's Playmate	17¢ a word.	All rights. Pays on publication.
Cicada	25¢ a word.	First and second rights. Pays on publication.
Click	25¢+ a word.	First English-language rights. Pays on publication.
Cosmo GIRL!	$1 a word.	All rights. Pays on publication.
Cracked	$100 a printed page.	All rights. Pays on acceptance.
Cricket	To 25¢ a word. Poetry, to $3 a line.	First English-language serial rights. Pays on publication.

Sample Rates and Policies

Magazine Title	Rates	Policies
Crusader	4-5¢ a word.	First and second rights. Pays on acceptance.
Current Health 1 & 2	$150+.	All rights. Pays on publication.
Devo'Zine	Features, $100. Meditations, $25.	First and second rights. Pays on acceptance.
Discovery Trails	7-10¢ a word.	One-time rights. Pays on acceptance.
Dolphin Log	Articles $100-300. Other, $15-100.	One-time, reprint, & worldwide translation rights. Pays on publication.
Dramatics	$50-400.	First rights. Pays on acceptance.
Dream/Girl	No payment. 2 copies.	First serial and reprint rights.
Encounter	6-8¢ a word.	First or one-time rights. Pays on acceptance.
Focus on the Family Clubhouse	$75-300.	One-time rights. Pays on acceptance.
Focus on the Family Clubhouse Jr.	To $300.	First North American rights. Pays on acceptance.
Fox Kids	$100-400.	All rights. Pays on publication.
The Friend	10¢ a word. Poetry, $25.	All rights. Pays on acceptance.
Go-Girl (webzine)	$50-75.	All or first rights. Pays on publication.
Guideposts for Kids (now online onlys)	$200-500.	All rights. Pays on acceptance.
Guideposts for Teens	$150-400.	All rights. Pays on acceptance.
High Adventure	5¢ a word.	First or all rights. Pays on acceptance.

Business & Career

Sample Rates and Policies

Magazine Title	Rates	Policies
Highlights for Children	Vary.	All rights. Pays on acceptance.
Hopscotch	5¢ a word.	First and second rights. Pays on publication.
Horsepower Magazine for Young Horse Lovers	$50-$75.	Rights negotiable. Pays on publication.
hot!	30-50¢ a word.	All rights. Pays on publication.
Humpty Dumpty	To 22¢ a word.	All rights. Pays on publication.
"In" Power	15¢ a word.	All rights. Pays on publication.
Insight	$50-125.	First rights. Pays on acceptance.
Jack And Jill	To 17¢ a word.	All rights. Pays on publication.
Jam Rag	$10-$50.	One-time rights. Pays on publication.
Jump	75¢-$1.25 a word.	All rights. Pays on publication.
Keynoter	$150-$350.	First North American serial rights. Pays on acceptance.
Keys for Kids	Devotionals, $15-20.	First and second rights. Pays on acceptance.
Kids Tribute	$75-150 Canadian.	First North American serial rights. Pays on acceptance.
kidsworld	$75-450 Canadian.	First rights. Pays 30 days after publication.
Ladybug	To 25¢ a word.	Rights vary. Pays on publication.
Latingirl	$1 a word.	All rights. Payment policy varies.

Sample Rates and Policies

Magazine Title	Rates	Policies
Listen	Crafts, $15. Poetry, 25¢ a line.	All rights. Pays on publication.
Listen Magazine	5-10¢ a word.	All rights. Pays on acceptance.
Live Wire	3-7¢ a word.	All rights. Pays on acceptance.
Looney Tunes™ Crafty Kids	Crafts, $25-300.	All rights. Pays on publication.
Muse	To 25¢ a word.	Rights policy varies. Pays within 60 days of acceptance.
My Friend	$35-50.	First North American serial rights. Pays on acceptance.
NASCAR RFT Racing for Teens	$50-150.	First rights. Pays on publication.
National Geographic World	$100-600.	All rights. Pays on acceptance.
Nature Friend	5¢ a word.	One-time rights. Pays on publication.
The New Era	$35-450.	All rights; reassigned on request. Pays on acceptance.
New Moon	6-12¢ a word.	All rights. Pays on publication.
On the Line, Story Friends	3-5¢ a word.	One-time rights. Pays on acceptance.
Our Little Friend	$25-50.	One-time rights. Pays on acceptance.
OWL	$200-500 Canadian.	World rights. Pays on acceptance.
Partners, Story Mates	2-5¢ a word. Poetry, 35-75¢ a line.	All, first, or one-time rights. Pays on acceptance.
Pockets	14¢ a word. Poetry, $25+.	First and second rights. Pays on acceptance.

Business & Career

Sample Rates and Policies

Magazine Title	Rates	Policies
Power and Light	5¢ a word.	Multiple-use rights. Pays on publication.
Power Station	10¢ a word.	All or one-time rights. Pays on acceptance.
Primary Treasure	$25-50.	One-time rights. Pays on acceptance.
Quantum	$200.	All rights. Pays on publication.
Read, America!	$50. Poetry, $10.	All rights. Pays on publication.
Scholastic DynaMath	$250-400.	All rights. Pays on acceptance.
Scholastic Scope	$100+.	Rights negotiable. Pays on acceptance.
School Mates	$50 per 1,000 words.	First rights. Pays on publication.
Science World	$200-650.	All rights. Pays on acceptance.
Seventeen	$1-1.50 a word.	First rights. Pays on acceptance.
Sharing the Victory	$50-200.	First serial rights. Pays on publication.
Skipping Stones	No payment. (nonprofit)	First rights.
Soccer JR.	$400-800.	All rights for picture story scripts. First North American, reprint rights. Pays on publication.
Spellbound	$5.	First World English-language rights. Pays on publication.
Spider	To 25¢ a word.	First English-language rights. Pays on publication.

Sample Rates and Policies

Magazine Title	Rates	Policies
Spike	$20-1,000.	Rights policy varies. Pays on acceptance.
SPIRIT	$200.	All rights. Pays on publication.
Sports Illustrated For Kids	$75-800.	All rights. Pays on acceptance.
Stone Soup	$25.	All rights. Pays on publication.
SuperScience	$75-600.	All rights. Pays on publication.
Synapse	No payment.	All rights.
Take Five	Devotionals, $30.	All rights. Pays on acceptance.
TC (Teenage Christian)	$10-25.	First and second rights. Pays on publication.
Teen	Fiction, $500.	All rights. Pays on acceptance.
Teen Celebrity	$200-500.	Exclusive rights for 3 months. Pays on publication.
Teens on Target	1 1/2¢ a word.	First or one-time rights. Pays on publication.
Thrasher	10¢ a word.	First North American serial rights. Pays on publication.
Tiger Beat	$50-200.	First North American serial rights. Pays on publication.
Today's Christian Teen	$150.	All rights. Pays on publication.
Together Time	Fiction, $25. Crafts, $15.	Multi-use rights. Pays on publication.
Tomorrow's Morning	50¢ a word.	Rights policy varies. Pays on publication.

Business & Career

Sample Rates and Policies

Magazine Title	Rates	Policies
Touch	2½-5¢ a word to $35.	First, second, and simultaneous rights. Pays on publication.
Turtle	22¢ a word.	All rights. Pays on publication.
U*S*Kids	20¢ a word. Poetry, $25.	All rights. Pays on publication.
Winner	5-10¢ a word.	First rights. Pays on acceptance.
Wonder Time	Fiction, $25.	Multi-use rights. Pays on production, 1 year before publication.
YES Mag	15¢ a word Canadian.	First rights. Pays on publication.
YES Magazine	$50-75.	All rights. Pays on publication.
YM	$100+.	First North American serial rights. Pays on acceptance.
Young Adult Today	$150.	Rights negotiable. Pays on publication.
Young & Alive	3-5¢ a word.	One-time rights. Pays on acceptance.
The Young Judaean	No payment.	All rights.
Young People's Press Online	No payment.	All rights.
Young Rider	10¢ a word.	First rights. Pays on publication.
Young Salvationist	15¢ a word.	First or one-time rights. Pays on acceptance.
Youth Challenge	15¢ a word.	First or one-time rights. Pays on publication.
Youth Update	15¢ a word.	First North American serial rights. Pays on acceptance.

Promotion

Author Visits: Hope, Expect, Ensure

By Toni Buzzeo

Author and illustrator visits can be among the most significant enrichment experiences in the lives of schoolchildren. The opportunity to meet with a real, live book creator enhances literacy and offers lasting connections that are difficult to create more effectively by any other means. For authors and illustrators, too, school visits can be meaningful and rewarding. The opportunity to meet with readers enhances a necessary sense of connection to your audience that can prove to be a source of inspiration and delight, as well as income!

"Ideal, inspiring visits—terrific connections—don't happen without the intention, hard work, and commitment of everyone involved," says Kay Winters, author of *The Teeny Tiny Ghost* books, *Tiger Trail*, *Wolf Watch*, and *Did You See What I Saw? Poems About School*. Winters believes it is essential for school and/or library personnel, children, and the author to work together for a successful visit. It's hard work. And it's worth every bit of preparation!"

The Ideal Visit

Given the hard work by everyone involved, what do that work and ideal visit look like when they come together?

The most important consideration is preparing the children for your visit. "The biggest difference I've seen is when the kids know I'm coming and are excited about it—maybe they've done some kind of art project or something that helps them connect with me even before I arrive," says Franny Billingsley, the author of *Well Wished* and *The Folk Keeper*.

Lee Wardlaw, whose books include *101 Ways to Bug Your Parents*; *We All Scream for Ice Cream: The Scoop on America's Favorite Dessert*; and *Hector's Hiccups*, agrees. "If the children have thought about or written down questions about me and my books ahead of time, and bring their questions to the presentation—so much the better! I love it, too, when teachers and other staff ask questions during the presentations. It's a plus to be greeted and thanked by the principal as well. Anything else is like icing on the cake. Delicious!" (In one particularly delicious example, a red carpet was actually rolled out for her entrance to the building!)

"The enthusiasm of the librarian makes all the difference in the world," says Helen Ketteman, whose latest books are *Armadillo Tattletale*, *Mama's Way*, and *Shoeshine Whittaker*. "I don't insist on much for my school visits, but I always insist that the kids are well-prepared. That is the sole most important factor, I think, in a successful school visit—and it hinges on the librarian. If she's had fun with the books, the kids will have had fun with them, too, and they'll be whipped into a frenzy of anticipation—a good librarian works wonders! The kids are the ones who benefit, because they'll come away from the author visit not only with useful information, but also with a new interest in reading and maybe writing and using their imagination. It's a fabulous thing when it works!"

The luckiest schools, like Dater Elementary School in Ramsey, New Jersey, have library media specialists like Mary Rose Morris to ensure this level of preparation.

"At a faculty meeting," says Morris, "teachers are asked to prepare for the visit by having their class work on a project about the author or illustrator. If they need assistance or suggestions, they can feel free to contact me or work with another class. I also notify the art teacher, music teacher, or other specialists to see how we can integrate this visit with their curriculum. We have parent volunteers who assist with the book orders, which are done about three months before the visit. The author or illustrator arriving at our building is greeted with banners of welcome and the halls are covered with work students have done in regard to their stories and illustrations. At times, students have performed skits from a story, written and recited poetry pertaining to the guest or one of the stories. It is important to demonstrate enthusiasm about the upcoming event and generate the excitement of having an author/illustrator visit our school."

For an inside view of the many faces of terrific visits, from school and library gigs to young author conferences and virtual chats, refer to my book, *Terrific Connections with Authors, Illustrators, and Storytellers: Real Space and Virtual Links*. Remember, if you know what an ideal visit looks like, you are that much closer to ensuring that it happens when you are hired to speak!

The Best Combination

At Longfellow Elementary School in Portland, Maine, where I am the Library Media Specialist, we follow the same elaborate preparations for a visit as Morris undertakes. But not every school contact is made by a library media specialist. Winters offers a heads up, emphasizing the importance of the librarian being on board and of the author knowing what to ask for.

"At schools where I have been hired by the PTA person and the librarian has not been kept on board," says Winters, "the books were never shown to the kids beforehand, the children were not prepared. It's like taking the kids on a field trip and never prepping them. The

Promotional Materials

Promotional materials, most often brochures or portfolios known as "author/illustrator packets," are worth the time they take to prepare. You can use these materials to attract speaking gigs initially and to inform and prepare a site for your visit. In packets, authors and illustrators often include biographies, program descriptions, articles they have written, review clips of their books, bibliographies with honors and awards noted, fee schedules, and references.

The very best packets, like that of author Lee Wardlaw also include a photo, sample book covers for displays, a letter to students, activity sheets and curriculum guides, a list of writing prompts, and a book order form. Wardlaw also emphasizes being responsive to the community. This southern California author includes a letter in Spanish with her other materials. The library media specialists I interviewed appreciate these added touches. Mary Rose Morris says, "I would like more updated photos and information. It would also be helpful to have book jackets, posters, and bookmarks." Mary Ann Albertine, LMS/ITS at the Harwich Elementary Library Media Center, Harwich, Cape Cod, Massachusetts, also asks for "lots of give-aways so each classroom can have something to display—book marks, book posters, book covers—and a website URL."

school and the children lose out. The author loses out because book sales are abysmal. It's important, if you are hired by the school PTA representative, to ask how the librarian will be involved. Many times that person works hand in glove with the librarian—the PTA person relieving the librarian of the paperwork that goes with the bookselling, the librarian doing the educating part of sharing the books with students and staff. That's the best combination!"

Determine your own needs, your own "bottom line," if you will. For some, like Barbara Haworth-Attard, expectations are few. "I bring my own bottled water, and I also bring my own lunch if the librarian/teacher does not invite me." Haworth-Attard is author of *Home Child*, *Love-Lies-Bleeding*, and *WyndMagic*. Others have a different bottom line.

Author/illustrator Katie Davis's titles include the upcoming *Scared Stiff*, and the companion volumes *Who Hops?* and *Who Hoots?* When she has author visits planned, she hopes for "prepared students, water, breaks, name tags, and food-not-from-the-cafeteria!"

Jane Kurtz asks schools to order her books to sell, among them *I'm Sorry, Almira Ann*; *Faraway Home*; and *River Friendly, River Wild*, so that she doesn't have to lug them along. Kurtz also asks schools to buy copies of her out-of-print books for the library so that the children will be familiar with them when she includes them in her presentations.

Other authors need an overhead projector—or ice water with lemon. Whatever your needs are, determine them in advance and then communicate them to your host! Many library media specialists have several phone

School Visits Pay

Income

For some authors and illustrators, the reason to do school and library visits is, in part, economic. "I do 20 visits a year and the income is good, better than the writing income," says author Kay Winters. For author Barbara Haworth-Attard, "School visits are exhausting and exhilarating all at the same time—but contribute half my income." Both would agree with the conclusion drawn by Elaine Marie Alphin, author of *Counterfeit Son, Telephones,* and *A Bear for Miguel:* "Certainly, supplemental income is a big attraction of school visits—but it's not the only one."

Book Sales

Visits provide an opportunity to sell books. Winters claims they increase total sales. "If you are really well known, and your books are selling like hot cakes, then you can stay home and write. School visits usually sell more books than autographing at bookstores or even speaking at conferences."

Kathleen Duey's experience proves this. "At a good school visit, I might sell 400 to 500 paperbacks. (One stellar example sold 700!) Most average between 100 to 250." Duey has written the American Diaries series, and many other titles for children and young adults.

Alphin adds, "I don't know how much school visits raise total sales, even if you sell a couple of hundred copies of a title at a school, but I do know that several of my publishers have told me they really appreciate authors who do school visits and are willing to work to promote a book by talking about it and doing signings. One PR person told me that she couldn't understand authors who didn't do this."

Audience Contact

The opportunity for audience contact is an even bigger draw for many authors and illustrators. Author Helen Ketteman says, "I don't need the money from school visits so much—not that it's not nice. I do it to spread the word about my books to the people who matter to me—the kids, teachers, and librarians." This is also true for author Lee Wardlaw. "Since I quit my teaching job in 1982, I've found school visits to be a great way to keep up with kids: how they dress, talk, think. Keeping in touch with my audience helped me to strengthen the characters in my books."

Alphin puts another spin on it. "We deal with marketing confusion, rejections, hostile reviews, questions about our Amazon.com rating, titles going out-of-print—the whole hassle of the business side of writing. Sometimes

School Visits Pay

it's disheartening and makes us forget why we got into this business. Looking out at a sea of rapt faces, feeling the kids' fascination with our books and with us for creating them, fielding questions that make us think about the ideas and messages in our books, and getting to sign some books for kids who really appreciate it can remind us of what we love about our craft and can also remind us that it's worthwhile to pursue it. We *are* reaching readers." Ketteman sometimes pushes herself and takes perhaps too much time away from her writing, for just this reason. "I've heard from teachers and librarians that after my visits the kids are jived to read—and to me, that's what it's all about."

Promotion
Winters advocates for school and library visits as a promotional tool, saying, "It gets your name and the titles of your books out there." Bonny Becker, author of *The Christmas Crocodile, Tickly Prickly,* and *An Ant's Day Off,* has seen this happen. "You reach a limited number of people at the school visit, with perhaps no obvious benefit at the time, but then because of it, your book gets mentioned on a list that has hundreds of members, many of whom are quite involved in the world of children's books. I know there are some valuable intangible spin-offs of doing visits."

Dian Curtis Regan, author of the Monster of the Month Club series, *Princess Nevermore,* and *The Friendship of Milly and Tug,* adds, "I do know that marketing departments claim they see arcs in book sales, post-school visits, so it does help, but unless that arc is huge, is it worth your time? I think the benefits are long-term, so you have to take that into consideration. New teachers and librarians meet you and become aware of your name and book titles, then, hopefully, remember both when future books come out."

Author Jane Kurtz concurs. "My own sense is that for a certain type of book, some speaking is pretty vital to keep it alive.... The independent booksellers used to be wonderful ambassadors who made sure books ended up in the hands of readers. Without the independents, going straight to the readers—with school visits and conferences—is filling the gap."

conversations with the prospective guest, as I do myself, to be sure they have made a note of each desire and given the guest plenty of opportunities to discuss details. Others prefer to use the mail. Most, however, have begun to rely heavily on e-mail for author/illustrator communications.

As Media Aide Rachel Woodyer of Grand Ridge Grade School, Grand Ridge, Illinois, says, "I have found e-mail to be the best because it is fast. People are not as likely to come to a phone as to be near a computer."

So be prepared with your own list of requests, from comfort items to equipment needs, and if your host doesn't contact you, feel free to contact him or her. In fact, one retired library media specialist advises, "Authors should communicate directly, not through their agents or publishers. They should tell the host what format they would like; any special equipment or needs. But deal with the host directly!"

Agreements and Check-ins

Too often, authors and illustrators don't insist on a contract for a school visit. Be sure that you do! You are being hired to work under specified conditions for an agreed upon fee. Both you and your host need that in writing, to be sure of no misunderstandings. Some schools have their own contract, which they will offer to send you. If so, or if you design your own, be certain that it includes:
- dates and times
- number and length of sessions each day
- number of students per session
- any additional events (such as book signings) and their times
- any amenities (such as meals) to be included.

If you haven't hammered out an agreement on the schedule, do so before you sign the contract.

Some authors, like Davis, include a book order form and a timetable with the contract. Others, like Wardlaw, have a *letter of agreement* rather than a contract. "In a sense, it's a trade agreement: I trade my best for their best," says Wardlaw.

After the contract or letter of agreement is signed, make sure that your communication doesn't end. Jan Cole, Library Media Specialist at Horace Mann Elementary, Duncan, Oklahoma, says, "I telephone a couple of times and ask the visitors' needs or wants and how I can make the trip as enjoyable for them as it will be for us." If your host doesn't call you, do call your host for a final follow-up conversation during the month before your arrival. This might be the time to make any last-minute determinations, and get one more sense of the people, the place, the needs. Mary Bowman-Kruhm, author of *"N" Is for New York; Money: Save It, Manage It, Spend It;* and *A Day in the Life of a Teacher*, suggests at this point "asking honestly for an appraisal of the composition of groups—what to expect from the students."

Boundaries and Flexibility

No matter how carefully you plan, how closely you read your contract, how accommodating your host, it is inevitable there will be a surprise or two. It is in the nature of schools and their fluidity that things change at the last minute. It may be that your host is so good at

Sample School Contract

To: [*Author Name*]
From: Toni Buzzeo, Library Media Specialist, and Joanne Fiore, Principal
Date:

The Longfellow Elementary School Library invites you to speak to Longfellow students in grades kindergarten through five on Wednesday, November 17, 2000, and Thursday, November 18, 2000. On each of the two days, you will meet with five groups of students in the library media center. Groups will be limited to two classes of children in all but one case, grade three, where three classes will be combined. Sessions with grades three through five will last 45 minutes. Sessions with kindergarten through grade two will last 35 minutes. The schedule will follow as soon as it is finalized.

A casual lunch will be scheduled each of the two days in the library where you will have the opportunity to relax for an hour and chat with teachers whose classes you have visited with that day. Your lunch will be provided.

On the evening of Wednesday, [*date*], the Longfellow Parent Teacher Organization will host a book sale and signing of your books in conjunction with our annual evening Book Fair gala, from 6:30-8:00 PM.

Please sign both copies of this agreement and return one to me.

We will look forward to your visit with our students as our school community busily prepares for next fall!

_____   _____
Toni Buzzeo, Library Media Specialist   Joanne Fiore, Principal

_____
Author

Business & Career

Sample Author Agreement

Marion the Librarian
ABC Elementary School
123 Once Upon a Time Lane
Anytown, USA

Dear Mr./Ms. Librarian:
Thank you for inviting me to ABC's annual Author Day. I look forward to meeting the staff and students on [date], and sharing with them my knowledge and experiences about the writing and publishing process.

    Enclosed is a copy of my Author Packet, which includes:
– an author bio and photo
– credit sheet, awards/honors list, and sample reviews/articles
– sample copies of book covers for possible promotional displays in the library and/or classrooms
    – a list of recommended books for teachers/librarians [*My list includes a title of my own and others:* Terrific Connections With Authors, Illustrators and Storytellers, *by Toni Buzzeo and Jane Kurtz;* What's Your Story?, *by Marion Dane Bauer; and* Author's Day, *by Daniel Pinkwater.*]
    – hand-out sheets the school may wish to photocopy and distribute to teachers. These sheets offer a selection of fun writing/reading activities to help prepare the students for my visit and to evaluate what the students have learned after I'm gone.

As discussed, I will arrive at [*time*] to set up, and will depart at [*time*]. Lunch will be provided by the school.

I will present the following 3 programs to be held in the [*library? multipurpose room? auditorium? classroom?*].
    – Program 1
    – Program 2
    – Program 3
    [*Here I briefly list the title of each presentation and a one-sentence synopsis; the grade levels or classes that will attend; the length of time needed, including a question-and-answer period; and any special materials I or the students will need, such as writing paper, microphone, overhead projector, etc.*]

Sample Author Agreement

To ensure that the students and teachers get the most out of my presentations, I ask that they be familiar with at least two of my books. [*List titles that are pertinent to the programs.*] The children, individually or as a class, may wish to write a list of questions they'd like to ask me and bring it to the program.

After the day's festivities, I will be available to autograph books in the [*location*] at [*time*]. I will need a staff or parent volunteer to help collect money. A book order form, to be sent home the day before my visit, is enclosed. [*Details concerning the book signing are also described here, such as who will supply the books, any discounts offered, etc. If I am supplying and selling the books, I usually offer the school 20 percent of the proceeds to help offset my honorarium.*]

My fee for the Author Day is [*amount*], plus expenses, payable the day of the visit. If the school must cancel the visit, and it cannot be rescheduled, ABC Elementary will pay one-third of my honorarium.

If ABC Elementary agrees to these terms, please sign the original copy of this letter and return it to me in the enclosed SASE. Ms. Librarian, if you have any questions, or suggestions on how to make my Author Visit more enjoyable for all, please feel free to contact me at your earliest convenience.

Sincerely,

Ms. Lee Wardlaw

adapting that you will never even realize what's gone wrong. At other times, you'll have to make a choice between maintaining your boundaries and being flexible.

Haworth-Attard says, "This is a tough one. I've sometimes had extra classes added at the last minute. If it is to be a presentation, which is mostly slides, I don't mind the extra bodies. Workshops, though, I try to keep to 50 or 60 children, tops. If they slide in another class, I grin and bear it and, as I think fairly fast on my feet, I adapt." You'll earn points if you can be adaptable, like Billingsley, who says, "I am very flexible, and I've never had any disasters—nor have I ever had to make any accommodations that seemed at all unreasonable. Maybe I've moved from a library to a cafeteria, or had more kids than I anticipated, but no big deal."

Each author, however, has a line to cross. "I'm inflexible about three things," says Wardlaw. "One, *breaks*. I'm human, and need to use the restroom now and then, just like everyone else! Two, more than three presentations is exhausting, and I'm not at my best after that, which isn't fair to the children, or to me. Three, my check is to be paid the day of my visit. Period."

Making and Keeping Contacts

So now that you know what to expect and ensure, how do you connect with schools?

Beth Lunsford, Media Specialist at City Park School, Dalton, Georgia, makes her contacts through Hobbit Hall Bookstore in Roswell, Georgia. If you are lucky enough to have an independent children's bookstore in your area, or even in your state, you might contact them, when you are ready to pursue visits. Other library media specialists, like Mary Ann Albertine, work through publishers, after receiving requests for specific authors from staff or students. Most, like Morris, Cole, and myself, learn of authors and illustrators through word of mouth, from our colleagues in other schools and libraries or at library, reading, and children's literature conferences. And now that the Internet has made the world so much smaller, Woodyer reminds us, "we ask on LM_NET of course!" LM_NET is a listserv of over 12,000 library media specialists in the U.S. and throughout the world.

Because so many contacts are made through personal recommendations, it is important to follow-up after good visits. Davis says, "I e-mail and thank the contact. I also ask for quotations for use in my materials. In fact, I got a great one from a superintendent this way! During my best performance, the ninth one on the third day, a woman walked in and watched the whole thing. I didn't know who she was until later. She had laughed throughout and loved what I did and gave me lots of nice compliments. And she bought two books! Everyone in the front office kept telling me sotto voce that 'Dr. R never laughs at anything!' and 'It takes a *lot* to impress her!' So of course I asked her to give me a quote and put it in my flyer!"

Billingsley offers to read and respond to anything that a child finishes writing after her workshop. Wardlaw always follows up with a letter to her

The Publisher's View on School Visits

Catherine Balkin, Library and Educational Marketing Director at Hyperion Books for Children, thinks that school visits are definitely helpful for authors and illustrators, for many of the same reasons that book creators themselves find them helpful: supplementing income, contact with the audience, the chance to see kids in action and listen to their language.

Cheryl Herman, Associate Marketing Manager, Author Promotions, at Simon & Schuster Children's Publishing, agrees. "School visits," she says, "are really the most direct way for authors and illustrators to interface with their audience—kids!"

What about book sales? Melanie Meeker, Coordinator of Author Events at Charlesbridge Publishing, notes that when she was first involved in setting up school visits, "most schools would order their books directly. Now, they do so to a lesser degree. Often, today, bookstores promote the visit and handle the book sales. Still," she adds, "the sales of those books come to us indirectly." While Balkin does not see any big sales spikes from school visits, she acknowledges that there are also very few returns.

The marketing people focus on other advantages for the publisher, however. Meeker notes that when authors and illustrators who do many school visits attend conferences, they are well-known to their audiences already. Librarians and teachers recognize them from their school gigs. Balkin calls this phenomenon "seeding."

"Once a library media specialist has had an author visit, he or she will always keep the author's or illustrator's books on the shelf and will watch for new books by that same person." Herman sees school visits as "definitely in the publishers' best interest. It is an opportunity to grow our authors, to grow their careers." Balkin adds that school visits are also great for "author care," noting that publishers who set them up go a long way toward making their authors and illustrators feel taken care of. Meeker adds, "There are no disadvantages to school visiting. Kids love it! Authors love it! It's wonderful!"

host, and sometimes a phone call. "I usually give the contact the name of a fellow author, whom I think they may like to host the following year. This keeps them thinking about continuing the Author Day!"

What a wonderful idea! Do your best, say thanks, and spread the word!

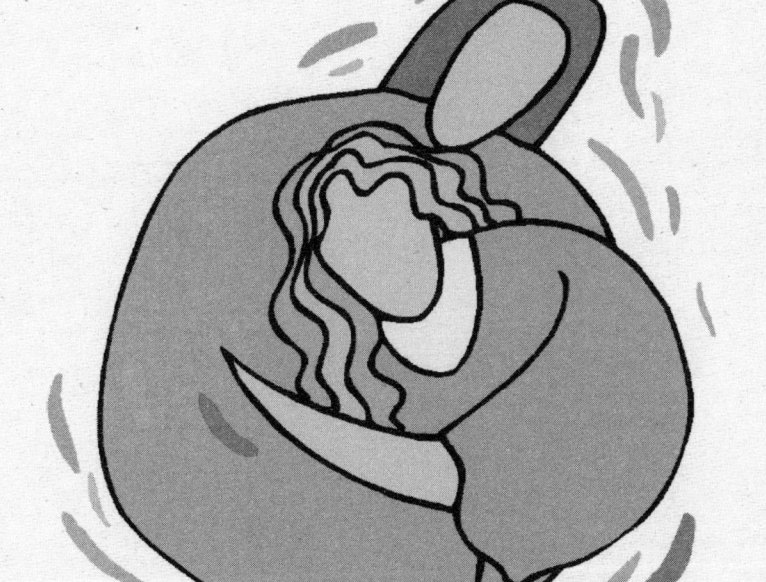

Reference & Research

Researching People

The Power of Our Family Stories

By Ruth Sachs

Her life reads like the clichéd soap opera. Clara married a young lieutenant in 1875. Before their fourth anniversary, they had a son and two daughters. Clara's Julius quickly earned promotions, moving from a statewide post to a national office. A couple of months before they marked five years of marriage, Julius developed a curious disease. Clara buried him eight days later.

That life, with its multitudinous details—tragic, joyous, mundane—and countless other lives, can provide writers with ideas for plot, inspiration for characters, facts for background.

Clara mourned two husbands, four siblings, and two of her young children. The surviving son fell in battle. One of her two grandchildren died at two. But she lived to nearly 90, and sprinkled in among the deaths are glimpses of cycles of joy. Her second husband started as a clerk at a sugar factory, and retired as Treasurer. Clara's daughter married well, and great nieces and nephews went out of their way to stay in touch with a beloved aunt. The life story of Clara Ossig will never become a made-for-TV movie. It is doubtful that a children's picture book will focus on the fate of her four-year-old daughter Helene. But it can furnish a well-structured outline for a short story or for a young adult novel about life in nineteenth-century Germany, or World War I, for nonfiction pieces on life, culture, even society and politics.

The facts of Clara's story come from a source I will put back on the shelf, but not before I have derived enough narrative to keep me happily submitting for at least a couple of weeks. If I had writer's block before, it is gone now.

The source? A genealogy buried in the microfiche of a Family History Center, the genealogy centers run by the Church of Jesus Christ of Latter-Day Saints (Mormons). Free.

Unharvested Tales

If your only contact with genealogical research consists of preprinted family trees with barely enough space for birth and death dates, or the overwhelming lack of information you discover if you purchase a database like Family Treemaker, you may have difficulty believing that pure genealogy can yield very useful results. Even with graphics like charts and trees, genealogy can appear to be endless lists of 'she was born' and 'he died', with great gaps that make up the stories of our lives.

To be sure, that cycle of born-and-died has its own mesmerizing effect on the genealogist. If a researcher is lucky enough to trace ancestors back to the seventeenth and eighteenth centuries, the life cycle rhythm is inescapable.

But the cache of stories knows no bounds. For every genealogical resource available, there is a separate and distinct genre of unharvested tales, tales woven from the broad cloth of daily existence, of calico curtains and white picket fences, immigrants' misery and settlers' sweat. Of women who died too young in childbirth and men who fell in senseless wars. Of children in wagon trains, of babies dying from yellow fever, of teens who married and had families before their acne cleared up.

A War or a Life

The source that tells the tale of Clara's life provided many details to help me flesh out the setting and plot. Her first married name was Sauer, meaning *sour*, adding a layer of meaning to the plot. She moved back and forth between a large Prussian city and a small town, spending her happier days in the small town. The city, now in Poland, had a distinctly military feel.

I know the specific name of the battle in World War I that claimed the life of her son. Captain Hans Sauer was fatally wounded at the front in France at the Battle of Rossignol-Titigny. Her daughter's "good marriage" was to a customs inspector, only a few months after World War I ended.

In fact, by the time I have finished reading the page and a half about Mrs. Clara Ossig, two or three stories have begun to take shape and write themselves on my computer screen. Do I want to focus on the historical aspects of her life and the upheaval that a world war brought to a family? I would need to research the Battle of Rossignol-Titigny if I took this approach.

Alternately, I could shine the spotlight on German history by means of Clara's life in particular. She was born the year after Germany's aborted attempt at democracy, into revolutionary fervor similar to our own Colonial period: Except that the students revolting on German campuses in 1848 were not successful, and democracy died. Her childhood was indisputably influenced by the remnants of that uprising, while her young adulthood saw Germany go to war with France, emerging not only victorious but also —for the first time in its history— united as a single nation. She lived through the rise of Communism, the first World War, and died a few months after Adolf Hitler came to power.

What a way to teach history! The personal touch adds a dimension that takes it out of the dry and distant past and makes it come alive.

But I am also drawn to Clara on a simply human level. The aspect of a grandmother, great-grandmother telling the family story to young children who still think *old* is fascinating. The outline can be taken out of Germany, put wherever I want, and it works. Our family sagas always enthrall.

In the Beginning

Novices to genealogy need not worry about their ignorance of the subject.

Most popular Internet service providers, such as America Online (AOL) and Microsoft Network, offer proprietary forums for researchers. If you are interested in tracking your own family, follow their directions to get started. The guidelines are generally well written.

If all you wish to do is tap the genealogy fountain for truth-based tales, other websites and basic sources will keep you writing for as long as you wish.

Yahoo, most often used as a search engine, is probably the simplest place to start. A portal justifiably touted for its good organization, www.yahoo.com lists its genealogy forum on its opening page. From there, information is nicely compartmentalized.

As an exercise in how such resources might be used for writing purposes, I chose the Surgener Home Page from Yahoo's index. A note from the compiler states that the Surgener family name is related to Sojourner, to which it eventually evolved. As a writer, I liked the implications of a name with hidden meaning, so I clicked on its link.

What a choice it turned out to be! Rowland *Sudgerner*, a 21-year-old from somewhere near London, swore the oath of allegiance and was transported to Virginia aboard the *Alice* on July 13, 1635. That's all we know about Rowland, but the records tell us quite a bit about John and Mary *Sojourner* of Virginia. (Remember that, historically, the same names of the same individuals may have inconsistencies of spelling.)

The researcher uncovered numerous land grants, buying and selling of property, and even John's will. He also found a legal document dated February 9, 1692: John Sojourner informed against John Collins for rustling two "beves" (beefs, or cows) from the plantation of William Baldwein.

As you can see from the records of Clara Ossig and John Sojourner, genealogical research does not purport to fill in every detail of a person's life. But in both cases, enough was written down past the born-and-died to draw up a good outline for a fiction article.

If I turn Clara's sorrow or John's propensity to rat on his neighbor into a short story, I will be making up plenty as I go along. The Ossig and Sojourner families will not call me to task if I write that Clara was a redhead and John was short, because I am not writing their family history. In fact, I will

Reference & Research

be changing some of what I know to be true to accommodate the story I am telling, as well as to stay out of hot water should I some day chance to meet the great-great-great-grandson of either family.

The Best of Sites

A genealogist who clearly understands the story-telling nature of family history writes for America Online's Genealogy Forum. You do not have to subscribe to AOL to read her work; the "Daily Genealogy Column" can be accessed on the Web. "Dear Myrtle" (www.DearMyrtle.com) combines the best of strict genealogy research—the nuts and bolts of where to find information if you are serious about your own family tree—with stories she finds along the way.

As dedicated a researcher as "Myrtle" is, she nearly overlooked an ancestress of her own named Parmilia Gist, who married into her Froman family. The Fromans, together with several other young couples, left Kentucky and moved to Missouri in the early 1800s. Myrtle writes that by 1850, Parmilia was widowed out on that frontier, left to raise several children by herself.

In one column, Myrtle mused that her serendipitous discovery made her aware "that strong-hearted women struggled to carve out a fair existence. . . . Often alone they battled the odds of the untamed prairies." Our stories tend to shine a spotlight on the men, leaving out the Parmilias and countless women like her. Their histories remain hidden in yellowed ledgers in the county clerk's office.

The Dear Myrtle column links to www.rootsweb.com, a site generally known as the Internet's oldest and largest genealogy community. For writers of historical fiction, a page of this website holds a treasure trove of first-person stories. On www.rootsweb.com/WWII, veterans and their relatives post narratives and biographies, sometimes with photographs, of memories they would like to have preserved. Despite the WWII in the web address, the site is open to veterans of any war, including Vietnam and the Persian Gulf.

At the site, Gaylord Merlin Yoder recounted that during the Battle of the Bulge, his squadron missed their target and dropped their payload in a patch of woods. Their mistake proved to be a winner, as they hit a German Panzer division parked there at the time.

Lewis Chinn's memory of life in a German prison camp during World War II opens a Pandora's box of questions appropriate for a Holocaust Remembrance Day discussion. He recalls the apparent theft of Red Cross parcels, one of which fed two men. He also remembers wondering if the prisoners would be gassed, "like the stories we heard about the Jews."

Keeping It Real

Since many of these men and women are still alive, their tales would not have to be fictionalized. Nonfiction writers could follow up with interviews to document history from eyewitnesses.

You will find that it is not hard to get genealogical researchers to talk. As an experiment for this article, I signed on to AOL's Family Treehouse chat. In a little under 30 minutes, I learned the following:

No one in the Family Treehouse chat thinks genealogy is dry and boring. Bob read his mother's journal and found out all the family secrets. Marie discovered that her great-uncle had been married three times. The family never knew that until she did the research and found the divorce decrees. B's great-grandparents were married December 1912 and her grandfather was born January 1913. Unnamed's mother had two children by his father before she found out he had never divorced his first wife. Queen found out that her husband's family founded Silver City, North Carolina, while her maternal grandmother's family was related to the Younger Gang. Queen added that one of her great-granduncles was a hobo that missed the train but the train didn't miss him.

These anecdotes that had chat room participants ROFL and <g>'ing from ear to ear were mixed in with serious talk about locations of documents, a Hardman who was born in Manchester and moved to Pennsylvania, and a Henry known to be a Methodist.

Jim Avery, a chat room regular, told me about a journal he found at an auction. A man named George Colby, from around Henniker, New Hampshire, kept a diary from 1900 through 1946. He recorded his trips to California, Oregon, and Alberta, where he worked as a carpenter and harvested hay. He also documented daily life, weather, deaths, and his sisters' families, along with a little local history. Jim intends to transcribe the journals and write a book based on Colby's life. He notes, "I know him (Colby) better than I know my own family"—the power of journaling and genealogy combined.

Yet often, knowledge of our own family bequeaths us stories so rare, so unbelievable, we almost need no other inspiration. My great-great-grandmother, the mayor's daughter, had two children out of wedlock (the first was stillborn) and married the father two months after her son was born. My great-grandmother on the other side of the family was sold to a wealthy, childless family, abused as an indentured servant. She married at 13, ran away with an alcoholic husband, bore nine children, and divorced in the 1940s.

The power of our family stories! Our synagogue hosted a "Lunch & Learn" on one small corner of genealogical research: Family Names. We have had more meaningful discussions in the past: abortion, family topics, the ethics of genetics. But more people showed up to ask questions about where they had come from than for any other topic. In some sense, our names defines who we are.

If we tell these stories, our own, and those we borrow from other people, we are creating a fiction based on a reality we know. Without fail, this is a reality that invites young and old to listen, to participate, to hear with the heart. It can be found within the confines of those born/died entries commonly known as genealogy.

Genealogy Resources

Books
- Ahmed, Salahuddin. *A Dictionary of Muslim Names.* New York: New York University Press, 1999.
- Eichholz, Alice. *Ancestry's Red Book: American State, County, and Town Sources.* Salt Lake City: Ancestry, Inc., 1992.
- *The Handybook for Genealogists.* Everton Publishers, ninth edition published in September 1999.
- Hansen, Kevan M. *Finding Your German Ancestors.* Salt Lake City: Ancestry, Inc., 1999.
- Helm, Matthew and April. *Genealogy Online for Dummies.* IDG Books, 1999.
- Herber, Mark D. Ancestral Trails: *The Complete Guide to British Genealogy and Family History.* Genealogical Publication Company.
- Horowitz, Lois. *Dozens of Cousins: Blue Genes, Horse Thieves, and Other Relative Surprises in Your Family Tree.* Berkeley, CA: Ten Speed Press, 1999.
- Laughlin, Michael C. *The Book of Irish Families: Great and Small.* Laughlin Press, 1998.
- McClure, Tony Mack. *Cherokee Proud.* Somerville, TN: Chu-Nan-Nee Books, 1998.
- Nelson, Lynn. *A Genealogist's Guide to Discovering Your Italian Roots.* Cincinnati, OH: Betterway Publications, 1997.
- Weiner, Miriam. *Jewish Roots in Ukraine and Moldova.* New York: YIVO Institute, 1999.
- Woodtor, Dee Parmer. *Finding a Place Called Home: A Guide to African-American Genealogy and Historical Identity.* New York: Random House, 1999.

Associations
- **African-American Genealogical Society of Northern California:** www.aagsnc.org, P. O. Box 27485, Oakland, CA 94602
- **Czechoslovak Genealogy Society International:** www.cgsi.org P. O. Box 16225, St. Paul, Minnesota 55116. E-Mail: CGSI@aol.com
- **Family History Centers:**
These are the indispensable research tools and they are part of every Latter-day Saints (LDS) church. To schedule an appointment to look up records on microfilm or microfiche, look under "Churches—LDS (Mormon)" in your local *Yellow Pages.* There is rarely a fee for reading, only fees for making copies. Staff is on hand to assist you with record searches.
- **Federation of Eastern European Family History Societies:** www.feefhs.org P. O. Box 510898, Salt Lake City, Utah 84151
- **Hispanic Genealogy Center:** www.hispanicgenealogy.com Murray Hill Station, P. O. Box 818, New York, NY 10156-0602

Genealogy Resources

- **International Association of Jewish Genealogical Societies:** www.jewishgen.org/ajgs, 4430 Mt. Paran Parkway NW, Atlanta, GA 30327-3747. E-Mail: HoMargol@aol.com
- **The Irish Ancestral Research Association (TIARA):** www.tiara.ie Dept. W, P. O. Box 619, Sudbury, MA 01776
- **National Genealogical Society:** www.ngsgenealogy.org 4527 17th Street N., Arlington, VA 22207
- **Palatines to America:** http://palam.org All German Ancestry. Call 614-236-8371 for chapter nearest you
- **Polish Genealogical Society of America:** www.pgsa.org 984 North Milwaukee Avenue, Chicago, IL 60622 E-Mail: PGSAmerica@aol.com
- **Scottish Genealogical Society:** www.sol.co.uk/s/scotgensoc Go to site, then e-mail for US locations (not stated on site)
- **Historical Societies:** If all else fails, look for the nearest historical society in your area. Without fail, these include genealogical discussion and research groups.

Websites

- **Ancestry.com:** www.ancestry.com
This site also doubles as America Online's (and Compuserve's) geneaology resource (Keyword:Genealogy). Users should be aware that the site leads the trend in charging for information, unheard of 10 years ago. Recommend using as last resort despite wealth of information.
- **Cyndi's List:** www.cyndislist.com
Over 73,000 links to useful (and trivial) genealogical websites.
- **DearMyrtle:** www.DearMyrtle.com
One of my favorites. This woman can tell stories, plus her site is well-organized and useful.
- **The Genealogy Home Page:** www.genhomepage.com
Sponsored by Family Tree Maker Online.
- **Genealogy.com:** www.genealogy.com
More information, formerly associated with Family Tree Maker.
- **International Blacksheep Society of Genealogists:** blacksheep.amity.org
There's a catch: To hear these stories, you have to produce a verifiable black sheep (social or criminal) in your own family. That's not all that hard.
- **It's All Relative:** www.iarelative.com
Slovak, Czech, and Eastern European Genealogy. Fun, fun site. Includes items such as Eastern European wedding traditions.
- **Jewish Genealogy:** www.jewishgen.org
Resources and links to good research areas.

Genealogy Resources

■ **National Archives:** www.nara.gov/genealogy
A government site with many free or nearly free research tools.
■ **The National Huguenot Society:** www.huguenot.netnation.com
An example of the fact that not all genealogy is strictly ethnic or national. This is a genealogy site linked to a specific religious group.
■ **RootsWeb.com:** www.rootsweb.com
Extraordinarily useful site, and they try to keep everything free of charge.
■ **Our Spanish Heritage:** www.geocities.com/heartland/ranch/5442
A small site, useful because it focuses on Spanish settlement in Texas and Mexico. Combines history with genealogy.
■ **UK & Ireland Genealogy:** www.genuki.org.uk
Helpful if you want to know anything about British history and people.
■ **Yahoo:** If all of the above isn't enough, go to www.yahoo.com. Follow the trail: Arts > Humanities > History > Genealogy and spend a couple of hours, or days, online! Then write stories.

Researching Place
Location, Location, Location

By Suzanne Lieurance

Sure, location is the most important factor for realtors and homeowners. It's also a major concern for writers, yet most don't have the luxury of working *on location*. Instead, they do the majority of their work at home, using a variety of research techniques to make specific locales come alive for their audiences. Here's how to uncover those special details that let readers *know* you've been to the places you're writing about—even if you haven't!

Travel Electronically

Lisa Harkrader lives in a small town in Kansas. A couple of months ago, she was writing a novel set in the Australian outback and needed to find out how to throw a nonreturning boomerang. She couldn't just take off for Down Under. Instead, Harkrader traveled the Internet. She located a website for a company in Australia that sells the boomerangs.

"I e-mailed the company, explaining who I was and what I was doing, and asked if they knew where I could find the information I needed," says Harkrader. "They e-mailed back with very detailed instructions on how to throw a nonreturning boomerang. These are the kinds of details that are hard to uncover when you can't actually visit a place, so you have to be creative and relentless in tracking them down."

Julia Beiker also lives in Kansas. When she was writing a story that takes place in Italy, she journeyed through the Internet, too. She joined an Italian genealogy group online to get a feel for how to enhance her story. Beiker says, "An Italian professor gave me expressions that would have been used by a boy during the time period of my story." (See "Researching People, The Power of Our Family Stories," and an accompanying list of online genealogy sources, page 201.)

Now here's a switch. Kristin Nitz lives in Italy and her current novel is set in Tuscany. "I used Yahoo (a search engine) to look at rentals in the Italian countryside," Nitz says. "The house and grounds I created for my setting are a composite of several of those villas."

Kim Williams-Justesen writes travel guides and usually does visit most of the places she includes in her guides. Yet she also goes online for some of her research. "I look at the government sites because it's amazing what you can find there, especially for state and national parks and historic sites," says Williams-Justesen. "I visit travel sites that might have reviews of places that I'm going to review—but I do this after I've visited a particular site, so their review doesn't color my own perception."

When Jane Buchanan, who writes historical fiction for kids, was working on a picture book set in 1910 Dorchester, Massachusetts, about a Polish family's first Thanksgiving celebration, she found, "The hardest part of that story was finding confirmation that factories in the Boston area would have been operating on Thanksgiving day in 1910. For that I used the Internet. I found articles on the library's magazine article index and tracked down their authors on the Web. I also came across a labor history listserv and people there were most helpful."

Study Maps

For writer Nancy Ferrell, the first step in researching location is to "obtain a map, as detailed as I can get, for the city and country I'm writing about. A map lets the writer know how far it is from point A to point B—important information that's often needed to make the action in a story credible."

Wendie Old, a children's librarian for more than 30 years who also writes fiction and nonfiction, agrees. "It helps to have a map. That way you're consistent as you move your characters from place to place."

Maps can be obtained from your local library, but the Internet is also a good place to find all kinds, everything from highway to weather maps.

When you're writing a historical book and "not on the scene," says, Suzanne Hilton, author of more than 20 books, "one aid is a topographical map that shows just the mountains, streams, and such—no highways, etc." She recommends the Library of Congress for "extremely early maps." Contact the Library of Congress about travel brochures, flyers, and pamphlets.

The picture books of Verla Kay take place in a variety of locations. Kay has written about the California Gold Rush, the railroad, covered wagons, and many other elements of U.S. history. "I've written successfully about places I've never been," says Kay, "but it's much easier when I've been there in person." She obtains brochures, flyers, and pamphlets from chambers of commerce, travel agencies, and the local visitors' bureaus for the locations she writes about, as a starting point for her research.

Williams-Justesen also sends away for materials. In one of her children's stories, a young girl goes to Ontario in search of a long lost uncle. To find out about Ontario, she says, "I sent away for brochures and maps and got a lot of really good stuff for free."

In the Neighborhood

With so many reference materials available online today, writers can sometimes forget about the resources at libraries. Besides local public libraries, college and university libraries offer a wealth of materials. Many have extensive archives of national magazines that include articles about locations all over the world. These magazines, old and new, often contain detailed photographs that can be immeasurably helpful for writers who need to see what a city or town looked like years ago or how it appears today.

"I can't emphasize enough the value of a good reference librarian," says Buchanan. "It's amazing, the things librarians can find that the average person simply wouldn't know existed. Never be afraid to ask for help. The librarian who is good won't give up until a source to answer your questions is found. It's amazing what you can find in a library if you know, or have help finding out, where to look!"

Other sources at your fingertips are the videos you can find at your library and video store. They have countless documentary videos that can provide writers with facts and tidbits about areas all over the world. Harkrader found additional information for her novel set in Australia this way. "To learn what aboriginal music sounded like," she says, "and to get a sense of the speech rhythms of aboriginal children from the Northern Territories, I found a nonfiction video in the library."

Most larger cities have their own magazines that can give writers a glimpse of what goes on there. San Diego, Santa Fe, Kansas City, Boston, New York, Atlanta, and many, many other cities publish magazines that contain a variety of articles about local spots writers can include in their fiction, or use as background information for their nonfiction. Many of these magazines have websites where writers can find articles from current and back issues. Other publications, like *Southern Living*, *Midwest Living*, and *Sunset Magazine* offer articles and advertisements about broader sections of the United States. (See "Regional Markets, In Your Own Backyard," pages 65.)

Large bookstore chains like Borders

Places, Please
A Few Great Resources for Researching Location

Maps
■ **The Weather Channel:** www.weather.com
For weather maps of all areas of the United States.
■ **GIS Data Depot:** www.gisdatadepot.com
For free topographical maps of many areas in the country.
■ **Library of Congress:** http://catalog.loc.gov
101 Independence Ave. S.E., Washington, D.C. 20540 (202) 707-5000.
A database of approximately 12 million records representing books, serials, computer files, manuscripts, cartographic materials, music, sound recordings, and visual materials in the Library's collections.
■ **Savewealth.com:** www.savewealth.com/links/travel/maps/index.html
For city maps and travel maps for regions all over the United States.

Magazines
■ *National Geographic:* http://www.nationalgeographic.com
Available by subscription, but you can see articles from past and current issues at the website.
■ *Trips Magazine:* www.tripsmag.com
Available at Borders Books, Barnes & Noble Booksellers, and Tower Records, as well as by subscription. Check out the website to see sample articles.
■ *British Heritage:* www.thehistorynet.com/BritishHeritage
The magazine of history, culture, travel, and adventure for those who love England, Scotland, Ireland, and Wales. British Heritage explores Britain's natural beauty, historic sites, famous and everyday people. See sample articles at the website.
■ *Historic Traveler:* www.thehistorynet.com/HistoricTraveler
6405 Flank Drive, Harrisburg, PA 17112.
The Guide to Great Historic Destinations. Each issue is packed with features and guides to historic places, hotels and inns, reenactments, tours, side trips and more. Complete with beautiful photography and maps.

Government Sites
■ **Govspot.com:** www.govspot.com/categories/statehomepages.htm
To locate state home pages, type in the name of the state you want to research.

Places, Please
A Few Great Resources for Researching Location

Online City Guides
- **LookSmart:** www.looksmart.com
Searchable data of information about cities in the United States.
- **ClickCity:** http://clickcity.com/clickcity_cfmfiles/newsite/header.cfm
Searchable database with information about cities and states throughout the United States.

Museums
- **The Franklin Institute Science Museum:** http://sln.fi.edu/
222 North 20th Street, Philadelphia, Pennsylvania 19103.
- **Smithsonian Museum:** www.si.edu/
For information about the museum write: Smithsonian Information, SI Building, Room 153, Washington, DC 20560-0010.

General Books
- **Encyclopedia Smithsonian** www.si.edu/resource/faq/start.htm
This online encyclopedia features answers to frequently asked questions about the Smithsonian and links to Smithsonian resources from A to Z.
- *Fodor's* **Travel Guides** www.crazydogtravel.com/fodor.html
Fodor publishes travel guides for cities and countries all over the world. You can find these guides at local bookstores or at online booksellers.
- **Lonely Planet Travel Guides and Phrase Books:** www.lonelyplanet.com
Guides to cities and countries (and various languages) all over the world. These guidebooks are available at Amazon.com or at the Lonely Planet website.
- **The Handy History Answer Book:** by Rebecca Nelson Ferguson. Available at local bookstores.

Books on Specific Times and Places
- *The Writer's Guide to Everyday Life in the 1800s,* by Marc McCutcheon
- *Everyday Life During the Civil War,* by Michael J. Varhola
- *The Writer's Guide to Everyday Life in the Wild West (from 1840-1900),* by Candy Moulton
- *The Writer's Guide to Everyday Life in Regency and Victorian England (from 1811-1901),* by Kristine Hughes
- *The Writer's Guide to Everyday Life in Renaissance England (1485-1649),* by Kathy Lynn Emerson
- *The Writer's Guide to Everyday Life in Colonial America (from 1607-1783),* by Dale Taylor

Places, Please

- *The Writer's Guide to Everyday Life from Prohibition Through World War II,* by Marc McCutcheon
- *Everyday Life in the Middle Ages (The British Isles from 500 to 1500),* by Sherrilyn Kenyon

One More Great Source
GORP (Great Outdoor Recreation Pages): http://www.gorp.com/gorp/location/us/us.htm
Information about every state, as well as national parks and other travel destinations.

and Barnes & Noble carry European magazines that cover topics like fashion, home furnishing, and architecture. These are sometimes helpful for getting a feel for a country the writer hasn't visited.

Travel to the Past

Writers can't actually travel back in time to see what a location was like long ago. Or can they? Never underestimate the power of museums.

When Hilton was researching her book *The Way It Was—1876,* she found a way to see how the World's Fair in Philadelphia would have looked that year. "At the Franklin Institute, there was a perfect scale model of the entire World's Fair of 1876. By scrunching down and looking through the gate, I could see the layout as a person entering the fair would," Hilton explains.

"Museums, libraries, and archives are treasure houses of old newspapers, diaries, and photos," says Jeri Chase Ferris, who writes biographies and historical fiction. "I'd say every one of these was an absolute necessity when researching the locations where my subjects have lived." (See "Reference Sites, Museums Online," page 229.)

Sometimes sources are closer to home, no matter how geographically distant. Elaine Marie Alphin needed background information about El Salvador when she was writing her award-winning book, *A Bear for Miguel.* "My family on my father's side is from El Salvador," says Alphin. "While the war was going on, my grandmother wrote me letters telling me how hard it was on the family, on my cousins. So I was drawing in part from their experiences."

Even if you don't have family letters about a faraway place, when writing about a specific place in an earlier time in history, many writers find it helpful to use diaries from that period. Many historical societies have a variety of diaries, according to date. Hilton suggests, "The University of Georgia put out a book called *American Diaries in Manuscript, 1580-1954, A Descriptive Bibliography.* It's an index to diaries *not* published, their dates, and where in the United States they can be found. I'm not sure you can still buy one, but it's a real find."

When Debra McArthur was researching her book about the Dust Bowl, she took an unusual approach for obtaining primary sources. McArthur is a college instructor in the Midwest, so she figured there were people around who had firsthand memories of the Dust Bowl, or knew someone else who did. To find them, McArthur created a flyer describing her project and asking for help. She placed the flyer in the college library and other high traffic areas throughout the campus when the college was having its alumini weekend.

Marty Crisp, author of 11 books, is another writer who likes to visit the location if at all possible. "In the case of my current project, set in England in 1599, I can't of course find 1599, but in England, I came pretty close!" she says. "I went to old manor houses and palaces searching for the perfect setting, and when I found it, it was practically a ruin. It was a manor house built in the 1580s and stripped down to its walls, but it was so much easier to furnish with my imagination than to strip out all the 1700s, 1800s, and 1900s things in other old houses that were in better repair."

Capture the Essence

Old has been lucky enough to live within driving distance of most of the locations where her subjects have lived and worked. "I visit, take pictures, talk to people there, take the tours and listen to the patter of the guides. Just the way things are said can be different, special, catchy," she says.

"Although it's not possible sometimes to visit the sites I write about, I certainly try," says Ferrell, who lives in Alaska. "There's nothing like actually being there and, once there, having some exciting hands-on experiences that help me transfer that excitement to my readers." When Ferrell wrote *The U.S. Coast Guard*, she arranged through the rear admiral to fly in a search-and-rescue helicopter in Sitka, Alaska, where she could take photographs from the aircraft.

Even popular fiction series like Sweet Valley or Baby-sitter's Club are set in definite locations. Writers have to know what the neighborhood is like where these characters live, what the town looks like, and so on—they have to create fictional towns that have the feel of real towns.

Sarah Verney has written for several series. "There's usually a series *bible* that describes the characters' personalities, physical descriptions, and even their houses and the town they live in," says Verney. For the Silver Blades and Sweet Valley stories she wrote, Verney found that the town descriptions included locations like "favorite stores, the pizza parlor, ice cream shop, the ice rink, the school, of course, and any place else the characters might hang out."

For her book *Gratefully Yours*, about a girl who rode an orphan train from New York to Nebraska in 1923, Buchanan thoroughly researched Nebraska, but as the deadline for completing the manuscript neared, she began to feel uneasy. "It would be immediately apparent to anyone who lived in Nebraska that I was a fraud, I was sure. I panicked," she says.

She told her husband she had to go to Nebraska. He politely pointed out why she couldn't go right then, so the

Reference & Research

book was published without Buchanan ever setting foot in Nebraska. A week after the book came out, an older woman told Buchanan that she had grown up on a farm in Nebraska. "I don't know how you did it," said the woman, "but you have captured it. This is where I grew up."

"I was thrilled, of course, and flattered, and also relieved," says Buchanan. "It was important to me to make the story believable, and also as accurate as possible."

There are all sorts of ways to research location. It doesn't really matter how you conduct your research—just so you convey the reality of place. As Hilton says, "I'm an avid researcher because some 10-year-old kid can tell if I'm guessing, and I don't want that to happen."

Researching Cultures

A Kaleidoscopic Voyage Around the World

By Carolyn P. Yoder

Today the field of world cultures, past and present, thrives in children's literature. More books are being written and the variety is great—from folktales and myths to contemporary fiction and nonfiction. The number of magazines devoted to the world and its peoples, or more general interest magazines that offer articles on the field, is growing. The quality of multicultural children's literature has also improved with age. Authors concerned with offering multidimensional portraits appreciate how people are similar but at the same time different—authors who live within and without the cultures they write about.

Beyond Funny Folklore

The pluses of multicultural literature far outweigh the minuses for many writers today. For Jane Yolen, author of more than 200 books of poetry and prose for children and adults, multicultural literature is "out of the funny folklore stage and the odd holiday stage and into real stuff."

Robert San Souci, who has brought to life peoples from California to the Caribbean to Japan, offers that "multicultural children's literature has blossomed in the past years, and generally, for the better. I think we've seen movement from the idea of those 'quaint' folks who live so 'colorfully' patronization, to genuine and worthy attempts to share insights into the richness of world cultures—while providing a way to bring diverse peoples together. Other cultures are no longer seen as just interesting backgrounds. They are viewed in multidimensional terms in the very best picture books and other works."

Barbara Elleman, the Distinguished Scholar of Children's Literature at Marquette University, feels that "more specifics or details are used in the writing, rather than generalities. Writers, therefore, are more cognizant of the differences and the similarities between cultures today."

For Harold Underdown, Editorial Director of Charlesbridge Publishing, writers are now able to be more specific because "there is far more writing done within 'minority' or foreign culture, or with real experience of them, than there was, say, 40 years ago."

But besides being more sensitive and insightful, today's literature has a special bonus by being more kid-friendly. Veteran writers and editors Judith Enderle and Stephanie Gordon, who have written their first multicultural title, *Something's Happening on Calabash Street,* suggest that "more children can now see themselves in books and magazines." Perhaps this is because children are being exposed to more of the world today.

Elsa Marston, who specializes in writing about peoples of the Middle East and Third World, finds that publishers are more open and more inclined than in the 1980s to cover lesser-known areas of the world. According to Florence Temko, who has authored more than 40 books on paper arts and folk crafts, this also pertains to the United States and its many cultural groups.

Writers and editors who worry that multicultural literature has so many good things going for it that it may become a hard market to break into, should be assured that many areas still need attention and fresh voices. Just stay away from the subgenres and categories that have been overdone.

Alexis O'Neill, who has written about her Irish heritage for *Cricket* and *Cobblestone,* stresses that "editors seem to have had their fill of folktales and myths. I suppose there was a glut of retellings." For Yolen, the following unintended pun offered by an agent sums up the problem: "Folktales are getting old fast." But O'Neill adds, "The pendulum will swing and they'll be in vogue again. It's just hard to say when! I think that editors might be sensitive to portraying a culture only in terms of its folktales or myths. They may be looking for contemporary stories that illuminate the culture today."

Carole Fiore, Library Program Specialist for the state library of Florida, thinks "the use of legends and myths to introduce a culture is wonderful," but also recognizes that "what is needed is factual material about the history of people and accurate information about how people live."

Even though there are more books that cover third-world cultures than ever before, Marston still finds that "really good ones are rare. It often seems to me that publishers regard fairy, traditional, and Arabian Nights-y tales as safer than books that would give a fair view of contemporary life." She adds that "books about so-called *nonpopular* cultures must be a little better than perfect, whereas very lightweight books can be published on *popular* cultures."

Sylvia Whitman, who specializes in history titles, agrees and points out that the Arab/Muslim world is still often misrepresented in ways that range from "oversimplification to outright vilification."

The reason for this lack of quality and quantity is most likely tied to economics, says Aaron Shepard, who writes folktales from around the world. "Publishers can generally sell folktales only from cultures represented in the curriculum. Many fascinating stories from less popular cultures cannot be profitably published. *Multicultural* is really a misnomer, since it generally refers to only a small selection of cultures of interest to American educators." Shepard says that in too many of these *popular* folktales, "the text is a mere backdrop to the pictures."

Elleman agrees that this "overabundance of folktales tends to dilute the quality." A weakness of today's folktales, she says, is that they "are more adult in tone than childlike. Children of color lack contemporary, everyday stories where they can find themselves."

San Souci adds, " I don't think there is an overabundance of *good* folktales or myths. In more recent years, there has been a much needed shakeout of inferior retellings—books that don't bother to get the tone, historical details, cultural niceties, etc., right because the author hasn't done any homework." But San Souci says some progress has been made. "The age of mix-and-match cultural elements that distorted presentations of such societies as Native American or African or Asian has pretty much fallen by the wayside. There are still bad books being published, but they are bad because of shallowness or poor storytelling, not the gross distortion that happened in years past."

Deborah Nourse Lattimore, who writes about ancient Near Eastern, pre-Columbian, and classical themes, offers advice for writers and editors who want to look beyond the standard folktale and obvious approach: "Change point of view, time, characters; find vacant quarters and work within."

How the Seeds Were Planted

Most writers who create stories from around the world have a love of traveling, a colorful past, a strong sense of place, or a lively curiosity, but they may also or simply have an appreciation of a good story.

San Souci has had a lifelong interest in the ways people live and think around the world. "Even as a child I was intrigued with the idea of traveling—at least in my imagination—all over the world and beyond it, into the realms of fantasy and science fiction. When I was introduced to world literature at an early age, I was able to understand and to connect in my mind with people from many different regions. It was a passport of sorts. Something of that sense of discovery, of commonality, of deep links is what I try to share in my retellings. Also important is the exploration of my own roots. In understanding who my forebears were, I have the feeling that I can understand more about who I am."

Lattimore's path started with her forebears as well. "I' ve been fascinated with world cultures and ancient peoples since I was a little girl growing up in an eclectically appointed house, filled with books and artifacts from trips my great-grandmother took well before I was born."

Reference & Research

O'Neill also finds her inspiration close to home. "One day I had been reading a very poor retelling of an Irish folktale and found myself getting angry at this writer for not understanding the rhythm and flow of the Irish voice. As corny as it sounds, I actually said 'Who am I?' The answer was that I was a Boston-born Irish American. I find it exciting to delve into my heritage and put voices on paper."

The fascination with peoples of the world is a combination of academic research and personal interest for Rosalie and Charles Baker, Editors of *Calliope* and *Footsteps*. "The evolvement and development of cultures and civilizations have always intrigued us, as have the similarities in beliefs and customs through the centuries. Studying the past and how various peoples handled their personal as well as their public lives is not only fascinating, but also remains key to understanding history itself."

The ways of people are often observed firsthand. Temko has visited 31 different countries where she has met with local artisans whenever possible. "They were usually very generous in letting me observe or participate in their work. I not only learned about their crafts, but had close contact with local people that helped me to understand their way of life."

Marston's ties to the Middle East and North Africa are personal. "My husband is from Lebanon, and I have lived and traveled in the Middle East on many occasions."

For some writers, travel time is short. Enderle and Gordon placed the story of *Something's Happening on Calabash Street* in their own backyard—Los Angeles—which has a diverse population. "We wanted to show how people of differing backgrounds can come together to celebrate and share part of their uniqueness."

Many writers are simply in love with a good story, whatever the culture that is its source or setting. Whitman says that "stories make life worth living. They give people a sense of where they belong in the sweep of time. They make sense of a chaotic world. I feel lucky that I'm able to develop some of my musings and share them."

For other authors the spark that sets the creative muscle in motion is curiosity. Shepard says that all it takes is "to be curious about the ways other cultures can be different from mine. The more different they are, the more curious I am."

Inside or Out

There has been much discussion about a writer's background and how it affects sensitivity, tone, and accuracy in multicultural writing. For most of the authors, editors, academics interviewed here, solid literature about the world should be based on quality and care and not on personal background.

Fiore suggests that, foremost, a good writer needs to be a keen and unbiased observer and reporter. Underdown adds that good writers must also have a "day-to-day intimacy" with the people they are writing about—"more experience of a culture than one would get from the typical tourist experiences. On one's experience with another culture, whether in this country or abroad, a person is struck by what is different, by the *exotic*. It takes longer to see the commonalties underneath the different customs."

Enderle and Gordon agree and stress that the connection to another culture must first be emotional. "If writers find a common thread and do research, it seems that outsiders should be able to portray other cultures. Just because you have never tasted golubtsi sauce shouldn't keep you from trying it and learning it's delicious."

O'Neill admits that even though "books written from the inside out by people from specific cultures tend to be truer to their cultural roots and the voices more authentic, there is a danger. Some editors place the cultural identity of the author above the work itself." The outsider, for O'Neill, "can bring to life what is taken for granted by a person on the inside. Outsiders can bring fresh eyes to the everyday and make links that are far reaching. They can see the universal in the specific."

Shepard also believes there is room for the insider and outsider. "Each brings a different perspective and insight. There is always something an outsider cannot know, but likewise, there is always something an insider fails to recognize."

Although Lattimore's advice seems to be directed to the outsider, the insider can also benefit: "Get to know the other culture very, very well. Talk to people, specialists, members of that society, academics, about customs, habits, language, etc. Respect them every step of the way, as you'd like someone to respect someone you cared about."

Whitman adds, "good writers approach both the familiar and foreign cultures as if they were anthropologists: They study context (history and sociology), establish the reliability of their informants, and observe, observe, observe before they venture a conclusion. They also try not to generalize too far beyond the small group under scrutiny."

The journey of the outsider is not easy. San Souci cautions the person writing about a culture not their own not to make assumptions about what is going on. "This is why extreme care must be taken to avoid even those small errors that can invalidate the story's verisimilitude, and if the story involves an attempt to present another culture, that can actually do a disservice in presenting a false image of a time, a place, a people."

Firsthand

To tell a fair and well-rounded story, a writer about cultures spends hours and hours on research, research that goes far beyond paper products—books, magazines, newspapers, journals. Movies, audiocassettes, genealogy, travel, interviews, living in an adopted home are just a few examples of other areas of research. Unlike a few years ago when online research was questioned, today most authors are realizing its value.

Shepard wishes he could visit every country he writes about, but that's far from possible, so nearly all his research is from home. "I use the encyclopedia, travel guides, old travelogues, and more and more the Internet. On the Web, in newsgroups, and on e-mail lists, you can often find members of the target culture who offer materials or can answer questions." San Souci follows a similar course of action, "Library research is always the heart of my retellings. I also consult journals, travel books, audiocassettes, videotapes, etc.—anything that will help me get a strong sense of people, place, historical setting. Since I'm a latecomer to the Internet, I've only begun to use it selectively to answer specific questions."

Temko tends to visit most of the places she writes about. "I rely on my own experiences of having observed them and researched them. Online research is extremely useful, but I like to supplement it by talking to people from that culture about a special point I am addressing."

O'Neill concurs that firsthand research is essential. "I use secondary sources and online research to fill in the gaps or help with the background, but there is no substitute for standing on the land, tasting the food, and hearing the voices of the people you are writing about."

For Lattimore, who writes about cultures of the past, travel for the sake of meeting *the* people of interest is impossible. To correct that, her primary research is "based on sources written or recorded by peoples living at the time, and secondary sources. Online research is good for finding sources, but not necessarily reading and taking notes. I'm afraid I simply prefer old-fashioned methods of actually holding the book or source material or seeing it live." Whitman strongly recommends first-person accounts. "They add interesting and varied voices that often open windows on the experience of women, minorities and non-elites." (For more detailed information on researching places, see "Researching Place, Location, Location, Location," page 209.)

In Review

Most authors seek reviews of their work from experts who are either academics well-versed in the subject or people who have grown up in or lived in a given culture.

Highlights for Children Senior Editor Marileta Robinson comments on the differences between the two types of review. "If you want to know if a piece is culturally sensitive, an academic expert may not be able to tell you that. On the other hand, asking community people for their reactions has its drawbacks. They might not want to hurt your feelings."

Underdown agrees with Robinson about the limitations of the academic review. "As an editor, I have learned to be skeptical of experts. Their ideas of accuracy can be stifling and irrelevant. I am far more concerned about getting the tone right, and academics usually have no ear for that."

Many writers seek a combination of reviews. Marston "wouldn't want to publish anything sensitive without reviews by two to three people, even though sometimes they may disagree on some points."

San Souci did just that for *Two Bear Cubs: A Miwok Story from California's Yosemite Valley*. The book "involved extensive on-site research, with invaluable help from Craig Bates, Curator of Ethnography at the Yosemite Museum, which maintains a research facility devoted to the history of the area and the Miwok in particular. This writing project was overseen by Les James, head of the American Indian Council of Mariposa County, who provided key details of interpretation."

According to the Bakers, one expert often leads to another and to new information. "Experts introduce us to others in the field who write for us, share their knowledge, and provide insights that we might have missed." Lattimore agrees. "I confer with experts at universities and libraries, as well as with members of that culture about which I am writing. Academics tend to be remote, removed from children's literature, but they can tell me huge amounts about sociology, which matters a great deal to me, as well as bibliography, archaeological data, and firsthand dealings with that culture, even the modern contacts."

Sounds Right

For authors, the hardest part of the writing process is stopping the research, gathering the notes, and organizing them into flowing and sensitive words. When the writing process finally begins, the author must keep in mind *tone*, perhaps the most important element in writing about people.

Yolen refers to tone as *voice*: "Getting the voice right sets everything else up." For Lattimore, the right tone "goes back to sociology and anthropological considerations. The people about whom you write should sound the way they did, at the time they lived." The wrong tone, on the other hand, "can

> **Leading Children's Magazines on World Cultures**
>
> ■ *AppleSeeds, Calliope, Cobblestone, Faces, Footsteps* (Cobblestone Publishing)
> ■ *Archaeology's dig!*
> ■ *Cricket, Spider, Muse, Click* (Carus Publishing, which purchased Cobblestone Publishing)
> ■ *Highlights for Children*
> ■ *New Moon*

spin a story into *inauthentic* at best and *dishonest* or *distortion* at worst," says San Souci.

Marston believes that it is important to keep a "careful, noncritical tone, while at the same time making some judgments." O'Neill reminds authors that "our writing will always be biased. The tone will always reflect our engagement with the subject." But despite this, Marston emphasizes that an author must avoid a tone that could be called "condescending, patronizing, or scandal-mongering." Underdown reveals that "unintended but obvious condescension is a flaw I see in the writing of many people beginning to write about other cultures."

What other elements are necessary for solid writing? A universal theme; a well-developed, accessible story; strong characters; a sense of place; and passion. O'Neill says, "When I love a subject, it's bound to show up on the page." Lattimore adds, "I think and deeply believe that if one loves what one does, that feeling will drive the art form and carry it above the ordinary."

It is the emotional link to others that motivates Enderle and Gordon— "the commonalties that link all people." For Robinson, "It's important to write about the human being, not the representative of the culture. Write from your heart and don't overdo exotic details." San Souci tries to strike a "balance between overstressing the unique or different aspects of another culture, while trying to make it seem overly familiar by downplaying or eliminating exotic—sometimes difficult—elements."

Balance comes into play in other areas of the writing process. According to Shepard, "It's always necessary to strike a balance between staying true to a folktale as it came from its culture and making that tale accessible and enjoyable to kids today."

Fiore stresses that "authors must understand the children and young adults they are writing for. That means talking with and listening to children the same age as those you want to read your work."

The Bakers not only want to make the story accessible to kids, but they also want to motivate them, "to make sure that the material presents an unbiased view and enough information for the readers to form an opinion about the person, time, culture."

On the Importance of Illustration

Deborah Nourse Lattimore: "Illustration fills the eyes. It expands drama, merriment, tension, and explains things like unfamiliar objects, equipment, costumes, portraits. It also brings a younger reader, and older readers, into visual contact and shortens the space between the known and the knowable."

Barbara Elleman: "In today's visual world, illustration is highly important. Whether art or photos are used depends on the subject. Captions are also essential and should speak to the image and should point out something new from what is given in the text, or at least show a new slant."

Jane Yolen: "Illustration simply changes one way of hearing the story—for good or bad."

Judy Enderle and **Stephanie Gordon:** "We stress over and over the importance of accuracy in art and ask that our editors be sure that details are correct. Illustrators must research in the same way that writers do. We are always glad to share information when asked, but authors and illustrators rarely have the opportunity to communicate."

Aaron Shepard: "Folktale retellings in picture books live or die according to the artists assigned to them."

Rosalie and **Charles Baker:** "Illustrating text is important, but more important is the choice of illustration. It must complement and add a dimension the text is not able to provide; it must be meaningful. Contemporary illustrations are great, when possible. Illustrators must do historical research or their work can distort the readers' view by providing *false* images. The illustrations should also reflect the particular culture or person involved and not be an outsider's view."

Alexis O'Neill: "What reader doesn't check out the photos and captions before diving into the text? What's hard is when the illustrations or photos are out of the author's control. I adore editors who run them by me first. After all, I'm the *expert* on the subject. Kids deserve accuracy in illustrations as much as in the text."

Carole Fiore: "Children are especially more visually literate than many adults and can be bombarded with numerous visual images. But care must be taken. Visuals must portray and enhance the message that the text is providing. Accuracy is extremely important."

Robert San Souci: "Illustrations—whether paintings, drawings, photographs—are absolutely vital in picture books to add breadth and depth to matter that can only be sketched in the necessarily limited text of a picture book. These help make the exotic elements more concrete, especially for younger readers."

Sylvia Whitman: "Illustrations amplify the text, drawing readers in, helping them hear the author's voice."

Elsa Marston: "Illustration captions should be written or reviewed by the author—not just handed to an editor with no specialized knowledge—to make up."

Writing About People of Yesterday & Today

Elsa Marston: "When writing about the past, you don't have to worry about offending sensibilities—certainly not so much. Information is generally more accessible through library research—though one must still make judgments when references disagree. Varying views on controversial subjects can still cause the writer trouble."

Robert San Souci: "I prefer to write about cultures of the distant or more recent past, since there is a fixed quality about them (though new archaeological and anthropological discoveries are constantly altering our perceptions about older societies). As a writer, I like the idea that I can get a firmer grasp on a past culture because I can focus on a specific historic time, and consult a wide range of resources that bring to bear the studies of many disciplines on how a society existed within the specific framing years. For me, contemporary cultures are quicksilver: fluid, volatile, ever-evolving."

Alexis O'Neill: "The past is safer than the present!"

Jane Yolen: "Far enough in the past and no one challenges you!"

Judy Enderle and **Stephanie Gordon:** "Cultures from the past would require historical research as well as ethnic research."

Rosalie and **Charles Baker:** "Rather than a difference we see many similarities and it is these similarities that we hope to share with our audience so that they will more fully appreciate how a study of the past helps them understand the present and prepare for the future."

Harold Underdown: "The big difference between past and present is that no one, ultimately, can be sure that they are writing accurately about the past, no matter how much research they do. One must also try even harder not to project one's own attitudes back into the past, and into one's characters in particular, because there is no reality check. It is *not* different in that one must try to bring that culture from the past to life with the same respect and concern for detail that one would need for a culture of the present."

Deborah Nourse Lattimore: "Perhaps the biggest difference between the past and present and writing about it is that the immediacy has flown away with the years. Recapturing that immediate contact is all. And, it ain't easy, either. I like to pretend I'm an ancient person and after reading texts written in that time, I say them aloud, while going for a walk."

The Authors: Their Works on Peoples of the World

Jane Yolen: *The Emperor and the Kite; The Seventh Mandarin; Not One Damsel in Distress; Gray Heroes; Mirror/Mirror; Favorite Folktales of the World; Greyling; Milk & Honey;* and the article "Notes from a Different Caroler" (*Horn Book*).

Aaron Shepard: *Master Man: A Tall Tale of Nigeria; Lady White Snake: A Tale from Chinese Opera; Forty Fortunes: A Tale of Iran; The Crystal Heart: A Vietnamese Legend; The Sea King's Daughter: A Russian Legend; Master Maid: A Tale of Norway; The Maiden of Northland: A Hero Tale of Finland; The Baker's Dozen: A Saint Nicholas Tale; The Legend of Slappy Hooper: An American Tall Tale; Savitri: A Tale of Ancient India;* and the article, "A Dozen Answers to the Multicultural Heckler," that appears on his web page. www.aaronshep.com

Rosalie and **Charles Baker:** *Classical Companion; Myths and Legends of Mount Olympus; Classical Ingenuity; Ancient Greeks; Ancient Romans.*

Alexis O'Neill: *Loud Emily; The Recess Queen;* "Seamus Kenny's Well" and "Liam McLafferty's Choice" (*Cricket*); "Ireland" (*Faces*).

Carole Fiore: *Libraries: Your Passport to the World* (Florida Library Youth Program).

Elsa Marston: *The Cliffs of Cairo; Lebanon: New Light in an Ancient Land; The Ancient Egyptians; Women in the Middle East: Tradition and Change; Free as the Desert Wind; Muhammad of Mecca, Prophet of Islam; The Phoenicians.*

Judy Enderle and **Stephanie Gordon:** *Something's Happening on Calabash Street.*

Florence Temko: Traditional Craft Series; *Funny Money from Africa; from Mexico; from North America; from the Caribbean; from Japan; from China;* Origami Favorites series, including *One Thousand Cranes; Origami Magic; Paper Pandas and Jumping Frogs, Origami and Its Uses;* and many more.

Sylvia Whitman: *Frontier Children; Uncle Sam Wants You; 'V' Is for Victory; Hernando de Soto and the Explorers of the American South; Tunisia: Arranging for Marriage; Vaqueros: The First Cowboys.*

Robert San Soucii: *Brave Margaret: An Irish Adventure; A Weave of Words; The Faithful Friend; Cendrillon: A Caribbean Cinderella; The Talking Eggs; The Legend of Scarface: A Blackfeet Tale; Two Bear Cubs: A Miwok Story from California's Yosemite Valley; Sukey and the Mermaid; The Samurai's Daughter; The Boy and His Ghost; The Secret of the Stones; Short & Shivery: Thirty Chilling Tales.*

Deborah Nourse Lattimore: *The Flame of Peace; The Dragon's Robe; Prince and the Golden Ax; Why There Is No Arguing in Heaven; Sailor Who Captured the Sea; Arabian Nights; Lady with the Ship on Her Head; The Winged Cat; Punga, the Goddess of Ugly; Medusa.*

Reference Sites

Museums Online

By Mark Haverstock

Following in the steps of the new electronic libraries, museums are now migrating into cyberspace. Without leaving the comforts of home, you can sample virtual exhibits, documents, and photographs. Many of the sites even let you turn back the clock and see images of exhibits past.

Though the number of museum sites on the Web is increasing rapidly, note that Internet access to a majority of their holdings may still be limited. Curators are scrambling to photograph, index, and present their exhibits using the Internet as a new avenue of outreach to patrons and serious researchers.

Keeping this in mind, most current sites are best at letting you search their indexes of materials, helping you narrow down where specific items are located—saving you phone calls and unnecessary trips. In situations where you still have to visit the museum in person, you'll be better prepared to do conventional research with a shopping list in hand.

The following is a sampling of popular, high-profile websites that offer resources to assist with the research for your next book or article.

■ **The Franklin Institute Online**
Philadelphia, PA. http://sln.fi.edu/

The Franklin Institute Science Museum is an informal science learning institution. Its mission is to encourage interest in science, to promote public understanding of science, and to strengthen science education. Although primarily a site geared toward educators and classrooms, it offers a wealth of general background information on mathematics and science in a historical perspective, as well as a multitude of web links in their Educational Hotlist section. Two notable resources:

inQuiry Attic: Contains a century's worth of scientific instruments. Each month, inQuiry Attic offers an online exploration of an object that would not otherwise be available for the public to see.

The Spotlights: Each one of the Spotlights incorporates outside Web resources into a package that can be used for research into a variety of fascinating topics.

■ **American Museum of Natural History**
New York, NY. www.amnh.org

The American Museum of Natural History is the largest natural history museum in the world. Since 1871 the museum has sponsored more than 1,000 scientific expeditions worldwide, amassing a collection of 30 million specimens and artifacts. The museum's exhibitions explore anthropology, archaeology, geology, mineralogy, paleontology, and biology. Notable anthropological halls include the Hall of South American Peoples, Hall of Asian Peoples, Hall of African Peoples, Peoples of the Pacific, the Hall of Mexico and Central America, and three halls devoted to the indigenous peoples of North America.

A good starting point for finding information and contacts is the AMNH research web page, www.research.amnh.org. A site search feature will allow you to find the contents of all the publicly available Web documents at this site. Highlights include: Hall of Planet Earth Virtual Tour: Tells the most significant stories of Earth, from its early evolution to the earthquakes and storms we encounter today. Fossil Halls: Displays the single largest and most diverse array of vertebrate fossils in the world.

Library Collections: Searchable index for over 485,000 volumes, including books, journals, pamphlets, and reprints and is rich in retrospective materials, some dating to the fifteenth century. New publications and current issues of journals are added on an ongoing basis. Major topics covered in the collection are zoology, geology and mineral sciences, paleontology, history of science, anthropology, and astronomy.

■ **The Metropolitan Museum of Art**
New York, NY
www.metmuseum.org

In formation since 1870, the Metropolitan Museum's collection now contains more than two million works of art from all over the world, ancient through modern times. About 3,500 objects are reproduced at the online site as a first installment, as well as the entire Department of European Paintings—with the online equivalent of wall labels. You can view highlights from the collection by selecting a curatorial department; by taking the director's tour; or by searching the online collection for artists, periods, or styles that interest you. Items of interest include:

My Met Gallery: Allows visitors to curate a private exhibition by saving their favorite works of art in a special area of the site. To use this feature, you must register with the site by signing the guest book.

Previous/Past Exhibitions: Online samples of past and present special exhibitions in the museum are available for viewing.

■ **Berkeley Art Museum and Pacific Film Archive**
Berkeley, CA
www.bampfa.berkeley.edu

The University of California Berkeley Art Museum and Pacific Film Archive collects and makes accessible art, film, and related educational resources. Its holdings include twentieth-century American and European paintings, sculpture, drawings, prints, photographs; Asian paintings and prints; Soviet, Japanese, and American avant-garde film and video; collection and special exhibitions. Searchable resources include:

Art: The *Online Multimedia Collection*

Guides are in-depth guides comprised of object records and essays by curators and scholars including overviews and organization of collections, as well as artists biographies and historical context of their creation and collection. Currently, the museum has the entire Hans Hofmann collection, with images, and the Theresa Cha conceptual art collection, as well as an overview of the Berkeley Art Museum collection grouped in thematic areas roughly following a chronology from the art of Medieval Euroupe through contemporary art.

Film: The *PFA Filmnotes Online:* are film notes from the Pacific Film Archives exhibition calendar, documenting a wide range of types of films, including: foreign, independent, classic, and avant-garde cinema. This searchable text resource contains over 12,000 film notes written between 1979 and the present.

CineFiles: A database of reviews, press kits, festival and showcase program notes, newspaper articles, and other documents from the Pacific Film Archive Library's clippings files, the Cinefiles files contain documents from a broad range of sources covering world cinema, past and present.

■ **Buffalo Bill Historical Center**
   Cody, Wyoming
   www.bbhc.org

The Buffalo Bill Historical Center is widely regarded as America's finest Western museum, featuring a library and five internationally acclaimed museums under one roof.

Buffalo Bill Museum: Examines both the personal and public lives of Buffalo Bill and seeks to interpret his story in the context of the history and myth of the American West.

Whitney Gallery of Western Art: Presents an outstanding collection of masterworks of the American West. Original paintings, sculptures and prints trace artistic interpretations of the West from the early nineteenth century to today.

Cody Firearms Museum: Contains the world's most comprehensive collection of American arms, as well as European arms dating back to the sixteenth century.

Plains Indian Museum: Features one of the country's largest and finest collections of Plains Indian art and artifacts. This museum explores the cultural histories, artistry and living traditions of the Plains Indian people, including the Arapaho, Crow, Kiowa, Cheyenne, Comanche, Blackfeet, Gros Ventre, Sioux, Shoshone, and Pawnee.

Draper Museum of Natural History: Integrates humanities with natural sciences to better interpret the Greater Yellowstone Ecosystem and adjacent intermountain basins.

McCracken Research Library: A specialized library and archives within the Buffalo Bill Historical Center. The collections include printed and electronic library materials and resources, original archives and manuscripts, photographs, microfilm, subject vertical files, and sound and video recordings. Subject areas relate to the history and culture of the American West, with major strengths in the following: Western American art and artists; the Plains Indians; Buffalo Bill and his Wild West; American firearms history and tech-

The Smithsonian Institution: Web Giant

The Smithsonian Institution in Washington, DC—www.si.edu—boasts one of the largest physical and online sites in the world. "It's a huge website–you could sit at your computer for scores of hours and not see it all," says Smithsonian Webmaster Peter House. "Content ranges from research papers to exhibitions to catalogues with pictures of objects and their descriptions." The Web experience is much different from visiting the physical museum. Objects can be viewed in a nonlinear fashion, as opposed to a single exhibit.

Smithsonian's website links to its 16 museums, including the National Air and Space Museum and the National Museum of Natural History. Additional links are provided to their research centers, such as the Archives of American Art and Smithsonian Astrophysical Observatory. There's also a high-end broadband museum site (for high speed DSL and cable connections) called the Virtual Smithsonian offering 3-D images, sound clips, and more than 100 videos at 2k.si.edu. For those who are modem-bound, a slower connection is available.

Over the past few years, the Smithsonian has been digitizing its catalogues and appending images to these records. The On-Line Collections site is the portal through which these collections will ultimately be available. Users will be able to use the portal site to search for topics or collections across the museums, and locate and browse the Smithsonian's treasures.

As you search the Smithsonian site, begin on the home page with the section "Where do I find?" It leads to the Encyclopedia Smithsonian, an index page of frequently asked questions and topics.

Smithsonian Institution Research Information System
SIRIS is the main archival catalogue, giving brief descriptions of its holdings, including cross-references to other collections. It is divided into the following:

■ *Libraries:*
Collections contain approximately 1.2 million volumes, including over 15,000 journal titles. Smithsonian collections are particularly strong in natural history, tropical biology, African-American ethnology and culture, astrophysics, astronomy and planetary sciences, American history, the history of science and technology, aviation history and space flight, postal history, fine arts and design, African art, Asian art, horticulture, conservation science, Chesapeake Bay area ecology, and museum administration. In addition, the Libraries hold a large collection of manufacturer's trade literature and catalogs and historically important rare books and manuscripts.

The Smithsonian Institution: Web Giant

■ *Archives & Manuscripts:*
Collections contain 220,000 archival records including manuscripts photographs, sound recordings, films, etc., for the seven archival repositories at the Smithsonian.

■ *Art Inventories:*
The Inventories contain more than 335,000 records describing American paintings and sculptures. The Inventory of American Paintings Executed before 1914 is a national census of paintings created by American artists working prior to 1914. The Inventory of American Sculpture is a national census of works created by artists born or active in the United States up through the twentieth century.

■ *Juley Photographic Collection:*
The Peter A. Juley & Son Collection at the National Museum of American Art is a large photographic archive that documents the work of approximately 10,000 American artists in 127,000 images.

■ *Research/Bibliographies:*
This catalogue describes specialized research bibliographies. References currently available are limited to the Museums Studies citations, the Cephalopod bibliography, Marine Mammals, and History of the Smithsonian bibliography databases.

■ *Smithsonian Chronology:*
Smithsonian Chronology is a list of significant events in the history of the Smithsonian Institution, from the life of James Smithson in the 1700s to the present. The catalogue contains circa 2,500 entries. Each entry consists of an event title, date, abstract, references, explanatory notes, and index terms.

nology; and the natural history of the northern Rocky Mountains and Great Plains.

■ **George Eastman House International Museum of Photography & Film**
Rochester, NY
www.eastman.org

George Eastman House, an independent nonprofit museum, collects and interprets images, films, literature, and equipment in the disciplines of photography and motion pictures—and it cares for the George Eastman legacy collections—to inspire discovery and learning for a regional, national, and international audience. It is the foremost museum of photography in the world. Highlights include:

Motion Picture Collection: Contains film titles encompassing features, shorts, documentaries, newsreels, and related amateur and video productions produced between 1894 and the present. The collection also includes historic artifacts of motion picture culture posters, star portraits, correspondence, music cue sheets, lobby cards, scripts, pre-cinema materials, and other paper documents.

Photography Collection: Includes more than 400,000 photographs and negatives dating from the invention of photography to the present day. Representative samples can be found in the online gallery.

■ **Museum of Science and Industry**
Chicago, IL
www.msichicago.org

The Museum of Science and Industry is one of the most visited museums in the world. Chicago businessman Julius Rosenwald created MSI, America's first center for "industrial enlightenment," as a vehicle for public science education. It was the first museum in North America to develop the idea of hands-on, interactive exhibits and the first museum to have participation of industry in its exhibits. The museum has 800 exhibits and more than 2,000 interactive units located in 350,000 square feet of exhibit space. Online highlights include:

Virtual Exhibits: Include "All Aboard the Silver Streak," "The U-505 Submarine," "International Space Station," and others.

Photo Archives: Sample photos from MSI's photograph collection include thousands of archival images of museum exhibits from the past, as well as photographs relating to the U-505 submarine, the Pioneer Zephyr train, the Chicago World's Fairs, and much more.

■ **Canadian Heritage Information Network (CHIN)**
www.chin.gc.ca

This is not a single site, but a gateway to museums, galleries, and heritage information in Canada and around the world. You can explore the collections in Canada's museums by browsing through samples of CHIN's comprehensive inventory of Canadian museum collections or spend time in the special thematic online exhibitions developed by Canadian museums working together and with museums around the world.

CHIN is a Special Operating Agency within the federal Department of Canadian Heritage. This electronic

Other Starting Points

The museums listed in this article are just a sampling of what you can find on the Internet. The following are links to hundreds of additional museum sites available. Check these to find specialized museums and historical societies.

- **Artcom Museum Tour:** artcom.com/museums
- **Art, Film, & Cultural Heritage Information Online:** www.bampfa.berkeley.edu/onlineres/artsonline.html
- **Art Museum Network:** www.amn.org
- **Bastrop ISD Libraries and Museums Links:** www.bastrop.isd.tenet.edu/museums.html
- **Florida Association of Museums:** www.flamuseums.org
- **Maine Archives and Museums:** www.mainemuseums.org
- **Museums Around the World:** emuseum.mankato.msus.edu/archaeology/museums/index.shtml
- **Museum Land:** www.museumland.com
- **Museum Network:** www.musee-online.org
- **Online Museums:** www.ops.org/benson/Online_museums.htm
- **Virtual Museum Links:** USA www.icom.org/vlmp/usa.html
- **World:** www.icom.org/vlmp/world.html

gateway to Canada's rich cultural and natural heritage offers services of interest to national and international online visitors, to museums, libraries, schools, colleges, and universities. Note that some parts of the site are restricted to registered users, but a free trial is available. Highlights include:

Virtual Exhibitions: Brings fascinating subjects in the sciences and humanities to life by combining text, pictures, video & sounds. These exhibitions can be used as resources for a multitude of subjects, such as history (Meiji: Tradition in Transition), art (Gestures and Words), and environmental studies (Endangered Species in Endangered Spaces).

Artefacts: Provides access to information on millions of museum objects, natural history specimens, and archaeological sites.

Sources

References: In Print & Online

By Mark Haverstock

This comprehensive catalogue of references covers print and Internet versions of works writers can use to begin and to extend their research. Several of the online sites offer free services; others are fee-based or may be available to patrons at public or university libraries.

Note that websites and links are subject to change. If a website or link is unavailable, try using a major search engine to search for the site.

General References

Here you can begin your search for books or periodicals on any topic. You can also check to see if an idea you have for a book has already been done and, if so, how long ago.

■ **Amazon.com** and **Barnes & Noble**
www.amazon.com
www.bn.com

Both commercial bookseller websites offer a free, easily accessible alternative to *Books in Print*. Each can be searched by author, title, and many entries provide brief synopses or reviews.

■ **Books in Print**
www.booksinprint.com
New York, NY: R.R. Bowker, 1948-, annual. Listings from more than 49,000 publishers of their books currently in print. The multivolume set can be searched by author or title.

In the Books in Print family are *Forthcoming Books* (bimonthly, 1966 -), *Paperbound Books in Print,* and *Books in Series.*

– *Subject Guide to Books in Print*

Books listed in *Books in Print* are assigned topical headings in this companion set. Contains nonfiction only. After your public library's catalogue, this is usually the next stop in an initial search for information. Indispensable for the writer.

– *Children's Books in Print*

New York, NY: R.R. Bowker, 1969-, annual. Following the same format as *Books in Print*, this reference lists over 88,000 books for children by author, title, and illustrator. It also contains information on 50 children's book awards: qualifications, past winners and when the award was established. A companion publication is the *Subject Guide to Children's Books in Print.* All of the *Books in Print* publications can be searched through online databases such as DIALOG and BRS or CD-ROM; ask if your library subscribes to these services. The website www.booksinprint.com combines all the *Books in Print* family as a paid online service with a free trial period. It includes these new features:

– *Bowker's Hooks to Holdings* allows libraries with Z39.50 compliant catalogues to let their professionals and patrons search the library's catalogue directly from booksinprint.com. Librarians and patrons can determine the availability and location of books already in the library's collection.

– *The Children's Room* lets you research, explore, and access every children's and young adult's book, audiocassette, and video title in the database. In addition to the usual searches by author, illustrator, title, and subject, you can search by age, grade, or Lexile level, as well as by fictitious characters, imaginary settings, awards, reviews in 22 authoritative sources, and much more.

– *The Forthcoming Book Room* allows users to search for book, audiocassettes, and videos released during the current month or due to be published in the next six months.

■ **Children's Catalogue**
New York: H.W. Wilson, 1909-, annual supplements, cumulated. Lists books by Dewey number, with a bibliographic citation (including price, grade level, description, and evaluation). Includes indexes and directory of publishers.

■ **Cumulative Book Index**
www.hwwilson.com
New York: H.W. Wilson, 1898- monthly except August, cumulated. English language books by author, title, subject. Especially helpful for writers who want to find books on any given subject, including fiction titles on that topic. Both the Children's Catalogue and Cumulative Book Index are available in CD-ROM format on a subscription basis or online at WilsonWeb with free trial.

■ **Ulrich's International Periodicals Directory**
ulrichsweb.com
New York, NY: R.R. Bowker, 1932-, annual (with updates 2/year). Provides bibliographic information on over 165,000 periodicals classified under 69 subjects, with subject cross-referencing and index. Includes serials available on CD-ROM and online, cessations, refereed serials (reviewed by an expert in the field). Ulrich's Hotline helps subscribers in solving research problems.

■ **Readers' Guide to Periodical Literature**
www.hwwilson.com
New York: H. W. Wilson, 1901- monthly with annual cumulation. An author and subject index to approximately 250 selected general interest periodicals. For specialized research, try some of the other Wilson guides, such as *Art Index, Social Sciences Index, Applied Science,* and *Technology Index.* Ask at the reference desk for these and many other specific subject indexes. *Readers' Guide* is available online as WilsonWeb on a subscription basis with free trial or in CD-ROM format.

Databases

Librarians at university and large public libraries can search national online services, which are collections of databases, saving you hundreds of hours of research time. Ask what is available, as there is usually a charge. Many libraries also now have databases for searching periodical information; a popular one is InfoTrac. Yours may also have CD-ROM encyclopedias and other research tools (many of the titles in this chapter are available on CD-ROM). For more information on databases and CD-ROMs, see *Gale Directory of Databases* (Detroit: Gale Research, every 6 months) and *CD-ROMs in Print* (Westport, CT: Meckler, annual).

Trade and Market Information

With these books you can target your article and book submissions, find an agent or a publisher, and keep up-to-date on children's books and news in the publishing world. Check your library, too, for specialty market guides (for example, *Religious Writers Marketplace*) by subject or region.

■ **Writer's Market**

Cincinnati: Writer's Digest Books, annual. A practical, comprehensive guide to the business side of writing. Lists book and magazine publishers with editors' names, what they are looking for, intended audience, submission guidelines, and how to obtain sample copies and writers' guidelines. Script, syndicate, and greeting card markets are also covered, as well as basic information on queries, manuscript format, rights, taxes. *Writer's Market Electronic Edition* is sold with book and accompanying CD-ROM.

Other titles of interest from Writer's Digest Books are:

–*Children's Writer's & Illustrator's Market:* Follows the same format as *Writer's Market,* including articles specifically aimed to inform and inspire the writer for children.

– *Novel & Short Story Writer's Market:* Follows the same format as *Writer's Market,* but created exclusively for fiction writers, it provides every fiction market, plus agents, articles, contests, and organizations.

■ **The Writer's Handbook**

Edited by Sylvia K. Burack. Boston: *The Writer,* annual. The first half of the book contains articles by authors about writing. The second half has lists of markets, how to contact, what they publish, number of words, pay, more. Lists a variety of magazines, book publishers, theaters, conferences, writers' colonies.

■ **Literary Market Place (LMP)**

www.literarymarketplace.com

New York, NY: R.R. Bowker, annual. Contains a wealth of information about the publishing industry. Check this if you need to find a certain type of publisher, help with photo research, public relations and promotion, an agent, proofreader, consultant, or contest. More than 2,000 pages of the names and addresses of anyone having anything to do with books.

Related titles are:

– *International Literary Marketplace* New Providence, MJ: R.R. Bowker, 1983- , annual. (Also available on CD-ROM.) This publication provides information similar to that provided in *Literary Market Place,* but on an international scale. It lists publishers in more than 160 countries, identifies major international booksellers and libraries, and provides other international publishing information. Some free services are available online for registered users.

■ **The Insider's Guide to Book Editors, Publishers, & Literary Agents,** 2001-2002

Jeff Herman. Rocklin, CA: Prima, 1999. Lists publishers' addresses, phone numbers, contact names, and what they publish. Also includes articles on writing and lists of organizations.

■ **International Directory of Little Magazines and Small Presses**

Len Fulton, ed. New York: Pushcart Press, annual. A listing of alternative, literary, and small press offerings. Companion volume: *Directory of Small Press & Magazine Editors & Publishers,* the name index to title above.

■ **Publishers Weekly**

New York: R.R. Bowker, 1872- , weekly. The magazine to read for information on the publishing world. See especially the spring and fall children's book announcement issues.

■ **Inkspot**

www.inkspot.com

An online resource and community for writers of all experience levels. Includes publishing and market news. Free e-mail newsletter available from site.

Reviews

The following contain reviews of new children's books and are well regarded in the field.

■ **Booklist**

www.ala.org/booklist/index.html

Chicago: American Library Association, 1905-, 22/year. Index plus selected features and reviews from past issues available online.

■ **The Horn Book Magazine**

www.std.com/Newbury/hbookweb/

Boston: *Horn Book Magazine,* 1925- bimonthly. The magazine is a standard in the children's literature field. The magazine has published a semiannual *Horn Book Guide* since 1989. On the website are a virtual history exhibit and some archived features and reviews.

■ **School Library Journal**

www.slj.com

New York: School Library Journal. 1954-, monthly. Features, columns, and useful news.

Biography

People are the primary makers of history and libraries are full of biographical sources. Whether all you need are birth and death dates, or a whole book about a famous person, this section will guide you to your needed information. Historical and present-day sources overlap, although some are specifically about one or the other.

■ **Biography.com**

www.biography.com

The website of the Biography channel on cable television, Biography.com contains a comprehensive list of historical figures and celebrities, along with brief biographies. It includes web pages for teachers, discussions, and more.

■ **Biography and Genealogy Master Index**

2nd ed. Detroit: Gale Research, 1980.

8 volumes. With annual updates, cumulated every five years. Original set contains 3.2 million citations to articles in standard works of collective biography; updates add thousands more each year. Biographical sources fill many shelves; start here to save time. Arranged by person's last name, followed by biographical sources person appears in. Online version available at libraries.

■ **Biography Index**
www.hwwilson.com
New York: H. W. Wilson, 1947- , quarterly, cumulated (now annually). Indexes biographical material, whether magazine, book, or chapter in a book, by name of subject. Also available on CD-ROM or online as WilsonWeb or on a subscription basis with free trial.

■ **Who's Who**
New York, NY: Marquis *Who's Who*. Publishes many titles, including *Who's Who*, 1849- , annual; *Who's Who in America*, 1899- , annual; *Who Was Who*, 1897- ; *Who Was Who in America*, 1897-; *Who Was Who in America Historical Volume, 1607-1896*; *Marquis Who's Who Publications: Index to all Books*, 1974- , biennial. Also available in CD-ROM and online through LEXIS-NEXIS.

■ **The International Who's Who**
London: Europa Publications, 1935-, annual. Short biographies of almost 20,000 living persons with dates, career, publications, interests, address, and phone. Also available on CD-ROM.

■ **Almanac of Famous People**
5th ed. Detroit: Gale Research, 1994. Brief biographical sketches of 27,000 persons, living and dead. Alphabetical by name, with indexes.

■ **Current Biography Yearbook**
www.hwwilson.com
New York: H.W. Wilson 1940- , monthly except December, cumulated annually. Long articles (several pages) of current persons of note, with biographical references at end. Also available in CD-ROM format and online, as WilsonWeb or on a subscription basis with free trial.

■ **Biography Today**
Detroit, MI: Omnigraphics, Inc. 1992- , three times yearly, cumulated annually. Profiles of contemporary people of interest to young readers.

■ **Newsmakers**
Detroit: Gale Research, 1988-, quarterly, with annual cumulation (supersedes Contemporary Newsmakers, 1985-87). Up-to-date biographical and career profiles of people in the news. Covers all fields, from business and international affairs to literature and the arts.

■ **The Dictionary of National Biography**
Founded in 1882 by George Smith. London: Oxford University 1908-9. Twenty-two volumes and nine supplements cover Britain's citizens from "earliest times" to 1900, including noteworthy colonial Americans. Evaluative and factual information.

■ **Dictionary of American Biography**
American Council of Learned Societies. New York: Charles Scribner's Sons, 1928-36, ongoing. 20 volumes, index

Reference & Research

volume, and supplement volumes with comprehensive index. Similar to the *Dictionary of National Biography*; presents lives of now dead Americans through essays by people who knew them. Also available in CD-ROM.

■ **The National Cyclopaedia of American Biography**
New York: James T. White, 1898- . Biographies of living and dead Americans. Not in alphabetical order, but each volume has an index and a cumulative index was published in 1984.

■ **Notable Americans: What They Did, from 1620 to the Present**
4th ed. Edited by Linda S. Hubbard. Detroit: Gale Research, 1988. Listing of names only. Includes candidates in presidential elections, members of Congress (including in the Confederacy), mayors, association executives, award winners, more.

■ **Research Guide to American Historical Biography**
Edited by Robert Muccigrosso. Washington, DC: Beacham, 1988-91. 3 volumes. Biographies of 278 famous Americans, followed by a listing of primary sources, fiction, juvenile biographies, archives, museums, societies devoted to the person.

■ **Biographical Directory of the American Congress 1774-1971**
bioguide.congress.gov/biosearch/biosearch.asp
Washington, DC: U.S. Government Printing Office, 1971. First part arranged chronologically by each Congress, including the Continental Congress; lists senators and representatives from each state and territory. Second part is arranged alphabetically by name; short biography.

■ **Notable American Women 1607-1950: A Biographical Dictionary**
Edited by Edward T. James. Cambridge, MA: Belknap Press of Harvard University Press, 1971. 3 volumes. Encyclopedic articles, with further reference sources at end.

■ **Notable American Women, the Modern Period**
Edited by Barbara Sicherman and Carol Hurd Green. Cambridge, MA: Belknap Press of Harvard University Press, 1980. 442 biographies, covering the late nineteenth- to the mid-twentieth centuries.

■ **Contemporary Black Biography**
Detroit: Gale Research, 1992- . 9 volumes as of 1995. Includes biographical and interview information, photographs, writings, awards, and sources. Most of the subjects are modern, although some are from earlier in the twentieth century.

■ **Encyclopedia of Frontier Biography**
Dan L. Thrapp. Lincoln: University of Nebraska Press. Short biographies of explorers, Indians, soldiers, outlaws, scouts, hunters, artists, and more. References for further reading under each entry. Also available on CD-ROM.

■ **American Historical Images on File: The Faces of America**
New York: Facts on File, 1990. Portrait (large photo, drawing, engraving,

painting) of subject with short biography. Artists, statesmen, musicians, sports figures, explorers, industrialists, journalists, many more. See also others in this series: *The Black Experience, Colonial and Revolutionary America, The Native American Experience,* and others.

■ **Corbis**
www.corbis.com
Commercial site containing vast collection of photos, incorporating Bettmann Archive. Portraits of artists, statesmen, musicians, sports figures, explorers, industrialists, journalists, many more. Thumbnail views available; pictures downloadable.

■ **Eponyms Dictionaries Index**
Detroit: Gale Research, 1977, with 1984 supplement. Where did Graham crackers, Ferris wheel, and the Taft-Hartley Act get their names? Find out here. Identifies biographical sources and dictionaries for 33,000 eponymous terms.

History
Read a newspaper article from the 1800s, a speech delivered in 1961, or an eyewitness account of a Colonial event. For writers of historical fiction and nonfiction, here is a guide to an exciting trip back in time. Included are general works, chronologies, and historical indexes; check out your library's reference works for histories of specific ethnic groups, countries, and fields of knowledge.

■ **World History: A Dictionary of Important People, Places, and Events, from Ancient Times to the Present**
Bruce Wetterau. New York: Henry Holt, 1995. Short entries on almost 10,000 subjects, plus chronologies.

■ **The Encyclopedia of World Facts and Dates**
Gorton Carruth. New York: HarperCollins, 1993. In chronological order, from the Big Bang 18 billion years ago to 1992. Covers all areas.

■ **The New York Public Library Book of Chronologies**
Bruce Wetterau. New York: Prentice-Hall, 1990. Differs from other books of this type in its arrangement by subject (more than 250 separate chronologies).

■ **The Timetables of History**
3rd rev. Bernard Grun. New York: Simon & Schuster, 1991. Follow tables from 5000 B.C. to the present to see what events occurred at the same time in history/politics, literature/theater, religion/philosophy, visual arts, music, science/technology, and daily life.

■ **Day by Day: the Eighties**
Edited by Ellen Metzler, Marc Aronson. New York: Facts on File, 1995. World events, U.S. politics and economy, science/technology, culture/leisure is listed for each month and day of decades from the 1940s to the 1980s.

■ **Chronicle of the 20th Century**
Liberty, MO: JL International Publishing, 1992. Each page represents one month of each year from 1900 on; short articles on what happened in all areas. See also *Chronicle of the World, America, French Revolution, Second World War,* and other titles by the same publisher.

Reference & Research

- **Chronicle of the 20th Century**
Dorling Kindersley, 1996. This book, with the same title as the preceding but from a different publisher, has full-color photographs, a simple and concise text, and a newspaper-style format to report the major events and people of the century, from world wars to the technological explosion. Also available in CD-ROM format.

- **Monarchs, Rulers, Dynasties, and Kingdoms of the World**
Compiled by R.F. Tapsell. New York: Facts on File, 1983. Lists over 13,000 rulers and dynasties by country in chronological order.

- **International Dictionary of Historic Places**
Chicago: Fitzroy Dearborn, 1995. 5 volumes: Americas, Northern Europe, Southern Europe, Middle East and Africa, Asia and Oceania. Several pages for each place, such as Boston's Freedom Trail, Hollywood, Santiago.

- **Dictionary of Historic Documents**
George C. Kohn. New York: Facts on File, 1991. Short explanations of more than 2,200 documents, including Code of Hammurabi, Ten Commandments, U.S. Pledge of Allegiance, Treaty of Paris, Cuban Constitution; with dates.

- **The Annals of America**
Chicago: Encyclopaedia Britannica, 1976. 20 volumes plus supplement volume 21 (1987). Speeches, letters, diaries, poems, book and magazine excerpts, songs, pictures, and background on important issues in American life by famous and little-known authors.

- **The Annals of the Civil War**
Cambridge, MA: Da Capo Press, 1994. 1878 volume is essentially a massive collection of eyewitness accounts of the Civil War. Besides battle scenes, the annals also cover the draft riots in New York and prisoner-of-war recollections.

- **Documents of American History**
10th ed. Edited by Henry Steele Commager and Milton Cantor. Englewood Cliffs, NJ: Prentice-Hall, 1988. 2 volumes. Includes proclamations, acts, decrees, decisions, speeches from 1492 to the present; collected by a noted historian.

- **Historical Statistics of the United States: Colonial Times to 1970**
White Plains, NY: Kraus International Publications, prepared by Bureau of the Census, 1989. 2 volumes. Need to know the population in 1790? Facts about immigrants in 1820? Exports in the 1600s? This reference has those numbers and much more. Available on CD-ROM.

- **Famous First Facts**
4th ed. Joseph Nathan Kane. New York: LW. Wilson, 1981. Lists more than 9,000 first happenings in American history from 1007 A.D. to 1980. Alphabetical by fact, with extensive indexing.

- **This Day in American History**
Ernie Gross. New York: Neal-Schuman, 1990. 11,000 entries under day of the year they happened.

- **This Day in History**
www.historychannel.com/thisday
Website sponsored by History Channel. Gives summary of historical events for current date or date of your choice.

- **The Negro Almanac: A Reference Work on the African American**
  5th ed. Compiled and edited by Harry A. Ploski and James Williams. Detroit: Gale Research, 1989. Comprehensive overview of black culture, with statistics, biographies, chronologies, and articles on legal, historic, labor, political, artistic, religious areas. 1,600+ pages.

- **The Writer's Guide to Everyday Life in the 1800s**
  Marc McCutcheon. Cincinnati: Writer's Digest Books, 1993. Covers clothing, language, transportation, furniture, money, medicine, dances, foods, crime, war. Includes chronologies of events, books, magazines, innovations, songs. See also *The Writer's Guide to Everyday Life: Prohibition to World War II*, by the same author (1995) and *The Writer's Guide to Everyday Life in the Middle Ages*, by Sherrilyn Kenyon (1995) and *The Writer's Guide to Everyday Life in the Renaissance*, by Kathy Lynn Emerson.

- **Poole's Index to Periodical Literature, 1802-1906**
  William Frederick Poole. Boston: Houghton Mifflin, 1882-1908. 2 volumes plus supplements. Helpful for the writer who wants to examine style of writing or read original texts from the nineteenth and early twentieth-century. *Author Index*, compiled by C. Edward Wall. Michigan: Pierian Press. Cumulative, 1971.

- **Famous First Facts About the States**
  David Stienecker. Woodbridge, CT: Blackbirch Press, 1995. Gives information on state birds, flowers, and trees, for all 50 states, along with notes on famous people born in each state and important dates in state history.

Local History Sources

To find out how the people of your community lived in the past and what events affected their lives, look for old newspapers, genealogies, and local history books of the era. Ask your librarian how to access these sources; some major libraries have sizable genealogy and local history collections.

- **United States Local Histories in the Library of Congress: Bibliography**
  Edited by Marion J. Kaminkow. Baltimore: Magna Carta, 1975. 4 volumes, 1 supplement (1986) with index. Arranged by region, then state. Includes city, title, place, publisher, date, number of pages. After you find the titles, you may be able to find these locally or through interlibrary loan.

News Sources

From current events reporting comes story ideas, people to contact for information and interviews, and the very latest in what's happening in any field. Back issues and volumes can be handy, too, for historical perspective.

- **Fact on File: World News Digest with Index**
  www.facts.com
  New York: Facts on File, 1941-, weekly with bound annual cumulation. Cumulative index issued every two months. Condenses the news of the week from more than 70 newspapers and news-

magazines around the world. Includes fact boxes, references to earlier articles, maps, tables. Covers government/politics, health, economy/finance, the arts, sports, environment, national/international events, business, science. Includes a color world atlas with index. CD-ROM available quarterly, cumulated annually. Available on the Web as a subscription service, with a free trial.

- **The CQ Researcher**
  www.cq.com
  (Formerly Editorial Research Reports). Washington, DC: Congressional Quarterly, 1923- , weekly. Each volume addresses one topic, such as organ transplants. Includes background, current views, the future, sources for more information, and subject and title indexes. Subscriber website.

- **Newspapers in Microform, United States and Newspapers in Microform, Foreign Countries**
  Washington, DC: Library of Congress, 1984. Covers 1948-1983. By state, city, with title index. Lists hundreds of libraries. Dates of publication and title changes helpful for researcher.

- **NewsBank**
  www.newsbank.com
  New Canaan, CT: NewsBank, 1981- monthly, with quarterly and annual cumulations. Provides subject access to articles from newspapers of more than 450 U.S. cities. Full text is on microfiche, index is printed. Has direction for use on each page. Searchable version, NewsBank Infoweb, available to subscribing schools and libraries.

Major Newspaper Indexes

The following newspaper indexes are in most large public libraries and are also available on CD-ROM. Searchable archives are available on the Internet, but may only include issues from recent years. Some may also charge fee for full-text downloads.

- **The New York Times Index**
  archives.nytimes.com
  1851-, semi-monthly.

- **Wall Street Journal Index**
  interactive.wsj.com
  1955-, monthly.

- **Washington Post Index**
  www.washingtonpost.com
  1971- , monthly.

- **USA Today Web Archives**
  www.usatoday.com
  1988- .

- **General Periodical Searches**
  The following websites offer a variety of full-text downloads from major periodicals. All provide article summaries and free search. They are fee-based and charge either flat access fee or per article.

- **Northern Light**
  www.northernlight.com
- **Electric Library**
  www.elibrary.com
- **Carl Uncover**
  uncweb.carl.org

Literature and Legend

Literature in general and children's literature in particular benefit from a good number of reference books. Specialized indexes abound to find poetry, essays, fairy tales, plays, songs, short stories, speeches, and book reviews.

■ **The Oxford Companion to Children's Literature**
Humphrey Carpenter and Mari Prichard. Oxford: Oxford University Press, 1984. Alphabetical listing of authors, characters, categories of children's literature, titles, and geographical areas (children's literature in various countries).

■ **Characters from Young Adult Literature**
Mary Ellen Snodgrass. Englewood, CO: Libraries Unlimited, 1991. Settings, synopsis, major and minor characters for each work, with author and character indexes.

■ **Oxford Dictionary of Nursery Rhymes**
Edited by Iona and Peter Opie. London: Oxford University Press, 1984. Arranged alphabetically by most prominent word (cat, father, London Bridge); gives origin and explanation.

■ **Calendar of Literary Facts**
Edited by Samuel J. Rogal. Detroit: Gale Research, 1991. Day-by-day: births and deaths of famous authors, publishers. By year: births, deaths, publications, events.

■ **Pseudonyms and Nicknames Dictionary**
Edited by Jennifer Mossman. Detroit: Gale Research, 1987. 2 volumes. 80,000 aliases, pen names, code names, stage names, etc., of 55,000 persons; provides real name, basic biographical information, and sources. Covers many fields.

■ **Brewer's Dictionary of Names**
Adrian Room. New York: Cassell, 1992. Defines people, places, and things in mythology, the Bible, history, politics, business, languages, literature, astronomy.

■ **Children's Writer's Word Book**
Alijandra Mogilner. Cincinnati, OH: Writer's Digest Books, 1992. Word lists by grade and a thesaurus using graded words.

■ **The Macmillan Visual Dictionary**
New York: Macmillan, 1995. Labels parts of objects such as tape measure, bulldozer, camera, baseball field, snake; names and shows types of glassware, tools, road signs, dresses, furniture. 25,000 terms in 600 subjects. A multilingual edition is also available.

■ **YourDictionary.com**
www.yourdictionary.com
Originally named *The Web of Online Dictionaries,* this site was launched in 1995 by Dr. Robert Beard at Bucknell University as a research tool for the world's linguistic community. This comprehensive Web portal specializes in information about any language. Look up a general or specialized word in English or foreign-language dictionaries.

■ **The Oxford English Dictionary**
2nd ed. Oxford: Clarendon, 1989.

20 volumes. First choice for looking up pronunciation, meaning, and historical origin of any word. For writers: Find out if an object, phrase, or word was used in the year you are writing about.

■ **Random House Historical Dictionary of American Slang**
Volume 1, A-G. Edited by J.E. Lighter. New York: Random House, 1994. Well-received first volume of proposed multivolume set. Includes when slang was first used, with year, author, and reference (can be book, magazine, television show, film). Usually several examples of usage under each word.

■ **The Macmillan Book of Proverbs, Maxims, and Famous Phrases**
Selected and arranged by Burton Stevenson. New York: Macmillan, 1987. Nearly 3,000 pages; traces sources (title, author, date). Arranged by subject, with index.

■ **A Dictionary of American Proverbs**
Edited by Stewart A. Kingsbury and Kelsie B. Harder. New York: Oxford University Press, 1992. Organized according to word; reveals the proverb source (first use and in the twentieth century) and distribution (by state).

■ **The Dictionary of Phrase and Fable**
www.bibliomania.com/Reference/PhraseAndFable/index.html
This classic work of reference by E. Cobham Brewer has been in popular demand since 1870. The dictionary is extensively cross referenced, listing terms and characters that appear in classic literature. This First Hypertext Edition is taken from Dr. Brewer's substantially revised and extended edition of 1894.

■ **Bartlett's Familiar Quotations**
www.cc.columbia.edu/acis/bartleby/bartlett
16th ed. Edited by Justin Kaplan. Boston: Little, Brown, and Company, 1992. Arranged in chronological order, with indexes by author and quote. Version also available on the Internet: It's the 9th Edition, copyright 1901, but still an excellent resource.

■ **The Quotations Page**
www.starlingtech.com/quotes/
This page was originally developed as a catalogue of quotation resources on the Internet; it has since evolved into a large-scale quotation site with many original resources. Also contains numerous links to other quotation sites.

■ **A Dictionary of Common Fallacies**
Philip Ward. Buffalo, NY: Prometheus, 1988. 2 volumes. Find out why mermaids don't exist, whales don't spout water, and the Declaration of Independence was not signed on July 4, 1776, and why so many people believe it was.

■ **Bulfinch's Mythology**
www.bulfinch.org
Edited by Richard P. Martin. New York: Modern Library, 1991. The classic in its field. Includes gods and goddesses (including Hindu and Norse), King Arthur and knights, other British hero tales, Charlemagne legends.

- **Encyclopedia Mythica**
pantheon.org/mythica
This is an encyclopedia on mythology, folklore, legends, and more. It contains over 5,700 definitions of gods and goddesses, supernatural beings and legendary creatures and monsters from all over the world.

- **Funk and Wagnalls Standard Dictionary of Folklore, Mythology and Legend**
Edited by Maria Leach. San Francisco: Harper & Row, 1984. More than 8,000 articles (some long, some short) on folk heroes, beliefs, spells, rhymes, festivals, dances, more.

Science

Information about science and technology is available at many levels of depth and difficulty. Investigate until you find the sources most comfortable for you. Not everyone can be an atomic physicist, but writers can read to understand basic principles and explain concepts to children.

- **McGraw-Hill Encyclopedia of Science & Technology**
7th ed. New York: McGraw-Hill, 1992. 20 volumes. 7,500 entries, 13,000 illustrations, analytical index, topical index, cross-references, study guides, list of contributing authors. CD-ROM and online versions available.

- **McGraw-Hill Dictionary of Scientific and Technical Terms**
5th ed. Edited by Sybil P. Parker. New York: McGraw-Hill, 1994. Includes pronunciation, field or subject, short definition. Handy appendices.

- **Dictionary of Scientific Literacy**
Richard P. Brennan. New York: John Wiley & Sons, 1992. Short explanation of words and phrases the average adult needs to know, from absolute zero to zygote with Doppler effect, global warming, radio telescope, much more.

- **Chemical Formulary**
New York: Chemical Publishing, 1933- . Ongoing multivolume set contains formulas for foods, drugs, cosmetics, cleaners, fabrics, adhesives, more. Good especially for historical research. *Cumulative Index* to volumes 1-25. Harry Bennett. New York: Chemical Publishing, 1987.

- **Milestones in Science and Technology: The Ready Reference Guide to Discoveries, Inventions, and Facts**
2nd ed. Ellis Mount and Barbara A. List. Phoenix, AZ: Oryx, 1994. 1,250 topics such as gasoline, rocket, porcelain, cable TV, zipper; includes explanation, field, and suggested reading.

- **Asimov's Chronology of Science & Discovery**
Isaac Asimov. New York: HarperCollins, 1994. Asimov died in 1992, but his name lives on in this updated version of one of his many books. From 4,000,000 B.C. to 1993 what was happening in math, medicine, technology, astronomy, agriculture, exploration, and more. Easy to understand.

- **The Timetables of Technology**
Bryan Bunch and Alexander Hellemans. New York: Simon & Schuster, 1993. Follow the advance of invention,

Reference & Research

discovery, publications, construction from 2,400,000 B.C. to the present in tables. See also *The Timetables of Science*, by the same authors.

- **McGraw-Hill Yearbook of Science & Technology**
  New York: McGraw-Hill, 1962-, annual. Supplement to the McGraw-Hill Encyclopedia of Science and Technology. Articles from AIDS to zeolite on the achievements in science and engineering, with charts, diagrams, graphs, photos.

- **Yearbook of Science and the Future**
  Chicago: Encyclopaedia Britannica, 1975-, annual. Science update in the familiar *Encyclopaedia Brittanica* format, to revise certain sections of that work; year in review takes in all scientific fields; more.

Field Guides

Field guides cover all areas of science. They are very helpful for identification, geographical location, and description. Some examples:

- **National Audubon Society Field Guide to African Wildlife**
  Peter C. Alden. New York: Alfred A. Knopf, 1995.

- **Simon & Schuster's Guide to Saltwater Fish and Fishing**
  Angelo Mojetta. New, York: Simon & Schuster, 1992.

Almanacs

Almanacs include retrospective information and basic standard information, and are generally more up-to-date than encyclopedias. This list includes general American almanacs, international, and specialized subject almanacs. General almanacs contain look-it-up-fast info: yearly data such as members of Congress, current events, and sports statistics, and general information such as maps, text of the Constitution, facts on nations and states, outline of history, and so on. The following are some of the most popular.

- **Information Please Almanac**
  www.infoplease.com
  Boston: Houghton Mifflin, 1947- , annual. Content also available on the website.

- **The World Almanac and Book of Facts**
  Mahwah, NJ: World Almanac Books, 1868-1876, 1886- annual.

- **Canadian Almanac & Directory**
  Toronto: Canadian Almanac & Directory Publishing, 1847- , annual. Provides geographical and political information. Lists hospitals, unions, organizations, television stations, magazines, publishers, libraries, museums.

- **The Annual Register World Events: A Review of the Year**
  New York: Stockton: 1758- , annual. Published in the U.K., copublished in U.S. and Canada. Country-by-country events and almanac-type information, international bodies (UN, NATO, African conferences, etc.), fields of religion, science, environment, architecture, arts, law, sports, more.

■ **Statesman's Year Book**
London: Macmillan/New York: St. Martin's, 1864-, annual. Bulk of the book is current information on countries (politics, economics, statistics, weather); small section on international organizations.

■ **Europa World Year Book**
London: Europa Publications, 1926- , annual since 1960. Provides detailed statistical and historical information about every country in the world.

■ **Demographic Yearbook**
www.undp.org/popin
New York: United Nations, 1948-, annual. Compilations of statistics for over 200 countries, such as population, life expectancy, marriage, divorce, deaths. Some data available on United Nations Population Information Network (POPIN) at the web address.

■ **CIA World Fact Book**
www.odci.gov/cia/publications/factbook/index.html
This source of important unclassified CIA data covers the nations of the world, from Afghanistan to Zimbabwe—area, political climate, international disputes, natural resources, environment, population, inflation rate, GDP, agriculture, industries, defense expenditures, national holidays, literacy rate, religion, legal system, labor force, and much more, and includes a map for every entry. CD-ROM and print versions available.

■ **Almanac of the 50 States: Basic Data Profiles with Comparative Tables**
Edited by Edith R. Hornor. Palo Alto, CA: Information Publications, 1985- , State-by-state statistics: geography, demographics, vital statistics, education, government, economics, communications. Tables ranking states in area, population, education, labor force, income, more.

■ **The Old Farmer's Almanac**
www.almanac.com
Dublin, NH: Yankee Publishing, 1792- , annual. Astronomy, farmer's calendar, weather predictions, entertaining articles and useful information. Selected information available on the website.

■ **The Weather Almanac**
7th ed. Detroit: Gale Research, 1996. Historical and current U.S. information. Lots of statistics for each city, plus articles on weather, air, storms, with charts, maps, photographs.

Atlases

For a standard geographical/political atlas, look for a recent copyright date. Changes have been too fast the past few years to trust an old one. Beyond that, there are atlases on just about any subject—sports, caves, railroads, politics, women, etc. so browse your reference section! Historical atlases concentrate on the past and can be general or specific for countries or events. Gazetteers are dictionaries of geographical place names.

■ **The International Atlas**
Chicago: Rand McNally, 1993. Views of the world, from regions, countries, down to individual cities. Multilingual.

- **Hammond New Century World Atlas**
  Maplewood, NJ: Hammond, 1996. Contains political, physical, topical maps. Hammond Atlas of the World available on CD-ROM.

- **Atlas of the World**
  Washington, DC: National Geographic Society, 1992, revised 6th edition. Includes infrared and satellite photos; the moon, the solar system, and a brief statistical overview of each country.

- **The Times Atlas of the World**
  9th ed. London: Times Books, 1992. Plates contain all types of maps, with easy-to-read key. Lists 210,000 place names in index.

- **The Dorling-Kindersley World Reference Atlas**
  London: Dorling-Kindersley, 1994. Colorful, country-by-country coverage. Maps, charts, graphs, statistics, world ranking, chronology, many facts.

- **Microsoft Encarta World Atlas**
  This CD-ROM based multimedia atlas contains over 1.7 million place names. Displays world music, flags and national anthems directly on the map. Informative new map "treks" explain key earth science topics like glaciers, volcanoes and deserts. The program offers 21 map styles, 11,000 articles and 6,500 images, videos, and audio files.

- **The Economist Atlas of the New Europe**
  New York: Henry Holt, 1992. Arranged by subject: history, communications, business, finance, politics, international relations, war, environment, people and culture, and, within each, by a country analysis. Big, colorful use of maps and charts.

- **Atlas of Contemporary America: Portrait of a Nation**
  Rodger Doyle. New York: Facts on File, 1994. Includes population density, ethnic dispersion, weather, taxes, political climate, much more.

- **Atlas of United States Environmental Issues**
  Robert J. Mason and Mark T. Mattson. New York: Macmillan, 1990. Maps, charts, and text used to illustrate water, waste, air, forest, energy, and other topics affecting the environment.

- **The Rand-McNally Commercial Atlas and Marketing Guide**
  Chicago: Rand McNally, annual. Need a map of railroads, military installations, or college population? This huge book is filled with statistics and maps. Provides population, economic, and geographical data for more than 128,000 U.S. places, with detailed maps.

- **Ancient History Atlas**
  Michael Grant. New York: Macmillan, 1971. By the acclaimed historian. 87 very clear, easy-to-read maps cover 1700 B.C. to 500 A.D. in the ancient Greek and Roman world.

- **The Times Atlas of World History**
  Edited by Geoffrey Barraclough. Maplewood, NJ: Hammond, 1993. A visual and written narrative of world

history from earliest times to the present. Detailed maps.

■ **Chambers World Gazetteer: An A-Z of Geographical Information**
5th ed. Edited by Dr. David Munro. Cambridge: Chambers, 1988. Place words (cities, countries, states, geographical sites) with pronunciation, location, information, sometimes a map.

■ **Omni Gazetteer of the United States of America**
Detroit: Omnigraphics, 1991. 11 volumes. Contains 1.5 million place names in the U.S. and its territories. Arranged by region, then by state, with an alphabetical list of places and information about each. Includes indexes. Also available on CD-ROM.

■ **The Map Catalogue.**
Edited by Joel Makower. 3rd ed. New York, Vintage, 1992. Sourcebook of maps to purchase (historical, county, wildlife, weather, and others) plus aerial photographs, educational materials, anything connected to maps or geography.

■ **Internet Oracle**
www.searchgateway.com/maps.htm
Collection of atlases, roadmaps, and driving directions. Site also contains other useful reference links.

Encyclopedias

Encyclopedias can be a good place to start a search, but they are almost never the place to end when writing for children. Editors of books and magazines alike today demand broader and deeper research for their readers. Encyclopedias as "sources of all knowledge" can be just one book or a multivolume set. For a review of various encyclopedias, see *Kister's Best Encyclopedias* (Phoenix: Oryx, 1994), where Kenneth Kister compares and evaluates general and specialized encyclopedias.

■ **Academic American Encyclopedia.**
Danbury, CT: Grolier

■ **Collier's Encyclopedia**
New York: P.F. Collier

■ **Compton's Encyclopedia**
Chicago: Compton's Learning/Encyclopaedia Britannica

■ **Encyclopedia Americana**
Danbury, CT: Grolier

■ **The New Book of Knowledge**
Danbury, CT: Grolier

■ **New Encyclopaedia Britannica**
Chicago: Encyclopaedia Britannica

■ **World Book Encyclopedia**
Chicago: World Book

CD-ROM Encyclopedias:
■ Academic American
■ Britannica
■ Compton's
■ Concise Columbia
■ Funk and Wagnalls
■ Grolier (Academic American Encyclopedia)
■ Information Finder (World Book Encyclopedia)
■ Microsoft Encarta
■ Random House

-253-

Encyclopedia Websites
- www.encyclopedia.com
  The Concise Columbia Electronic Encyclopedia, Third Edition

- search.britannica.com/search?adv
  (Encyclopaedia Britannica
  encarta.msn.com (Microsoft Encarta)

- www.funkandwagnalls.com
  Funk and Wagnalls Encyclopedia

- www.refdesk.com/myency.html
  My Virtual Encyclopedia

Subject encyclopedias:
Choose from dozens available at your local library. Just a quick scan of the shelves can lead you to encyclopedias on computer science, comics, crime, cities, states, science fiction, mammals, medicine, music, art, antiques, espionage, extraterrestrials, the Renaissance, religions, Western lawmen, and world coins. The following are examples of two multivolume sets that are worth checking.

- **Oxford Illustrated Encyclopedia**
  New York: Oxford University Press, 1993. 8 volumes: 1. The Physical World. 2. The Natural World. 3. World History from Earliest Times to 1800. 4. World History from 1800 to the Present Day. 5. The Arts. 6. Invention and Technology. 7. The Universe. 8. Peoples and Culture. Edited by experts in each field; sumptuous illustrations.

- **World Geographical Encyclopedia**
  New York: McGraw-Hill, 1995. 5 volumes: 1. Africa. 2. The Americas. 3. Asia. 4. Europe. 5. Oceania and index. Geography, history, economics, and the politics of each country, plus beautiful color photos.

Government Documents

The U.S. government, the largest publisher in the world, is a source of information that all writers should keep in mind when beginning their research. If you can think of a subject, the government has probably published a book, pamphlet, periodical, or statistic about it.

- **Monthly Catalogue of U.S. Government Publications**
  Washington, DC: U.S. Government Printing Office, 1895- , monthly, with supplements, cumulations, and indexes. All branches, agencies, and departments are represented in this up-to-date list.

- **Statistical Abstract of the United States**
  Washington, DC: U.S. Department of Commerce, Bureau of the Census, 1878-, annual. More than just population numbers; for example, attendance for various arts activities by sex, race, age, education level, and income, or average annual expenditure on consumer goods by region and size of household. If you need numbers, look here first.

- **The United States Government Manual**
  Washington, DC: Office of the Federal Register, National Archives and Administration, General Services, annual. Lists names and addresses of government offices and their head people.

■ **Fedworld**
www.fedworld.gov

This portal to government agencies is a comprehensive central access point for searching, locating, ordering, and acquiring government and business information.

Idea Generation

Ideas

Moving Ideas

Stuck in the Middle Again

By Lisa Harkrader

You started with a great story idea. You were excited. You couldn't wait to get it down on paper. And for a while, the story flowed.

But now you're beating your head against the computer screen. You're stuck in the middle. Again. And you need another great idea, or combination of ideas, to get you out.

"I always get stuck in the middle of a story," says Mary E. Pearson, author of *David v. God*. "I am absolutely convinced that I've lost all control. I've veered off the path, am hopelessly lost, and will never find my end to the story." Novelist and screenwriter Kathy Mackel agrees. "It's part of the process. I don't even think of it as being stuck anymore."

The Wall

Jane Kurtz, author of 13 books, including *River Friendly, River Wild* and *Faraway Home*, can't think of a single book where she hasn't been stuck at some point. "I say I've 'hit the wall,' the way they talk about in running. I think I can't come up with anything, but then I somehow push through and get a second wind. So far I've always found new insight."

How can you force yourself to write, to push through, when you have no idea what comes next?

Pearson gives herself a daily goal. "Usually a thousand words. Even if I don't make my goal, I've eeked out a few more words, and amazingly, when I look back at them the next day, they look pretty good."

"I give myself permission to write bad stuff, stuff that stinks," says Mackel. "Then I find the one thing that doesn't stink, and throw out the rest."

Throwing out parts of your story, even parts that stink, can be difficult. What's not working is at least familiar. What might work is completely unknown. Sometimes you simply have to trick yourself into forging into that unknown territory.

"I tell myself I'll just play with it," says Kurtz. "I can always go back to the old version. But I usually like the new version better." For her book, *Waterhole Waiting*, she created a new computer file called "Waterhole Working" so that her mind knew it was a working draft, not the real manuscript. "It took the pressure off," she says.

Other writers cut the parts of their manuscript that aren't working and paste them into a file called "Outtakes" or "Saved Pieces." Those saved chunks of writing might never find their way

Ideas

back into the story, but the outtake file serves as a security blanket, allowing the writer to experiment with new ideas without losing the old. As Mackel says, "I'll never write something the same way again. If I want to bring something back, sometimes just a phrase or description, it's there."

Ignore It & It Will Come

If forcing yourself to write doesn't work, try the opposite—quit. When you give your conscious mind a rest, your subconscious will often deliver exactly what you need.

Kurtz uses this approach often. When she finds herself at a sticking point, she'll stop for the day. "Then, while I'm washing dishes or doing laundry, the next step will come. I try to be patient and pay attention."

Your subconscious is never more in control than when you're asleep, and writers can use it to their advantage. "I get the best ideas in half dreams in the middle of the night or as I'm waking up," says Linda Joy Singleton, author of the Regeneration science fiction series.

Some writers actively call that half-dream state to the forefront. "I get into the recliner," says Mackel, "pull a blanket over me, and go into a half dream. I watch my characters act. I let the images flow."

Katie Davis, writer and illustrator of *Who Hops?*, *Who Hoots?*, and *I Hate to Go to Bed*, does something similar. "I close my eyes and visualize an expansive space. There are no walls. Nothing to stop my imagination. And I imagine my characters doing extreme things. Later I can whittle those things down from the extremely ridiculous to the realistically ridiculous."

What's Wrong with This Picture?

If you can pinpoint the reason you've stalled, it will often generate ideas to help you get started again.

When Mackel was writing *Straight from the Horse's Mouth*, she completed seven chapters and became stuck. "Then I realized I didn't know what the bad guys wanted," she says. "Many times the protagonist is reacting to the antagonist. What drives a good story is what the antagonist wants."

Singleton has faced a similar problem in the series books she's written. "I have many different characters with different motivations. Sometimes their motivations and my plot might conflict."

Often, writers focus so intently on character and plot, they don't realize the impact setting has on their story. If you've run out of ideas, take a look at your setting. Is there anything in it you can use to get started again?

In *Can of Worms*, Mackel's main character is heavily into computers. Mackel used those computers to get the character into trouble, and then to get him out. In the sequel, *Eggs in One Basket*, Mackel's main character is a football player with a musician girlfriend, and again, the athletic environment and musical instruments figure into the plot. "Let the environment move the action forward," Mackel advises. If the environment isn't moving the action forward, can a change of setting help? "Absolutely," she says.

Consult Your Road Map

"Sometimes that 'stuckness' can happen because you've allowed an attractive subplot or even an intriguing scene to send you off on a tangent that doesn't

Unsticking the Middle

Try these tricks to help shake new ideas loose:

- **Take a walk.** Or a drive or a shower. Let your subconscious chew on the problem.
- **Juggle many balls.** Keep several projects in various stages of completion. If you can't move forward on one, let it cool while you work on something else.
- **Run a 15-minute sprint.** Set a timer and plow ahead in your story for 15 minutes. Even if what you write is awful, you'll probably find at least one glimmer of a good idea that, like a grain of sand in an oyster, will gather more good ideas around it.
- **Do the opposite.** List all the ideas you've come up with, then list the exact opposite next to it. For example, if the only way you can see your main character reacting is to cry, think about what would happen if she laughed instead.
- **Trick yourself.** Save a new version of the story and call it *test page* or *notes*. Change the font, change the margins, change whatever you need so that it doesn't look like a real manuscript page.
- **Study the masters.** See how other writers worked through similar story problems. "Other writers are my best teachers," says Jane Kurtz. "If you're a surgeon, you aren't expected to invent each surgical procedure yourself. You'll study those who went before you."
- **Seek professional help.** No, not a therapist, although being stuck for new ideas can make you think you need one! Show your story to your critique group or other writers and let them help you brainstorm.

---

support your story," says Pearson.

If that happens, Pearson often reviews or revises the plot one-liners she created before she started writing. "I always have two—one for my external plot, one for my internal plot. These one-liners are not the synopses I might use in a cover letter, but short-takes on my character's goals and growth."

For her novel *Scribbler of Dreams*, Pearson's one-liners are: *External*—Kait wants Bram and lies about her identity to keep him. *Internal*—Kait sees the foundation of her life crumbling away when she discovers her family has been living a lie for generations.

"These are short, to the point, and help me focus on the character goals," Pearson says. "If I start going off on tangents, I can look back and ask, 'Does this have anything to do with Kait's goal of keeping Bram? Is the emotion Kait's feeling related to the dissillusionment she is experiencing?' It helps to revisit these goals so the purpose of the middle is clear again."

Serve It with a Twist

What if your story has an overused or trite theme—something under the bed,

Fresh Twists on Old Ideas: What Editors Say

"We see lots of 'old person as hero' stories," says Mary Lou Carney, Editor of *Guideposts for Kids*, which is to be published exclusively online, and *Guideposts for Teens*. "The ball goes into the yard of the mean old man next door, and guess what? He's not mean."

Story Friends Editor Rose Mary Stutzman sees these kinds of stories, too. "Kindly grandparents get overworked. I see so many stories in which the grandmother teaches a wonderful lesson to the child. Nice idea, but it gets old."

Is there any way to make a grandparent story fresh? "If you want to write a generational story, make the kid the hero," says Carney.

John Allen, Editor of *Cricket* and *Cicada*, sees another kind of grandparent story. "By my rough estimate, I've witnessed the fictional deaths of over 2,500 grandparents in my six years at *Cricket*," he says. "It's almost as though there's a movement afoot among writers to kill off the elderly, albeit in a quiet way, giving the old codgers a chance to pass on a few last words of wisdom before they go."

One dying grandparent story that worked for *Cricket* was "My Grandma Can Fly," by Chris Pease. Allen explains why: "The author used his theme as a skeletal structure on which to hang a sweet, funny fantasy story. The author included a multitude of small, quirky details to keep the focus on the fantasy while fleshing out the characters. Also, Pease wrote with a lot of humor, and being funny means all the difference—with any story."

Stutzman agrees. "Humor seems to be the key. Or perhaps it's surprise. Certainly humor and surprise are interrelated." She knows instinctively when she's found a story with a fresh twist. "The first-grader inside me gives a great

the littlest Christmas tree, the new kid at school? How do you find an idea that will give it a fresh twist?

"By putting your own experiences and voice in the story," says Singleton. "Go past your initial ideas. Keep digging deeper for your own stamp of originality. Instead of Cinderella's slipper, it could be a basketball shoe. The pumpkin coach could be an orange bicycle. Think past the ordinary."

In the novel *Can of Worms*, and in the screenplay adaptation Mackel wrote for the Disney Channel, the main character doesn't fit in and he has a football player picking on him. "That has been done so often, it's become an American myth," says Mackel. "The twist is, where does he go to get help? Mike goes to outer space."

Davis has often been praised for taking old themes, such as being afraid or not wanting to go to bed, and breathing new life into them. She believes it's because she's not only writing for kids, she still is a kid. "My 7-year-old self or

> ## *Fresh Twists on Old Ideas:*
> ## *What Editors Say*
>
> sigh of joy and satisfaction. It's even better if the first-grader's broad, satisfied smile turns into a laugh."
>
> A common thread in worn-out story ideas is preachiness. Carney, sees too many superficial girl relationship stories and too many Bible-thumping kid stories where the main character remembers something the pastor said and it convinces him not to do something bad. For *Cicada,* Allen sees many stories about why you shouldn't smoke, kids with cancer, and the evils of seeking popularity.
>
> What can you do to make sure your story doesn't slip into the preachy mode?
>
> Carney uses "My Brothers Ate My Homework," by Pam Zollman, as an example. "Not doing your homework is a very easy problem for adults to preach about. Zollman wrote it in first person, so you were the kid who didn't do your homework. It couldn't be preachy, because you were the one who didn't plan ahead. If you're a very good writer, first person is a way to approach the topic and make sure you're not writing as the adult."
>
> Writers can also elevate their stories above a well-worn or preachy theme by using lots of dialogue. "You can't stand behind the pulpit and do dialogue," says Carney. Another technique is to layer the conflict, not stop with the most obvious conflict. Up the ante. Create characters with depth and imagination. "The best stories are about people; they aren't about issues," says Allen. Carney agrees, putting the idea of boring, cut-out characters metaphorically: "Paper dolls went out a long time ago."

my 12-year-old self is not someone from the past. She's still alive inside me."

Being Stuck: It's a Good Thing

If you've tried all the tricks, analyzed your story till your eyes have crossed, and still can't come up with new ideas to jump-start your story, it doesn't mean you've failed. In fact, it means just the opposite: You're a writer who won't settle for mediocrity.

"I'd like to meet the writer who doesn't get stuck," says Mackel. She laughs. "Or maybe I wouldn't. A writer who has everything worked out ahead of time and doesn't get stuck is probably missing an opportunity to do something better."

"It's part of stretching yourself as an author," says Kurtz. "You don't get stuck if you aren't trying something ambitious enough. You don't get stuck if you're working on something very simple or formulaic." Davis sums it up, albeit brashly: "Writers who suck don't get stuck."

Surefire Ideas

How to Find More Topics Than You Can Write About

By Katherine Swarts

"Where do you get your ideas?" The question is a cliché of the writing business, competing with "show, don't tell" and "write what you know" for the title of phrase-most-often-heard-by-writers. But it is a valid question, most often asked by beginning writers out of frustration or inexperience.

Any writer can take a closer look at their immediate world, beginning even with an apparently humdrum daily life: Surely you haven't spent your life locked in a closet (and there have even been books about people who did!). Count your blessings—and your interests—and find more than enough to write about whether you've never been published or you're an experienced writer ready to re-energize. Here's a checklist to spark those ideas.

Nostalgia

■ *Traditions:* What were your favorite childhood family traditions? How did you continue them—or blend them with your spouse's family traditions—as an adult? Recreate a special moment in your childhood and let readers experience the "good old days" vicariously.

■ *Family history:* Were you the same age as your target market in the 1970s, the 1950s, the Great Depression? Was your family large or small, rural or urban, rich or poor?

■ *Link past and future:* Did you grow up before computers, before space travel, before television? What were the nearest equivalents in your era? What were your speculations about the future? Now that the year 2000 has come and gone, the market is ripe for articles on how that year was once considered a landmark date for a futuristic world—and how close or far off the speculations were. While space colonies and electric cars are still in the earliest stages of development, the CD player and the Internet were science fiction even in the early 1980s.

■ *Naughty and nice:* Be careful about using nostalgia or the past in children's writing, however. Children enjoy reading about youngsters like themselves, regardless of time or culture, but a "when I was your age" tone is a guaranteed turnoff. None of us were really as hardworking and respectful as we like to believe. If you have parents or teachers living, they can be an excellent source of naughty tales from your life to mix with the nice. If you admit to being a typical child, children will read your writing.

Work and Play

■ *Old pleasures:* What did you enjoy as a child? Woodwork? Scouts? Baseball? Embroidery? Beyond nostalgia, these hobbies have wonderful potential for how-to articles. Many traditional crafts and programs still exist. Just do your research first to make sure your terms and allusions aren't out of date.

■ *Field research:* What are your own children interested in? Do the equivalent of field research and ask them to introduce you to their favorite websites, TV shows, and hobbies. Interview them and their friends for articles, and let their enthusiasm (a primary ingredient of interesting writing) shine through.

■ *New interests:* What are your current hobbies? Teenagers and even younger children enjoy many of the same activities adults do, whether it's bowling, bird-watching, or cooking. Make sure your suggestions are age-appropriate, however. A 12-year-old can build a campfire alone, but a 6-year-old had better not try. Remember that readers come from a variety of economic backgrounds and upbringings; don't extol the virtues of expensive camping trips if most of your target market lives in the inner city. If you do want to write a camping article for these readers, try profiling a program dedicated to introducing urban children to the wild.

■ *Careers:* Work, as well as leisure, can be an excellent source of ideas. Modern children are encouraged to think about future careers at an early age. You may think no one would be interested in your day job: Who wants to grow up to be a janitor, a secretary, or a full-time homemaker? But if your work has little obvious prestige, it's still necessary to the functioning of society. Books on the life of a mail carrier or a construction worker can be fascinating. If your novel needs an interesting adult character, a librarian or trash collector may have potential.

Newspapers & Other Periodicals

■ *Looking around:* Convinced that your life isn't as dull or as void of ideas as you thought? The same goes for your town or neighborhood. Maybe you don't live in Hawaii or Hollywood, or anywhere else that seems sufficiently glamorous. But many who live in the big city, or even in the South Seas, think the same—"Nothing ever happens around here." Actually, it does.

■ *Newspapers:* Don't just read the front page of the local paper. Check the regional section for events or people that might interest a wider readership. Look up seasonal listings of community events, such as Christmas musicals or Fourth of July celebrations. Look especially for events geared toward children or families. Attend one and write a first-person piece. Take your children and include their observations. With annual events, always include information on plans for next year, so that your article will be up to date when published.

■ *Regionals:* Look also at regional magazines—periodicals covering your state, city, or area. Not only do they provide ideas on interesting events and people—regionals make excellent markets themselves. Local writers have a natural edge with regionals, not to mention less competition. (See the article on regional magazines, "Regional Markets, In Your Own Backyard," page 65.)

■ *Community news:* Take the local and regional angle to its smallest scale. Most small towns and city neighborhoods publish weekly community newspapers that feature the interesting local tidbits rarely noticed by metropolitan dailies—school programs encouraging children in volunteer work, a 10-year-old already laying plans for a career in science, town development news that will affect the environment. Even an elementary school's periodic newsletter to parents about events and people, or a high school newspaper, can prompt ideas.

Libraries

■ *Popular locally:* It's not as if you haven't thought of using the library to come up with ideas. But find ideas there in a less traditional way. The library's potential as a source of local information goes much further than the stacks of books and magazines. Small libraries can be better sources of direct information than those in the largest city. Small-town librarians are often friendlier, more personal, and more knowledgeable on general matters because there are no teams of librarians to specialize in various subjects. Nearly all libraries, however, have a children's librarian. Ask your children's librarian what topics or series are popular in your area, and start your research by reading the frequently checked out books yourself.

■ *Personal interest:* Ask the children's librarian about personal experiences at the library. You can generate all sorts of ideas: a humorous article ("Mind Your Manners in the Library!"), a mystery ("The Day the Library Computer Checked Out"), or a career article.

■ *Regionals:* After talking with the librarians, check the community bulletin board most libraries have for postings of local events. Don't forget to check the shelf with regional books for listings of local attractions. Fascinating but less-than-famous places make first-rate article topics. Look also for information on state parks and bits of local history.

■ *Special events:* Don't forget that libraries host special events, programs, and exhibits, many of which are geared toward children. Listen in on a story hour, or volunteer for an after-school program and write a how-to article on the crafts used. Your library probably publishes a monthly calendar of events; ask your children's librarian for a copy, or check the library's website.

■ *Internet:* The wide reach of the Internet is a strong partner of the local library for a writer looking for topics. Your city or county government, school system, and local Chamber of Commerce probably have websites. Look for information on local history, community events, and special programs and organizations. While checking histories, see if any group has an anniversary coming up. A timely article on the hundredth birthday of a local organization may be just what your favorite regional market needs.

Calendars

■ *Think ahead:* Since timeliness counts for so much in selling what you write, look for topics that will be of interest at certain seasons or dates. Remember when planning a seasonal or anniversary article that magazines don't buy a piece tonight and publish it tomorrow. The typical publisher is working on the Christmas issue during summer vacation. Lead times vary—and are listed in writers' guidelines—but few magazines accept seasonal articles less than six months in advance and some want material a year before publication. A year's lead is a good idea in any case, as it leaves time to query other markets in the event of rejection.

■ *Less obvious:* Most periodicals are deluged with Christmas submissions, not to mention material for Valentine's Day, Halloween, Independence Day, and other well-known holidays. Landmark anniversaries for famous historical events—the fiftieth anniversary of D-Day, the hundredth anniversary of the San Francisco earthquake—are also obvious. But lesser-known anniversaries and events can also furnish material. An article on a major local hurricane usually gains points with an editor if the query mentions that the disaster is approaching its hundredth anniversary.

■ *Religious celebrations:* Get hold of a religious calendar or find a website that lists lesser-known holidays and events. Every religion has special events and milestones, such as Pentecost, Purim, and the many festivals of the Eastern religions. A Catholic magazine might run an article on a saint in the month of his feast day, or legends might make an interesting lead for an article in a general interest publication. It's a tradition that if you eat goose on Michaelmas Day, for example, you'll have money all year. Where do such traditions start? Why a goose? How have attitudes toward money changed through history? Look at the library for *Chase's Annual Events* and other references of annual events, unusual festivals, and little-known anniversaries. (See also "References: In Print and Online," page 237.)

■ *Internet:* Celebrations and anniversary projects are also common in schools. See if your children's classes are reading a novel 50 years after publication, celebrating Isaac Newton's birthday, or planning a commemorative event for the town's founding anniversary. Keep mining all these sources for ideas, and soon you'll have your own commemorative event to celebrate—a record number of publishing credits!

Ideas

A Start with Statistics

Ideas for articles, stories, books can come from anywhere. They may stir deep within our minds or hearts out of our life experience and knowledge, or they may spark with a fact that we happen to encounter or that we seek out and unearth. We've gathered facts in the form of statistics, rankings, and simple facts to ignite those sparks. Fire them up, dig deep in yourself, and produce your unique creation.

Popular Culture

■ The most common surname in the English-speaking world is Smith: About 2,382,500 Smiths reside in the U.S.

■ The largest Teddy Bear Picnic ever was attended by 33,573 bears and their owners in 1995 at the Dublin Zoo in Dublin, Ireland.

■ The most overdue book was one in German borrowed from Sidney Sussex College, Cambridge, England, by Colonel Robert Walpole circa 1667. It was found by Professor Sir John Plumb and returned 288 years later. No fine was charged.

■ The most valuable comic in the U.S. is Action Comics No. 1, estimated to be worth $105,000. It was published in 1938 and marked the original appearance of Superman.

■ The favorite Girl Scout cookie is Thin Mints, which accounts for 26 percent of all cookie sales.

■ The world's biggest piggy bank, named Maximillion, is 15-feet, 5-inches long; 8-feet, 8-inches tall; and 21-feet 4.5-inches in circumference. It was built by the Canadian Imperial Bank of Commerce in Canada in 1995.

■ The world's tallest snowman was built in 1995 by a team of local residents of Ohkura Village, Yamagata, Japan. It took them 10 days and nights to build the 96-foot, 7-inch snowman.

■ The world's longest zipper was made by Yoshida (Netherlands) Ltd. It was 9,353.56 feet long and had 2,565,900 teeth.

■ The largest jack-o'-lantern was carved from an 827-pound pumpkin at Nut Tree, California, in 1992.

- The largest hamburger was made in 1989 at the Outagamie County Fair in Seymour, Wisconsin. It weighed 5,520 pounds and was 21 feet across.

- The world's largest rubber ducky race took place on the River Avon in Bath, England, with 100,000 plastic ducks.

- The biggest mousetrap is a 9-foot, 10-inch long, fully functional trap designed to spark children's interest in science and physics, and was built by students in Lisbon, Ohio.

- The greatest reported diameter for a bubble-gum bubble is 23 inches, by Susan Montgomery Williams in 1994.

- The biggest bagel weighed 563 pounds, and measured 59.25 inches in diameter and 12.5 inches in height. It was made by Kraft Food and Lender's Bagels in 1996.

- The best-selling car of all time is the Volkswagen Beetle, with an estimated 21,220,000 produced.

- The laziest animal in the world is the koala, who sleeps 22 hours per day.

- The most popular goldfish name is Jaws.

- The most common phobia is arachnaphobia or the fear of spiders.

- The most popular girl's name in the U.S. is Brittany; the most popular boy's name is Michael. Fifty years ago, the most popular names were Mary and Robert, and 100 years ago, Mary and John.

- The top milk-consuming country is Iceland, with 184.1 quarts per capita annual consumption.

- The most effective fitness activity is swimming.

- Jack is the most common movie character name.

- The largest reference library in the world is the Library of Congress, with more than 29,000,000 volumes.

- Elton John's average monthly credit card bill is approximately $413,000.

- The most landed-on square in *Monopoly* is Illinois Avenue.

- The most expensive *Monopoly* set, valued at $2 million, was created by San Francisco jeweler Sidney Mobell in 1988. The board is 23-carat gold and the dice spots are 42 full-cut diamonds.

- The most popular candy in the U.S. is the Reese's Peanut Butter Cup, with 5 percent of the market.

- The most common place name in the U.S. is Fairview.

- The top toy in the U.S. is Barbie and her related products.

- The Swiss drink more soft drinks than anyone in the world, with 110 quarts per capita annual consumption.

- The best-selling single record worldwide is Bing Crosby's "White Christmas," with more than 30,000,000 copies sold.

- The highest recorded mileage for a car is 1,613,281 miles for a Volkswagen Beetle. Sadly, "Old Faithful" was totaled in an accident in 1997.

- The youngest college graduate is Michael Kearney, who received his B.A. in anthropology from the University of South Alabama in 1994 when he was 10 years and 4 months old.

- The top calorie-consuming country in the world is Ireland.

- The record for the largest sum of money ever rejected by a pop star for an advertising deal is $12 million, by Bruce Springsteen in 1987. The money had been offered by Chrysler for the use of Springsteen's "Born in the USA" in a car commercial.

- The state with the highest recycling rate is New Jersey.

- The most popular American pet is the cat, with more than 66,150,000 registered. They are followed by dogs with 58,200,000 registered.

- The most published author of all time is William Shakespeare.

- The most expensive film script is Clark Gable's script for *Gone With the Wind*, which sold at Christie's auction house for $244,500 in 1996.

- The youngest person to receive an official gallantry award is Julius Rosenberg of Winnepeg, Canada, given the Medal of Bravery in 1994 for stopping a black bear that attacked his three-year-old sister when he was five. He saved his sister's life by growling at the bear.

- The youngest number one box-office star is Shirley Temple who was seven when she became number one in 1935.

- New Jersey businessman Charles "Chuck" Feeney has given away nearly all of his $4.1 billion fortune. He owns neither a car nor a house and wears a wristwatch that cost $16. Most of his money has gone into education and research in Ireland.

- The richest pet in Hollywood was Ava Gardner's corgi Morgan. He was left a monthly salary and his own limousine and maid when Gardner died in 1990. Morgan lived off his inheritance in a Hollywood mansion for seven years until he died in 1997. He was buried in Gregory Peck's backyard.

- The longest hiccupping fit was endured by Charles Osborne of Anthon, Iowa, who began hiccupping in 1922 while he was trying to weigh a hog before slaughtering it and continued until February 1990. He was unable to find a cure but did lead a normal life, marrying twice and fathering eight children.

- The most famous canine rescuer of all time is Barry, a St. Bernard who saved more than 40 people during his 12-year career in the Swiss Alps. His best known rescue was of a boy who lay half frozen under an avalanche in which his mother died. Barry spread himself across the boy's body to warm him and licked the child's face to wake him up, then carried him to a nearby house.

Ideas

- The youngest person to make a solo circumnavigation is David Dicks of Australia who was 18 years, 41 days old when he completed his trip of 264 days, 16 hours, and 49 minutes.

- The stuffed body of Toto, the dog who starred alongside Judy Garland in *The Wizard of Oz*, sold for $3,680 at auction in 1996.

- Walter Cavanaugh of Santa Clara, California, holds the record for the most credit cards. He has 1,397 different credit cards, which together are worth more than $1.65 million in credit. He keeps his collection in the world's longest wallet, which is 250 feet long and weighs 38.5 pounds.

- John Reznikoff of Stamford, Connecticut, collects the hair of long-dead celebrities. Some of the famous hair in his collection, insured for $1 million, belonged to Abraham Lincoln, John F. Kennedy, Marilyn Monroe, and Elvis Presley.

- The most expensive movie poster is from the 1932 Universal Studios film *The Mummy*, which sold for a record $453,000 in March 1997. Only two known copies of the poster exist.

- Niek Vermeulen of the Netherlands has a record-breaking collection of 2,112 distinct airsickness bags from 470 airlines.

- The record for the greatest distance covered while leapfrogging is 996 miles, 352 yards, by 14 students from Stanford University, California. They began on May 16, 1991, and stopped 244 hours, 43 minutes later, on May 26.

- Children 10 to 17 were found to be willing to provide personal family information, including name and address, for a free gift from a favorite store's website, according to a study by the Annenberg Public Policy Center reported in *American Demographics*. 45 percent would give information online for a $100 gift; 29 percent of their parents said they would do the same. In other statistics, 60 percent of parents are more concerned that teenagers would provide such information than younger children.

- Americans annually consume more than 7 billion pounds of candy and gum, or more than about 24 pounds a person, spending more than $22 billion. The Danes lead the world in sugar consumption, however, at 37 pounds each.

- Los Angeles County, California, has more than 500 companies that make toys.

- Among the top new toys sold in 2000 were Poo-Chi Robotic Dog, Pokémon Rocket Booster, Celebration Barbie, and *Who Wants to be a Millionaire* board game. Among the top entertainment software was *Diablo 2*, *Dirpy 64: Crystal*, *The Sims*, *Pokémon Yellow*, and *Tony Hawks Pro Skater*.

- More than 43 million people own more than 61 million dogs and 74 million cats in the U.S., according to the American Pet Association. More than 28 million dog owners and 37 million cat owners buy their pets Christmas presents.

- Horses, owned for recreation or commerce, number 6.9 million in the U.S.

725,000 are race horses or breeders and about 5 million are show or recreation horses. The American Horse Council reports that the horse industry contributes more to the GDP than the movie, railroad, furniture, and tobacco industries.

■ About 3,000 products are made from petroleum, including eyeglasses, deodorant, ink, and bubble gum.

Society
■ Every year, 22 million school days are lost due to the common cold.

■ One in five students in grades 9 through 12 has contemplated suicide in the past year. Almost 8 percent report attempting suicide.

■ The birth rate for teenagers in 1998 was 51.1 live births per 1,000 women ages 15 to 19 years, 2 percent lower than 1997 and 18 percent lower than 1991 when it reached its most recent peak.

■ 29.8 percent of 15-to-19-year-old women are using contraception.

■ Of the children under age five who died in traffic crashes, 51 percent were unrestrained.

■ It is estimated that the total annual cost of toy-related injuries treated in hospital emergency rooms among children 4 and under is approximately $385 million.

■ Private schools in the U.S. number more than 27,000, 25 percent of the total number of schools but containing only 11 percent of all students. About 77 percent of private schools are in rural areas or small towns, according to *American Demographics* magazine.

■ 88.4 percent of adolescents report that they never, or rarely, wear a bicycle helmet.

■ From 1975 to 1998, an estimated 4,193 children's lives were saved by safety belts and child restraint systems.

■ Only 18 percent of American youth ages 6 to 19 eat the recommended five daily servings of fruit and vegetables.

■ Most organized sports-related injuries, 60 percent, occur during practice rather than during games.

■ Youths working on farms account for 40 percent of all fatalities to workers under the age of 18. Over one-half of those deaths are transportation related.

■ Unintentional injuries account for 41 percent of deaths for children 5 to 14.

■ Seven fatalities directly related to nonprofessional football took place during the 1998 season; all deaths resulted from injuries to the brain. Of the seven, six were associated with high school football and one was associated with college football.

■ From 1987 to 1997, intoxication rates decreased for drivers in all age groups. The greatest decrease was for 16-to-20-year-old drivers. An estimated 17,359 lives have been saved by the 21-year-old minimum drinking age laws since 1975.

Ideas

- 7.7 percent of all children in the U.S. live in homes with a grandparent; 75 percent of those homes are maintained by the grandparent.

- In 1998, 68 percent of American children lived with two parents, down from 77 percent in 1980.

- Between 1980 and 1997, the percentage of children living in two-parent families in which both mother and father worked full-time all year increased from 17 percent to 31 percent.

- Teenagers represented 10 percent of the U.S. population in 1998 and accounted for 14 percent of all motor-vehicle-related deaths.

- Nearly half of Americans 12 to 21 are not vigorously active on a regular basis.

- About 14 percent of young people report no recent physical activity. Inactivity is more common among females (14 percent) than males (7 percent).

- Children under 18 without health insurance make up 14 percent of the population.

- 23.7 percent of high school seniors report smoking marijuana in the past month; 2 percent report using cocaine in the past month.

- Among high school students, 51 percent of girls and 68 percent of boys play on a school or community sports team.

- Although average blood lead levels in children ages one to five have dropped since 1976, close to 1 million children have blood lead levels associated with adverse effects.

- 11 percent of adolescents 12 to 17, and 14 percent of children 6 to 11, are overweight; an increase of 6 percent since 1976-1980.

- The percentage of tenth- and twelfth-grade students who reported smoking daily dropped in 1998 after generally increasing since 1992. Among tenth graders, the percentage dropped from 18 percent in 1997 to 16 percent in 1998 and among twelfth graders, it dropped from its recent high of 25 percent in 1997 to 22 percent in 1998.

- 81 percent of children ages 19 to 35 months have received the DTP vaccination.

- Of children 13 to 18, 20 percent have a poor diet.

- Teenagers account for 12.5 percent of all births; 7.3 percent of teen mothers receive late or no prenatal care.

- A higher percentage of children ages three to four were enrolled in preschool in 1997 than in 1998, 48 percent compared with 45 percent.

- A family member reads daily to 57 percent of children ages three to five.

- In 1998, about 8 percent of the nation's 16-to-19-year-olds were neither enrolled in school nor working, a decrease from 9 percent the prior year.

- 14 percent of eighth-grade students, 24 percent of tenth-grade students, and 32 percent of twelfth-grade students reported having five or more alcoholic beverages in a row in the last two weeks.

- In 1997, 19 percent of American children lived in families with cash incomes below the poverty level. The percentage of children in poverty has stayed near 20 percent since 1981.

- Injuries from motor vehicles and firearms are the primary causes of death among youths ages 15 to 19. Motor vehicle traffic-related injuries accounted for 36 percent of deaths in this age group, while 27 percent of deaths were from firearms.

- Average math scores have increased for all ages between 1982 and 1996.

- In 1997, 86 percent of young adults 18 to 24 had completed high school, either with a diploma or an alternative credential such as a GED test. The high school completion rate has increased since 1980 when it was 84 percent.

- Girls have consistently higher reading scores than boys at all ages while boys outperform girls in math at all ages.

- Between 1980 and 1997 the percentage of serious violent crime involving juveniles has ranged from 19 percent in 1982 to 26 percent in 1993; in 1997, 23 percent of all serious violent crime involved a juvenile.

- In 1998, 31 percent of high school graduates ages 25 to 29 had earned a bachelor's or higher degree. This percentage increased from 26 percent to 28 percent from 1980 to 1995, then increased 3 percent between 1995 and 1996 and has remained stable since.

- One in 33 children and 1 in 8 teenagers suffers from depression.

- Of youth gang members, 92 percent are male and 8 percent are female. Only 1.5 percent of youth gangs are female dominated.

- In 1998, female high school graduates were more likely than males to have taken biology, chemistry, and algebra II.

- Between 1994 and 1998, Internet access in public schools increased from 35 percent to 89 percent of schools.

- In 1997, the dropout rate for students ages 16 to 24 was 11 percent, a slight decrease from the 1990 figure.

- In 1997-1998, the estimated current expenditure per student in average daily attendance was $6,624.

- Between 1987 and 1997, the percentage of high school graduates going directly to college increased from 57 percent to 67 percent.

- In 1984-1985, there were 631,983 computers in schools, a ratio of 62.7 students per computer; by 1997-1998 this ratio dropped to 6.4 students per computer with a total of 8,049,875 computers in schools.

Ideas

- 38.4 percent of youths 18 to 24 do volunteer work, spending an average of 2.8 hours per week.

- The country with the highest ratio of university students is Canada, with 7,197 university students per 100,000 people. The U.S. is second with 5,653 per 100,000.

- The most common murder weapon in the U.S. is the handgun; in the U.K. the most common murder weapon is a sharp instrument.

- Forty-nine percent of children report feeling very safe in school.

- Getting bossed around is cited by 17 percent of children as the worst thing about being a kid; 26 percent of parents cite crime as the worst thing about being a kid.

- In 1997, 91.5 percent of students said they were taught about AIDS and HIV in school, up from 83.3 percent in 1991.

- Of the calories consumed by teenagers, 20 percent come from sugar.

- ADHD affects approximately 3 to 5 percent of children.

- National public school expenditures on behalf of students with ADHD exceeded $3 billion in 1995.

- Forty-five percent of children 9 to 11 think that being a good friend is the most important factor used by students in their schools to decide who fits in. For children ages 12 to 14, the most important factor is clothes.

- U.S. fourth-grade students perform above the international average in both mathematics and science achievement. Eighth-graders score below the international average in mathematics achievement and above average in science achievement. Twelfth-grade students score below the international average in mathematics and science.

- In 1995, approximately 13 percent of students 12 to 19 knew a student who brought a gun to school.

- The representation of women among science and engineering doctorate recipients continues to increase. Women received 33 percent of all those doctorates awarded in 1997, compared with 27 percent in 1988.

- In 1987, 27 percent of high schools offered community service opportunities to their students. By 1999, more than 80 percent of public high schools were doing so.

- Between 1986-1987 and 1996-1997, the number of bachelor degrees awarded to men increased by 8 percent and those awarded to women rose by 28 percent.

- Between 1985-1986 and 1995-1996, inflation-adjusted scholarships and fellowships rose 84 percent at public colleges and 67 percent at private colleges.

- Sixty-six percent of kindergarten students are proficient in recognizing their letters and 29 percent are proficient in understanding the beginning sounds. In math, nearly all first-time kindergartners are proficient in number and shape recognition and 58 percent are proficient in understanding relative size.

■ Between 1988-1989 and 1998-1999, prices at public colleges have risen 22 percent, and prices at private colleges have increased by 28 percent, after adjustment for inflation. For the 1998-1999 academic year, prices for undergraduate tuition, room, and board were estimated to be $7093 at public colleges, and $19,410 at private colleges.

■ Between 1987 and 1997, the percentage increase of women enrolling in graduate school far exceeded that of men. The number of male full-time graduate students increased by 22 percent, compared to 68 percent for full-time women students.

■ The Children's Rights Council ranked Maine as the best state to raise children, based on rates of abuse and neglect, immunization, school dropout, poverty, infant and child mortality, divorce, and other criteria. It was followed by Massachusetts, Connecticut, Vermont, New Hampshire, North Dakota, and Maryland.

■ Families in the U.S. use enough gasoline each year to cover a football field 40 miles deep.

■ The National Trust for Historic Preservation lists the most endangered historical sites in the U.S. as (1) Anderson Cottage (Washington, D.C.), a presidential summer house where Lincoln drafted the Emancipation Proclamation; (2) Dwight D. Eisenhower VA Medical Center (Leavenworth, KS), built as a home for disabled veterans of the Civil War; (3) the Hudson River Valley (New York), because industry and power plants threaten its natural beauty and the river towns; (4) historical neighborhood schools across the country.

■ About one-quarter of the energy used in the U.S. comes from natural gas, more than any other source.

■ A paper mill uses the same amount of energy at the same rate as a city of 100,000 people.

■ Wyoming produces more coal than any other state, typically amounting to 278 tons annually.

■ Coal mining has a lower injury rate than farming, construction, or retail.

■ The U.S. lists more than 1,000 species as endangered or threatened. Half of all counties in the country are home to such a species, whether an animal, insect, or plant.

■ Over the last 100 years, the earth's temperature has increased 1°C (1.8°F).

■ The sea level has risen 1 to 2 millimeters annually, from melting ice and expansion of ocean water. At that rate, the U.S. Geological Survey predicts that Glacier National Park will have no glaciers left by the middle of the century and Iceland's glaciers will be gone by 2200.

Ideas

- 20,000 years ago, the sea level was 125 meters below its level today. If it were to rise another 10 meters, about a quarter of the people in the U.S. would be flooded out.

- At California's Salton Sea, a single incident killed up to 150,000 water birds.

- In 1993 in Milwaukee, 403,000 people were sickened and 104 died of the largest waterborne disease outbreak in U.S. history.

- From 900,000 to 2 million people become ill annually from drinking water.

- When Congress issued the last land grants meant to encourage railroad expansion, in 1871, 80 railroads had received land amounting to twice the size of Colorado.

- During the 1880s and 1890s, railroads added 176,000 kilometers of track and built seven transcontinental routes. At the end of World War I, that number was 400,000 kilometers.

- The deadliest recorded earthquake in history—830,000 people—occurred in Shensi province, China, in 1556.

- An earthquake redirected the Mississippi River in Missouri in 1811 during the largest series of earthquakes recorded in North America.

- A 1970 tidal wave killed 200,000 and left 100,000 missing in East Pakistan.

- The worst epidemic in U.S. history occurred in 1918, when more than 500,000 people died from the Spanish influenza.

- The worst polio epidemic in U.S. history was in 1916: 27,363 reported cases and more than 7,000 deaths.

- AIDS deaths in 1981: 425,357. AIDS deaths in 1998: 17,047.

- The U.S. government estimates that three to four million children live within one mile of a hazardous waste site.

- Twenty-four new nations have been established since 1990. Most were carved from the former Soviet Union, Eastern Europe, and the Balkans.

- Ranked by the United Nations according to quality of life, in 1999 Canada was the world's most livable country, followed by Norway, the U.S., Australia, and Iceland. The least livable were Sierra Leone, Niger, Burkina Faso, Ethiopia, and Burundi.

- Transparency International, based in Berlin, ranked Cameroon as the most corrupt in the world. Denmark, at number one, was the least corrupt, and the U.S. was seventeenth out of 85.

- Apart from Antarctica, Greenland has the lowest population density in the world, followed by the Western Sahara, Mongolia, Namibia, and Australia. The most populous areas are Monaco, Singapore, Malta, the Maldives, and Bahrain.

- The highest infant mortality rates in 1998 were in Angola, Afghanistan,

Sierra Leone, Mozambique, and Liberia. The lowest were in Sweden, Singapore, Finland, Japan, and Norway.

■ The highest life expectancy rates in 1998 were in Andorra (83.46), San Marino (81.14), Japan (80.70), Singapore (80.05), and Australia (79.75). The lowest were in Mozambique (37.52), Malawi (37.58), Zimbabwe (37.78), Angola (38.31), and Botswana (39.27).

■ The 10 most widely spoken languages in the world are Mandarin Chinese (885 million), Spanish (332 million), English (322 million), Bengali (189 million), Hindi (182 million), Portuguese (170 million), Russian (170 million), Japanese (125 million), German (98 million), and Wu Chinese (77.2 million).

■ A decade ago, a child born in southern Africa had a life expectancy of 60. In 2005, according to the Population Reference Bureau, a newborn will have a life expectancy of 45, due primarily to HIV/AIDS.

Polls and Surveys

■ A Gallup Organization report indicated that 66 percent of students 13 to 17 said school fighting was a big problem, up 18 percent over the preceding year. Twenty percent of the students said they had been in a fight.

■ Of teens surveyed about dates in American history by the Gallup Organization, 42 percent knew Columbus discovered America in 1492; 39 percent knew states' rights were a Civil War issue; 25 percent knew the U.S. declared independence in 1776. The survey found that suburban teens were more likely to know these facts than rural or urban teens.

■ Three-quarters of Americans shower or bathe every day, according to a CNN/USA Today/Gallup poll, compared to approximately a third of Americans in 1950.

■ Gallup reports that 60 percent of Americans exercise in some way daily, while only 24 percent did in 1961.

■ Today, 70 percent of Americans say a girl can call a boy for a date. 80 percent of men agree, but only 62 percent of women. In 1950, according to the Gallup Organization, only 29 percent thought it appropriate.

■ The Gallup Organization found that 70 percent of Americans believe that physical attractiveness is important to be happy and get ahead in society. Among older respondents, 31 percent say their own appearance is above average, while 56 percent of those 18 to 29 rate themselves as above average. 76 percent of Americans in the poll said they were satisfied with their looks.

■ A Gallup poll found that Tiger Woods is considered by Americans to be the greatest athlete currently playing sports. He was followed by Michael Jordan, Mark McGwire, and Cal Ripken Jr. Americans' favorite spectator sports, another Gallup poll revealed, are football (33 percent), basketball (16 percent), and baseball (13 percent). Ice hockey and auto racing were far behind (5 percent each).

Ideas

- In an earlier Gallup poll, Americans named Michael Jordan athlete of the century, followed by Muhammad Ali, Babe Ruth, Jim Thorpe, and Jesse Owens.

- In a survey performed for Earth Day, the Gallup Organization found that 76 percent of Americans thought that the environmental movement had a great or moderate effect on U.S. policies. That number compares to 85 percent for the civil rights movement, 82 percent for women's rights, 75 percent for abortion rights, 74 percent for gun control, 67 percent for consumer rights, 59 percent for gay and lesbian rights, and 50 percent for animal rights.

- Fifty-five percent of Americans are "sympathetic" toward and another 16 percent are "active" in the environmental movement, according to the Gallup poll.

- Most Americans prefer dollar bills to dollar coins, according to a Gallup survey that found 53 percent like paper, and 22 percent, metal. 31 percent of those 18 to 29 prefer the coin, compared to 20 percent of those 30 to 49, and 18 percent of those 10 to 64.

- Most Americans read a book every year, says a Gallup poll. At 84 percent of the population, that has remained consistent over a score of years. The same poll indicated that women read more than men; age doesn't factor considerably in the amount reading.

- A study performed by YALSA and Smartgirl.com found that among 3,072 11-to-18-year-olds surveyed, 72 percent said they read for fun. 36 percent said they "read constantly for their own personal satisfaction," and 81 percent of girls and 62 percent of boys would read more if they had time. More than 66 percent reported reading magazines; 77 percent of the girls read teen fashion magazines and about 50 percent of boys read video game magazines; 59 percent of the respondents read newspapers.

- The Office for Intellectual Freedom reports that in the 1990s, the books most often challenged in libraries were the Scary Stories series; *Daddy's Roommate; I Know Why the Caged Bird Sings; The Chocolate War; The Adventures of Huckleberry Finn; Of Mice and Men; Forever; Bridge to Terabithia; Heather Has Two Mommies; The Catcher in the Rye; The Giver;* and *My Brother Sam Is Dead.*

- The American Library Association reported 472 official challenges, in which groups or individuals wanted books removed from the libraries and schools.

- The top American schools, according to rankings by U.S. News and World Report, are (1) Princeton; (2) Harvard; (3) Yale; (4) California Institute of Technology; (5) Massachusetts Institute of Technology; in a tie, (6) Stanford and the University of Pennsylvania; (8) Duke; (9) Dartmouth; and in a tie, (10) Columbia, Cornell, and the University of Chicago.

- The U.S. Census shows that at least 329 languages are spoken in the U.S.

- About 70 percent of public libraries provide Internet access, with rural libraries 16 percent behind other areas.

- The largest libraries in the country are the Library of Congress (24 million volumes); Harvard University (13.6 million); New York Public Library (11.4 million); Yale University (9.9 million); Queen's Borough Public Library (New York) (9.2 million); and University of Illinois–Urbana (9 million).

- The most widely held library book in America is *In Search of Excellence: Lessons from America's Best-run Companies,* followed by *Megatrends: Ten New Directions Transforming Our Lives* and *A Manual for Writers of Term Papers, Theses, and Dissertations*. Three children's books make the list of top 100 books found on library shelves: *The Way Things Work* (number 24); *Polar Express* (50); and *Owl Moon* (94). The first work of fiction on the list is number 34, *Lake Wobegon Days,* followed by *Beloved: A Novel,* at 35.

- The word that won the first national spelling bee contest in 1925 was gladiolus. The winning words from 1990 to 2000 were: fibranne, antipyretic, lyceum, kamikaze, antediluvian, xanthosis, vivisepulture, euonym, chiaroscurist, logorrhea, and demarche.

- The *Columbia Journalism Review* ranks the best newspapers as (1) *New York Times;* (2) *Washington Post;* (3) *Wall Street Journal;* (4) *Los Angeles Times;* (5) *Dallas Morning News;* (6) *Chicago Tribune;* (7) *Boston Globe;* (8) *San Jose Mercury News;* (9) *St. Petersburg Times;* (10) *The Sun* (Baltimore).

- The World Development Report 2000 indicates that half the population of the world live on less than two dollars a day, and almost half of those live on less than one dollar a day.

- In 1979, a woman earned about 63 percent of what a man earned. Today, that number is 75.8 percent.

- The Population Reference Bureau reports that half of all 10-to-19-year-olds around the world have had sex by 16 years and virtually all of them have had sex by 20.

- Risk of death from pregnancy is twice as high for ages 15 to 19 as for ages 20 to 24, according to the World Health Organization.

- The world population's percentage of children has decreased from 1950's 34 percent to 30 percent. By 2050, predicts the United Nations, children will make up 20 percent of the population and the number of people over 60 will have increased from today's 10 percent to 22 percent.

- *Interactions* magazine estimates that every second, more than 2,700 photographs are taken and 80 percent of them are taken on vacations.

- Children make or influence 40 percent of all purchases in the U.S., according to *Interactions*.

- Video games outsold box office revenues for the first time in history in 1999.

Ideas

■ A Kaiser Family Foundation survey found that 74 percent of teens, 13 to 18, thought it "a good thing to make a conscious decision not to have sex until some later time" and 76 percent said they knew someone who had chosen to delay becoming sexually active.

■ On an average day, 31 percent of children watch one to three hours of television. 17 percent watch more than five hours and 17 percent watch none at all. 53 percent of children have a TV in their rooms. 33 percent have a video game player and 29 percent have a VCR; 24 percent have cable or satellite service. (Kaiser Family Foundation)

■ The Kaiser Family Foundation asked children what they would choose to have on a desert island with them. The results were: computer with Internet access, 33 percent; CDs, tapes, or radio, 24 percent; TV, 13 percent; video games, 13 percent; books or magazines, 8 percent; videos, 3 percent.

■ Sixty-nine percent of children live in homes with computers. 42 percent use a computer on a typical day, for an average of one hour, 26 minutes. (Kaiser Family Foundation)

■ Three-quarters or more of voters 18 to 24 support tougher gun control, patient rights to sue health plans, funding of sex education in schools, greater health coverage for the uninsured, and more gay hate crime protection, according to a survey by the Kaiser Family Foundation. 70 percent of the respondents said politicians are out of touch with people their age and that the presidential election will have little impact on their lives.

Competitive Ideas

What's Out There?

By Susan Tierney

An important step in any book project is market research, a process closely integrated with idea development. By researching published titles, you can learn how thoroughly a topic is covered and determine how to shape your own working ideas.

Competition research begins with titles, authors, publishers, and audience. Where are the gaps in these? What has been well covered? Sometimes a search comes up empty and there appear to be no books on a topic or slant. While that's potentially good news for a writer confident of an idea, it is also a possible indicator that the subject won't work easily and an idea needs to be thought through again.

Even a simple gathering of titles in bibliography form can help you refine a new idea. The Internet has made research of this kind substantially easier, but it doesn't replace library research. Focus, slant, and style of existing titles will need a close, hands-on look.

Begin with booksellers such as Amazon.com or Barnesandnoble.com, and look also for online resources related to your topic. (The computer-shy can still easily consult the *Subject Index to the Children's Books in Print*.) Gather the titles you can and follow leads. If a title stands out as similar to your own idea, see if you can find a review of the book on the bookseller site, or see what the publisher site has to say. If you come across relevant book series, seek them out at the publisher websites, or order catalogues, and let your mind roam over the subjects listed. Trips to the library are the next necessary step as you begin to focus in even more closely.

Competition research has a second important role: It is regularly included in book and article proposals submitted to prospective publishers, to demonstrate how the proposed book will fill a need in the market. (For more details on proposals and market research, see "Book Proposals, A Crack in the Door," page 151, and "Market Research, Scope Out the Competition," page 159.)

Below are selected ideas with titles that represent the first step in a possible market research/idea generation process. Each search below used a variety of resources. None is complete, but the titles and suggestions illustrate how a writer might proceed to pull together an idea, discover needs, and add a new book to what's out there.

Ideas

Idea One:

Indonesian President Suharto resigned under pressure in 1998, after an economic crisis and increasing student protests.

Competitive works—the search:
A search of online booksellers on this event branched through keywords such as Indonesia, Suharto, world government, Asian history, world conflict, world leaders; it was limited to middle-grade and young adult titles.

Virtually all the books found are directed at the library market. Books about culture are listed below as potentially of interest for a work on the subject of modern Indonesia. Not listed—as too far off the central event—are works on natural history, folktales, crafts, or the famous eruption of Krakatoa. If few juvenile books directly treat modern politics in Indonesia, the nation itself is well covered. That is likely to mean that readers and editors are interested in the topic broadly, and a new book on a modern subject might well find a market. So, how to refine the idea? How to reach in a new direction? See the ideas that follow the bibliographic listings.

Current titles:
- *East Timor: Island in Turmoil* (World in Conflict series). Taro McGuinn. Lerner Publishing Group, 1998. 104 pages. YA.
- *Indonesia* (Worldfocus). Susi Arnott. Heineman Library, June 1997. 31 pages. 9-12. From a British publisher.
- *Indonesia* (Countries of the World). Mark Cramer, Frederick Fisher. Gareth Stevens Publishing, January 2000. 9-12.
- *Indonesia* (Cultures of the World). Gouri Mirpuri. Benchmark Books, January 1994. 128 pages. 9-12.
- *Indonesia* (Festivals of the World). Elizabeth Berg. Gareth Stevens, September 1997. 32 pages. 9-12.
- *Indonesia* (Globe-Trotters Club). Robin Lim. Carolrhoda Books, September 2000. 48 pages. 9-12.
- *Indonesia* (Major World Nations). Garry Lyle. Chelsea House, December 1998. 104 pages. 9-12.
- *Indonesia in Pictures*. Tom Gerst (Editor), et al. Lerner Publishing, April, 1995. 64 pages. New edition of book originally published by Sterling. 9-12.
- *Pak in Indonesia* (My Future). Alain Cheneviere, et al. Lerner Publishing, July 1996. 60 pages. 9-12.

Out-of-print titles:
- *Indonesia*. Nance Lui Fyson. Raintree/Steck-Vaughn Publishers, April 1990. 9-12.
- *Indonesia*. Sylvia McNair. Children's Press, October 1996. 126 pages. 9-12.
- *Volcanoes, Betjaks, and 'Dragons': Let's Travel to Indonesia Together* (Windows on the World). Jeannette P. Windham. Global Age Publishing, September 1995. 9-12.
- *Ancient Indonesia and Its Influence in Modern Times*. Donald E. Weatherbee. September 1974. 9-12.
- *The Land and People of Indonesia*. Datus C. Smith, Jr. HarperCollins Children's Books, January 1983. 9-12.

Series of potential interest:
Learning more about series is another way to help develop ideas. Amazon. com

and Barnesandnoble.com both often include book reviews from such publications as *Booklist, Kirkus Reviews,* and *School Library Journal* that can be very useful in providing a sense of a series. You'll still also need to study catalogues, read the full reviews themselves, and of course read some of the books. Do the titles give you other ideas about how to handle your own?

- Asian History on File. Diagram Group, Facts on File, Inc. An extensive binder series for schools on regional history, with maps, charts, index, bibliography. Facts on File also publishes a related title, *Major Political Events in Indochina 1945-1990.* Darren Sagar. 256 pages. 1991.
- Enchantment of the World, Second Series. Children's Press. A geography series that also covers climate, plants, animals, history; government, economy, arts, culture, religion, daily life; for grades five to nine. The current list of titles does not include Indonesia.
- In World History. Enslow Publishers. The only series title found online was *Philip II and Alexander the Great Unify Greece in World History,* by Don Nardo; the Enslow site currently doesn't highlight this series.
- Turning Points in History. Chelsea House. Generals, people, scientists, statesmen who changed the world.
- World Leaders Past and Present. Chelsea House. Series titles cover Mikail Gorbachev, Nelson and Winnie Mandela, Lech Walesa, Kim Dae-jung, Alexander Dubcek, Francois and Jean Claude Duvalier, the Gemayels, Worteck Jarzelski, Ferdinand Marcos, Sukarno, among many others.

Possible ideas:
After even this preliminary research into the competition, here are a set of ideas that come to mind on this event.

- a young adult title on the student protest in Indonesia and the cultural and economic effects on children.
- a young adult or middle-grade biography of Suharto.
- a young adult or middle-grade title on Indonesian life today, and the changes of the last decades.
- a young adult history of student protests from nineteenth-century France to twentieth-century Europe and America in the 1960s to current protests, especially at world trade meetings and for environmental issues.
- a middle-grade title on modern leaders, focusing on Asia and how it is changing.
- a middle-grade or young adult title on leaders who have faced coups, resignations, impeachments, and other difficulties.

Idea Two:
A hundred years ago, Constantine Stanislavski created Method Acting, a process in which actors must see and hear in their performances as if in real life, to create "natural" reactions.

Competitive works—the search:
An online search came up with no titles for children on Stanislavski himself or specifically on acting methods. The key

words were acting, theater, drama, teaching drama, playwrights. The search results were wide ranging and could have led even further afield almost immediately, with titles on movie stars, puppetry, activity kits with plays, novels with theaters as settings, education methods, plays and skits for classroom and church teaching, many books on teaching individual classics (*Everyman, Tartuffe, A Doll's House, Death of a Salesman*), and myriad titles on Shakespeare and the Globe. Included below are titles focused on learning how to act, the workings of theater, and other performance topics, although it is by no means a comprehensive list. Note that Stanislavski's own book, *An Actor Prepares*, is still read widely, and would be appropriate for older teens.

Current titles:
- *Actor* (Careers Without College). Kathryn A. Quinlan. Capstone Press, March 1998. 9-12.
- *Anyone Can Produce Plays With Kids: The Absolute Basics of Staging Your Own At-Home, In-School, Round-The-Neighborhood Plays* (Young Actor Series). L. E. McCullough. Smith & Kraus, September 1998. 192 pages.
- *Beginning Drama 11-14.* Jonothan Neelands. Calendars Island, September, 1998. 96 pages. 11-14.
- *Building Works Theater.* John Malam. NTC/Contemporary Publishing, April 2000. 32 pages. 9-12. The workings of theater, on stage and off, and a brief history.
- *Director: Film, TV, Radio, and Stage* (Career Exploration). Lewann Sotnak. Capstone Press, January 2000. 48 pages. 9-12.
- *Easy Stage Lighting.* Tim Freeman. Lillenas Publishing, January 1996.
- *House of Games: Making Theatre from Everyday Life.* Chris Johnston. Routledge, September 1998. 320 pages. For all ages, including for schools. Covers acting methods.
- *Lessons for the Stage: An Approach to Acting.* Julian S. Schlusberg. Shoestring Press, April 1994. 245 pages. YA and high school teachers. A practical manual for teaching acting methods.
- *Magnificent Monologues for Kids* (Hollywood 101). Chambers Stevens, et al. Sandcastle Publishing, February 1999. 80 pages. 9-12. For kids' acting classes.
- *Theater* (Great Lives). David Weitzman. Simon & Schuster, November 1996. 9-12. Covers 26 people important to the theater, through history.
- *24-Carat Commercials for Kids: Everything Kids Need to Know to Break into Commercials* (Hollywood 101.) Chambers Stevens, Renee Rolle-Whatley (Editor). Sandcastle Publishing, May 1999. 96 pages. 9-12. For kids' acting classes.
- *The Young Actor's Book of Improvisation: Dramatic Situations from Shakespeare to Spielberg.* Sandra Caruso, Susan Kosoff. Heineman Books, June 1998. Volumes for ages 7-11 and 12-16.

Possible ideas:
While there are many books on the theater, it is interesting that nothing seems to hit the idea of Stanislavski. With Method Acting such an important part of twentieth-century dra-

matic history, the subject seems a good possibility for development.

- novel for any age set in early twentieth-century Russia and the theater, based on Stanislavski.
- a biography of Stanislavski, for any age.
- a book on people who had major influences on the theater and acting, any age.
- a book for elementary, middle, or high school students on the way method acting works.
- a self-help book that uses principles of method acting to work out problems, for groups of children.
- changes in the theater throughout history, from the Greeks to medieval drama to the Renaissance and to modern times; an educational title or one with extensive illustrations, in the tradition of DK Eyewitness books, for example.
- the arts at the turn of the century, particularly in Russia, for young adults.
- a career book that uses the methods of Stanislavski to help young actors pursue acting.

Idea Three:

In 1978, scientists discovered a body orbiting Pluto that may or may not be a moon.

Competitive works—the search:
Space as a subject of children's books can be matched in quantity and quality only by dinosaurs. The strong likelihood that some publisher somewhere will be looking for a new book on space is balanced by the difficulty in finding a new angle, or, if there is a new discovery to report, to do a book before the competition.

Current titles:
- *Clyde Tombaugh and the Search for Planet X* (Carolrhoda On My Own Books). Margaret K. Wetterer, Laurie A. Caple (illustrator). Carolrhoda, October 1996. 48 pages. 5-11. Story of the man who discovered Pluto, his love of telescopes and astronomy.
- *A Double Planet? Pluto & Charon.* Isaac Asimov, Greg Walz-Chojnacki, Frank Reddy. Gareth Stevens, January 1996. 32 pages.
- *The Planet Hunters: The Search for the Outer Planets.* Dennis Brindell Fadin. Simon & Schuster, September 1997. 160 pages. 12+. The story of the people behind astronomy.
- *Pluto* (True Books). Larry Dane Brimner, Children's Press, August 1999. 48 pages. 9-12.
- *Pluto* (First Books). Robert Daily. Franklin Watts, 1994. Grades 4-6.
- *Pluto* (Gateway Solar System). Gregory L. Vogt. (grades 2-4) 1996, Millbrook Press, 1996. Grades 2-4.
- *Postcards from Pluto: A Tour of the Solar System.* Loreen Leedy. Holiday House, September 1993. 32 pages. 5-8.
- *Outer Planets: Uranus, Neptune, Pluto.* Duncan Brewer. Marshall Cavendish, September 1992. 64 pages. 12+.

Out-of-print titles:
- *How Did We Find Out about Pluto?* Isaac Asmiov, Erika Kors (illustrator) Walker & Company, February 1991. 61 pages. 9-12.

- *Mapping the Planets and Space* (Maps & Mapmakers) Martyn Bramwell, George Fryer. Lerner Publications, July 1998. 48 pages.

Series of potential interest:
- Planet Library. Lerner Publishing Group. 9-12.
- Science Project Ideas. Enslow Publishers. Includes titles on the sun and moon. 96 pages each. 9-14.
- Countdown to Space. Enslow Publishers. 9-12.
- Watts Library: Space. Franklin Watts. 9-12.
- DK Discoveries. DK Publishing. 48 pages. 9-12.

Possible ideas:
- the facts that make Pluto unique as a planet and the controversy over the designation in 1999.
- the role of moons in defining astronomical bodies.
- space orbits; Pluto and Neptune cross orbits, the only planets to do so.
- light-curves, which were behind the discovery of Pluto's moon.
- the science behind discovery of planets and other bodies; Pluto was discovered by calculations from irregularities of Uranus and Neptune.

Idea Four:

Judo was created as a sport in Japan in 1882, although it is based on ancient principles of self-defense from China, Tibet, and India.

Competitive works—the search:
So many titles directly discuss Judo, it might be difficult to sell another book on the techniques of the martial arts. The list below is just a fraction of the titles that come up under online searches for Judo and martial arts. But Judo's origin and history may suggest other approaches that could be used as a framework for teaching your readers the sport.

A search for children's books on Japanese sports came up with nothing, but some interesting adult books come up in a search, and these might provide a new slant for a cultural book that uses sports and history as an interesting starting point.

Current titles:
- *Combat: Fencing, Judo, Wrestling, Boxing, Taekwondo, and Lots, Lots More* (Zeke's Olympic Pocket Guide.) Jason Page. Lerner Publishing, August 2000. 9-12.
- *Judo* (Action Sports Series). Bill Gutman, Peter Ford (illustrator). Capstone Press, December 1995. 48 pages. 9-12.
- *Karate and Judo* (How to Play the All-Star Way). Thomas Nardi, et al. Raintree/Steck-Vaughn, April 1998. 9-12.
- *Learning Martial Arts* (New Action Sports) Steve Potts. Capstone Press, January 1996. 48 pages. 9-12.
- *Mastering Martial Arts* (New Action Sports). Steve Potts. Capstone Press, January 1996. 48 pages. 9-12.
- *Martial Arts.* Bob Knotts. Children's Book Press, March 2000. 48 pages. 8-10.
- *The Martial Arts Almanac.* Vinh-Hoi Ngo, Neal Yamamoto (illustrator). Lowell House, October 1997. 88 pages. 9-12.

- *Martial Arts Training Diary for Kids.* Art Brisacher. Turtle Press, September, 1997. 96 pages. 9-12.
- *Superguides: Martial Arts.* David Mitchell. DK Publishing, February 2000. 72 pages. 9-12.
- T*he Tigers Eye, the Birds Fist: A Beginner's Guide to the Martial Arts.* Louise Rafkin, Leslie McGrath (illustrator). Little Brown, April 1997. 144 pages. 9-12. Includes history and legend.
- *The Ultimate Martial Arts Encyclopedia for Kids.* Hoi Gno. Lowell House, November 2000. 160 pages. 8-12.
- *Young Martial Arts Enthusiast.* David Mitchell. DK Publishing, April 1997. 64 pages. 9-12.

Out-of-print titles:
- *Martial Arts Masters: The Greatest Teachers, Fighters, and Performers.* Ngo Vinh-Hoi. Lowell House, October 1996. 8-12.

Adult titles on Japanese sports:
In addition to the many other books on tae kwon do, karate, kickboxing, and akido are adult titles on Japanese athletics and arts that might lead to ideas for children's books. While weapons in themselves might not be a subject most editors would accept on first glance, the artistic and philosophical concepts behind the art of swordsmanship could be a way of approaching a multicultural subject for children. Samurai swordsmen were expected to be knowledgeable also of music and poetry.

- *The Art of Japanese Swordsmanship: A Manual of Eishin-Ryu Iaido.* Nicklaus Suino. Weatherhill, June 1994.
- *Bokken Art of the Japanese Sword.* Dave Lowry, Mike Lee (Editor). Ohara Publications, December 1985.
- *Bushido: The Soul of Japan : An Exposition of Japanese Thought.* Inazo Nitobe. Charles E. Tuttle Co., August 1994.

Possible ideas:
- sports developed over centuries in different cultures, middle-grade.
- the connection of sports with mental and spiritual health, YA.
- how a sport like Judo, and other martial arts, reflects a society, middle grade or YA.
- history of Japan, China, Tibet, through the perspective of a sport.

Ideas

Agent, Contest, & Conference Listings

Listings

Agents

Allred & Allred Literary Agents
7834 Alabama Avenue
Canoga Park, CA 91304

This agency specializes in books from new and unpublished clients. It represents juvenile books, textbooks, scholarly books, and short story collections in many genres including biography, nutrition, crafts, sports, science fiction, and historical.
Established: 1990
Contact: Robert Allred
Current clients: Brad Roberts, Pam Robolo, and Warren Patterson.
Submissions: Query. Send first 10 pages of manuscript. Include cover letter and 1-2 page synopsis. SASE. Responds to queries in 3 weeks; manuscripts in 2 months.
Client requirements: Published and unpublished.
Fees: None.
Contract: Written contract for 1 year. 10% on domestic sales; 10% on foreign.
Categories: Middle-grade fiction and nonfiction (8-12); young adult (12-18) and adult (18+) fiction and nonfiction.
Needs: At this time we are looking for middle-grade to young adult manuscripts.

Alp Arts Co.
Suite 7
221 Fox Rd.
Golden, CO 80403

A member of SCBWI, this agency, which specializes in children's books, represents 40 clients and handles 100% juvenile or young adult proposals.
Established: 1994
Contact: Sandy Ferguson Fuller
Current clients: Bonnie Turner, Holly Huth, Pattie Schnetzler.
Submissions: Query with SASE. For picture books and easy readers, send complete manuscript.
Client requirements: Published and unpublished.
Fees: $25 submission fee for nonpublished authors. Basic consultation fee: $60 for picture books/easy readers; $90 for middle grade or young adult. Other fees vary.
Contract: 10-15% on domestic sales.
Categories: Juvenile picture books (0-4 years); easy-to-read (4-7); story picture books (4-10); middle-grade fiction and nonfiction (8-12); and young adult (12-18).
Needs: We would like to see children's and young adult book manuscripts.

Listings

Joseph Anthony Agency
15 Locust Court
R.D. 20
Mays Landing, NJ 08330

Literary agent Joseph Anthony deals in picture books, easy readers, middle-grade fiction and series books.
Established: 1964
Contact: Joseph Anthony, President
Submissions: Complete manuscript with SASE.
Client requirements: Published and unpublished.
Fees: Reading fee, $40. Other fees vary.
Contract: No contract until manuscript is sold. Commission, 15% domestic; 20% foreign.
Categories: Concept books (0-4 years); early picture books (0-4); easy-to-read (4-7); story picture books (4-10); chapter books (5-10); middle-grade (8-12); young adult (12-18); series. Nonfiction only: how-to, general interest, educational.
Needs: We need Christmas stories and manuscripts under 300 words or over 10,000 words.

Author Author Literary Agency Ltd.
P.O. Box 56534
Lougheed Mall R.P.O.
Burnaby, B.C. V3J 7W2 Canada

A member of the Writers Guild of Alberta, this agency welcomes new writers; 25% of its clientele are children's authors of both fiction and nonfiction.
Established: 1992
Contact: Pat Litke
Current clients: Represents 20 clients.
Submissions: Send three sample chapters or query with book proposal and author's bio. Enclose SAE/IRC. Considers simultaneous queries and submissions.
Client requirements: Published and unpublished.
Fees: Reading fee, $75 per proposal.
Contract: 15% domestic (Canadian); 20% foreign (non-Canadian).
Categories: Fiction and nonfiction: easy-to-read (4-7 years); story picture books (4-10); chapter books (5-10); middle-grade (8-12); young adult (12-18).
Needs: The market is competitive. Pay attention to form and substance, as well as presentation and appearance. Be professional in your approach.

Andrea Brown Literary Agency, Inc.
P.O. Box 1027
Montara, CA 94037

A member of the Association of Author's Representatives and SCBWI, this agency specializes in all genres of children's fiction and nonfiction books.
Established: 1981
Contact: Laura Rennert, Associate Agent
Current clients: Mike Thaler, Mel Glenn
Submissions: For picture books, submit complete manuscript. SASE. All others, query with SASE.
Client requirements: Published and unpublished.
Fees: None
Contract: 15% domestic; 20% foreign.
Categories: Fiction and nonfiction. Concept books (0-4 years); toddler books (0-4); early picture books (0-4); easy-to-read (4-7); story picture books (4-10); chapter books (5-10); middle-grade (8-12); young adult (12-18);

activity books; novelty; how-to; general interest; and photo essays.
Needs: Science, high-tech, geography, history books in all categories and for all ages are needed. We are also looking for books for early readers. We need writers who can write challenging and sophisticated material for today's 21st century kids. Writers should think commercially and write with a fresh voice.

Pema Browne Ltd.
HCR Box 104B
Pine Road
Neversink, NY 12765-9603

This agency handles juvenile and children's picture books, as well as adult nonfiction and novels.
Established: 1966
Contact: Pema Browne, President.
Current clients: Lezlie Evans, Linda Graham Barber, Linda Cargill.
Submissions: Query with SASE. Does not accept simultaneous submissions. Responds to queries in 3 weeks.
Client requirements: Published and unpublished.
Fees: None.
Contract: 15% domestic; 20% foreign.
Categories: Fiction and nonfiction: concept, toddler books, and early picture books (0-4 years); easy-to-read (4-7); story picture books (4-10); chapter books (5-10); middle-grade (8-12); YA (12-18); activity books; novelty; series. How-to; general interest; reference.
Needs: We are seeking middle-grade and picture books. We are interested in all genres if the manuscripts are unique, well written, and presented in a professional manner.

Catalog Literary Agency
P.O. Box 2964
Vancouver, WA 98668

For 15 years, this literary agency has had a roster of clients ranging from children's authors to adult novelists. They are not interested in seeing poetry manuscripts.
Established: 1986
Contact: Douglas Storey, Agent
Current clients: Handles 70 clients.
Submissions: Query with SASE. Accepts simultaneous and multiple submissions. Enclose an SASE for return of manuscript. Responds to queries in 2 weeks; manuscripts in 3 weeks.
Client requirements: Published and unpublished.
Fees: No reading fee. However, there is a $250 handling fee for each project.
Contract: One-year contract. 15% domestic; 20% foreign.
Categories: Fiction and nonfiction: Easy-to-read books (4-7 years); story picture books (4-10); chapter books (5-10); middle-grade (8-12); young adult (12-18); activity books; series; educational, how-to, general interest; photo essays; reference.
Needs: We are interested in every genre except poetry or religious works.

Creative Literary Agency
P.O. Box 506
Birmingham, MI 48009-0506

Juvenile books, adult novels and nonfiction are handled by this agency whose 10 clients represent published and unpublished authors.
Contact: Michele Rooney
Submissions: Query with SASE. Will

accept simultaneous submissions. Responds to queries in 2 weeks; manuscripts in 6 weeks
Client requirements: Published and unpublished.
Fees: Reading fee, $145, includes evaluation and critique. (Refunded upon author's first sale). Additional marketing fee.
Contract: 10% domestic; 15% foreign. Written contract, binding for 60 days.
Categories: Juvenile nonfiction; juvenile fiction; young adult fiction.
Needs: We are actively seeking juvenile fiction and nonfiction in the genres of humor, nature, fantasy, inspirational, and sports.

Ruth Cohen, Inc. Literary Agency
P.O. Box 7626
Menlo Park, CA 94025

Currently handles 35% juvenile work and is looking for new or previously published authors.
Established: 1982
Contact: Ruth Cohen or Sally Driscoll
Current clients: Represents 45 clients.
Submissions: Send outline plus 2 sample chapters. SASE. Does not accept unsolicited manuscripts. Responds to queries in 3 weeks.
Client requirements: Published and unpublished.
Fees: None.
Contract: 15% domestic; 20% foreign. Written contract, binding for 1 year.
Categories: Juvenile fiction and nonfiction; picture books; young adult.
Needs: We want to see well-written and well-crafted manuscripts. We do not accept poetry, Westerns, film scripts, or how-to books.

Educational Design Services, Inc.
P.O. Box 253
Wantagh, NY 11793-0253

This agency, which represents 17 clients, only handles text materials for the K-12 education market.
Established: 1981
Contact: Bertram Linder, President or Edwin Selzer, Vice President
Submissions: Queries with SASE or complete manuscripts with SASE.
Client requirements: Published and unpublished.
Fees: None.
Contract: 15% domestic; 25% foreign.
Categories: Nonfiction only. Middle-grade (8-12 years); young adult (12-18); activity books; bilingual; hi/lo; educational.
Needs: We are looking for K-12 text materials for the education market.

Peter Elek Associates
Box 223
Canal Street Station
New York, NY 10013-2610

With a roster of 20 clients, this agency specializes in children's picture books and fiction and nonfiction.
Established: 1979
Contact: Lauren Macta
Current clients: Laura Cornell and Barbara Hehner.
Submissions: Query with an outline or proposal and SASE.
Client requirements: Published and unpublished.
Fees: None.
Contract: 15% domestic; 20% foreign.
Categories: Fiction and nonfiction: story picture books (4-10 years).

Needs: Looks for fresh, lively, original material.

Ethan Ellenberg Literary Agency
548 Broadway, #5E
New York, NY 10012

This agency handles a wide range of children's books from early concept material to young adult fiction.
Established: 1984
Contact: Ethan Ellenberg, President
Current clients: Julia Noonan, Eric Rohmann, and Sara Banks.
Submissions: Query with SASE or submit complete manuscript. SASE. Accepts simultaneous and multiple submissions.
Client requirements: Published and unpublished.
Fees: None.
Contract: Two-year exclusive contract; 15% domestic.
Categories: Fiction for concept books, toddler books, and early picture books (0-4 years); easy-to-read (4-7); story picture books (4-10); chapter books (5-10); middle-grade (8-12); young adult (12-18); and series.
Needs: We're actively looking for talent of all kinds especially in the genres of literary and commercial fiction, children's books, and breakthrough nonfiction. We do not accept poetry.

Flannery Literary
1140 Wickfield Court
Naperville, IL 60563-3300

Representing 33 clients, most of whom are previously unpublished, Flannery Literary specializes in children's fiction and nonfiction and young adult.
Established: 1992
Contact: Jennifer Flannery
Submissions: Query with SASE.
Client requirements: Published and unpublished.
Fees: None.
Contract: Written contract, with 30 day cancellation clause. 15% domestic; 20% foreign.
Categories: Fiction and nonfiction: concept, toddler, and early picture books (0-4 years); easy-to-read (4-7); story picture books (4-10); chapter books (5-10); middle-grade (8-12); YA (12-18).
Needs: We are currently looking for picture books and YA novels. Be sure to include a brief but captivating query letter.

Fran Literary Agency
7235 Split Creek
San Antonio, TX 78238-3627

This agency represents 33 clients. Sixty percent of its clients are new or previously unpublished. The Fran Literary Agency handles juvenile fiction and nonfiction, as well as young adult.
Established: 1993
Contact: Fran Rathman, Kathy Kenney
Current clients: Francisca Consejal, Daniel Greene.
Submissions: Send complete manuscript with SASE. Accepts simultaneous and multiple submissions.
Client requirements: Published and unpublished.
Fees: Processing fee, $25. Written criticism service, fee varies.
Contract: 15% domestic; 20% foreign.
Categories: Fiction and nonfiction: early picture books (0-4 years); story picture books (4-10); chapter books

Listings

(5-10); middle-grade (8-12); YA (12-18); bilingual.

Needs: We are currently looking for sports fiction; juvenile nonfiction; self-help/personal improvement; and bilingual books.

Gem Literary Services
4717 Poe Rd.
Medina, OH 44256

This agency's list is composed of 25% juvenile books and 70% of its clients are new or previously unpublished authors. It handles both juvenile fiction and nonfiction.
Established: 1996
Contact: Laura Weber
Current clients: Eliza Warren, Christina Jared, Dan Tossounian.
Submissions: Query with synopsis or send complete manuscript with synopsis and biography. SASE. Accepts simultaneous submissions. Responds to queries in 2 weeks; to manuscripts in 1 month.
Client requirements: Published and and unpublished.
Fees: $75-$175 for office expenses; refunded after sale of book. No reading fee.
Contract: 15% domestic; 20% foreign.
Categories: Fiction and nonfiction: concept, toddler, and early picture books (0-4 years); easy-to-read (4-7); story picture books (4-10); chapter books (5-10); middle-grade (8-12); young adult (12-18); adult. Activity books; novelty; series. Nonfiction: educational, how-to, general interest, photo essays, reference.
Needs: We are looking for nonfiction for girls. Remember the age you are writing for and use age-appropriate language.

Independent Publishing Agency:
A Literary and Entertainment Agency
P.O. Box 176
Southport, CT 06490-0176

Fifty percent of this agency's clients are new or previously unpublished writers. Handles juvenile fiction and nonfiction.
Established: 1990
Contact: Henry Berry.
Submissions: Send a synopsis and 2 sample chapters; for picture books, send entire manuscript. SASE.
Client requirements: Published and unpublished.
Fees: Reading fee, $250 for evaluation/critique of manuscript.
Contract: 15% domestic; 20% foreign.
Categories: Fiction and nonfiction: story picture books (4-10 years); young adult.
Needs: We are looking for juvenile picture books: fiction and nonfiction.

Joy Literary Agency
P.O. Box 957-856
Hoffman Estates, IL 60195-7856

Nearly all of the clients at the Joy Literary Agency, which handles juvenile nonfiction and young adult fiction, are new or unpublished writers.
Contact: Carol Joy
Submissions: Query with outline or proposal. SASE.
Client requirements: Published and unpublished.
Fees: None.
Contract: 15% on domestic sales. Offers

a written contract, binding for 2 years.
Categories: Juvenile nonfiction; young adult.
Needs: We are open to new writers. Include SASE with query.

Barbara S. Kouts, Literary Agent
P.O. Box 560
Bellport, NY 11713

In business for over 20 years, Barbara Kouts specializes in juvenile books from board books to young adult.
Established: 1980
Contact: Barbara Kouts
Current clients: Robert San Souci, Han Nolan, Roland Smith.
Submissions: Query only with SASE. Accepts multiple and simultaneous submissions.
Client requirements: Published and unpublished.
Fees: None.
Contract: 15% domestic.
Categories: Fiction and nonfiction: concept, toddler, and early picture books (0-4 years); easy-to-read (4-7); story picture books (4-10); chapter books (5-10); middle-grade (8-12); young adult (12-18); adult (18+).
Needs: We are open to all genres except romance and science fiction.

Karen Lewis & Company
P.O. Box 741623
Dallas, TX 75374

With a client list of 35, Karen Lewis & Company represents juvenile fiction and nonfiction for middle-grade through adult readers.
Established: 1995
Contact: Karen Lewis

Current clients: Wendy Jacobs, Rosary O' Neill, Baron Birtcher.
Submissions: Query with sample chapters. SASE. Accepts simultaneous submissions.
Client requirements: Published and unpublished.
Fees: None.
Contract: One-year contract with a 30-day cancellation policy; 15% domestic; 20% foreign.
Categories: Fiction and nonfiction: middle-grade (8-12 years); young adult (12-18); adult (18+); bilingual.
Needs: We need books that speak to young readers in original ways.

Ray Lincoln Literary Agency
Elkins Park House
Suite 107-B
7900 Old York Road
Elkins Park, PA 19027

This agency primarily looks for children's fiction since 30% of the books it handles are juvenile.
Established: 1974
Contact: Mrs. Ray Lincoln
Current clients: Jerry Spinelli, Susan Katz, Barbara Robinson.
Submissions: Query first with SASE. Then, if requested, submit outline, 2 sample chapters, and SASE.
Client requirements: Published and unpublished.
Fees: None.
Contract: 15% commission on domestic sales; 20% on foreign.
Categories: Juvenile to young adult fiction.
Needs: Children's manuscripts should have a polished writing style and fresh point of view.

Barbara Markowitz Agency
117 North Mansfield Avenue
Los Angeles, CA 90036

With 21 years in the literary business, the Barbara Markowitz Agency handles both published and unpublished children's authors.
Established: 1980
Contact: Barbara Markowitz
Current clients: Barbara O'Connor, William Durbin, Mary Batten.
Submissions: Query with first 3 chapters. Include SASE. Accepts simultaneous and multiple submissions.
Client requirements: Published and unpublished.
Fees: No reading fee. Postage fee varies.
Contract: 15% domestic; 20% foreign.
Categories: Fiction and nonfiction: middle-grade (8-12 years); young adult (12-18); adult (18+).
Needs: We would like to see historical and contemporary fiction. Do not send submissions over 40,000 words. We do not accept poetry, fables, fantasy, or fairy tales.

McLean Literary Associates
2205 157th Lane SW
Tenino, WA 98589-9490

McLean Literary Associates represents published and unpublished authors in children's fiction. Most of their clients write for the adult fiction and nonfiction markets, however, juveniles comprise 10% of their business.
Established: 1984
Contact: Donna McLean Nixon
Submissions: Query first with SASE.
Client requirements: Published and unpublished writers.
Fees: Reading fee, $100. Evaluation fee varies.
Contract: 15% domestic; 20% foreign.
Categories: Juvenile fiction.
Needs: We do not accept poetry.

Mews Books Ltd.
20 Bluewater Hill
Westport, CT 06880

This agency specializes in children's authors whose works encompass preschool through young adult.
Established: 1970
Contact: Sidney B. Kramer, President
Current clients: Richard Scarry, Harvey Weiss, Steven W. Moje.
Submissions: Query with outline and 2 sample chapters. SASE. Does not accept simultaneous or multiple submissions. This agency will return materials only with an SASE.
Client requirements: Published and unpublished.
Fees: No reading fee. If material is accepted, a circulation fee and office costs are applied.
Contract: Three-year exclusive contract; 15% commission on domestic sales.
Categories: Fiction and nonfiction: concept, toddler, and early picture books (0-4 years); easy-to-read (4-7); story picture books (4-10); chapter books (5-10); middle-grade (8-12); young adult (12-18); adult (18+); series. Nonfiction only: activity books; bilingual; educational; how-to; reference.
Needs: We are looking for professional, quality material in all genres. We also offer a consultation service through which writers can obtain advice on publishing and contract issues.

Dee Mura Enterprises, Inc.
269 West Shore Drive
Massapequa, NY 11758-8225

Since 1987, this agency has worked with published and unpublished writers in all genres. Juvenile books make up 15% of its business.
Established: 1987
Contact: Dee Mura, Ken Nyquist.
Submissions: Query with bio and SASE. Considers simultaneous queries.
Client requirements: Published and unpublished.
Fees: No reading fee. Office fees charged.
Contract: 15% domestic; 20-25% foreign.
Categories: Juvenile nonfiction; young adult fiction.
Needs: We are open to nonfiction manuscripts with a unique touch.

Jean V. Naggar Literary Agency
216 East 75th Street
New York, NY 10021

With a client list of 100, the Jean V. Naggar Literary Agency specializes in novels and nonfiction; 15% of its business is made up of juvenile books. Though it mostly works with previously published children's authors, it does take on a few unpublished clients.
Established: 1978
Contact: Frances Kuffel
Current clients: Nancy Willard, Tom Birdseye, Marty Crisp.
Submissions: Query only. SASE. No simultaneous or multiple submissions.
Client requirements: Works with previously published authors but will accept a few unpublished authors.
Fees: None. Office expenses extra.
Contract: Standard author-agent written contract; 15% domestic; 20% foreign.
Categories: Fiction and nonfiction: concept, toddler, and early picture books (0-4 years); easy-to-read (4-7); story picture books (4-10); chapter books (5-10); middle-grade (8-12); young adult (12-18).
Needs: We accept professional-quality queries only.

National Writers Literary Agency
3140 South Peoria #295
Aurora, CO 80014

Representing published and unpublished juvenile authors in almost every genre, 20% of this agency's business is with children's books.
Established: 1981
Contact: Andrew Whelchel, President
Current clients: Andrew Coleman, Gloria Chisholm.
Submissions: Query with SASE. Accepts simultaneous and multiple submissions.
Client requirements: Published and unpublished.
Fees: None.
Contract: One-year written contract with 30-day termination notice; 10% commission on previously published authors; 15% on unpublished clients; 20% on foreign sales.
Categories: Fiction and nonfiction: concept, toddler, and early picture books (0-4 years); easy-to-read (4-7); story picture books (4-10); chapter books (5-10); middle-grade (8-12); young adult (12-18); adult (18+); activity books; bilingual; hi/lo; novelty;

Listings

series. Nonfiction only: educational, how-to, general interest, photo essays, reference.
Needs: We are open to anything that is well-written.

Norma-Lewis Agency
Suite 602
311 West 43rd Street
New York, NY 10036

This agency's clients are new or previously unpublished writers of juvenile fiction and nonfiction for preschool through high school age readers.
Established: 1980
Contact: Norma Liebert
Submissions: Query with writing samples; enclose SASE. Does not accept simultaneous or multiple submissions.
Client requirements: Published and unpublished.
Fees: None.
Contract: 15% domestic; 20% foreign.
Categories: Fiction and nonfiction: concept, toddler, and early picture books (0-4 years); easy-to-read (4-7); story picture books (4-10); chapter books (5-10); middle-grade (8-12); young adult (12-18); adult (18+). Nonfiction only: how-to; general interest.

Janis Renaud, Literary Agent
Dept. 341
20465 Douglas Crescent
Langley, British Columbia V3A 4B6
Canada

This agency actively seeks new writers and works with them to help them get published.
Established: 1998
Contact: Janis Renaud

Submissions: Query with bio and SAE/IRC. For fiction, include a brief synopsis, a chapter outline, and first chapter. For nonfiction, include a chapter outline and writing credits.
Client requirements: Published and unpublished.
Fees: One-time marketing fee to defer costs.
Contract: One-year written contract, with 60-day termination notice; 15% domestic; 20% foreign.
Categories: Juvenile fiction and nonfiction; young adult fiction.
Needs: We actively seek all genres. At this time we are particularly interested in young adult fiction. Poetry or science fiction are not accepted.

Scott Treimel New York
434 Lafayette Street
New York, NY 10003

Specializing in children's books from concept books through young adult novels, 30% of this agency's clients are unpublished writers.
Established: 1995
Contact: Scott Treimel
Submissions: Query with SASE. For picture books, send entire manuscript. Does not accept simultaneous or multiple submissions.
Client requirements: Published and unpublished.
Fees: No reading fee.
Contract: 15% domestic; 20% foreign.
Categories: Fiction and nonfiction: story picture books (4-10 years); chapter books (5-10); middle-grade (8-12); young adult (12-18).
Needs: We are looking for picture books, chapter books, middle-grade fic-

tion and nonfiction, and young adult fiction.

Writers House
3368 Governor Drive #224F
San Diego, CA 92112

Writers House has two offices: one on the East Coast (21 West 26th St., New York, NY 10010) and the other on the West Coast. Half of its clients are unpublished authors.
Established: 1974
Contact: Steven Malk (CA); Susan Cohen (NY)
Current clients: Karen Romano Young, Franny Billingsley, Elise Primavera.
Submissions: Queries only. SASE.
Client requirements: Published and unpublished.
Fees: None.
Contract: One-year contract: 15% domestic; 20% foreign.
Categories: We accept juvenile fiction and nonfiction from picture books to young adult.

Writers' Contests & Awards

Jane Addams Children's Book Award
Ginny Moore Kruse
1708 Regent Street
Madison, WI 53705

Presented annually since 1953, the Jane Addams Children's Book Award is given to a book that most effectively promotes the cause of peace, social justice, world community, and the equality of the sexes and all races.

Entries should be for ages two through fourteen. Themes may include: solving problems courageously and non-violently; overcoming prejudice; approaching life with self-confidence; broadening outlook to appreciate a variety of cultures; and understanding human needs with compassion.

Books may be submitted by publishers, or requested by the committee and should be for children of preschool through high school ages. All entries must have been published in the year preceding the contest.
Deadline: April 1.
Representative winners: *Through My Eyes*, Ruby Bridges; *Molly Bannaky*, Alice McGill.
Announcements: Announcement of the contest is made each year on September 6, Jane Addams's birth date.
Award: Winners receive a hand-illuminated scroll; silver seals are also placed on the book jacket by the publisher. Honor scrolls may also be awarded.

Aesop Prize and Aesop Accolades
Judy Sierra
Box 428
2887 College Avenue #1
Berkeley, CA 94705

These contests are held annually by the Children's Folklore Section of the American Folklore Society. They honor fiction and nonfiction books published in the year preceding the contest.

Folklore should be central to the book's content and the understanding of folklore should be enhanced by the book itself. All folklore sources must be fully acknowledged and referenced within the publication.

Send one copy of each submission to each committee member. Send an SASE for complete details and a list of committee members.
Deadline: September 20.
Representative winners: *King Solomon and His Magic Ring*, Elie Wiesel; *Trickster and the Fainting Birds*, Howard Norman.

Announcements: Winning books will be announced in November.
Award: To be announced.

Alcuin Citations
Alcuin Society
P.O. Box 3216
Vancouver, BC V6B 3X8
Canada

Recognizing the work of Canadian book designers and publishers for the past 18 years, the Alcuin Citations are awarded for excellence in book design and production. The citations are awarded in five categories: fiction, nonfiction (unillustrated), nonfiction (illustrated), poetry, and pictorial.

Eligible books must be published in Canada in the year preceding the contest. There is an entry fee of $10 per book submitted. Send an SASE for further information and an entry form.
Deadline: March 31.
Representative winners: *The Magic Mustache*, Andree Lauzon (Annick Press); *A Barbeque for Charlotte*, Marc Tetro (McArthur & Company).
Announcements: Winners are announced in May.
Award: An award certificate is presented at the annual meeting.

American Association of University Women Award for Juvenile Literature
North Carolina Literary and Historical Association
4610 Mail Service Center
Raleigh, NC 27699-4610

Each year, this award is presented for the year's best work of juvenile literature by a writer from North Carolina. Only books published in the year preceding the award will be eligible. Entries should contain subject matter relevant to North Carolina, and feature an imaginative quality.
Deadline: July 15.
Announcements: Contest is announced in March. Winners are announced at the North Carolina Literary and Historical Association's annual meeting in November.
Award: Winners are honored at the annual meeting with an awards ceremony.

Américas Award for Children's and Young Adult Literature
Consortium of Latin American Studies Programs c/o Center for Latin America
University of Wisconsin-Milwaukee
P.O. Box 413
Milwaukee, WI 53201

The Américas Award is given in recognition of U.S. works of fiction, poetry, folklore, or selected nonfiction published in the previous year in English or Spanish. All entries must authentically and engagingly portray Latin America, the Carribbean, or Latinos in the United States. This award seeks to reach beyond geographic borders, as well as multicultural-international boundaries, focusing instead on cultural heritages within the hemisphere. Winners are chosen based on distinctive literary quality; cultural contextualization; exceptional integration of text, illustration and design; and potential for classroom use.
Deadline: January 15.
Representative winners: *Crash-*

boomlove: A Novel in Verse, Juan Felipe Herrera (New Mexico Press, 1999); *Cuba: After the Revolution*, Bernard Wolf (Dutton, 1999).
Announcements: Winners are announced in the spring.
Award: Letter of citation to author and publisher, and a cash prize of $200.

Amy Writing Awards
The Amy Foundation
P.O. Box 16091
Lansing, MI 48901
website: www.amyfound.org

The Amy Foundation Writing Awards program is designed to recognize creative, skillful writing that presents the biblical position on issues affecting the world today in a sensitive, thought-provoking manner.

The contest is open to all writers, and there are no word length requirements. Entries must have been published in a secular, non-religious publication and must contain scripture. All entries must contain direct quotes from the Bible. There is no entry fee. Send an SASE for complete guidelines.
Deadline: December 31.
Announcements: Winners are announced on May 1.
Award: First-place winners receive a cash award of $10,000.

Hans Christian Andersen Awards
International Board on Books for Young People
IBBY Secretariat, Nonnenweg 12
Postfach, CH-4003
Basel, Switzerland

Every other year, IBBY presents the Hans Christian Andersen Awards to an author and an illustrator whose complete works have made a lasting contribution to children's literature. Nominations are made by the National Sections of IBBY and recipients are selected by a distinguished international jury of children's literature specialists.
Deadline: August 15.
Representative winners: Ana Maria Machado, Katherine Paterson, and Uri Orlev.
Announcements: Winners are announced at the Children's Book Fair in Italy.
Award: Winners receive a gold medal and diploma at an awards reception.

ASPCA Henry Berg Children's Book Award
American Society for the Prevention of Cruelty to Animals
424 East 92nd Street
New York, NY 10128-6804

This annual award is named for the founder of the ASPCA and presented to honor those books that promote the humane ethics of compassion and respect for all living things. Fiction, nonfiction, collections of stories, and poetry are accepted.

Any English language book is eligible as long as it was published in the year preceding the contest. Send six copies of each entry along with a detailed plot summary, including the moral theme of the story.
Deadline: October 31.
Announcements: Award and honor recipients will be announced in June.
Award: Winners are presented with an award at a reception in June.

Listings

Atlantic Writing Competition
Writers' Federation of Nova Scotia
1113 Marginal Road
Halifax, NS B3H 4P7

The Writers' Federation of Nova Scotia encourages all writers in Atlantic Canada to explore their talents by sending in new, untried work to any of the five categories of this competition: writing for children, short story, poetry, novel, and magazine article.

Because the goal of this competition is to help writers grow and experiment, the judges will return written comments when the competition is concluded. Entrants must be a resident in the Atlantic Provinces for at least six months prior to the deadline, and are asked to use a pen name on the manuscript to ensure impartiality of the judges. Only one entry per category will be eligible. Manuscripts will not be returned. Entry fee is $15 for non-members; $10 for members.

Deadline: August 4.
Announcements: Winners will be announced at a Gala Celebration of Writers and Writing in March. All entrants are invited to attend.
Award: Cash prizes ranging from $50–$200 are awarded in each category.

Baker's Plays High School Playwriting Contest
Baker's Plays
P.O. Box 699222
Quincy, MA 02269-9222

This annual contest is open to any high school student. Entries should be about "the high school experience," but may also be about any subject, and of any length, so long as the play is easily produced on the high school stage.

All entries must be accompanied by the signature of a sponsoring high school drama or English teacher. Multiple submissions and co-authored scripts are welcome. Submissions must be firmly bound, typed, and come with an SASE.

Deadline: January 30.
Announcements: Winners will be notified in May.
Award: First-place winners receive $500, and the winning play will be published by Baker's Plays. Second- and third-place winners receive cash awards of $250 and $100 respectively.

John and Patricia Beatty Award
California Library Association
Suite 300
717 K Street
Sacramento, CA 95814-3406

Honoring a distinguished book for children or young adults that best promotes an awareness of California and its people, a committee of librarians selects the winning title from books published in the United States within a given year.

The award is presented by the California Library Association in memory of John and Patricia Beatty, who wrote eleven books of fiction for young people. Each year this award is gaining in reputation and prestige due to the excellence of the books it has honored.

Deadline: Write for 2001 deadline.
Representative winner: *The Perilous Journey of the Donner Party*, Marian Calabro (Clarion, 2000).
Announcements: Contest is announced

during National Library Week in April. Winners are announced at the CLA Annual Conference in November.
Award: A cash prize of $500 and an engraved plaque are presented at the Beatty Awards Breakfast, during the CLA Annual Conference.

Geoffrey Bilson Award for Historical Fiction
The Canadian Children's Book Center
35 Spadina Road
Toronto, ON M5R 2S9
Canada

This contest looks to honor excellence in historical fiction for young people by a Canadian author. Entries should be historically authentic, inform the reader significantly. Entries must be written by residents of Canada, and should be published in the year preceding the contest.

Winners are chosen by a jury, appointed by the Canadian Children's Book Center, with a member of the Our Choice Committee acting as chairman.
Deadline: May 15.
Representative winners: *The Wreckers,* Ian Lawrence; *Good-Bye Marianne,* Irene N. Watts; *To Dance at the Palais Royale,* Janet McNaughton.
Announcements: Winners will be notified in November.
Award: Winners are presented with a cash award of $1,000 and a certificate.

Black-Eyed Susan Award
Awards Committee
P.O. Box 21127
Baltimore, MD 21228

Since 1992, this state award has been presented in several categories. The purpose of the award is to promote literacy and lifelong reading habits by encouraging students to read quality, contemporary literature. Nominees should broaden the human experience and provide accurate, factual information. Everyone is eligible to suggest titles for the master list of nominees.

Maryland students read the books and vote for the one book they consider to be most outstanding in each category. Votes from across the state are sent in and tallied to determine the winners.
Deadline: April 30.
Representative winners: *Danger Zone,* David Klass; *Ella Enchanted,* Gail Carson Levine; *101 Ways to Bug Your Parents,* Lee Wardlaw.
Award: Winners receive a pewter plate engraved with the year and the Black-Eyed Susan Book Award logo.

Walter M. and Grace C. Bonderman Youth Theatre Playwriting Competition
Indiana University-Purdue University at Indianapolis
Suite 309
425 University Boulevard
Indianapolis, IN 46202-5140

Held every other year, this contest seeks to encourage writers to create artistic scripts for young audiences. Entries must be previously unpublished.

Entries are intended for an audience of children in grades 3 through 12. Author should suggest appropriate age category on the entry form.

Plays should run about 45 minutes. Musicals will not be accepted. No si-

multaneous submissions; no entry fee. Send an SASE for further guidelines.
Deadline: September 1, 2002.
Announcements: Competition is announced in the spring; winners are announced in January.
Award: Top four winners receive $1,000 and staged readings of their plays.

Boston Globe-Horn Book Awards
Karen Walsh
The Horn Book, Inc.
Suite 200
56 Roland Street
Boston, MA 02129
www.hbook.com/bghbrules

Since 1967, *The Boston Globe* and The Horn Book, Inc. have annually co-sponsored these awards for excellence in literature for children and young adults. Books to be considered are submitted by publishers in four categories: fiction, poetry, nonfiction, and picture book. Please specify category before submitting. Eligible books will have been published in the year preceding the contest.

A copy of each entry should be sent to each of the three judges. Send an SASE or check the website for further guidelines.
Deadline: May 15.
Representative winners: *The Folk Keeper*, Franny Billingsley; *Sir Walter Ralegh and the Quest for El Dorado*, Marc Aronson; *Henry Hikes to Fitchburg*, D. B. Johnson.
Announcements: Contest is announced in February; winners are announced in October.
Award: Winners in each category receive $500 and an engraved silver bowl. Honor recipients receive an engraved silver plate. In the case of dual winners in one category, prize money will be divided.

Brant Point Literary Prize
P.O. Box 18203
Beverly Hills, CA 90209-4203
www.brantpointprize.com

Sponsored by What's Inside Press, this award recognizes excellence in children's and young adult writings that are based on a specific theme, which varies from year to year. The 2000 theme was "Triumph." From the submissions received, the judges select the one that most uniquely embodies the selected theme.

All entries must be previously unpublished, and accompanied by an application form. Entry fee, $40. Manuscripts will not be returned.
Deadline: March 31.
Announcements: Winners will be notified by mail.
Award: Grand-Prize winners receive $2,500, a publishing contract with What's Inside Press, LLC, with a minimum first run printing of 10,000. Each book will be embossed with the prize logo.

Ann Connor Brimer Award
Nova Scotia Library Association
P.O. Box 36036
Halifax, NS B3J 3S9
Canada

Since 1990, this award seeks to promote the diversity and breadth of Atlantic writers. The awards recognize excellence in writing for children up to the age of 15.

Fiction and nonfiction published in Canada between May of the year preceding the contest and April 30 are eligible. Send an SASE for complete competition guidelines and further information.
Deadline: April 30.
Representative Winners: *Make or Break Spring*, Janet McNaughton; *The House of Wooden Santas*, Kevin Major.
Announcements: Winner is announced in September.
Award: Winner receives $1,000 at an award ceremony in November.

Buckeye Children's Book Award
State Library of Ohio
65 South Front Street
Columbus, OH 43215

The Buckeye Children's Book Award was designed to encourage children in Ohio to read literature, to promote teacher and librarian involvement in children's literature programs, and to give recognition to the authors of children's literature.

The awards are presented in three categories: Kindergarten through second-grade; third- through fifth-grade; and sixth- through eighth grade. Students are given the master voting list, and may vote for one book in each category. The master list consists of books by American authors that were published in the past three years.
Deadline: February 2001.
Representative winners: *Verdi*, Janell Cannon; *Wayside School Gets a Little Stranger*, Louis Sachar; *Seedfolks*, Paul Fleischman.
Announcements: Winners are announced in February or March.
Award: Winning books become part of the Buckeye Children's Book Hall of Fame, housed in the Columbus Metropolitan Library.

Byline Magazine **Contests**
Contests, *Byline Magazine*
P.O. Box 130596
Edmond, OK 73013

Each month, *Byline Magazine* presents four contests to challenge and inspire writers. Categories change each month. Some of the past month's categories include short story, children's story, and picture book.

All contest entries must be unpublished; multiple entries are permitted. Entry fees range from $3 to $5. Name, address, phone number, and contest category should be listed on the front page of the manuscript. Do not include a cover sheet.

Send an SASE or visit the website at www.bylinemag.com/contests/htm for monthly categories and guidelines.
Deadline: Deadlines vary.
Announcements: Contest winners are announced three months after the deadline.
Award: Winners receive cash prizes and possible publication in *Byline*.

Randolph Caldecott Medal
American Library Association
50 E. Huron
Chicago, IL 60611
website: ww.ala.org/alsc

The Caldecott medal is awarded annually to the artist of the most

Listings

distinguished American picture book for children.

The contest is open to all U.S. citizens. Illustrations must be original artwork and demonstrate excellence in execution of the artistic technique and of pictorial interpretation of the story, theme, or concept and illustration style. Send an SASE or visit the website for complete guidelines.

Deadline: December 31.

Representative winners: *Joseph Had a Little Overcoat,* Simms Taback (Viking); 2000 Honor Books: *A Child's Calendar,* Trina Schart Hyman (Holiday House); *Sector 7,* David Wiesner (Clarion Books).

Announcements: Competition is announced annually; winners are announced at the Mid-Winter Meeting.

Award: The Caldecott Medal is presented at an awards banquet.

California Writers Contest
Friends of the Sacramento Public
 Library
Suite 309, Department TA
828 I Street
Sacramento, CA 95814

Looking to encourage and reward California writers, this annual award is sponsored by the Friends of the Sacramento Public Library. The award is open to California residents in the following categories: script, short story, first chapter of a novel, poem, nonfiction article, book or article for children, and first chapter of a young adult fiction or nonfiction book.

Word length limits and guidelines vary for each category. All entries must be previously unpublished. Limit 5 entries per competition; entry fee $5. Manuscripts will not be returned. Send an SASE for complete guidelines.

Deadline: August 18.

Announcements: Winners are announced at a writers' conference in October.

Award: Cash awards ranging from $50 to $200 are given in each category.

***Calliope* Fiction Contest**
Calliope
P.O. Box 466
Moraga, CA 94556-0466

In its ninth year, this annual fiction contest is sponsored by the Writers' Special Interest Group of American Mensa. It looks to create a fun writing experience for members, subscribers, and entrants. The contest accepts most types of quality fiction including: magical realism, science fiction, fantasy, light horror, mystery, romance, and young adult/juvenile. It does not accept violence or graphic themes.

All entries must be original; reprints are not accepted. Entries should not exceed 2,500 words, and author's names should only appear on a separate cover sheet. Five entries per writer will be permitted. Entry fees are: members/subscribers, one free entry, $2 each additional story; non-members, $2 per submission. All entries must come by regular mail, not via the Internet. Send an SASE for further guidelines.

Deadline: Entries are accepted between April 16 and September 30.

Representative winners: Owen Williamson, Stina Branson, Jim Hayes.

Announcements: Winners will be notified both by mail, and in the

January/February issue of *Calliope*.
Award: First- through third-place winners will receive cash prizes based on the entry fees received. All winners and honorable mentions will receive certificates suitable for framing. Winners may also be published in *Calliope*.

Canadian Library Association's Book of the Year for Children Award
Moose Jaw Public Library
461 Langdon Crescent
Moose Jaw, SK S6H 0X6
Canada
website: www.cla.ca

Sponsored by the Canadian Library Association, this annual award is presented to the year's best book for children that was published in Canada during the year preceding the contest. All nominated titles must be written by a Canadian citizen or a permanent resident of Canada.

Any work that is an act of creative writing such as fiction, poetry, or retelling of traditional literature is eligible for consideration. Send an SASE for complete guidelines.
Deadline: Nominations should be sent by January 1.
Representative winners: *Sunwing*, Kenneth Oppel; *Stephen Fair*, Tim Wynne-Jones; *Uncle Ronald*, Brian Doyle.
Announcements: Winners are announced at the CLA annual conference in June.
Award: Winners are presented with a medal at an award ceremony during the Canadian Library Association's annual conference.

Canadian Library Awards Young Adult Canadian Book Award
North York Public Library
GS/HU Department
5120 Yonge Street
North York, ON M2N 5N9
Canada
website: www.cla.ca

Recognizing an author of an outstanding, English language, Canadian book that appeals to young adults between the ages of 13 and 18. Entries must be works of fiction in either novel or short story collection form.

Nominated titles must be published in Canada and written by either a Canadian citizen or resident of Canada. All entries must have been published in the year preceding the contest. Send an SASE for complete contest guidelines.
Deadline: December 31.
Representative winners: *Alone at Ninety Foot*, Katherine Holubitsky; *Janey's Girl*, Gayle Friesen.
Announcements: Call for nominations begins in October. Winners are announced in June at the CLA annual conference.
Award: Winners receive a leatherbound book with the title, author, and award seal embossed in gold on the cover.

Raymond Carver Short Story Contest
Humboldt State University
Department of English
Arcata, CA 95521

Honoring Raymond Carver and his connection to the Humboldt State

Listings

University English department, this annual contest is open to all U.S. citizens. It accepts previously unpublished short stories that are a maximum of 6,000 words (about 25 pages).

Send two copies of each story. Include a cover sheet with author's name, address, phone number, and e-mail address. Author's name must not appear on manuscript. Entry fee, $10.
Deadline: December 1.
Announcements: Winners will be announced in June.
Award: First-place winners receive $500 and publication in *TOYON*, the literary magazine of Humboldt State University. Second-place winners receive $250 and publication in *TOYON*.

Rebecca Caudill Young Readers' Book Award
Illinois Reading Council
P.O. Box 6536
Naperville, IL 60567-6536

This award was developed to encourage children and young adults to read for personal satisfaction. Books are nominated by children in grades 4 through 8. A master list of 20 titles is sent to participating elementary and middle schools. Students read the books and vote on their favorites each February. This program may be sponsored by public libraries if the schools in the area choose not to participate.
Deadline: Students vote in February.
Representative winners: *Ella Enchanted*, Gail Carson Levine; *Frindle*, Andrew Clements.
Announcements: Winning title is announced in March.
Award: Winners receive a plaque.

***Children's Writer* Contests**
Children's Writer
95 Long Ridge Road
West Redding, CT 06896

Each year, *Children's Writer* sponsors three contests with different themes, for unpublished fiction and nonfiction. Winning entries are judged on originality, writing quality, characterization, plot, and age-appropriateness.

Themes and age ranges vary for each contest. Submission lengths range from 350 to 1,500 words. Subscribers to *Children's Writer* do not have to pay an entry fee. Entry fee for non-subscribers is $10, which entitles entrant to a free eight-month subscription.
Deadline: February, June, and October.
Representative winner: *Ride a Wild Nightmare*, Justin Stanchfield.
Announcements: Winners are announced in *Children's Writer*.
Award: Cash prizes of $250–$1,000 are awarded to winners. Grand-prize winners are published in *Children's Writer*.

Mr. Christie's Book Award
2150 Lake Shore Boulevard West
Toronto, ON M8V 1A3
Canada

This annual awards program honors excellence in the writing and illustration of Canadian children's literature and encourages the development and publishing of high-quality children's books. Their goal is to promote a love of reading in young people. All entries must be published in Canada during the year preceding the contest.

Entries are accepted in English and French. Submissions should be sent to

each of the five judges. Send an SASE for judges' list and contest guidelines.
Deadline: January 31.
Announcements: Winners are announced in May.
Award: A cash award of $7,500 is awarded to the winner.

Christopher Award
The Christophers
12 East 48th Street
New York, NY 10017

The Christopher Awards are presented each year in several different categories including juvenile books, television specials, motion pictures, and books. These awards recognize creative works that go beyond entertainment to educate and inspire their audience. To be eligible for the book categories, entries must be original titles published in the year preceding the contest. No entry fee.

Send four copies of each title with a press kit, press release, or catalogue copy. Send an SASE for guidelines.
Deadline: November.
Representative winner: *Free the Children*, Craig Kielburger with Kevin Major.
Announcements: Winners are announced in February.
Award: Bronze medallions are given to the winners at a ceremony in February.

CNW/FFWA Florida State Writing Competition
CNW/FFWA
P.O. Box A
North Stratford, NH 03590
website: www.writers-editors.com

This annual competition is open to all writers, and presents awards in 11 categories including: children's literature, fiction, and nonfiction.

All entries must be previously unpublished. Multiple entries are accepted, provided each entry is accompanied by the entry fee of $10 for entries under 3,000 words, and $20 for entries over 3,000 words. Entries not following contest rules will be disqualified. Send an SASE for complete guidelines.

Entries are judged on format, grammar, clarity, structure, transitions, and impact. Author's name should not appear on manuscript. Include a separate cover letter with name, address, and title of manuscript. Entries should not be stapled; use paper clips only. Manuscripts are not returned; send an SASE for winners' list.
Deadline: March 15.
Representative winners: *The Secret of Ocotilo Canyon*, Mary Knapp; *Stampede*, Jennifer McCormick.
Announcements: Announcements of winners are made by May 31.
Award: Winners receive cash awards ranging from $25 to $75 for first- through third-place. First-place winners also receive a certificate.

Colorado Book Awards
Colorado Center for the Book
2123 Downing Street
Denver, CO 80205

The Colorado Book Awards are presented annually to Colorado authors who exemplify the best writing in the state during the year preceding the contest. The purpose of the award is to honor Colorado authors and promote

Listings

their books throughout Colorado and the United States.

Eligible authors must be Colorado citizens for three of the twelve months prior to the award. Books may be any subject matter, and the awards committee reserves the right to determine new awards categories based on the books that are entered. A special honor will be given to an individual who has made an outstanding contribution to Colorado's literary heritage. Send an SASE for an entry form and further guidelines.
Deadline: January 15.
Representative winners: *Through the Eyes of the Children,* Diane Hirschinger Gallegos; *A Good Doctor's Son,* Steven Schwartz; *Innocents on the Ice,* John Behrendt.
Announcements: Winners are announced in October.
Award: Winners are celebrated at an awards reception in their honor.

Dana Awards
Mary Elizabeth Parker, Chair
7207 Townsend Forest Court
Browns Summit, NC 27214-9634
www.pipeline.com/~danaawards

The purpose of the Dana Awards is monetary encouragement for work that has not yet been recognized. All submissions should be unawarded, unpublished, and not under promise of publication at the time of submission. Entries should contain clear, well-developed themes and be written in a style that exhibits love of language and mastery of the craft.

The awards are offered in three categories; poetry, short fiction, and novel. Novels are not accepted in the children or teen genres. Send an SASE or visit the website for guidelines. Send email questions to danaawards@pipeline.com

Include a cover sheet, with name, address, phone, and e-mail address. Author's name should not appear on manuscript. Multiple submissions are accepted. Entry fees, one short story or five poems, $10; novel entries, $20.
Deadline: October 31.
Representative winners: *The Half-Way Covenant,* Jacob M. Appel; *The Butcher's Rose,* Joette Hayashigawa.
Award: Winners receive cash awards of $1,000 in each category.

Marguerite de Angeli Contest
Delacorte Press/Random House, Inc.
1540 Broadway
New York, NY 10036

This contest looks to encourage the writing of contemporary and historical children's fiction set in North America for readers ages 7 through 10. It is open to U.S. and Canadian authors who have not previously published a novel for middle-grade readers.

Submissions should be between 40 and 144 pages in length and written for an audience of readers ages 7 through 10. Include a brief plot summary with cover letter. Each entrant may only submit two manuscripts for consideration of this award. Manuscripts under consideration for this award should not be submitted to any other publisher.
Deadline: Manuscripts should be postmarked between April 1 and June 30.
Announcements: Winners will be

announced before October 31 in *School Library Journal, Book Links, Publishers Weekly,* and other trade publications.
Award: Winners receive a contract for a hardcover and paperback edition of their work, $1,500 in cash, and $3,500 cash advance against royalties.

Delacorte Press Prize for a First Young Adult Novel
Bantam Doubleday Dell BFYR
1540 Broadway
New York, NY 10036

Open to U.S. and Canadian authors who have not previously published a young adult novel, the Delacorte Press Prize looks to encourage the writing of contemporary young adult fiction.

Entries should be written for a 12- to 18-year-old audience. Manuscripts should be no shorter than 100 and no longer than 224 typewritten pages. Photocopies are acceptable if legible and printed on quality paper. Send an SASE for return of manuscript. Only two manuscripts per person will be considered for the prize. Send an SASE for complete contest guidelines.
Deadline: December 31.
Representative winners: *Night Flying,* Rita Murphy; *A Door Near Here,* Heather G. Quarles.
Announcements: Contest results will be announced no later than April 30. Winners will be announced in *Publishers Weekly* and *School Library Journal.*
Award: The prize of a book contract covering world rights for a hardcover and a paperback edition, including a $6,000 advance on royalties are awarded. A cash prize of $1,500 will also be presented to the winner.

Distinguished Achievement Awards
The Association of Educational Publishers
201 Mullica Hill Road
Glassboro, NJ 08028
www.edpress.org

Sponsored by EdPress, these annual awards honor quality educational publishing. EdPress recognizes the industry's very best writing, editing, art, and design in print publications and audio/visual media. Entries are accepted in 64 award categories including short story, short nonfiction, and software for children, young adults, and adults.

All entries must have been published in the year preceding the contest. Send an SASE or visit the website for complete guidelines.
Deadline: January 14.
Announcements: Winners are announced in the spring.
Award: Winners in each category receive a plaque at the EdPress annual awards banquet in Washington, D.C.

Arthur Ellis Award
Crime Writers of Canada
3007 Kingston Road
Box 113
Scarborough, ON M1M 1P1
Canada

Sponsored by the Crime Writers of Canada, this award was established in 1984. It honors the best work published by Canadian authors during the previous year. Awards are presented in five categories: best novel, best first novel, best short story, best juvenile, and best true crime.

Entries may deal with espionage, suspense, crime, thriller fiction, and mystery. Entrants must be residents of Canada or Canadian citizens living in other countries. Send an SASE for complete guidelines.
Deadline: January 31.
Representative winners: *Sins of the Father,* Norah McClintock; *Sudden Blow,* Liz Kelly; *No Claim to Mercy,* Derek Finkle.
Announcements: Winners are announced in May.
Award: Award winners receive the "Arthur Statuette."

Empire State Award
New York Library Association,
Youth Services Section
252 Hudson Street
Albany, NY 12210-1802

The Empire State Award honors a body of work from a New York author that represents excellence in children's or young adult literature and has made a significant contribution to literature for young people. Members of the Youth Services Section of the New York Library Association are eligible to submit suggestions to the Committee Chair. Committee members will consider these suggestions along with their own. Send an SASE for complete contest information
Deadline: November 30.
Representative winners: Peter Spier, Jean Craighead George, Richard Peck.
Announcements: Winners are announced in May at the spring conference of the New York Library Association.
Award: An engraved medallion is presented to the winning author.

Shubert Fendrich Memorial Playwriting Contest
Pioneer Drama Service
P.O. Box 4267
Englewood, CO 80155-4267
website: www.pioneerdrama.com

In tribute to the founder of the Pioneer Drama Service, Shubert Fendrich, this annual contest is offered to encourage the development of quality theatrical material for educational and community theatres. Unpublished plays on any subject will be accepted. Entries should have a running time of 20 to 90 minutes, and must have been produced at least once.

Subject matter should be suitable for family-oriented audiences and theater groups. Send an SASE or visit the website for complete guidelines.
Deadline: March 1.
Announcements: Winner will be announced June 1.
Award: Contest winner will receive a $1,000 royalty advance in addition to publication.

Dorothy Canfield Fisher Book Award
Vermont Department of Libraries
109 State Street
Montpelier, VT 05609-0601

The purpose of this award is to encourage Vermont children to become enthusiastic and discriminating readers. During the year, children read books from the current list of 30 titles. In the early spring they vote for their favorite book. All forms of writing are considered including fiction, nonfiction, short stories, and poetry. All

public libraries and schools in Vermont receive the master list of books each year. Send an SASE for complete contest guidelines.
Deadline: Voting takes place in April.
Representative titles: *Gypsy Rizka, Speak,* and *Seal Island School* are on this year's master list.
Announcements: Winners are chosen no later than October 31.
Award: Winner receives a scroll illustrated by a Vermont artist, presented at an award ceremony.

Norma Fleck Award
33 Spadina Road
Toronto, ON M5R 2S9
Canada

Established by her family to honor her extraordinary contribution to Canadian children's literature, the Norma Fleck Award is given annually to an author or illustrator of Canadian nonfiction for children. Exceptional quality, informative and captivating presentation, and breadth and depth of information are some of the key criteria in selecting the annual winner.

Recipients are chosen by jury, with each member possessing a deep understanding of Canadian children's books, as well as a professional involvement in the book. Send an SASE for complete guidelines.
Deadline: April 30.
Representative winner: *By Truck to the North*, Andy Turnbull and Deborah Pearson.
Announcements: Winners are announced in November.
Award: A $10,000 cash award will be presented to the winner.

Foster City International Writers' Contest
Foster City Art and Culture Committee
650 Shell Boulevard
Foster City, CA 94404

This annual contest is sponsored by the Peninsula Press Club and is open to all writers. It looks to recognize new writers of fiction, humor, children's stories, rhymed verse, and blank verse.

Entries may be fiction, to 3,000 words; children's stories, to 2,000 words; and rhymed and blank verse that does not exceed two double-spaced pages. One piece per entry fee, $10. All entries must be written in English and previously unpublished.

Include a 3x5 card with each entry containing author's name, title of entry, phone number, address, and category. Author's name should not appear on the manuscript itself. Entries will not be returned.
Deadline: October 31.
Announcements: Competition is announced in the spring. Winners are announced in December.
Award: First place winners receive $250. Honorable mentions receive $125.

H. E. Francis Award Short Story Competition
English Department
University of Alabama, Huntsville
Huntsville, AL 35899

Sponsored by the Ruth Hindman Foundation and the University of Alabama at Huntsville, English Department, this annual contest accepts previously unpublished manuscripts only. Entries are judged by a panel of recognized, award-winning authors, directors of creative writing programs, and editors of literary journals.

Manuscripts should not exceed 500 words. Multiple submissions are accepted. Entry fee, $15 per submission. Include three copies of each manuscript. Author's name should not appear on manuscript. Include a cover letter with author's name, title, address, and phone number. Send an SASE for complete guidelines.

Deadline: December 31.
Representative winner: *How the Dead Live,* Gina Oschner.
Announcements: Winners are announced in March.
Award: A $1,000 cash award is presented to the winner.

Don Freeman Memorial Grant-In-Aid
Society of Children's Book Writers and Illustrators
Suite 296
345 North Maple Drive
Beverly Hills, CA 90210
website: www.scbwi.org/grants.htm

This grant-in-aid was established by the SCBWI to enable picture book artists to further their understanding, training, and work in the picture book genre. It is available to both full and associate members of SCBWI who intend to make picture books their chief contribution to the field of children's literature.

Applicants are required to submit artwork: either a rough book-dummy accompanied by two finished illustrations or ten finished illustrations suitable for picture book portfolio presentation. Further specifications will be sent with application.

Deadline: Applications available beginning June 1 and are accepted between January 10 and February 10.
Representative winner: Yuyi Morales.
Announcements: Requests for applications may be made beginning June 1 of each year. Completed applications and accompanying materials will be accepted after January 10 and must be postmarked no later than February 10.
Award: Winner receives a grant of $1,500; runner-up receives a grant of $500.

Georgia Children's Book Award and Georgia Children's Picture Story Book Award
Department of Language Education
125 Aderhold Hall
University of Georgia
Athens, GA 30602

Promoting reading for pleasure, these annual awards are voted on by children in the primary grades. Upon receiving nominations, a committee of teachers and librarians prepares a list of 20 titles for each award. Titles are then sent to Georgia classrooms that have agreed to participate.

Nominated titles should be appropriate for students in grades four to eight, and those nominated for the picture storybook category should appeal to students in kindergarten to grade four. Nominees must have literary merit and be free of stereotypes. All nominees must be written in English, and published within five years of the

competition. Authors must be residents of the U.S. or Canada.
Deadline: December.
Representative winners: *No, David,* David Shannon; *Leo the Magnificent Cat,* Ann M. Martin/Emily Arnold McCully; *Dog Breath,* Dav Pilkey.
Announcements: Winners will be announced in May.
Award: Winners receive a cash award of $1,000 and a plaque presented at the University of Georgia Children's Literature Conference.

Golden Archer Awards
Wisconsin Educational Media Association
Mary Ann Blahnik
Sturgeon Bay Public Schools
1230 Michigan Street
Sturgeon Bay, WI 54235

These awards are presented in three categories: primary, intermediate, and middle/junior high. Nominations for books are solicited from students. Librarians then choose five nominations that meet the eligibility criteria. Books should be recognized as noteworthy in quality and of special interest to children. Books must have been published in the United States and should be currently in print and readily available.

A nominations committee determines the titles for each age level to be a part of the competition. This list of titles is sent to each librarian that is a member of the Wisconsin Educational Media Association, and others upon request. They then vote on the winners.
Deadline: Final votes are due March 15.
Representative winners: Jack Prelutsky, Kevin Henkes, Joseph Bruchac.

Announcements: Winners are announced in April.
Award: Winners are presented with bronze medals and certficates.

Golden Kite Awards
Society of Children's Book Writers and Illustrators
8271 Beverly Boulevard
Los Angeles, CA 90048
website: www.scbwi.org

The Golden Kite Award is the only award presented to children's book authors and artists by their fellow authors and artists. Awards are presented to the most outstanding children's books published during the preceding year that were written or illustrated by members of SCBWI. Golden Kite Statuettes are given in four categories: fiction, nonfiction, picture book text, and picture book illustration. Honor books are also awarded in each category.

Winning books are those that the judges feel exhibit excellence in writing or illustration, and genuinely appeal to the interest of children. Books may be submitted between February 1 and December 15. Send one copy of the entry to each judge in the specific category, and one copy to the SCBWI office. Send an SASE or visit the website for guidelines.
Deadline: December 15.
Representative winners: *Speak,* Laurie Halse Anderson; *Space Station Science: Life in Free Fall,* Marianne J. Dyson.
Announcements: Winners are notified in April.
Award: Golden Kite Statuettes are presented to the winners. Plaques are presented for Honor Book winners.

Gold Medallion Book Awards
Evangelical Christian Publishers
 Association
Suite 2
1969 East Broadway Road
Tempe, AZ 85282
website: www.davisual.com/ecpa2000

For over 20 years the Gold Medallion Book Awards have been recognizing excellence in evangelical Christian literature. Entries are evaluated on the content, design, literary quality, and significance of contribution. Awards are presented in several categories including preschool, elementary, youth, reference, marriage, Christian education, family and parenting, and nonfiction.

Books must be submitted by publishers. Entry fee, $125 per title for ECPA members; $275 for nonmembers. Send an SASE for complete category list and guidelines.

Deadline: December.
Representative winners: *Because I Love You,* Max Lucado; *Fresh Faith,* Jim Cymbals and Nancy Pearcey.
Announcements: Entry forms are sent in October. Winners are announced at the annual Gold Medallion Book Awards Banquet.
Award: Winners receive a plaque at the annual banquet.

Governor General's Literary Awards
The Canada Council for the Arts
P.O. Box 1047
350 Albert Street
Ottawa, ON K1P 5V8
Canada

Established in 1975, these awards are presented to the best books written by citizens of Canada. Recipients are selected by two separate juries; one for English-language books, and one for French-language books. Entries may be fiction, nonfiction, poetry, drama, children's literature (text), children's literature (illustration), and translation. All entries must have at least 48 pages, except for picture books, which have a minimum of 24 pages. Books with more than one author/illustrator are not eligible. Send an SASE for complete guidelines and further information.

Deadline: Books published between September 1 and April 30 of the award year have a May 15 deadline. Books published between May 1 and September 30 of the award year have a deadline of October 15.
Representative Winners: *The Hollow Tree,* Janet Lunn; *A Child's Treasury of Nursery Rhymes,* Kady MacDonald Denton.
Announcements: The list of nominated books is announced in October, and winners in mid-November.
Award: Each winner receives $15,000 and a specially bound copy of their book. They are honored with a reception and dinner.

**Lorian Hemingway Short Story
 Competition**
P.O. Box 993
Key West, FL 33041

This contest was established to recognize and encourage the efforts of those who have not yet achieved major success in the world of publishing. Short stories of up to 3,000 words are accepted in several genres of fiction.

Entry fee, $10 per submission

postmarked before June 1; $15 per submission postmarked between June 1 and June 15. Multiple entries are accepted. Send a SASE for additional information and guidelines.
Deadline: June 15.
Announcements: Winners are announced in August.
Award: Winners of this contest receive a cash award of $1,000. Honorable mention receives $500.

Highlights for Children Fiction Contest
Highlights for Children
803 Church Street
Honesdale, PA 18431

Sponsored by *Highlights for Children*, this contest offers monetary awards for works of fiction in each year's designated theme. The most recent theme was sports stories for children. Stories may be any length up to 900 words. Stories for beginning readers should not exceed 500 words. Manuscripts or envelopes should be clearly marked Fiction Contest. Those not marked will be considered as regular submissions to *Highlights*. Enclose an SASE with each entry. No entry fees or form are required. All entries will be considered for publication in *Highlights for Children*.
Deadline: Entries must be postmarked between January 1 and February 28.
Announcements: Contest is announced in September. Winners will be announced in June.
Award: Each of the three winning entries will receive a cash award of $1,000, and will be published in *Highlights for Children*.

Insight Writing Contest
Insight Magazine
55 West Oak Ridge Drive
Hagerstown, MD 21740
website: www.insightmagazine.com

Sponsored by *Insight Magazine*, this contest honors previously unpublished work from a teen's point of view that deals with issues of concerns to today's teenagers. Entries should be written with a distinct Christian spiritual angle.

Prizes are awarded in three categories: student short story, general short story, and student poetry. Authors entering the student categories must be under the age of 21.

Submissions are judged on grammar, storyline, description, and dialogue. All entries must be typed, and may be sent via standard mail or e-mail to insight@rhpa.org.

All entries will be considered for publication. *Insight Magazine* retains first rights to publish the winning entries. Send an SASE or e-mail for further information.
Deadline: June 1.
Announcements: Competition is announced in the February issue of *Insight Magazine*. Winners are announced in a special winners' issue.
Award: Winners receive cash prizes ranging from $150 to $250 and publication in *Insight*.

Inspirational Writers Alive! Competition
Texas Christian Writer's Forum
6028 Greenmont
Houston, TX 77092

This annual contest serves to help

Listings

aspiring writers in the inspirational/religious markets and to encourage writers in their efforts to write for future publication. The competition consists of five categories: short story, short story for children or teens, article, daily devotions, and poetry. Individual requirements vary for each category.

Entry fee $10. Submissions must be unpublished. Include a cover sheet with name, address, and title of work. Send a SASE for complete competition guidelines and further information.
Deadline: May 15.
Announcements: Winners are announced at the Texas Christian Writers Forum.
Award: Winners receive cash awards ranging from $10 to $24 and a certificate of merit.

IRA Children's Book Awards
International Reading Association
P.O. Box 8139
Newark, DE 19714-8139
website: www.reading.org

These awards are presented annually for an author's first or second published book in the genres of fiction and nonfiction. Within each genre two awards will be presented; one for younger readers (ages 4–10) and one for older readers (ages 10–17).

Books may be entered into the competition by the author or publisher. Entries should be free from racism and sexism, and should encourage young people to read by providing them with something they will delight in and profit from by reading.

Entries should be sent directly to the designated IRA Children's Book Award Subcommittee Members. Send an SASE for further details.
Deadline: November 1.
Representative winners: *The Snake and the Scientist*, Sy Montgomery; *Molly Bannaky*, Alice McGill; *Eleanor's Story: An American Girl in Hitler's Germany*, Eleanor Ramrath Garner.
Award: A cash award of $500 and a medal are presented to the winner.

Barbara Karlin Grant
Society of Children's Book Writers and
  Illustrators (SCBWI)
Suite 296
345 North Maple Drive
Beverly Hills, CA 90210
www.scbwi.org/grants

The Barbara Karlin Grant was established to recognize and encourage the work of aspiring picture book writers. It is available to both full and associate members of SCBWI who have never had a picture book published.

One picture book manuscript per applicant may be submitted. The text may be an original story, work of nonfiction, or a re-telling or adaptation of a fairy tale, folktale, or legend. Complete guidelines and application forms available with an SASE, or visit the website.
Deadline: Request for application may be made beginning October 1 of each year. Completed applications are accepted between April 1 and May 15.
Representative winners: Toni Buzzeo, Andrea Beaty.
Announcements: Requests for applications are made beginning October 1 of each year.
Award: Winners receive $1,500; runner-ups receive $500.

Ezra Jack Keats New Writers Award
The New York Public Library
Early Childhood Resource and Information Center
66 Leroy Street
New York, NY 10014

This annual award honors books that portray the universal qualities of childhood, strong family and adult relationships, and the multicultural nature of our world. This annual award is given to a new writer of picture books for ages 9 and under. All entries should reflect the style of the award-winning author and illustrator, Ezra Jack Keats.

Authors entering this contest should have published no more than five books. Limit five entries per competition; no entry fee. Winners must be present to accept this award.
Deadline: December 15.
Representative winners: *Elizabeti's Doll*, Stephanie Stuve-Bodeen; *Calling of the Doves*, Juan Felipe Herrera.
Announcements: Award winner is announced in January.
Award: Winners receive a cash award of $1,000 and an Ezra Jack Keats silver medallion.

Robert F. Kennedy Book Award
Robert F. Kennedy Memorial
Suite 200
1367 Connecticut Avenue NW
Washington, D.C. 20036
website: www.rfkmemorial.org

This award is presented to the book that most faithfully and forcefully reflects Robert Kennedy's purposes—his concern for the poor and powerless, his struggle for truth in justice, his conviction that a decent society must assure all young people a fair chance, and his faith that a free democracy can act to remedy disparities of power and opportunity. Entries may be fiction and nonfiction, and must have been published in the year of the contest. Entries may be submitted by authors or publishers, and multiple entries are accepted. Entry fee, $25. Send an SASE, or visit the website for complete contest guidelines.
Deadline: January 31.
Representative winners: *Walking with the Wind: A Memoir of the Moment*, Congressman John Lewis; *Earth in the Balance: Ecology and the Human Spirit*, Al Gore.
Announcements: Winners are announced in the spring.
Award: Winners of this award receive a $2,500 prize.

Coretta Scott King Award
American Library Association
50 East Huron
Chicago, IL 60611

The Coretta Scott King Award is presented annually by the Coretta Scott King Task Force of the American Library Association's Social Responsibilities Round Table. Award recipients are authors and illustrators of African descent whose distinguished books promote an understanding and appreciation of the "American Dream."

The award celebrates the life and work of Dr. Martin Luther King Jr., and honors his widow, Coretta Scott King. Winners are chosen by a seven-member national award jury.
Deadline: Ongoing.

Representative winners: *Bud, Not Buddy,* Christopher Paul Curtis; *Heaven,* Angela Johnson.
Award: Winners receive a framed citation, an honorarium, and a set of Encyclopaedia Brittanica or World Book Encyclopedias.

Magazine Merit Awards
Society of Children's Book Writers
   and Illustrators
8271 Beverly Blvd.
Los Angeles, CA 90048

SCBWI presents the Magazine Merit Awards to honor their members' outstanding original magazine work published during that year. They are presented in four categories: fiction, nonfiction, illustration, and poetry.

Recipients must be members of SCBWI, and all are encouraged to join. Every magazine piece published for young people by an SCBWI member is eligible during the year of original publication.

Members must submit their own work. Proof of publication is required. Send four copies of the published work; illustrators may send color photocopies or tearsheets. Send an SASE for complete guidelines and further information.

Deadline: December 15.
Representative winners: *Stinksgiving,* Lisa Harkrader; *The Magic of Masks,* Mary Amato.
Announcements: Contest is announced in January. Winners are announced in April.
Award: Winners receive a plaque at an awards dinner. Honor certificates are awarded in each category.

David McCord Children's Literature Citation
Framingham State College
100 State Street
P.O. Box 9101
Framingham, MA 01701-9101

Since 1986 the Curriculum Library, with the Nobscot Reading Council of the International Reading Association, has sponsored the David McCord Children's Literature Citation to recognize his long and enduring contribution to children and their literature. It seeks to honor an author or illustrator whose body of work has made a significant contribution to excellence in the field of children's literature.

A committee of four librarians and teachers select the annual winner.
Deadline: Ongoing.
Representative winners: Jack Prelutsky, Kevin Henkes, Joseph Bruchac.
Announcements: Winners are announced in November.
Award: The winner is celebrated at the David McCord Children's Literature Festival in November.

McElderry Picture Book Prize
Simon & Schuster Children's
   Publishing
1230 Avenue of the Americas
New York, NY 10020

Encouraging new literary and artistic talent in the picture book field, this competition awards a book contract and an advance against royalties to its winner. Previously unpublished writers are asked to submit a book that they have both written and illustrated.

All manuscripts must be in English.

Entrants under contract with a literary or artist's agent are not eligible. Multiple submissions are not accepted; no entry fee. Send an SASE for return of complete guidelines.
Deadline: Entries must be postmarked between April 1 and December 31.
Announcements: Winner will be announced in the spring.
Award: A book contract with an advance of $12,500 against 10% hardcover and 6% paperback royalties.

The Vicky Metcalf Awards
Canadian Authors Association Awards
P.O. Box 419
320 South Shores Road
Campbelford, ON K0L 1L0
Canada

Established in 1963, these awards are named for Toronto librarian Vicky Metcalf. They seek to honor inspirational writing for Canadian youth. The awards are presented in three categories. The Body of Work Award goes to a Canadian author who has published a minimum of four books that are inspirational to young people. The Short Story Award is for a Canadian author of a short story written in English. The Editor's Award is given to the editor of the winning short story, if it is published in a Canadian periodical, anthology, or collection. Requirements and guidelines vary for each category.

The prizes in this competition are given "solely to stimulate writing for children by Canadian writers." Send an SASE for complete contest guidelines, and specific category requirements.
Deadline: December 31.
Representative winners: *Leaving the Iron Lung,* Anne Carter; *Chicken Lady,* W. D. Valgardson.
Announcements: Awards are presented at a banquet during CAA's annual conference in June.
Award: Body of Work winner receives $10,000; Short Story Award winners receive $3,000; and Editor's Award winner receives $1,000.

Milkweed Editions Prize for Children's Literature
Milkweed Editions
Suite 400
430 First Avenue North
Minneapolis, MN 55401-1743

The Milkweed Prize for Children's Literature is awarded to the best novel for children ages 8 through 13. Milkweed Press focuses on this important age group of middle-grade readers because they feel this group is not as well served by major publishers.

All submissions must be previously unpublished. Picture books and collections of stories are not eligible.
Deadline: Ongoing.
Representative winners: *The Dog with Golden Eyes,* Frances Wilbur; *Behind the Bedroom Wall,* Laura Williams.
Announcements: Winners are chosen no later than October 31.
Award: A $10,000 cash advance is awarded to the winning author.

Milkweed National Fiction Prize
Milkweed Editions
Suite 400
430 First Avenue North
Minneapolis, MN 55401-1743

Milkweed Editions is looking for

manuscripts of high literary quality that embody humane values and contribute to cultural understanding for its National Fiction Prize contest. Entries consist of the best works of fiction accepted for publication by Milkweed in the calendar year, by a writer not previously published by Milkweed. Submission directly to the contest is no longer necessary.

Manuscripts should be one of the following: a novel, collection of short stories, one or more novellas, or a combination of short stories and one or more novellas.

Deadline: Ongoing.
Representative winners: *Falling Dark*, Tim Tharp; *Tivolem*, Victor Rangel-Ribiero; *The Tree of Red Stars*, Tessa Bridal.
Announcements: Winners announced upon publication.
Award: A cash advance of $5,000 on royalties will be given to the winner.

Minnesota Book Awards
Minnesota Center for the Book
987 East Ivy Avenue
Saint Paul, MN 55106
website: www.mnbooks.org

This awards program honors Minnesota writers, illustrators, and editors. Entries may be submitted in 10 categories: young adult; children; anthology and collections; autobiography; fine press; history and biography; nature and Minnesota; poetry; mystery; novel and short story; and popular fiction.

Entries must carry a copyright date of the year of the contest. All submissions must be accompanied by an entry form and three copies of the book. Send SASE for complete category list and guidelines. No entry fee is required.

Deadline: December 15
Representative winners: *The Quiltmaker's Gift, Dating Miss Universe, Dove Song, An Early Winter.*
Announcements: Winners will be notified in April.
Award: Winners are honored at an awards celebration.

Mythopoeic Awards
Eleanor Farrell
P.O. Box 320486
San Francisco, CA 94132-0486

Each year the Mythopoeic Society sponsors four writing awards: Fantasy Award for Adult Literature, Fantasy Award for Children's Literature, Scholarship Award in Inklings Studies, Scholarship Award in General Myth and Fantasy Studies.

Books are nominated and judged by members of the Mythopoeic Society, and must have been published in the year preceding the contest. Send an SASE or visit the website for complete guidelines and further information.

Deadline: February 28.
Representative winners: *Tamsin,* Peter S. Beagle; *The Folk Keeper,* Franny Billingsley; *Dark Lord of Derkholm,* Diana Wynne Jones.
Announcements: Competition is announced in December; winners are announced at the annual Mythopoeic Conference in July or August.
Award: Winners are presented with a statuette of a lion, intended to evoke Aslan from C.S. Lewis's Chronicles of Narnia.

National Book Awards
National Book Foundation
9th Floor
260 Fifth Avenue
New York, NY 10001
www.publishersweekly.com/NBF

The National Book Awards are presented in four categories: fiction, nonfiction, young people's literature, and poetry. The awards look to enhance the public's awareness of exceptional books written by Americans, and to encourage a love of reading. Eligible entries can be full-length books of fiction and general nonfiction, and collections of essays by one author. All books must be published in the United States, in the year preceding the contest.
Deadline: July 10.
Representative winners: *Waiting*, Ha Jin; *When Zachary Bear Came to Town*, Kimberly Willis Holt.
Announcements: Winners are announced in November.
Award: One winner in each category receives a cash prize of $10,000.

National Children's Theatre Festival Playwriting Competition
Actors' Playhouse
280 Miracle Way
Coral Gables, FL 33134

Sponsored by Actors' Playhouse, this annual competition seeks original musicals. Eligible entries will be unpublished scripts, but works that have had limited production exposure, workshops, or staged readings are encouraged.

Scripts should be written for an audience of children ages 5 to 12, but should also appeal to adults. All entries must have a maximum of eight adult actors to play any number of roles. Scripts should have a running time between 45- and 60-minutes. Send an SASE for official entry form and complete guidelines.
Deadline: August 1.
Announcements: Winners will be notified in November.
Award: First-place musicals receive $1,000. Second-place winners receive a $100 honorarium.

National Written and Illustrated By ... Awards Contest for Students
Landmark Editions, Inc.
P.O. Box 270169
Kansas City, MO 64127

Encouraging and celebrating creativity, this annual contest is open to students in three categories: 6- to 9-years old; 10- to 13-years-old; or 14- to 19-years-old. Most genres are acceptable including biography, humor, science fiction, and mystery. Text may be written in prose or poetry. The text and illustrations should run between 16 and 24 pages.

Books are judged on the merits of originality and the writing and illustrating skills displayed. Entry fee, $2. All entries must be accompanied by an entry form, and must be signed by a teacher or librarian to qualify. Send an SASE for entry form and complete guidelines.
Deadline: May 1.
Announcements: Winners will be notified in October.
Award: Winners receive a publishing contract.

Listings

John Newbery Medal
Association for Library Service to
  Children
American Library Association (ALA)
50 East Huron Street
Chicago, IL 60611
website: www.ala.org

Awarded annually by the Association for Library Service to Children, a division of the American Library Association, the Newbery Medal is presented to the author of the most distinguished contribution to American literature for children.

Entries must be written by citizens of the United States, and published in the year preceding the contest. Entries should display respect for children's understandings, abilities, and appreciations. Entries may include co-authored books.
Deadline: December 31.
Representative winners: 2000 Winner: *Bud, Not Buddy,* Christopher Paul Curtis (Delacorte). 2000 Honor books: *Getting Near to Baby,* Audrey Couloumbis (Putnam); *Our Only May Amelia,* Jennifer L. Holm (HarperCollins)
Announcements: Winners are announced at the ALA mid-winter meeting in January or February.
Award: The Newbery Medal is presented at an awards banquet.

New Voices Award
Lee & Low Books
95 Madison Avenue
New York, NY 10016

Established in 2000, this award is presented to a writer of color for a picture book. Manuscripts should address the needs of children of color with stories that they can identify with and relate to. Entries should promote a greater understanding of one another.

Entries should be up to 1,500 words; no entry fee. Limit two entries per person. Send an SASE for the return of manuscript.
Deadline: Entries must be postmarked between January 1 and September 30.
Award: Winners receive a cash grant and a publication contract including an advance on royalties. Honor Award winners receive a cash grant of $500.

***No Noun-Sense* Contests**
No Noun-Sense
Box 147-2211
No. 4 Road
Richmond, BC V6X 3X1
Canada
website: www.nonounsense.com

This website sponsors contests that are open to all writers. The contests are offered in several categories including writing for children, fiction, and romance. It accepts previously unpublished work only.

No entry fee; no length requirements. Include a cover page with name, address, phone number, title, and word count. Submissions can be e-mailed to editor@webprospects.com. Send an SASE or visit the website for guidelines.
Deadline: May 21.
Announcements: Winning entries are announced in June.
Award: First- through third-place winners receive cash prizes ranging from $25 to $200.

NWA Short Story Contest
National Writers Association
3140 S. Peoria Street #295
Aurora, CO 80014

The purpose of the National Writers Association Short Story Contest is to encourage the development of creative skills, recognize and reward outstanding ability in the area of short story writing. Any genre of short story may be entered. Judging will be based on originality, marketability, research, and reader interest. Copies of the judges' evaluation sheets will be sent to entrants who send an SASE with their entry. Entry fee, $15 per submission.

Entrants can have their manuscripts critiqued for a fee of $5 per thousand words.
Deadline: July 1.
Announcements: Contest opens each April.
Award: First- through third-place winners receive cash awards. Fourth- through tenth-place winners will receive a book. Honorable mentions receive certificates.

Scott O'Dell Award
1700 East 56th Street
Chicago, IL 60637

Honoring quality writing in the field of historical fiction, this award is presented yearly. Entries must be written by an American citizen and published during the previous year, and have a setting in North, South, or Central America. Entries are usually submitted by publishers, although authors may submit their own work. Send an SASE for guidelines and entry forms.

Deadline: December 31.
Announcements: Winners are announced in the spring.
Award: Winners receive a cash prize of $5,000.

Once Upon a World Award
Museum of Tolerance
9786 West Pico Boulevard
Los Angeles, CA 90035

This award commends children's literature with themes of tolerance and diversity. Books should reinforce mutual understanding and illustrate the effects of stereotyping and intolerance, allowing the child to sympathize with the underdog.

All submissions must be in English, and must have been published in the preceding year. Submissions should be written for children ages 6 to 10 and may be fiction, nonfiction, or poetry. Send an SASE for complete guidelines.
Deadline: August 4.
Representative Winner: *So Far from the Sea*, Eve Bunting.
Announcements: Winners are announced in October.
Award: Winners receive a cash award of $1,000.

Orbis Pictus Award for Outstanding Nonfiction for Children
National Council of Teachers of English (NCTE)
64 Juniper Hill Road
White Plains, NY 10607

This annual award was established to promote and recognize excellence in the writing of nonfiction for children. The name of the contest commemorates

Johannes Amos Comenius's book *Orbis Pictus—The World in Pictures*.

Nominations of individual titles may come from the membership of NCTE and from the educational community. Any nonfiction book of informational literature that has as its central purpose the sharing of information that was published in the year preceding the contest is eligible.

Send nominations to the committee chair and include the author's name, title, publisher, copyright date, and an explanation of why you liked the book.

Deadline: November 30.

Representative Winner: *Shipwreck at the Bottom of the World: The Extraordinary True Story of Schackleton and the Endurance*, Jennifer Armstrong.

Announcements: Winners are announced in March or April.

Award: Winners receive a plaque presented in November during the Books for Children Luncheon at the Annual NCTE Convention. Five Honor books receive certificates of recognition.

Pacific Northwest Library Association's Young Readers Choice Award
Marshall Public Library
113 S. Garfield
Pocatello, ID 83204
website: www.pnla.org

The Pacific Northwest Library Association's Young Reader's Choice Award is the oldest children's choice award in the U.S. and Canada. It was established in 1940 in the hopes that every child would have an opportunity to find a book that interests and entertains them. Nominations are taken from children, teacher, parents, and librarians of the Pacific Northwest including Washington, Oregon, Alaska, Idaho, Montana, British Columbia, and Alberta.

Nominated titles must be published three years prior to the award year and printed in the U.S. or Canada. Titles are voted on by students in fourth through twelfth grade.

Deadline: February 1.

Representative winners: *A Mouse Called Wolf*, Dick King-Smith; *Ella Enchanted*, Gail Carson Levine; *Wringer*, Jerry Spinelli.

Announcements: Winners are announced in April.

Award: Winners of this contest receive $150 and a silver medal presented at an annual meeting and banquet.

Paterson Prize for Books for Young People
Maria Mazziotti Gilan, Director
Poetry Center
Passaic County Community College
One College Boulevard
Paterson, NJ 07505-1179

Established to honor outstanding children's books that are considered the best books for young people published in the preceding year. The prize is awarded in three categories: Pre-K–Grade 3; Grades 4–6; and Grades 7–12. Short stories, collections, short nonfiction, books, and poetry will be accepted.

Publishers should submit three copies of each entry with an official entry form. Entries will not be returned; they are donated to the Poetry Center Library at Passaic County

College. Include an SASE for the list of winners.
Deadline: March 15.
Representative Winner: *King of Dragons*, Carol Fenner.
Announcements: Winners will be announced in *The Poets & Writers Newsletter*.
Award: A cash award of $500 is offered in each category.

PEN Center USA West USA Literary Award in Children's Literature
PEN Center USA West
Suite 41
672 S. Lafayette Park Place
Los Angeles, CA 90057

Recognizing outstanding works published or produced by writers who live in the western United States. Winners are selected in ten categories including fiction, poetry, nonfiction, drama, and journalism.

The competition is open to authors and translators who live west of the Mississippi River. Entries may be submitted by authors, publishers, agents, or publicists. Entries must have been published in the year preceding the contest. Send four copies of each entry; entry fee $20 per submission. Send an SASE for complete guidelines and further contest information.
Deadline: December 31.
Representative winners: *Village of a Million Spirits*, Ian MacMillan; *Weslandia*, Paul Fleischman.
Announcements: Winners are announced in May.
Award: Winners in each category receive $1,000 and are honored at a ceremony in Los Angeles.

PEN/Norma Klein Award for Children's Fiction
PEN American Center
568 Broadway
New York, NY 10012

Established in 1990, the PEN/Norma Klein Award for Children's Fiction commemorates the late children's book author. The biennial prize recognizes an emerging voice of literary merit among American writers of children's fiction. Candidates for the award are new authors whose books demonstrate the adventuresome and innovative spirit that characterizes the best children's literature.

Candidates nominate themselves. Nomination letters should describe the author's work in some detail, and include a list of the candidate's publications. Do not send books with nominations, the judges may request them later. Entries are judged by a panel of three distinguished children's book authors.
Deadline: December 15.
Representative winners: Cynthia Grant, Graham Salisbury, Angela Johnson, and Rita Williams-Garcia.
Announcements: Winners are announced in the spring.
Award: A cash award of $3,000 will be given to the winner.

***Pockets* Magazine Fiction-Writing Contest**
Lynn Gilliam, Associate Editor
P.O. Box 340004
Nashville, TN 37203-0004
www.upperroom.org

In its eleventh year, this fiction-writing contest is sponsored by *Pockets*

Listings

magazine. There are no pre-selected fiction themes, although historical fiction will not be accepted.

All submissions must be previously published and be between 1,000 and 1,600 words. Include a cover sheet with author's name, Social Security number, address, title, word count, and "Fiction Contest." Author's name should not appear on manuscript itself.

Submissions will only be returned if they are accompanied by an SASE. Electronic submissions are not accepted. Send an SASE for further guidelines, or visit the website.

Deadline: Entries must be postmarked between March 1 and August 15.
Representative winner: *Star of Hope*, Pamela Beres.
Announcements: Winners will be notified by November 1.
Award: Winners receive $1,000.

Edgar Allan Poe Awards
Mystery Writers of America, Inc.
6th Floor
17 E. 47th Street
New York, NY 10017
www.mysterynet.com/awards

The "Edgars," named after Mystery Writers of America's "patron saint" Edgar Allan Poe, are awarded to authors of distinguished work in various categories of the mystery genre. Categories include: Best Young Adult Mystery, Best Juvenile Mystery, Best Novel, Best Short Story, and Best Critical/Biographical Work.

Entries must be published in the U. S. in the year preceding the contest. Each category has specific rules. Send an SASE for a complete listing, or check the website for further information.
Deadline: Deadlines vary.
Representative winners: *The Killer's Cousin*, Nancy Werlin; *Sammy Keyes and the Hotel Thief*, Wendelin Van Draanen; *The Widower's Two-Step*, Rick Riordan.
Announcements: Nominations are announced in February; winners are announced at the annual Edgars awards banquet.
Award: An "Edgar" bust is given to each winner. Nominees each receive a scroll.

Michael L. Printz Award for Excellence in Young Adult Literature
American Library Association
50 E. Huron
Chicago, IL 60611
website: www.ala.org

The Michael L. Printz Award is presented to a book that exemplifies literary excellence in young adult literature. Entries may be fiction, nonfiction, poetry, or an anthology. All entries must be published in the year preceding the contest. Submissions should be for young adults ages 12 to 18. Winners will be chosen by a selection committee, and as many as four honor books will also be awarded.

ALA committee members may nominate any number of titles. All nominations are kept confidential. Judges note that winning titles won't necessarily have a profound message, and that controversy is not something they avoid. They are looking for books that readers will talk about. Send an SASE or visit the website for complete

guidelines and information.
Deadline: December 31.
Representative winner: *Monster*, Walter Dean Myers.
Announcements: Winners are notified at the ALA mid-winter conference.
Award: Winner is celebrated at an ALA award ceremony.

Quill & Scroll International Writing/Photography Contest
Quill & Scroll Society
School of Journalism and Mass Communication
University of Iowa
Iowa City, IA 52242
website: www.uiowa.edu/~quill-sc

These awards seek to recognize student journalists for their writing, reporting, and photojournalism. Awards are presented in 12 categories including editorial, editorial cartoon, news story, feature story, and review columns.

Entry fee, $2 per entry. Entries not accompanied by the school registration form and entry fee will be disqualified. Each entry must have been published in a high school or professional newspaper in the year preceding the contest. Entries must be the work of a currently enrolled high school student. Each school is limited to four entries per division.
Deadline: Entries must be postmarked no later than February of each year.
Announcements: Winners will be announced in March 2001.
Award: Winners receive a National Award Gold Key, and if they are high school seniors, are eligible to apply for a $500 scholarship.

Pleasant T. Rowland Prize for Fiction for Girls
Pleasant Company Publications
8400 Fairway Place
Middleton, WI 53562

Named for the former educator and publisher of educational material, this annual contest presents awards to the best literature for girls ages 8 to 12. The purpose of the competition is to honor authors who successfully capture the spirit of contemporary American girls and show how the lives of today's girls are touched and affected by the events shaping the United States today.

All submissions must be previously unpublished, and feature a female protagonist between the ages of 8 and 12. Entries are judged on character development and overall quality. Historical fiction and collections of short stories or poetry are not eligible. Multiple submissions are not accepted. All entries must be written by residents of the U.S.
Deadline: Write for 2001 deadline.
Representative winner: *The Secret Voice of Gina Zhang*, Dori Jone Yang.
Announcements: Winners are announced in March.
Award: Winning author receives a cash advance of $10,000 and a publishing contract.

SCBWI Work-In-Progress Grants
Society of Children's Book Writers and Illustrators
345 Maple Drive, Suite 296
Beverly Hills, CA 90210
www.scbwi.org

The Society of Children's Book Writers and Illustrators offers these grants to assist and support those working in the children's book market. They are offered in four categories: general, contemporary novel for young people, nonfiction research, and a work whose author has never had a book published. Runner-up grants are also awarded. Send an SASE for an application and complete guidelines.

Projects that are under contract are not eligible for the SCBWI Grants.
Deadline: Completed applications are accepted between February 1 and March 1.
Representative winners: Paula Yoo, Cara Haycak, Jonathan Solomon.
Announcements: Requests for applications are made in October; winners announced in the following September.
Award: Winning grants are for $1,500. Runner-up grants are $500.

Seventeen Magazine Fiction Contest
Seventeen Magazine
850 Third Avenue
New York, NY 10022

This annual contest looks for original fiction by authors ages 13 through 21. Entries should be previously unpublished and no more than 4,000 words in length.

Multiple submissions are accepted; no entry fee. Include author's name, address, telephone number, date of birth, and signature on the top right corner of the first page of each entry.

Submissions are judged by the editors of *Seventeen*. Manuscripts will not be returned. Send an SASE for complete contest information.
Deadline: Write for 2001 deadline.
Announcements: Announcements are made in *Seventeen*; winners are notified late in the year.
Award: The Grand-Prize winner receives $1,000 and publication in *Seventeen Magazine*. Other winners receive cash awards ranging from $50 to $1,000.

Skipping Stones Awards
Skipping Stones
P.O. Box 3939
Eugene, OR 97403
wesbite: www.efn.org/~skipping

In its eighth year, this contest focuses on cultural and ethnic diversity. It honors exceptional contributions to ecological and multicultural education. It offers awards in four categories: Ecology & Nature, Educational Videos, Multicultural & International, and Teaching Resources. Judges look for authenticity, presentation.

Entries must be previously published and may be short stories, short nonfiction, poetry, plays, collections, and videos. E-mail questions to skipping@efn.org. Each category has specific guidelines. Send an SASE or visit the website for complete category requirements and entry forms.
Deadline: January 15.
Representative winners: *Grandaddy's Gift*, Margaree King Mitchell; *Tomás and the Library Lady*, Pat Mora; *A Rainbow at Night*, Bruce Hucko.
Announcements: Competition is announced in August. Winners are announced in April.
Award: Honor award certificates and award seals are presented to the winners. Winning entries are also reviewed in *Skipping Stones Magazine*.

Kay Snow Writing Awards
Suite 5A
9045 SW Barbour Boulevard
Portland, OR 97219-4027

The purpose of this annual contest is to help writers reach professional goals in writing in a broad range of categories including: adult fiction, adult nonfiction, poetry, juvenile short story or article, screenwriting, and student writer (18 and under).

All entries must be typed, double-spaced. Title and category must be on the upper left corner of each page. Each entry must be accompanied by a 3x5 card with the author's name, address, phone, title of entry, and category. Cards should be placed in a plain white, sealed envelope, labeled with category and title only.

Submit three copies of each entry. Entry fee is $10 for members; $15 for nonmembers. Manuscripts will not be returned.
Deadline: May 15.
Representative winners: Sharon Michaud, Kathryn Umbarger, Paula Terry, Kit Ehrman.
Announcements: Finalists will be notified by mail prior to the annual conference in August. Awards will be presented at the banquet.
Award: Cash awards ranging from $50 to $300 are given to the winners in each category.

Society of Midland Authors Awards
P.O. Box 10419
Chicago, IL 60610

The Society of Midland Authors presents these annual awards to encourage writers to practice their art in the heartland. The awards are presented in several categories including juvenile fiction, juvenile nonfiction, poetry, adult fiction, adult nonfiction, and biography. The competition is open to writers living in the Midwest only.

Books should be at least 2,000 words. Multiple submissions are accepted; no entry fee. Send an SASE for complete guidelines.
Deadline: January 30.
Representative winners: *Trapped Between the Lash and the Gun*, Arvella Whitmore; *Black Hands, White Sails: The Story of African-American Whalers*, Patricia C. McKissack and Fredrick L. McKissack; *Algebra of Night*, Willis Barnstone.
Announcements: Winners are announced at the Society's annual banquet in May.
Award: Winners receive cash prizes.

Southwest Writers Workshop Contest
1338-B Wyoming Blvd. NE
Albuquerque, NM 87112
website: www.southwestwriters.org

This annual contest is sponsored by the Southwest Writers Workshop in conjunction with their annual workshop. It offers writers an opportunity to have their work read and judged by professional editors and agents. Each entry also receives a written critique by a judge or a qualified published author.

The contest is offered in several categories including: novels with the subcategories of: children's picture book, science fiction or fantasy, spiritual essay, among others; short stories including literary, romance, and mystery.

Submit two copies of each entry. Author's name must not appear on manuscript itself. Author's name should be on the contest entry form only. Visit the website for a complete list of categories and genres.
Deadline: May 1.
Representative winners: Ngan Dan, Mallory Jensen, Summer Aubrey.
Announcements: Finalists in each category will be notified by mail. Winners are announced in September.
Award: Cash prizes ranging from $100–$250 are awarded to the winners.

The Spur Awards
Western Writers of America
W. C. Jameson
60 Sandpiper
Conway, AR 72032
website: www.westernwriters.org

Given annually for distinguished writing about the American West, these awards are among the oldest and most prestigious in American literature. The awards are offered in several categories including: best Western novel, best short story, best juvenile fiction, and best juvenile nonfiction.

All entries must be set in the American West, the early frontier, or relate to the Western frontier experience. All submissions must have been published in the year preceding the contest. Authors may submit multiple works in one category provided they are by different publishers.
Deadline: January 31.
Representative winner: *Walking with the Wind: A Memoir of the Moment,* Congressman John Lewis.
Announcements: Winners are announced in the spring.
Award: Winners of this award receive a $2,500 prize.

Stanley Drama Award
Wagner College
Department of Theatre and Speech
631 Howard Avenue
Staten Island, NY 10301

This annual competition accepts original, full-length plays, musicals, or one-act plays that have not been produced professionally or published in trade book form. Writers entering musicals should submit a manuscript accompanied by an audio cassette with all of the music included in the play.

Only one submission per playwright will be considered. Previously entered plays are not eligible. An entry fee of $20 must accompany each submission. Send an SASE for an application form and complete contest guidelines.
Deadline: October 1.
Announcements: Winners are announced in April.
Award: Winning playwright receives $2,000.

Stepping Stones Annual Writing Contest
P.O. Box 8863
Springfield, MO 65801

Stepping Stones, formerly known as Goodin Williams Goodwin Literary Associates, presents this annual contest for writers of children's stories. Its purpose is to promote writing for children by encouraging children's writers, and giving them an opportunity to submit their work in competition.

Fiction, to 1,000 words, and poetry, to 20 lines, are accepted. Entries should not be illustrated or in book format. Entry fee, $5. All entries must be accompanied by a completed contest entry form. Send an SASE for guidelines and entry form.
Deadline: July 31.
Announcements: Winners are announced approximately 60 days after the deadline.
Award: First- through fourth-place winners receive cash prizes ranging from $10 to $80.

The Sugarman Family Award for Jewish Children's Literature
District of Columbia Jewish
   Community Center
1529 Sixteenth Street NW
Washington, D.C. 20036

Held biennially, this award serves a purpose of enriching children's appreciation of literature and culture, and to inspire and encourage other writers and illustrators of Jewish literature for children. All entries must have been published in the year preceding the contest.

Entries may be picture books, fiction, and nonfiction, but must be targeted to children ages 3 to 16. Entries should reflect Jewish concepts, trends, and traditions, and should be presented from the Judaic point of view. Send an SASE for complete guidelines and further information.
Deadline: December 31, 2002.
Announcements: Winners are announced at an awards ceremony in the spring.
Award: Winners are presented with $750 at an awards ceremony.

Sydney Taylor Book Awards
Association of Jewish Libraries
1327 Wyntercreek Lane
Dunwoody, GA 30338

The Sydney Taylor Awards were established to honor outstanding children's books with positive Jewish content. All submissions should be fictional, and must be written in English. Material should deepen the understanding of Judaism for all children, and reveal aspects of Jewish life. Short stories and collections are not eligible.

Entries should be between 64 and 200 pages in length, double-spaced. Author's name should not appear anywhere on manuscript. Multiple submissions are not accepted. Manuscripts will not be read without an accompanying release form. No entry fee. Send SASE for release forms, complete contest guidelines, and further information.
Deadline: January 15.
Representative winners: Jack Prelutsky, Kevin Henkes, Joseph Bruchac.
Announcements: Winners are announced in November.
Award: The winner is celebrated at the David McCord Children's Literature Festival in November.

Teddy Children's Book Award
Austin Writers League
#E-2
1501 West 5th Street
Austin, TX 78758
www.writersleague.org

This award looks to honor the best children's or adult book published in the year preceding the contest. All

Listings

members of the Austin Writers League are invited to submit entries. Although submissions to this contest must be written by AWL members, entrants can join the league when entering the contest. Send an SASE or visit the website for guidelines.
Deadline: March 15.
Representative winners: Kimberly Willis Holt, John Erickson, Diane Gonzalez Bertrand.
Announcements: Winners are announced in September at a ceremony honoring the finalists.
Award: Winners receive a cash prize of $1,000 and a "Teddy Bear Trophy."

Vegetarian Essay Contest
The Vegetarian Resource Group
P.O. Box 1463
Baltimore, MD 21203
website: www.vrg.org/essay

This annual essay contest looks to increase awareness of the vegetarian lifestyle. It is open to children ages 8 to 18 and entrants need not be vegetarians to participate.

Any aspect of vegetarianism such as culture, health, ethics, or the environment, should be discussed in a two- to three-page essay that is based on interviews, research, and/or personal opinion. There are three categories of entries: 8 and under, 9 to 13, and 14 to 18.
Deadline: May 1.
Announcements: Winners are announced in early autumn.
Award: A $50 savings bond will be awarded in each age range. Winning essays will be published in *Vegetarian Journal*.

Stella Wade Children's Story Award
Amelia Magazine
329 E Street
Bakersfield, CA 93304

Amelia Magazine has been sponsoring this annual award since 1988. The contest looks for unpublished children's stories that are innovative, fresh, and contain strong characterization.

Entries should be up to 1,500 words and accompanied by the $7.50 entry fee for each submission. Multiple entries are accepted.
Deadline: August 15.
Announcements: Contest is announced continually in *Amelia*. Winners receive notification by mail within 12 weeks.
Award: Winners receive publication in *Amelia* and a cash award of $125.

Western Heritage Awards
National Cowboy Hall of Fame
1700 N.E. 63rd Street
Oklahoma City, OK 73111

This contest honors authors who contribute to the preservation of Western heritage. It is sponsored by the National Cowboy Hall of Fame. All submissions must deal with the American West or Western experience and can be in the form of a novel, art book, juvenile book, magazine article, short story, or poetry.

Each entry is judged on quality of writing, originality, and organization. Winners are chosen by a panel of three judges. Send an SASE for details.
Deadline: November 30.
Announcements: Competition is announced in January. Winners are an-

nounced by mail in the spring.
Award: Winners receive "Wrangler Trophies" during a ceremony at the National Cowboy Hall of Fame.

Jackie White Memorial National Children's Award
Columbia Entertainment Company
Betsy Phillips, Director
309 Parkade Blvd.
Columbia, MO 65202-1447

This contest seeks to encourage the writing of large cast plays suitable for production by the Columbia Entertainment Company's Children's Theatre School. Entrants should submit original, unpublished plays ranging from one to one-and-a-half-hours in length. Plays should have speaking roles for 20 to 30 characters, with at least 10 characters developed in some detail. Plays should be for all audiences, but be geared towards middle-grade students. Previously produced plays are also accepted.
Deadline: June 1.
Announcements: Contest is announced in January. Winners are notified in August.
Award: Winners receive $250 and the production of their play by the Columbia Entertainment Company.

William Allen White Children's Book Award
Emporia State University
Box 4051
1200 Commercial Street
Emporia, KS 66801-5092
website: www.emporia.edu/libsv/

Established by Emporia State University, the William Allen White Children's Book Award was put in place to honor the memory of one of the state's most distinguished citizens by encouraging the boys and girls of Kansas to read and enjoy good books.

Each year a master list is compiled by the Book Selection Committee, which represents educational institutions in Kansas. Books on the list must be nominated by a member of the Book Selection Committee. Suggestions for nomination may be submitted to the Executive Secretary of the William Allen White Children's Book Award program.

All nominations must have been published in English, during the year preceding the contest. Only books whose authors reside in the United States, Canada, or Mexico are eligible.

Children in fourth through eighth grade read the books from the master list and vote on the winner.
Deadline: April 1.
Representative winners: *White Water*, P. J. Petersen; *Frindle,* Andrew Clements; *Mick Harte Was Here,* Barbara Park.
Announcements: Winners are announced at the end of April.
Award: Winners receive the bronze White Award Medal, designed by Elden Tefft. Winners are celebrated at a luncheon or dinner.

Laura Ingalls Wilder Award
American Library Association
50 East Huron Street
Chicago, IL 60611

Recognizing an author or illustrator whose books have, over a period of years, made a substantial and lasting contribution to literature for children. The Laura Ingalls Wilder Award is presented every three years. Nominees are U.S. residents, and must have had their books published in the United States.

Nominees are presented to the award committee by members of ALA.
Deadline: Ongoing.
Representative winners: Russell Freedman, Virginia Hamilton, Marcia Brown, Jean Fritz.
Award: Winner receives a medal at an awards presentation.

Paul A. Witty Short Story Award
International Reading Association
P.O. Box 8139
Newark, DE 19714-8139
website: www.reading.org

The annual award is presented to the author of an original short story published for the first time in the year preceding the contest. Entries must be published in a periodical for children. Stories being entered in this competition should serve as a literary standard that encourages young readers to read periodicals.

Publishers or authors may submit entries, which should be sent to each member of the awards committee. Send an SASE or visit the website to request entry forms and competition guidelines.
Deadline: December 1.
Representative winners: Bill Pronzini, William J. Buchanan, Teresa Bateman.
Announcements: Winners are announced in January.
Award: A cash award of $1,000 is awarded to the winner at the annual IRA Convention.

Women in the Arts Annual Contests
Women in the Arts
P.O. Box 2907
Decatur, IL 62524-2907

This annual contest has been encouraging new writers and seasoned professionals since 1995. It offers awards in several categories including fiction, nonfiction, fiction for children, and essay. The majority of its entries come from unpublished writers.

Entry fee, $2 per submission. Include a cover letter with name, address, phone number, title of submission, category, and word count. Manuscripts will not be returned. Send an SASE for category length requirements and complete guidelines.
Deadline: November 15.
Announcements: Winners are notified in January.
Award: A $50 savings bond will be awarded in each age range.

Carter G. Woodson Book Award
National Council for the Social Studies
Manager of Awards and Special Projects
3501 Newark Street NW
Washington, D.C. 20016
www.ncss.org

The National Council for the Social Studies established this award for the most distinguished social science books appropriate for young readers that depict ethnicity in the United States. It seeks to encourage the writing, publishing, and dissemination of outstanding social science books for young readers. The award is presented in two categories: elementary and secondary. Honor books in each category will also be named.

This competition accepts work published in the United States during the preceding year. Send an SASE for competition guidelines.
Deadline: February.
Representative titles: *Story Painter: The Life of Jacob Lawrence,* John Duggleby; *Edmonia Lewis: Wildfire in Marble,* Rinna Evelyn Wolfe.
Announcements: Competition is announced in January. Winners are chosen in the spring.
Award: Certificates are given to the winners in each category during the NCSS annual conference in the fall.

***Writer's Digest* Writing Competition**
Writer's Digest
1507 Dana Avenue
Cincinnati, OH 45207
www.writersdigest.com

Writer's Digest presents this annual contest in several categories including: genre short story, children's fiction, personal essay, stage play script, and inspirational. Entries must be original, unpublished and unproduced. Entrants may enter the contest as many times as they like.

Categories must be listed in the upper left corner of the manuscript. Judges reserve the right to recategorize entries. Each entry must be accompanied by an official entry form and the required entry fee of $10. Send an SASE or visit the website for complete information and length limits. Exact word count must be listed on the first page of each entry. Entries exceeding the word or page limits will be automatically disqualified.
Deadline: May 31.
Representative winners: *The Keepsake Thief,* Maureen Mayer; *The Woman Who Waits,* Gary O'Shaughnessy.
Announcements: Contest announced in January; winners are announced in the November issue of *Writer's Digest.*
Award: The Grand-Prize winners receive a $1,500 cash award and a trip to New York City to meet with four editors or agents; other prizes include cash awards ranging from $25–$750 and books from *Writer's Digest.*

***Writers' Journal* Writing Contests**
Val-Tech Media
P.O. Box 394
Perham, MN 56573-0394
website: www.sowashco.com/writersjournal

Writers' Journal offers these writing contests throughout the year in several different categories. Among the categories are: short story, horror/ghost, romance, and travel writing. Guidelines vary for each contest. Send an SASE or visit the website for complete details. Enclose a #10 SASE for winners' list.

All entries should be previously unpublished. Submit two copies of each entry. Reading fees vary. Send an SASE for details.
Deadline: Deadlines vary for each contest; write for details.
Announcements: Winners are announced in *Writers' Journal.*
Award: Winners receive publication and cash prizes ranging from $15-$50.

Writers' Union of Canada Writing for Children Competition
Writers' Union of Canada
24 Ryerson Avenue
Toronto, ON M5T 2P3
Canada
website: www.writersunion.ca

This competition is held for Canadian citizens or landed immigrants who have not yet been published in book format, and do not have a contract with a publisher.

Fiction and nonfiction prose for children (no illustrations) are accepted up to 1,500 words. All entries must be unpublished and written in English. Entry fee, $15 per entry. Include a cover letter with name, address, phone number, word count, and whether the submission is fiction or nonfiction. Author's name should not appear on the manuscript itself. Manuscripts will not be returned. Send an SASE or visit the website for complete details.

Deadline: April 23.
Representative winner: *How Cold Was It?*, Jane Barclay.
Announcements: Winners will be notified in July.
Award: Winners receive $1,500. Winning entry and 11 finalists will also be submitted to a Canadian publisher of children's books.

The Writing Conference, Inc. Writing Contest
The Writing Conference, Inc.
P.O. Box 27288
Shawnee Mission, KS 66225-7288
www.writingconference.com

The Writing Conference, Inc. sponsors this annual contest for elementary, junior, and high school students. Entries may be a narrative, an essay, or a poem. Only one entry per person is permitted. All entries must be original and can not have been published previously.

Topics for this annual contest change each year. Send an SASE or visit the website for topics and entry forms. Students should not put their names on the entry itself, only on the entry form.

Deadline: January 8.
Representative winners: Cassie Morrow, Ada Smith, Lindsay Costlow.
Announcements: Competition announced in the fall; winners announced in February.
Award: Winning entries are published in *The Writer's Slate*, and along with their parents, will be guests at the annual conference.

Young Hoosier Book Awards
Carmel Clay Public Library
Carmel, IN 46032

Since 1992, this annual award has been encouraging recreational reading in Indiana students. The award consists of three categories: kindergarten through third-grade; fourth- through sixth-grade; and sixth- through eighth-grade.

Each year students, teachers, parents, and media specialists submit suggestions for nominations for this award. Nominations must adhere to all the guidelines. Send an SASE for complete list. Students then read a certain number of books on the list.

In April, the students vote on their favorite book.

Deadline: Voting results are due in April.
Representative winners: *Double Trouble in Walla Walla*, Andrew Clements; *My Little Sister Ate One Hare*, Bill Grossman.
Announcements: Winners are announced at the end of April.
Award: An engraved plaque is awarded to the winners.

Charlotte Zolotow Award
Cooperative Children's Book Center
4290 Helen C. White Hall
600 North Park Street
Madison, WI 53706

Honoring the distinguished children's book author, this award is given to the author of the best picture book text published in the year preceding the contest. All entries must be written by a citizen of, and published in, the United States. Entries may be of any genre of writing including fiction, nonfiction, poetry, or folklore, as long as it is presented in a picture book format and aimed at a young audience.

Winners are chosen by a committee of children's literature experts. Send an SASE for complete guidelines.
Deadline: December.
Representative winners: *When Sophie Gets Angry—Really, Really Angry...*, Molly Bang; *Three Cheers for Catherine the Great*, Cari Best.
Announcements: Winners are announced in January.
Award: A bronze medallion and cash prize of $1,000 are given to the winner.

Writers' Conferences

Conferences Devoted to Writing for Children – General Conferences

Celebration of Children's Literature
Montgomery College Continuing Education
51 Mannakee Street
Rockville, MD 20850

In an effort to provide continuing education for writers, teachers, librarians, and artists, this conference was organized 12 years ago for book lovers to receive inspiration as well as information on the children's literature market.
Date: April.
Subjects: Last year's topics included "The Roots of Storytelling," "Small Hands—Big Ideas," and "Finding the Right Publisher."
Speakers: At the 2000 conference, Judith O'Malley, Beth Mende Conny, and Sheila Hamanaka were guest speakers.
Costs: $60–$80.
Contact: Sandra Sonner, Senior Program Director.

Children's Literature: Landmarks, Boundaries, and Watersheds
Children's Literature Association
P.O. Box 138
Battle Creek, MI 49016-0138

This four-day conference involves full days of panels and workshops on everything from fantasy and genre boundaries to ethnic children's literature. Besides a roster of well-known children's authors and illustrators, the conference also features banquets, excursions, and local entertainment.
Date: June
Subjects: Last year's conference themes included "Crossing Cultural Boundaries," "New Girls and Their Champions," and "The Harry Potter Phenomenon."
Speakers: At last year's conference, Nancy Willard, Carolivia Herron, and Monica Hughes were featured.
Location: The 2000 conference was held at the Hotel Roanoke in Roanoke, VA.
Costs: Costs range from $120-$140 for members; $165-$185 for nonmembers. Fee does not include banquet.
Contact: Kathy Kiessling.

Children's Literature Conference
University College for Continuing Education at Hofstra University
UCCE, Hofstra University
Hempstead, NY 11549

Since 1986, the aim of this conference has been to bring together writers,

illustrators, librarians, educators, editors, booksellers and others interested in quality children's literature. The program features sessions with two speakers, six special interest groups from which registrants may choose two, and a panel of two children's editors who will critique first pages of randomly selected manuscripts.
Date: April 21, 2001.
Subjects: Conference workshops in the past featured submission procedures, writing poetry, illustrating picture books, and writing nonfiction.
Speakers: Last year's speakers included Ted and Betsy Lewin, Penny Colman, and Susan Beth Pfeffer.
Location: Hofstra University.
Costs: $72.
Contact: Kenneth Henwood, Director, Liberal Arts Studies.

Highlights Foundation Writers' Workshop
Highlights Foundation
814 Court Street
Honesdale, PA 18431

With a 3:1 student-faculty ratio, writers have ample opportunity to meet with the faculty on an individual basis during this annual conference. It also features contests, lectures, and a chance to network with writers, editors, and publishers. The week-long conference offers workshops covering both fiction and nonfiction for the children's market. Each participant receives at least three private conferences with faculty members.
Date: July.
Subjects: Topics presented at the 2000 conference centered on humor, science fiction, poetry, and young adult fiction and nonfiction.
Speakers: In past years, Laurence Pringle, Patricia Lee Gauch, and Peter Jacobi have been featured, along with the editorial staff of *Highlights for Children*.
Location: Chautauqua, New York.
Costs: $1,485 for first-time attendees; for returning writers, costs are higher.
Contact: Kent Brown, Executive Director.

In Celebration of Children's Literature
Professional Development Center
University of Southern Maine
305 Bailey Hall
Gorham, ME 04038

This three-day institute provides motivation for writers, storytellers, poets, teachers, and librarians and offers strategies for sharing literature with children of all ages. The format includes guest lectures, informal sessions, workshops, and book discussions. The conference aims to immerse participants into the world of children's literature.
Date: July.
Subjects: Last year's topics included "Writing for all Ages," "Sailing the Craft of Children's Poetry," and "Pictures for the Words."
Speakers: Elizabeth Winthrop, Paul Zelinsky, and J. Patrick Lewis were among the 2000 faculty.
Location: University of Southern Maine (Gorham campus).
Costs: $180 for the three-day program, including lunch.
Contact: Joyce Martin, Coordinator.

Robert Quackenbush's Children's Book Writing & Illustrating Workshop
Robert Quackenbush Studios
460 East 79th Street
New York, NY 10021

Held annually since 1982, this special five-day workshop provides participants with the chance to study with author and illustrator Robert Quackenbush. With an emphasis on picture books, the goal of this workshop is to learn how to create books for children and to overcome creative blocks. Classes for up to 10 people are held in the artist's studio on Manhattan's Upper East Side.
Date: July.
Subjects: Topics include how to work with a publisher to produce a book and how to develop a manuscript.
Speakers: Robert Quackenbush.
Location: New York City.
Costs: 2000 costs: $650; $100, non-refundable deposit.
Contact: Robert Quackenbush, Director.

Spoleto Workshop on Writing for Children
Spoleto Arts Symposia
60 West End Avenue, Suite 3-A
New York, NY 10025

In 2001, the Spoleto Writers' Workshop is holding its seventh annual session in Spoleto, Italy. Writers' workshops, consultations with faculty, manuscript critiques, readings, and writing sessions are on its agenda. Programs on children's fiction and nonfiction and writing for young adults will be featured.
Date: TBA.
Subjects: Fiction, nonfiction, young adult.
Speakers: James Magnuson was a former guest.
Location: Spoleto, Italy.
Costs: 2000 costs: $1,150 to $1,400.
Contact: Clinton J. Everett, Executive Director.

Wildacres Writing Workshop— Writing for Children
233 South Elm Street
Greensboro, NC 27401
www.wildacres.com

This conference specializes in critiquing students' work in classes no larger than 10. Attendees must submit a one-page writing sample
Date: July.
Subjects: Picture books, middle-grade, young adult, and creative nonfiction.
Speakers: Faculty at the 2000 conference included Cheryl Zach, Margaret Davol, Marcia Thornton Jones, and Jacqueline Ogburn.
Location: Wildacres grounds in the mountains of Little Switzerland, NC.
Costs: $480, includes workshop fees, one manuscript critique, a double-occupancy room, and meals.
Contact: Judith Hill, Director.

Listings

Conferences Devoted to Writing for Children – Society of Children's Book Writers & Illustrators

Alabama
Spring Mingle 2001!
SCBWI, Southern Breeze Chapter
P.O. Box 26282
Birmingham, AL 35260

This annual conference, which is held in either Alabama, Georgia, or Mississippi, on a rotating basis, emphasizes professionalism in the field of children's literature. Geared towards writers and illustrators, this three-day conference also features manuscript critiques and portfolio reviews.
Date: February 23–25, 2001.
Subjects: Last year's topic was on "Promotion with Pizazz."
Speakers: Richard Peck and Patricia Lee Gauch, as well as an illustrator, will be this year's speakers.
Location: Jackson, Mississippi.
Costs: Members, $90–$120; nonmembers, $100–$140.
Contact: Joan Broerman.

Writing and Illustrating for Kids
SCBWI, Southern Breeze
P.O. Box 26282
Birmingham, AL 35260

Held each October, this fall conference features over 30 workshops for beginning writers to published authors. Topics range from writing for preschool readers all the way up to young adults and deal with plot, characterization, chapter books, and novels.
Date: October.
Subjects: Topics include poetry, craft and technique, basics for beginners, and working with an editor.
Speakers: Kathi Appelt will be the keynote speaker. Rebecca Kai Dotlich, Elizabeth Harding, and Fiona Simpson will also appear at the 2001 conference.
Location: Birmingham, Alabama.
Cost: Members, $70–$100; nonmembers, $80–$120.
Contact: Joan Broerman, Regional Advisor.

California
March in Modesto
SCBWI, North Central California
P.O. Box 307
Davis, CA 95617

Published authors, an illustrator, and an editor are part of this yearly conference that provides information and opportunities for writing picture books through young adult novels.
Date: March.
Subjects: Topics include an editor's viewpoint, illustrating for the children's book market, and middle-grade to young adult fiction.
Speakers: TBA.
Location: Modesto.
Costs: $40–$50 including lunch.
Contact: Tricia Gardella or Tekla White.

National Conference on Writing and Illustrating
8271 Beverly Boulevard
Los Angeles, CA 90048
www.scbwi.org

Now in its 30th year, the National

Conference meets twice yearly during the summer and winter. Many award-winning authors, illustrators, editors, and publishers will present lecture workshops and individual consultations.
Date: Winter conference, February 17–18; Summer Conference, August 3–7 (tentative).
Subjects: Winter Conference will focus on sales and marketing.
Speakers: East Coast-based publishers, editors, and art directors will be featured at the Winter Conference.
Location: The Winter Conference will meet at the Roosevelt Hotel, Manhattan, NY: Summer Conference has yet to be announced.
Costs: $35 for members; $40 for nonmembers.
Contact: Lin Oliver, Executive Director.

San Diego Regional Conference
16048 Lofty Trail Drive
San Diego, CA 92127

This day-long conference offers guidance and encouragement to authors and illustrators from all levels of experience. Sessions are lead by noted and award-winning professionals.
Date: January 27.
Subjects: "Basics for Beginners" will discuss the process of submitting queries and manuscripts.
Speakers: Award-winning authors Jane Yolen and Edith Hope Fine; and freelance book designer, Kaelin Chappell.
Location: Quality Resort in San Diego's Mission Valley, 875 Hotel Circle South.
Costs: $75 for members, $85 for nonmembers.
Contact: Arlene Bartle.

Canada
Canada Conference
130 Wren Street RR#1
Dunrobin, ON K0A 1T0
Canada

Each year the Canadian chapter of the Society of Children's Book Writers & Illustrators presents a one-day program to help writers hone their craft and to achieve publication. The conference features panel discussions, portfolio critiques, and book signings.
Date: May.
Subjects: Lectures, workshops, and social events are part of this gathering.
Speakers: Past faculty have included Stephen Mooser, Kara Vincinelli, and Janet Wilson.
Location: Ottawa, Ontario, Canada.
Cost: TBA.
Contact: Noreen Kruzich Violetta, Regional Advisor, at 613-832-1288.

Iowa
Back to School Conference
SCBWI Iowa
1462 Old Freeport Place
Bettendorf, IA 52722-7001

The goal of this one-day conference is to meet the needs and desires of SCBWI for education in the field of children's literature. It is open to both members and nonmembers.
Date: September, October, and May.
Subjects: Children's literature and art, literary agents, and marketing.
Speakers: The faculty in 2000 featured Jacqueline Briggs Martin, Carol Gorman, and Ellen Jacobson.
Location: Iowa.
Costs: TBA.

Listings

Contact: Connie Heckert, Regional Advisor, at hecklit@aol.com.

Michigan
Biannual Conference/Retreat in the Even Years
5060 Sequoia Southeast
Grand Rapids, MI 40512

Held every other year, the purpose of this retreat by the Michigan chapter of SCBWI is to nurture and educate children's writers and illustrators and offer them opportunities to network and receive critiques from editors.
Date: 3 days in October, 2002.
Subjects: Small group critiques; past sessions have focused on illustration, picture books, and novels.
Speakers: Last year's retreat featured Carol Fenner.
Location: Michigan.
Costs: $250–$300.
Contact: Todd Budita.

Nevada
Northern Nevada Spring Conference
www.scbwi.org

The Northern Nevada Chapter of the SCBWI organizes this annual conference. Speakers will include an editor, agent, author, and a tax expert.
Date: June (date to be announced).
Subjects: To be announced.
Speakers: The speakers at the 2000 conference included Boyds Mills Press Editor Beth Troop, and authors Stephanie Jacob Gordon and Judith Ross Enderle.
Location: To be announced.
Costs: $30; $55 with manuscript critique.

Contact: E-mail a mailing address to Ginny Castleman, Regional Advisor, for additional information.

New England
Spring Conference
SCBWI New England
17 Morton Street
Newton, MA 02459-1013

Each year the SCBWI New England Spring Conference is held in a different location for working writers and illustrators. Workshops focus on fiction, nonfiction, young adult, marketing, and publishing.
Date: May 18–19, 2001.
Subjects: This year's conference topics include the "Nuts & Bolts" of creating books for children; and "To Market, To Market" focusing on connecting with readers and publishers.
Speakers: Guest speakers for 2001 include author Joanna Cole as well as editors and agents.
Location: Sturbridge Host Hotel in Sturbridge, Massachusetts.
Costs: $150. Lodging is extra.
Contact: John Bell, Regional Advisor.

New York
SCBWI Conference for Children's Book Illustrators and Author/Illustrators
32 Hillside Avenue
Monsey, NY 10952

Since 1986, this annual conference has provided an opportunity for illustrators to have their portfolios reviewed by art buyers and agents from the publishing industry. Submission guidelines are available at the above address.

Date: First or second Monday in May.
Subjects: Lectures present advice on all areas of illustrating fiction and nonfiction children's material, from concept to finish.
Speakers: Past lecturers have included Paul Zakris, Art Director for Simon & Schuster Books for Young Readers; and Author/Illustrator Maggie Smith.
Location: The Society of Illustrators, 128 East 63rd Street, New York, NY, 10021.
Costs: $90–$100. Please request guidelines for additional information.
Contact: Frieda Gates, Director.

North Carolina
Pathways to Publishing
SCBWI-Carolinas
104 Barnhill Place
Chapel Hill, NC 27514-9924

This conference offers participants a full day of working with published SCBWI authors, illustrators, and other professionals in the children's literature field.
Date: To be announced.
Subjects: Sessions include manuscript and illustration critiques, discussions on the roles of authors, agents, editors, and illustrators.
Speakers: Last year's lecturers included Author in Residence at Western Carolina University Dr. Gloria Houston, and Susan Raab, a marketer of children's and parenting books.
Location: North Carolina Bar Center, Weston Parkway, Cary, North Carolina.
Costs: $60–$75; accommodations available for an additional $54–$75.
Contact: Write to above address for additional information.

Utah
Spring Into Action: A Hands-On Workshop
1194 East 11000 South
Sany, UT 84094

This workshop features sessions and manuscript critiques with local and noted authors and editors.
Date: April 20–21.
Subjects: To be announced.
Speakers: Authors Aaron Shepard and Karen Clemmens Warrick.
Location: Westminster College of Salt Lake City, 1840 South 1300 East.
Costs: Friday only, $40; Saturday only, $80; Friday and Saturday, $115. Manuscript critiques (up to 5 pages) available for $25.
Contact: Kim Williams-Justesen, Regional Advisor.

Washington
Writing and Illustrating for Children
SCBWI Washington
14816 205th Avenue SE
Renton, WA 98059
www.scbwi-washington.org

Now in its tenth year, this SCBWI conference aims to improve writing and illustrating skills and to provide education, information, and advice to writers. Registration is on a first-come, first-serve basis.
Date: April 7, 2001.
Subjects: For 2001, the topics to be covered include picture books; writing for magazines; and working with an agent.
Speakers: This year's speakers will include Keith Baker, Peg Kehret, and Peggy King Anderson.

Listings

Location: Seattle Pacific University.
Costs: SCBWI members, $55; non-members, $65. Critique, $10.
Contact: Sue Ford, Regional Advisor.

Wisconsin
Fall Retreat for Working Writers
SCBWI-Wisconsin
51243 Redtail Rd.
Gays Mills, WI 54631

This retreat for working writers is in its 12th year. It continues to provide writing and marketing information as well as networking opportunities and critiques for writers.
Date: October.
Subjects: Topics covered include picture books, middle-grade and young adult fiction and nonfiction, and writing for magazines.
Speakers: For last year's conference, Jane Resh Thomas, Harold Underdown, and Cailyn Dlouhey were among the guest speakers.
Location: Wisconsin.
Costs: $220-$250.
Contact: Patricia Curtis Pfitsch.

Conferences with Sessions on Writing for Children – University or Regional Conferences

Annual Writers Conference at Oakland University
College of Arts and Sciences and Detroit Women Writers
231 Varner Hall
Oakland University
Rochester, MI 48309-4401
www.oakland.edu/contin-ed/writerconf/

Since 1961, this conference has been a collaboration between Oakland University and the Detroit Women Writers organization. It currently attracts over 400 attendees every year.
Date: 1½ days during the 2nd or 3rd week of October.
Subjects: Children's topics from the 2000 conference were "Writing for Children—Pre-school to Second Grade," "Reliable Web Resources for Writing Children's Books and Stories," and "How to Write Children's Nonfiction."
Speakers: The 2000 conference lecturers included Wong Herbert Yee, Jane Briggs Bunting, and Virginia Low Burns.
Location: Oakland University.
Costs: $85, with additional fees for writing workshops and manuscript critiques.
Contact: Gloria J. Boddy, Director.

Aspen Summer Words Writing Retreat and Literary Festival
Aspen Writers' Foundation
P.O. Box 7726
Aspen, CO 81612
www.aspenwriters.org

Founded in 1976 by poet Kurt Brown, this conference aims to educate and inform adult and children's writers, and to provide a forum for sharing ideas. The Writing Retreat offers workshops in fiction, memoir, essay, and poetry writing, and requires an application process. The Literary Festival has more than 20 events for writers, and is open to all.
Date: Third week in June.
Subjects: The topic from the 2000 Festival was, "The Patchwork Craft of Writing for Children."
Speakers: The 2000 speaker on children's writing was Lois Lowry.
Location: Aspen Institute and four other locations throughout Aspen.
Costs: $325 for the Retreat; $175 for the Festival. Lodging, $60 a night for a shared room; $120 a night for a single.
Contact: Julie Comins, Executive Director.

California Writers' Club Conference at Asilomar
3975 Kim Court
Sebastopol, CA 95472
www.calwriters.com

This conference offers hands-on workshops, seminars, critiques, and contests, while urging attendees to participate in guided tours and oceanside walks through this California State Park. Seminars are limited to 25 participants each, although participants can enjoy other conference activities.
Date: To be announced.
Subjects: Children's topics have included "Defrost Before Writing That

Children's Novel," and "Dogsled Your Way to Children's Nonfiction."
Speakers: Last year's speakers included children's author Sherry Shahan, and Marcia Preston, Publisher of *Byline Magazine*.
Location: Asilomar, part of the California State Park system.
Costs: $450 fee includes conference privileges, shared accommodations, and some meals. A $35 discount is available to CWC members, or fees paid in advance.
Contact: Gilbert Mansergh, Director (GPMansergh@aol.com).

Cat Writers' Association Annual Writers Conference
P.O. Box 1904
Sherman, TX 75091-1904

Since 1993, the Cat Writers' Association has held their three-day writing conference in order to provide expert help for writers to get published. Another aim of the Cat Writers' Association is to promote and reward writing that features cats.
Date: November.
Subjects: Last year's conference featured a panel of children's writers, illustrators, and an agent. Some of the topics covered in the 16 sessions include writing for children, online rights for writers, and writing for magazines.
Speakers: TBA.
Location: TBA.
Costs: Members, $55; nonmembers, $88. Lodging is extra.
Contact: Amy D. Shojai, Conference Chairman.

Clarion West Fantasy and Science Fiction Writers Workshop
Suite 350
340 Fifteenth Avenue East
Seattle, Washington 98112
www.sff.net/clarionwest

This workshop offers an intensive, six-week program for those interested in professional careers in science fiction, fantasy, and horror. Its focus is primarily adult literature, although some young adult topics are addressed. Every week, a new instructor—a professional writer or editor—teaches the class. Request application guidelines from the above address.
Date: 6 weeks during summer.
Subjects: To be announced.
Speakers: Authors John Crowley, Paul Park, and Pat Murphy were instructors with the 2000 Workshop.
Location: Seattle Central Community College.
Costs: $1,400 tuition; college credits can be obtained at an additional cost. Dormitories are available at Seattle University for $850. Scholarships are also available.
Contact: Leslie Howle, Administrator.

Craft of Writing Conference
P.O. Box 310560
Denton, TX 76203-0560

With an emphasis on exploring the changes taking place within the publishing industry, this annual conference for writers, established in 1982, features over 30 workshops and a panel of faculty members. A manuscript critique and contest, as well as book signings, are also part of this program.

Date: October.
Subjects: Children's fiction and non-fiction and young adult publishing.
Speakers: TBA.
Location: University of North Texas in Denton, Texas.
Costs: $149 for one day; $199 for two days.
Contact: Gina Thompson.

Critique Retreat for Writing Women
Jam-Packed Press
P.O. Box 14282
Pittsburgh, PA 15239

Fledgling through professional writers can attend the five critique sessions or participate in open discussions with a faculty of editors, writers, and publishers. Writing techniques, marketing your work, finding an agent, networking, and help with the Internet are covered in this three-day retreat.
Date: June, September, October.
Subjects: Workshops focus on writing for children and young adults, publishing, marketing, humor, and memoirs.
Speakers: TBA.
Location: St. Joseph Center in Greensburg, Pennsylvania.
Costs: $195 to $225 includes lodging and five meals.
Contact: Judith Burnett Schneider or Mary Jo Rulnick at 724-325-4964.

Gig Harbor Writers Conference
P.O. Box 826
Gig Harbor, WA 98335-0826

Through workshops and lectures focusing on children's fiction and non-fiction, writers have the opportunity to meet with authors and editors. This three-day conference is now in its fourth year.
Date: May 4–6, 2001.
Subjects: Workshops have featured topics on juvenile historicals, plotting, and real characters.
Speakers: For 2000, young adult author Randall Platt was part of the faculty.
Location: Gig Harbor, Washington.
Costs: $119–$149.
Contact: Kathleen O'Brien, Director, at 253-265-1904.

Hofstra University Summer Writers' Conference
Hofstra University
Hempstead, NY 11549
www.hofstra.edu

This conference provides aspiring writers the opportunity to work with established authors of a variety of genres, including children's writing. Students may attend workshops that offer more than 25 contact hours with a professional author. Hofstra's Summer High School Students Writers' Conference is also available for high school students with a serious interest in writing.
Date: 2 weeks in July.
Subjects: The 2000 workshop included "Writing for Children."
Speakers: Last year's workshop leader for children's writing was author Judith Logan Lehne.
Location: Hofstra University campus.
Costs: Tuition is $400 for one workshop or $625 for two. Graduate and undergraduate credits available at an additional cost. Hofstra residence halls are available for $350 during the two week conference.

Contact: Write to above address or e-mail: uccelibarts@hofstra.edu for additional information.

Manhattanville Summer Writers' Week
Manhattanville College
2900 Purchase Street
Purchase, NY 10577

This week-long conference offers writers the opportunity to hone their skills while working closely with professional writers and writing teachers. A special workshop is also offered to benefit beginning writers who want to master the elements of creative writing. There are also readings and a lecture, a session with editors and agents, and three workshops on different aspects of writing and editing.
Date: June 25-29, 2001.
Subjects: Last year's workshops included children's/young adult literature, and the young adult novel.
Speakers: Richard Peck and Dorothy Markinko spoke at the 2000 workshops.
Costs: Non-credit; $560; 2 graduate credits, $810; registration fee, $30.
Contact: Manhattanville College School of Graduate & Professional Studies, 914-694-3425.

National Writers Association Foundation Conference
3140 South Peoria Street, #295
Aurora, CO 80014
www.nationalwriters.com

Initially introduced in 1926 as a writing workshop, this annual event now provides education and assistance to writers of both children's and adult material in all its genres. Also available are one-on-one discussions with editors and agents.
Date: Second weekend of June.
Subjects: Previous subjects included "The Book to Film Process," and "Working with Small Publishers."
Speakers: 2000 speakers included Jonathan Treisman and Dorrie O'Brien.
Location: Renaissance Hotel, Denver (www.renaissance.com).
Costs: $195 for NWA members; $215 for non-members. Rooms are available at the Renaissance Hotel for about $70 per night.
Contact: Sandy Welchel, Director.

Of Dark and Stormy Nights
P.O. Box 1944
Muncie, IN 47308-1944

Sponsored by the Midwest Chapter of the Mystery Writers of America, this annual conference is the longest-running workshop for writers of mysteries and true crime in the U.S. It offers a few mystery-writing workshops for children and young adults.
Date: June 9.
Subjects: Topics from last year's sessions included "Getting Kids Interested in Reading and Writing" and "Writing for Older Youngsters and Younger Adults."
Speakers: Last year's faculty included Janet Riehecky and Marlis Day.
Location: Holiday Inn Rolling Meadows, Meadows, Illinois, outside of Chicago.
Costs: $150, meals included. Holiday Inn rooms available to conference attendees for approximately $98 a night.
Contact: Bill Spurgeon, Director.

Ozark Creative Writers, Inc.
75 Robinwood Drive
Little Rock, AR 72227

Held annually since 1967, the Ozarks Creative Writers, Inc. brings writers, editors, agents, screenwriters, and producers together to learn from one another.
Date: Three days during the second weekend in October
Subjects: Topics mainly cover writing for adults, with usually one lecture presented by a professional in the children's writing field. Topics include poetry, scripts, marketing, and success stories.
Speakers: The 2000 conference included Dan Slater, Senior Editor for Penguin Putnam; and Carolyn Wall, Fiction Editor for *Byline* magazine.
Location: The Inn of the Ozarks, Eureka Springs, AR.
Costs: $50–$60. Friday and Saturday evening banquets are $16–$19. Lodging is not included.
Contact: Marcia Camp, Program Coordinator.

Perspectives in Children's Literature
University of Massachusetts
226 Furcolo Hall, #2-22639
Amherst, MA 01003-3035

Since 1971, authors, illustrators, teachers, librarians, and students are welcome at this one-day conference featuring workshops, lectures, reading, and social events. Writers can choose two workshops from five selections.
Date: April.
Subjects: Past workshops have included "What's Funny in Children's Books," "Transforming Memories into Fiction," and current issues in children's literature.
Speaker: TBA.
Location: University of Massachusetts at Amherst.
Costs: $55, which includes lunch. $50 for students & SCBWI members.
Contact: Karin Dean, Coordinator, at 413-545-1116, or fax to 413-545-2879.

Philadelphia Writers' Conference
107 Newington Drive
Hatboro, PA 19040-4508

For three days, beginning writers as well as published ones can partake of four concurrent workshops; a roundtable buffet featuring a panel of agents and editors; a manuscript critique; a bookfair; and an annual awards banquet.
Date: June.
Subjects: Last year's theme was "Perseverance Pays," with the focus on children's literature, nonfiction, and writing for the juvenile and young adult market.
Speakers: TBA.
Costs: $160-$180. Buffet and banquet extra. Scholarships available.
Contact: I. Murden, Registrar, at 215-744-1417, or fax to 215-442-1987.

Remember the Magic 2001 Summer Conference
The International Women's Writing Guild
P.O. Box 810
Gracie Station
New York, NY 10028

Sponsored by The International Women's Writing Guild, a network of

Listings

women writers, this week-long conference at Skidmore College hosts over 70 daily workshops. Women of all ages and backgrounds attend writing and critique sessions, and open readings of works-in-progress.
Date: August.
Subjects: The 2000 conference included writing children's picture books and writing fairy tales, as well as a practical guide to creating plot, character, and dialogue in young adult fiction.
Speakers: Past faculty included Alexandra Wallner, Susan Baugh, and Sandra Gardner.
Location: Skidmore College, Saratoga Springs, New York.
Costs: Prices range from $60–$65 for a one-day registration to $740–$760 for a one-week registration with room and board.
Contact: Hannelore Hahn, Executive Director.

South Florida Writers Conference
5016 SW 72nd Avenue
Miami, FL 33155

Co-sponsored by the University of Miami and the National Writers Association, this conference features over 40 courses and over 20 speakers. Special events include a panel discussion, keynote speaker, celebrity author book signing, chat sessions, and awards breakfast and conference panel.
Date: March.
Subjects: At the 2000 conference, some of the topics included capturing a niche in the children's market; who gets an agent and how; and how to make plots work for you.
Speakers: Past speakers included Joyce Sweeney and Evelyn Mayerson.
Costs: $139; for Saturday events only (no banquet), $119.
Contact: Warren Zeiller, Conference Coordinator, 305-661-9446; or e-mail to prehistory@aol.com.

Vancouver International Writers Festival
1398 Cartwright Street
Vancouver, BC V6H 3R8
Canada
website: www.writersfest.bc.ca

This annual festival encourages an appreciation of the written word and promotes literacy by providing a forum where readers and writers of all ages can interact. Half of the events offered are for children's literature.
Date: Five days in October. Check website for dates and a schedule of events.
Subjects: Participants can listen to noted authors read and discuss their work, as well as learn techniques for improving their own writing and getting it published.
Speakers: Previous speakers have included Kenneth Oppel, Dennis Foon, Catherine Gildiner.
Location: Granville Island, Vancouver.
Costs: Tickets range from $8–$22 (Canadian).
Contact: Alma Lee, Artistic Director.

Victoria School of Writing
Box 8152
Victoria, BC V8W 3R8
Canada
ww.islandnet.com/vicwrite

The purpose of this conference is to improve the writing ability of its

participants by offering intensive, small workshops mentored by established writers. One of the seven or eight workshops deals exclusively with the art of writing for children.
Date: 4–5 days during the third week of July.
Subjects: To be announced.
Location: The Victoria School, in Victoria's Lake Hill district.
Costs: $475 Canadian; includes some meals. Accommodations for four nights and meals are available for $208 in Canadian dollars.
Contact: Gil Parker, Chair.

Whidbey Island Writer's Conference
5456 Pleasant View Lane
Freeland, WA 98249
www.whidbey.com/writers

Offering full sessions for children's authors, this conference aims to blend the benefits of a small gathering of writers with the resources of a larger conference in a "personal setting."
Date: March 2–4.
Subjects: "Success in Children's Writing," and "From Idea to Printed Page."
Speakers: Ann Paul, Kirby Larson, and Brenda Guiberson.
Location: South Whidbey High School.
Costs: $258, luncheons included.
Contact: Celeste Mergens, Director.

Write Now! Workshop
Creative Copy Ink
P.O. Box 50993
Phoenix, AZ 85076-0993

This workshop offers writers a one-day opportunity to meet with professional writers and participate in hands-on writing sessions. Of the nine workshops offered, writers may choose a total of three, which range from writing children's books to character development.
Date: February.
Subjects: Topics presented at the 2000 workshop included "Brainstorming Your Ideas," "Inspiring the Masses," and "Early Readers."
Speakers: Mona Gansberg Hodgson and Lauraine Snelling were part of the 2000 faculty.
Location: Phoenix, Arizona.
Costs: $39 for early registration; $49 thereafter.
Contact: Kitty Bucholtz, Director.

Write on the Sound
Edmonds Arts Commission
700 Main Street
Edmonds, WA 98020

This conference provides workshops on a variety of topics for all levels and genres, lead by noted authors, educators, and trade professionals. Manuscript critiques and contests are also offered.
Date: First weekend in October.
Subjects: 2000 children's topics were "Sizzling Mysteries" and "Nuts and Bolts of Children's Writing."
Speakers: The 2000 conference speakers included Henriette Klauser, William Dietrich, and manuscript critiques by Gloria Rempton.
Location: Edmonds Arts Commission
Costs: $85 for 2 days, $50 for 1 day. Contest entries, $10 mailed in advance with entry; request brochure for guidelines and theme. Lodging not included.
Contact: Frances Chapin, Edmonds Cultural Resources Coordinator.

Writers Institute
University of Wisconsin at Madison
Liberal Studies and the Arts
610 Langdon Street
Madison, WI 53703

Since 1989, this annual conference has welcomed writers of both fiction and nonfiction. It encourages and assists the writing of all genres and for every age group.
Date: July 12–13.
Subjects: Children's topics for this year will cover historical fiction, nonfiction, and the basics of writing and selling children's and young adult material.
Location: University of Wisconsin, Madison campus.
Costs: $195, and an additional $35 for critiques. Accommodations available at the Lowell Center for $60, with a full breakfast included.
Contact: Christine DeSmet, Director.

Writers Retreat Workshop
P.O. Box 139
South Lancaster, MA 01561

Since 1987, this 10-day workshop has provided writers with an intensive experience in one-on-one dialogues with instructors; brainstorming sessions with staff; a faculty of visiting authors and editors offering the latest marketing advice; and writing sessions, assignments, and classes on crafting a novel. Workshops are taught in the method of Gary Provost's step-by-step course for crafting your novel for publication. Each attendee must submit a one-page summary of a novel they are working on.
Date: May 25–June 3, 2001.
Subjects: The focus of the children's topics for this workshop center on children's fiction and nonfiction and writing for young adults.
Speakers: For 2001, Elizabeth Lyon, Don Maass, and Michelle Brummer will be on the faculty, along with authors and publishers.
Location: Marydale Retreat Center in Northern Kentucky.
Costs: $1,635, which includes all meals, lodging, classes, consultations, and classroom materials.
Contact: Gail Provost Stockwell, Director, at 800-642-2494.

Writing, Creativity and Ritual: A Retreat for Women
995 Chapman Road
Yorktown, NY 10598

For 10 days in Glastonbury, England, site of King Arthur's Avalon, writers explore the creative process through workshops, guided imagery, critiquing, dialogue, and other writing exercises. In addition, this retreat offers three days of sightseeing to Jane Austen's home; Stonehenge; and other sites of interest.
Date: July 27–August 6, 2001.
Subjects: Children's and young adult fiction and nonfiction, humor, mystery, and science fiction/fantasy.
Speakers: TBA.
Location: The Abbey House in Glastonbury, England
Costs: $1,750 to $2,000 including meals, lodging, and conference materials.
Contact: Emily Hanlon, Retreat Leader, at 914-962-4432, or by e-mail at emily@emilyhanlon.com.

Writing Your Future
Willamette Writers
9045 SW Barbur Blvd.
Portland, OR 97219
www.willamettewriters.com

This three-day conference brings together Northwest writers in order to participate in workshops and to network with agents and editors.
Date: August.
Subjects: Last year's workshops focused on fiction and nonfiction for preschool through young adult; rewriting; humor in stories; and using the Internet.
Speakers: Judy Cox and Nicole Rubel were part of the 2000 faculty.
Costs: $246 with early registration; otherwise, $276.
Contact: Cherie Walter, Conference Chair.

Conferences with Sessions on Writing for Children – Religious Writing Conferences

American Christian Writers
P.O. Box 110390
Nashville, TN 37222
www.ecpa.org/acw

Now in its 15th year, this organization schedules 36 conferences every year in 36 major cities throughout the country in an effort to reach as many Christian writers as possible. Conferences usually last one, two, or three days and are held in conference hotels. Approximately 20% of topics deal with writing for children.
Date: Request conference schedule or visit the above website for information on dates and locations in your area.
Costs: $99–$169.
Contact: Reg A. Forder, Director.

Festival of Faith and Writing
Calvin College
3201 Burton Southeast
Grand Rapids, MI 49546

This biennial festival is held at Calvin College, a liberal arts undergraduate institution committed to a reformed faith. It explores the craft of spiritual writing for both adults and children.
Date: April 18–20, 2002.
Subjects: The 2000 conference topics included "Retelling a Biblical Tale for Children" and "Writing to Nurture the Spiritual Imagination of Children."
Speakers: Festival 2000 lecturers included Jane Yolen, Sandy Sasso, and Ashley Bryan.
Location: Calvin College.
Costs: $125–$135 for the Festival; accommodations at local hotels average around $75–$80 nightly; meals are not included in the registration fee.
Contact: Gary Schmidt, Professor of English, Calvin College.

Montrose Christian Writers' Conference
5 Locust Street
Montrose, PA 18801
www.montrosebible.org

This annual event encourages powerful, Christian writing, flowing from a personal relationship with God. All writers of adult and young adult literature are welcome.
Date: 4½ days in late July.
Subjects: Last year's topics included "How to Get Published," "Inspirational Writing," and "Teens Can Write, Too!"
Speakers: Last year's speakers included Publishing Assistant Shirley Brinkerhoff, from Boyds Mills Press; and young adult author Nancy Rue.
Location: Montrose Conference grounds.
Costs: Tuition is $110, with critiques available for $25.
Contact: Patti Souder, Director.

New Jersey Society of Christian Writers Fall Seminar
New Jersey Society of Christian Writers
P.O. Box 405
Millville, NJ 08332-0405

Founded in 1992, The New Jersey Society of Christian Writers membership includes beginning to professional

writers who produce material for the secular media to proclaim the good news of salvation. Their one-day seminar in the fall is devoted to aiding writers reach their full potential in the Christian market.
Date: November.
Subjects: The 2000 seminar included topics on "Developing Your Creativity," "Article Writing," "Beware: 21 Pitfalls Ahead," and "Selling What You Write."
Speakers: Susan Titus Osborn was last year's guest speaker.
Location: Millville, New Jersey.
Costs: $75.
Contact: Dr. Mary Ann Diorio, Founder/Director, at 856-327-1231.

St. David's Christian Writers' Conference
87 Pines Road East
Hadley, PA 16130

Held thrice yearly, this Christian conference features manuscript critiques, keynote speakers, lectures, panels, writing sessions, and one-on-one appointments with editors.
Date: April, May, and June.
Subjects: Sample workshops include writing for children, juvenile fiction, E-publishing, and devotionals.
Speakers: Faculty for the 2000 conference included Rose Mary Stutzman, Amanda Lynch, and Jim Watkins.
Location: TBA
Costs: One-day workshop, $35–$40. Five-day workshop, $235. Room and board extra.
Contact: Audrey Stallsmith, Registrar.

The Writing Academy Summer Seminar
301 Brookside Lane
Seven Fields, PA 16046
www.wams.org

This seminar invites writers from across the United States and Canada who "share a passion for telling the story of God's good news to a hurting world." It offers encouragement, inspiration, and a peer-reading session in which participants share their works-in-progress.
Dates: 3½ days during the first weekend in August
Subjects: Topics focus on writing for all ages. Among the lectures at the 2000 seminar were, "Clarify the Message," and "Poetry and Hymn Lyrics."
Speakers: Last year's lecturers included J. Nestingen and G. Grindal.
Location: Mount Olivet Retreat Center, Farmington, MN.
Costs: $255 for double-occupancy rooms, $325 for single rooms.
Contact: Nancy James, Director.

Indexes

Subject Index

Topics, publishers, and companies are included in this Subject Index. For authors, editors, and other individuals, see the Name Index, page 384. For titles of books, magazines, articles, stories, and series, see the Title Index, page 390.

A

Able Minds 61
Abrams 12
Absey and Company 18
Academics. *See* Experts.
Accuracy 223
Acknowledgments 161, 163
Acquisitions and mergers 8, 9
Action 83, 99, 102, 108
Active voice 143
Activity books 89, 90, 153, 158, 162
ADD/ADHD newsletter 72
Adjectives 147
Adventure books 14
Adverbs 141, 146
Advertising 33, 35, 43, 45
Aesop Prize 88
Africa World Press 18
African Americans 50, 112
  authors 88
  awards 111, 115, 116, 117, 128
  books 11, 113
  history 50
  magazines 50
  markets, girls 43
  markets, parents 44

AG Fiction 10
  See also American Girl; Pleasant Company.
Agents 118, 166, 169, 171, 293-303
Agreements, on spec 174
  See also Contracts.
Aladdin Paperbacks 80
  See also Simon & Schuster.
Alfred A. Knopf 12, 17
Alloy Books 18
Alloy Online 16, 89
Allworth Press 62
Amazon.com 8, 22, 78, 157, 163, 168, 190, 283
America Online (AOL) 93, 203, 204
American Bar Association 179
American Booksellers Association 163
American Folklore Society 88
American Girl Collection 10, 90
American Indian Council of Mariposa County 223
American Library Association (ALA) 88, 108, 109, 110, 111, 112, 116
American Society of Journalists and Authors (ASJA) 165, 166
Anchorage Press 102
Animals, as characters 78, 83

Index

-369-

Anthologies 114, 166
Archives 214
Art books 13
Art Education *36*
Arthur books 87
AskJeeves 91
Association for Library Service to Children (ALSC) 112
Association of American Publishers 8
Atheneum Books for Young Readers 13, 88, 91, 95
ATL Press 18
AtRandom 23
Attorneys 169
Audience 101
Author Visits 187-198
Author's Day 194
Authors Guild 119, 169, 174
Authors' rights 119
Autobiography 159
Avisson Press 18
Awards 88, 111-122
  Aesop Prize 88
  American Library Association (ALA) 112
  Boston Globe-Horn Book Award 131
  Coretta Scott King New Talent Award 116, 117
  Coretta Scott King Award 111, 115, 116, 117, 128
  Caldecott Medal 10, 11, 77, 88, 95, 111, 112, 117, 120, 122, 134
  Golden Kite 88, 117, 119, 121, 128
  Hans Christian Andersen Author Award 88
  Jane Addams Peace Award 88
  Library of Congress living legends 88
  Los Angeles Times Book Prize 88
  Magazine Merit Award 113
  Margaret A. Edwards Award 88
  Michael L. Printz Award 88, 111, 115, 116, 122, 126, 127
  National Book Award 10, 11, 95, 111, 115, 119, 120, 121, 128, 131-133
  National Jewish Book Award 88
  New England Book Award 88
  Newbery Medal 10, 11, 77, 88, 111, 112, 113, 114, 117, 120
  Whitbread Children's Book of the Year 116

B

Baby Faire Inc. 44
Baby Gap 44
Backlist 28
Baker's Plays 102
Bantam Doubleday Dell 12, 166
Barnes & Noble 8, 214
  BarnesandNoble.com 23, 168, 283
Beginnings, fiction 101, 105
Benchmark Books 94
Best-sellers 12, 14, 22, 91
Bick Publishing House 18
Binney & Smith 34, 96
Biography 162, 214
Blackbirch Press 13
Blue Sky Press 18
Bob Jones University 20
Bologna Book Fair 13
Book clubs 8, 16, 42, 82
Book Expo 16
Book-of-the-Month Club 16, 42
Book producers 167
Book proposals 151-158, 283
Book reviews 116
Book sales 10, 14, 22, 168, 189, *190*

e-books 23
retailers, 168
sales records 16
Books-a-Million 8
Booksellers 8, 16, 283
See also Amazon.com; Barnes & Noble; Book sales; Borders.
bookstores 211
chains 8, 211
K-Mart 16
T.J. Maxx 16
Target 16
Wal-Mart 16
Book tie-ins 9
Borders 8, 11, 211
Boys
books 92
magazines 35
Branden Publishing 18
Brochures 189

C

Caldecott Medal 10, 77, 88, 95, 111, 112, 117, 120, 122, 134
Cambridge Physics Outlet 89
Canadian publishers 18, 20, 21
Candlewick Press 90, 94
See also Walker and Company.
Candy Cane Press 90
Cartwheel Books 77, 78, 80, 82, 83
Carus Publishing (Cricket Publishing) 15, 34, 50, 58, 91, 92, 94, 100, 224
See also Cobblestone Publishing.
Catalogues 163, 283
CD-ROMS 91, 94, 111, 112, 165, 166, 175
Celebrity authors 27-28
Censorship 119

Chaosium 18
Chapbooks.com 93
Chapter books 83
Chapter, sample 152, 153, 154, 155, 156, 159, 160
Characters 14, 77, 78, 81, 82, 86, 101, 102, 105, 108-110, 190, 260, 261
Charlesbridge Publishing 153, 197, 217
Chelsea House 13
Child Care Information Exchange 36
Children's Better Health Institute 58
Children's Book Council 163
Children's Literature Web Guide 174
Children's Press
See Grolier, Inc.
Children's Writing Resource Center 174
Church of Jesus Christ of Latter-Day Saints 201
City Park School 196
Clarion Books 15
Classics 47, 48
Clichés 141
CNN Interactive 94
Cobblestone Publishing 15, 34, 49, 50, 92, 95, 224
See also Carus Publishing.
COHM 179
College markets 89
Comic book 104, 159
Coming-of-age books 131
Competition 283
Competition research 159, 160, 163
Complete manuscript 153, 154
Concordia Publishing 152, 153, 154, 155
Condé Nast 42, 92
Conferences, writers' 347-365

Conflict 99, 101, 105
Contacts 196, 198
  See also Experts.
Contemporary Drama Service 106
Contemporary fiction 83
Contests 130, 305-345
Contracts 165-171, 177
  agents and attorneys 169
  all rights 165, 167, 170
  boilerplate 170
  contracts 192
  duration 165, 169
  electronic rights 165, 166, 169, 170
  exclusive rights 169
  first rights 169, 177
  licensing clause 174
  negotiation 169, 170, 171, 174, 176, 177
  new media 165
  payment 174, 176
  retaining rights 166, 169, 170
  school visits 192, 194, 195
  subsidiary rights 166
  Tasini, lawsuit 165
  termination clauses 169
  work-for-hire 165, 166, 167
Copyright law 165, 170
Coretta Scott King Award 88, 111, 115, 116, 117, 128
Coretta Scott King Illustrator Award 117
Coretta Scott King New Talent Award 116, 117
Coteau Books 18
Courier Corporation 89
Court Wayne Press 90
Cover letter 152, 154, 156, 159
Crafts
  books 162
  magazines 71

Creative Editions 18
Cricket Books 19
Cricket Publishing.
  See Carus Publishing.
Critical Thinking Books & Software 19
Critique groups 152
Crown Books 8, 11, 17, 91, 94
Cultures 217-224, 226
  contemporary stories 217, 218
  folktales and myths 217
  magazines, world cultures 217
Curriculum 13, 30, 82, 88, 218
  See also Educational publishing.
  author visits 188, 189
  church curriculum 99

D

Databases 165, 170, 201
Dater Elementary School 188
Dawn Publications 19
Delacorte Press 10, 12, 88, 113, 128
Delacorte Prize 130
Dénouement 100
Devotionals 154
Dial Books 77, 78
Dialogue 102, 105, 108-110, 145, 263
Different Books 19
Discovery Enterprises 19
Disney Channel 262
Disney Publishing 9, 90
Dorling Kindersley (DK Publishing) 8, 89
Dover Publications 89
Drafts 259
Drama 99-110
TheDrama.com 94

Dramatic Publishing 106
Dutton Children's Books 91
  See also Penguin Group.

E

Early readers 9, 77-86, 90, 153
E-books 166, 168, 171
E-commerce 8
Edge Books 15
Educational publishing 8, 26, 27, 35, 37, 38, 39, 51, 52, 77, 81, 83, 89, 90, 93, 158.
  See also Time, Inc.
  Canadian schools and libraries 90
  educational activities 94
  Educational Resources Information Center (ERIC) 60
  educational websites 55
Eerdmans Books for Young Readers 19
Eldridge Publishing Company 107
Electronic Elementary 61
Electronic publishing 165, 166, 169, 171
Electronic rights 165, 166, 169, 170, 173
Element Books 19
Emergent readers 51, 77, 81, 82, 92
Encore Performance Publishing 19, 107
Encore Software 94
Endings, fiction 109
English as a Second Language (ESL) 164
Environment 59, 151, 158
E-publishing 23
Everyday Learning/Creative Publications 8

Experts 156, 223
Exposition 108-110
E-zines 44, 61, 62

F

Fairy tales 218
Family.com 66
Family Heritage series 91
Family History Center 201
Family Treehouse 204
Family Treemaker 201
Fantasy 219
Fantasy books 14
Farrar, Straus & Giroux 19, 87, 88, 161
Fashion magazines 42
Fiction 12, 14, 95-106
  series 155, 215
Florida Library Youth Program 227
Folk crafts 218
Folktales 217, 218, 219, 220, 225
Format, book proposals 152
Fox books 77, 86
Frances Foster Books 19
Franklin Watts 8, 29
Free Spirit Publishing 19, 151, 152, 156, 158
Front Street Books 14, 19
Frontlist 28

G

Genealogy 201-205, 209
  Dear Myrtle 204
  Genealogy Forum 204
  resources 206, 207, 208
Geography 13

Index

Getting to Know the World's Greatest Artists series 13
Gibbs Smith Publishers 91
Girls
  books 158, 162
  magazines 35
  websites 60, 61
Girl Scouts of the USA, 61
Gold Award 128
Golden Books 9, 94
Golden Kite Award 88, 111, 117, 118, 119, 128
Golden Lamp Award 49
Gores Technology Group 94
G.P. Putnam's Sons
  See Penguin Group.
Grand Ridge Grade School 192
Graphic novel 159
Great Source 93
Greenwillow Press 88
Greyling 227
Grolier, Inc. 8, 13, 29, 89
  See also Scholastic.
    Franklin Watts 8
    Orchard Books 8
Gryphon House 16, 26, 27
Guideposts Publishing 90
Gulliver Books 95

H

H&S Media 42, 92
Hampton Roads Publishing 20
Handprint Books 91
Hans Christian Andersen Author Award 88
Harcourt, Inc. 21, 88, 95, 109
Harper and Row 77
HarperCollins Children's Books 7, 11, 13, 16, 19, 43, 80, 87, 88, 90, 91, 94, 115, 166
Harwich Elementary Library Media Center 189
Hearst Magazines 43
Hendrick-Long Publishing 20
Henry Holt and Company 15, 62, 87, 91, 94, 159, 162, 164
Heuer Publishing 20
Historical fiction 90, 110, 153, 210, 214
History 49, 50, 105, 155, 202, 211, 218, 226
  as background 105
  cultures 218
  historic sites 210
  historical societies 214
  research 202, 214, 215, 225, 226
HIT Entertainment PLC 11
Hobbit Hall Bookstore 196
Holiday House 122
Holloway House Publishing 20
Horace Mann Elementary 192
Houghton Mifflin Books for Children 12, 15, 93
How-to articles 71
Humor 153, 158, 262
HungryMinds.com 89
Hyperion Books for Children 88, 90, 166, 197

I

Ideals Books 80, 90
Ideas 259-290
  checklist 265-268
IDG 89
I.E. Clark Publications 18
Illustration 78, 80, 81, 111, 112, 116,

134, 135, 136, 160, 225
Imaginarium 93
Impact Publishers 20
Instructional Fair Group 8
International Reading Association (IRA) 11
Internet 23, 33, 55-60, 89, 91, 151, 168, 170, 174, 196, 203, 204, 209, 210, 221, 222
See also Websites.
iPublish.com 23

J

Jane Addams Peace Award 88
Jean V. Naggar Literary Agency 166
Jewish Publication Society 20
JL Hammett Company 93
Journey Books 20
Judaica Press 20
Jump at the Sun 88

K

Kaeden Books 77, 82, 83
Kalmbach Publishing 92, 107
Kendall/Hunt Publishing 178
Kingfisher Books 17
Klutz Press 89

L

Label books 82
Launches 14, 91
  book imprints 17, 23, 26, 91
  consumer magazines 33
Laura Geringer Books 19

Licensing 91
  magazines 15, 33, 34, 92
  picture books 91
The Learning Company 93, 94
Learning Network 93
Lerner Publishing 152, 156
Letter of agreement 192
Librarians and media specialists 187, 188, 189, 192, 196
  See also Markets, school and library.
Library of Congress 88, 163, 211
Licensing 9, 16, 174
Lillenas Publishing 20
Line Publications 42
Listservs 210
Little, Brown and Company 12, 21, 87, 90, 166
Little Simon 87
  See also Simon & Schuster.
LM_NET 196
Lobster Press 20
Log Cabin Publishing 71
Londoll, Inc. 8
Longfellow Elementary School 188, 193
The Loose Leaf Book Company 93
Los Angeles Times Book Prize for young adult fiction 88

M

Macmillan Children's Books 29
Magazine Merit Award 117, 118
Magazine Publishers of America 33, 42
Magazines 33, 211
  African-American 44
  boys 40
  city 211

closings 33, 35
cultures 224
educational 34, 36, 37, 39, 51
e-zines 55-60
girls 43
history 49
in research 211
Internet 55-60
middle-grade 33, 42
music 40
new magazines 33
parenting 43, 44
preschool 45
school and library 35, 50
sports 34, 40
teen 33, 40, 42
Maps 210
Margaret A. Edwards Award 88
Market analysis 153, 154, 156, 157, 159-164
Marketing, author promotions 197
Market research 159-164, 173, 283
Markets 8, 153
  college 89
  direct mail 35, 89
  easy readers 81, 82, 83
  educational 9, 26, 30, 81, 82, 89, 90, 158
  grocery stores 16
  home 8, 50
  mass-market 163
  mass-merchandisers 16
  middle-grade 14, 24, 25
  niche 159, 164
  nonfiction books 13, 31, 82
  parenting 27, 158
  preschool 89
  regional 65-69
  school and library 8, 13, 17, 29, 34, 35, 45, 52, 82, 89, 153, 163
  sports 40
  trade 17, 26, 163
  Wright Group 81
  young adult 15, 16, 18, 35
Marquette University 217
Martha Stewart Living Omnimedia 44
Matchbox Books 11, 90
  See also Pleasant Company.
Mattel 90, 93, 95
May Davenport 19
Mayhaven Publishing 20
McGraw-Hill Company 8, 52, 90
Media Central 163
Media, rights 165
Megan Tingley Books 21, 90
Melanie Kroupa Books 10
Memoirs 159
Meredith Corporation 33, 96
Mergers and acquisitions 89
Meriwether Publishing 20, 106
Michael diCapua Books 90
Michael L. Printz Award 88, 111, 115, 116, 122, 126, 127
Microsoft 23
Microsoft Network 203
Middle-grade 12, 14, 24, 25, 33, 42, 44, 100, 115, 158
Middles, fiction 108
Midlist books 168, 171
Millbrook Press 7, 8, 11, 13, 17, 91, 94
Modern Library 23
Monarch Publications 40
Mondo Publishing 77, 78, 82, 83
Mormons 201
Motivation 259, 260
Mountain Lake Software 61
Multiculturalism 43, 116, 151, 158, 217, 218, 219, 220, 221
Multiple submissions 157

Museums 213, 214, 223
  online 229-235
Music 40
Myths 217, 218

N

Narrators 105
National Book Award 10, 95, 111, 115, 119, 120, 121, 131
National Book Foundation 120
National Censorship Coalition 119
National Jewish Book Award 88
National Wildlife Federation 45, 59
National Writer's Union (NWU) 165-171
Naturegraph Publishers 21
Nelvana Ltd. 89
New Discovery Books 30
New England Book Award 88
New media 165
New writers 83, 99, 116, 154
Newbery Medal 10, 11, 77, 88, 93, 111, 112, 113, 114, 117, 120, 128-130
Newpapers 65
Nonfiction 91, 118, 153, 157, 160, 161
  books 13, 16, 30, 82
  magazines 15, 92, 118
  proposals 153, 159-164
Noodle Kidoodle 89
North-South Books 91, 95
Novelty books 9, 90
NTC/Contemporary Publishing 8

O

On-demand publishing 168, 169, 171
Online community 62
On-spec agreements 174
Outlines 153, 154, 155, 156, 159
Out-of-print books 168, 169, 189

P

Pacing 108
Paperbacks 82, 168
Parachute Press 16, 91, 94
Parade Publications 96
Parent Channel 93
Parenthoodweb.com 66
Parenting 158
  books 16, 26, 27, 28
  magazines 43, 44, 65, 92
Payment 173-179
  file-keeping 177
  rates 175
  reprints 179
  school visits 190-191, 195
PBS Kids Books 90
Peachtree Publishers 21
Pearson 8, 35, 89, 93
  See also Penguin Group.
  Addison Wesley Longman 8
  Allyn & Bacon 8
  DK Publishing (Dorling Kindersley), 8, 89
  Macmillan USA 8
  Pearson Education 8, 92
  Prentice Hall School 8
  Scott Foresman 8
Pegasus Library and Education Services 90

Penguin Group 8, 18, 89, 162
  See also Pearson.
  Allen Lane 8
  Avery 8
  Berkley Books 8
  Dutton 8
  Frederick Warne 8
  G.P. Putnam's Sons 87
  Hamish Hamilton 8
  Ladybird 8
  Michael Joseph 8
  Plume 8
  Puffin 8
  Putnam 8, 86
  Riverhead 8
  Viking 8
Personification 101
Peter Bedrick Books 13
Petersen Publishing Company 96
Photographs 160, 225
Picture books 12, 78, 91, 111, 112, 153, 158, 211, 225
Pinwheel Publishing 91
Pioneer Drama Service 107
Pitspopany Press 21
The Place in the Woods 21
Plays 92, 99-110
  markets 106, 107
Pleasant Company 10, 90, 95, 125, 160, 162
  See also American Girl.
Plot 99, 108, 110, 113, 261
  See also Story.
Pokémon 9
Preachiness 263
Prentice Hall 52
Preschool 89, 112
  books 9, 14, 26, 80, 89, 91, 112
  magazines 36, 37, 38, 39, 45, 57
Primary sources 13

  See also Research.
Primedia 40, 42, 44, 95
Printing 168
Problem, story 100
Prometric 89
Promotion 187-198
  author/illustrator packets 189, 194
  publishers' views 197
  school visits 187-198
Proofreading 152
Proposal, book 151-158, 160, 161, 163, 283
  competition 159
  complete manuscript 153, 154
  format 152, 153
  nonfiction 159, 160
  publisher lists 161
  publishing history 154
Protagonist 109, 110
PTA 188, 189
Public Broadcasting Service (PBS) 9, 90, 93
Publishers Information Bureau 33
Putnam
  See Penguin Group.
Puzzles 60, 153

Q

Query 62, 69, 71, 153, 164, 174

R

R.R. Bowker 163
Rainbow Books 21
Raintree/Steck-Vaughn 13, 29, 30
Random House 9, 23, 29, 77, 90, 94, 128

Reading programs 82
Ready to Learn Service 90
Red Deer Press 21
Reference publishing 89
References 211, 237-242
Regeneration series 260
Regional Markets 65-69
  See also Markets.
Rejection 158
Religious publishing 99, 153
  curriculum 99
  plays 106-107
  short story 105
  Sunday School papers 105
Reluctant readers 30
Reprints 174, 175, 177, 179
Research 151, 154, 201-256, 283
  archives 214
  bibliography 283
  competition 160, 163, 283
  diaries 214
  first-person accounts 222
  genealogy 201-205
  historical societies 214
  location resources 212
  magazines 211, 212
  maps 210, 212
  markets 157, 159, 283
  museums 213, 214
  newspapers 214
  online 222, 283
  people 201-205
  places 209-216
  primary resources 222
  publisher lists 151
  secondary sources 222
  sources 154
  state and national parks 214
  times and places 213
  travel guides 213

  videos 211
Résumé 83, 152, 153, 156, 159
Retellings 219, 225
Review, manuscript 223
Revision 154
Rhyme and rhythm 80
Richard Jackson Books 91
Rights 165, 166, 173, 174, 175
  abridgement 166
  agents and attorneys 169
  all rights 165, 167, 170, 175
  anthologies 166
  duration of contract 166, 169
  electronic rights 165, 166, 169, 170
  exclusive 169
  file-keeping 178
  first North American rights 175
  first rights 169, 175
  first serial rights 175
  foreign 166
  markets 177
  negotiating 169, 170, 171
  new media 165
  one-time rights 174, 175
  rates and policies chart 180, 181, 182, 183, 184, 185, 186
  reprint rights 175, 177
  retention 166, 169, 170
  second rights 175, 179
  subrights department 166
  subsidiary 166, 171, 175
  time limits 169
  work-for-hire 165, 166, 167
Rightscenter.com 166
Roberts Rinehart Publishers 90
Robins Lane Press 16, 26, 28
Rocky River Publishers 21
Rodale Press 40, 92
Royalties 168
Running Press Book Publishers 21

Index

S

St. Martin's Press 22
Saint Mary's Press 21
Sample text 154, 156, 159, 160
SCBWI
  See Society of Children's Book Writers & Illustrators.
Scenes 102, 105, 109
Scholastic 8, 9, 13, 18, 52, 78, 82, 88, 89, 93
  See also Grolier, Inc.
  magazines 34, 51, 53
  Scholastic Paperbacks 9
  school and library 53
School visits 187-198
Science 89, 158
Science fiction 219, 260
Screenplays 99, 100
Search engines 170, 203, 209
SeaStar Books 21, 91, 95
Self-help and advice, books 158, 162
Self-publishing 168
Sets 102
Setting 103
17th Street Productions 16, 89
Short stories 99, 100, 105, 118
Short Story International 178
Sierra Club Books for Children 91
Silver Whistle 21
Simon & Schuster 9, 12, 13, 17, 22, 23, 30, 77, 80, 87, 88, 91, 94, 171, 197
Simon Spotlight 9, 90
  See also Simon & Schuster.
Small presses 18, 27
Social history 162
Society of Children's Book Writers and Illustrators (SCBWI) 88, 117, 118, 119, 128, 174

Software 61, 63, 84, 93, 94
Sources
  See Research.
Special interest publications 71
Specialty publishing 168
Sports 34, 40, 96
  sports fiction 12
State Historical Society of Iowa 96
State Library of Florida 218
Steadwell Books 30
  See also Raintree/Steck-Vaughn.
Stepping Stone Books 77
Sterling Books 91
Sterling Publishing 152, 156, 158
Story 86, 99, 220
  See also Plot.
  beginning, middle, end 101, 108, 109
  catalysts 108
  climax 109
  conflict 99, 100, 101
  cultures 220, 221, 224
  dénouement 100
  pacing 108
  personification 101
  problem 100
  scenes 102, 105, 109
  setting 103
  structure 99, 100, 101, 110
  style 110
  turning point 99
Structure 99, 100, 101, 110
Student Channel 93
Submissions 157
  multiple 157
  unsolicited 83, 157
Subsidiary rights 166, 171
  See also Contracts; Rights.
Sylvan Learning Systems 89
Synopsis 154, 155, 156

T

Table of contents 152, 153, 154, 156
Tabloids 65
Tasini ruling 165
Teacher Channel 93
Teachers' guides 158
Technical publishers 167
Techniques 39
Technology 60
  See also CD-ROMs; Internet; Websites.
Teens
  See Young adults.
Ten Speed Press 162
Textbook publishers 167
Theme 261
Third World Press 21
Thomson Corporation 89
Thomson Learning 30
Tilbury House 151, 153, 158
Time, Inc. 34, 51, 52
  See also The Big Picture; Time For Kids; Time For Kids World Report.
Time Warner 23
Times Mirror Magazines 40
Tone 219, 220, 222, 223
  See also Voice.
Torstar Corporation 89
Toys 'R' Us 93
Trade books 168
Traditional Craft Series 227
TransWorld Media 40
Travel guides 209, 213
Tribune Company, education division 8, 90
  See also McGraw-Hill.
Tricycle Press 159, 162
Triplepoint, Inc. 89

'tweens 33, 42
Twenty-First Century Books 14
Two-Can Publishing 91

U

UAHC Press 22
United Parenting Publications (UPP) 65, 66, 69, 71
United States Copyright Office 179
Unsolicited manuscripts 83, 157

V

Vermont Folklife Center 91
Viking Children's Books 10, 11, 12, 87, 88, 161, 162
Vocabulary 78, 82, 83
Voice 156, 223
  See also Tone.

W

Walker and Company 90, 95
  See also Candlewick Press.
Websites 16, 110, 151, 167, 170, 203, 210, 283
  ABC News 4 Kids 57
  Alloy.com 16
  altavista.com 170
  Amazing Adventure Series: Stories of Imagination 57
  AskJeeves 56
  authors 189
  Babysitters Club 23
  Berit's Best Sites for Children 56
  book sales 23

Boys' Life 58
chickaDEE Net 59
Children's Better Health Institute 58
Club Girl Tech 60, 61
Colorado Alliance of Research Libraries 56
Consumer Reports Online 44
Cricket magazines 58
culture research 221
Cyberkids 61
Cyberteens 61
Daily Genealogy Column 204
DearMyrtle.com 204
Dodoland 57
Electronic Elementary 61
e-zines 63
Fathering Magazine 57
FreeZone 60, 63
FreshLimeSoda 61
FutureScan 57
genealogy 203, 207
Girl Power! 57
Girl Scouts 61
A Girl's World 61
gp4k.com 35
Highlights for Children 45
Just 4 Girls 61
A Kid's Life 57
Kids' Castle 57
Kidtalk News Family Magazine 57
KidzMagazine 61
location research 209
lycos.com 170
magazineoutlet.com 73
magazine-rack.com 73
Magazines for Libraries 56
mediafinder.com 73
Michigan Electronic Library 56
MidLink 55, 63

museums 229-235
National Geographic World 58
newsdirectory.com 73
Nightmare Room 94
northernlight.com 170
online community 62
Outer-Net Links for Kids: Ezines and Magazines 56
Parents and Children Together Online 55, 60
Penguin Group 16
periodicals online 165
publisher sites 163, 283
publishing sources 163
rightscenter.com 166
rootsweb.com 204
search engines 170
Seventeen Online 59
Soccer Jr. 34
Sports Illustrated For Kids 59
stephenking.com 171
StoryPlace: The Children's Digital Library 57
Syndicate Media Group 94
teenstylemag.com 92
Teenvoice.com 61
Time For Kids 59
uncweb.carl.org 170
USA Plays For Kids 110
website 94
writers' guidelines 23
Yahoo! 56
yahoo.com 170, 203
Yak's Corner 57
YES Mag 59
Youthline USA 57
Zillions 44
zooba.com 162
What's Inside Press 22
Whitbread Children's Book of the

Year Award 116
Wiley Children's Books 22
William Morrow 22
Williams-Justesen, Kim 209, 211
Winslow Press 22
Woodbine House 22
Work-for-hire 165, 166, 167
  See also Contracts; Rights.
World Wide Web
  See Internet; Websites.
The Wright Group 8, 77, 81, 82, 83
Writer's Guild of America 174
Writers' guidelines 23, 151, 154

X

Xlibris 168

Y

Yahoo 203, 209
Yosemite Museum 223
Young adults 99
  books 14, 15, 16, 88, 105, 115,
    123, 126, 127, 129
  magazines 33, 35, 40, 42, 43, 99
Young Adult Library Services Association (YALSA) 114, 126

Z

Zany Brainy 89
Zenith Entertainment 91
Zoboomafoo 9

Name Index

*This index includes authors, editors, and other individuals.
For topics, publishers, and companies, see the Subject Index, page 369.
For books, magazines, articles, stories, and series,
see the Title Index, page 390.*

A

Aardema, Verna 95
Adler, David 87
Albertine, Mary Ann 189, 196
Aliki 88
Allen, John 99, 102, 104, 105, 108, 109, 262, 263
Allen, Moira Anderson 62
Almond, David 116, 119
Alphin, Elaine Marie 109, 190, 214
Amen, Carol 174, 179
Anderson, Laurie Halse 88, 112, 115, 117, 119-121
Anderson, Walter 35
Arima, Elaine 162
Aronson, Marc 92, 159, 162, 164
Asher, Sandy 88, 102, 103, 105, 108, 109, 110
Astley, Amy 42
Ayers, Katherine 12

B

Babbitt, Natalie 87
Bagdlasarian, Adam, 11, 121
Baker, Charles & Rosalie 47, 48, 49, 220, 223, 225, 226, 227
Balkin, Catherine 197
Bancroft, Gloria 81, 82, 83
Bang, Molly 112
Bartoletti, Susan Campbell 119
Bates, Craig 223
Bauer, Marion Dane 194
Baum, L. Frank 87
Baynes, Pauline 87
Becker, Bonny 191
Becker, Larry 95
Beckman, Richard 42
Bedrick, Peter 13
Beiker, Julia 209
Bellows, Melina Grosa 44
Benenson, Lisa 95
Bergerson, Chris 61, 62, 63
Bicknell, Liz 94
Billingsley, Franny 187, 196
Bishop, Gerald 45
Blackwood, Gary 99, 100, 102, 108-110
Block, Francesca Lia 12, 14
Blume, Judy 88
Bond, Felicia 12
Boughton, Simon 17, 91, 94
Bowman-Kruhm, Mary 192
Bradburn, Frances 115, 122, 126-127

Braithwaite, Jill 152, 154, 157
Breen, Karen 93
Bridwell, Norman 93
Brothers, Ellen 95
Brown, Marc 87
Browne, Anthony 88
Broyles, Anne 158
Buchanan, Jane 210, 215, 216
Budhos, Marina Tamar 162, 164
Burack, Sylvia K. 92
Burgett, Gordon 166
Buscaglia, Marti 92
Buzzeo, Toni 188, 193, 196

C

Cadnum, Michael, 11, 121
Campbell, Don G. 22
Carney, Mary Lou 35, 262, 263
Carr, Kelly 95
Cart, Michael 122
Casement, Charles 27
Christopher, Matt 12
Clark, Christine 45
Cole, Jan 192, 196
Collard, Sneed B. III 118, 161, 163
Coman, Carolyn, 11, 121
Cooney, Barbara 95
Corbett, Corynne 43
Corey, Orlin 106
Cormier, Robert 88, 95
Crichton, Michael 23
Crisp, Marty 215
Crutcher, Chris 88
Csatari, Jeff 40
Curtis, Christopher Paul 10, 11, 88, 113, 119, 128-130
Cushman, Karen 12

D

Davis, Jill 160, 161, 162, 164, 192
Davis, Katie 189, 196, 260, 262
Dawson, Ted 49
de Brunhoff, Laurent 12
dePaola, Tommie 87
de Regniers, Beatrice Schenk 95
Dott, Jack 40
Draper, Sharon 117
Dr. Seuss 80, 94
Duey, Kathleen 190
Dyson, Marianne 88

E

Elleman, Barbara 217, 218, 225
Elliot, Jennifer 151, 158
End, Hedy 42
Enderle, Judith 217, 220, 221, 224, 225, 226, 227
Essex, Christopher 55, 60
Evans, John 42

F

Falligant, Erin 160, 162, 163
Feldcamp, John 168
Ferrell, Nancy 210, 215
Ferris, Jeri Chase 214
Fiedelholtz, Sara 92
Field, Syd 99, 100
Fiore, Carole 218, 220, 224, 225, 227
Florea, Jesse 173, 177
Flower, Mary 169
Franceschelli, Christopher 91
Freedman, Russell 113

G

Gale, David 94
Garland, Eric 43
Garton, Keith 34, 51, 52
Geiger, Nicole 159, 160, 162, 164
Gerver, Jane 78, 80, 82, 86
Giff, Patricia Reilly 12
Gilbert, Frances 152, 154, 156, 158
Giuduci, Vittorio 13
Gordon, Stephanie 217, 220, 221, 224, 225, 226, 227
Goss, Brian 60, 62, 63
Grove, Karen 109, 110

H

Hallinan, Patrick K. 80
Harkrader, Lisa 118, 209
Harvey, Brett 165, 169, 170
Herman, Cheryl 197
Herman, Jeff 171
Hill, Eric 87
Hilton, Suzanne 210, 214, 216
Hirschfeld, Robert 12
Hirschman, Susan 77
Hoban, Russell 77
Hoff, Syd 77
Holabird, Katharine 90
Holt, Kimberly Willis 119, 120, 131-133
Hopkins, Lee Bennett 13
Hopkinson, Deborah 88
Hoppe, Anne 77, 80, 83
Hort, Lenny 108-110
Huff, Sandy 174, 176, 179

I

Ibbotson, Eva 14
Imamura, Kevin 40
Iverson, Annemarie 95

J

James, Les 223
Jean, Terri 72
Johns, Linda 72
Johnson, Donna 45
Johnson, Sylvia A. 13

K

Karl, Jean 95
Katz, Susan 7, 14
Kaufman, Ronne 78, 81, 82
Kay, Verla 211
Keating, Joanne 71
Keegan, Denise 42
Keller, Emily 60, 62, 63
Keller, Martin 40, 92
Kerr, M.E. 12
Ketteman, Helen 188, 190, 191
Kiefer, Barbara 112, 122
King, Dr. Martin Luther 116
King, Stephen 23, 171
Kisseloff, Jeff 162
Kossmann, Walter 30
Krieger, Ellen 80, 81, 83, 86
Kuhn, Betsy 13
Kurtz, Jane 189, 191, 194, 259, 260, 261, 263

L

Lamb, Wendy 113, 114, 128
Lattimore, Deborah Nourse 219, 221, 222, 223, 224, 225, 226, 227
LeGuin, Ursula 88
Leon, Dorothy 118
Lewis, C.S. 87
Linder, Diana J. 71, 72
Lobel, Arnold 77, 86
Lunsford, Beth 196
Lyons, Lisa 99, 104

M

Machada, Ana Maria 88
Mackel, Kathy 259, 260, 262, 263
Mantel, Paul 12
Marcello, Patricia Cronin 155
Marshall, Jim 77, 86
Marshall, Marcia 13
Marston, Elsa 100, 108-110, 218, 220, 223, 224, 225, 226, 227
McArthur, Debra 214, 215
McCarthy, Pat 71, 72
McClafferty, Carla 161, 164
McCormick, Patricia 14
McCullen, Caroline 55, 63
McCullers, Carson *131*
McLoone, Margo 13
Meeker, Melanie 197
Minarik, Else Homelund 77
Mooser, Stephen 117, 119
Morris, Mary Rose 188, 196
Myers, Christopher 111, 115
Myers, Walter Dean 88, 115
Myracle, Lauren 104

N

Nierman, Kevin 162
Nitz, Kristin 209
Nolan, Han 121
Norman, Howard 88
Numeroff, Laura 12
Nunn, Kate 94

O

O'Malley, Judy 92
O'Neill, Alexis 218, 220, 221, 222, 224, 225, 226, 227
Old, Wendie 210, 215
Olswanger, Anna 118
Osborne, Mary Pope 86
Ottaviano, Christy 94

P

Pape, Ray 106
Parent, Kip 166
Park, Barbara 86
Partridge, Elizabeth 161
Paterson, Katherine 88
Paulsen, Gary 12, 14
Pearson, Mary E. 259, 261
Pease, Chris 262
Perry, Michael 107
Petersen, Kristina 9
Pinkney, Brian 88
Pinkwater, Daniel 81, 194
Platzner, Linda 95
Pohn, Ali 60
Pollard, Barbara K. 162
Poploff, Michelle 94
Postlewait, Beula 174

Preston, Elizabeth 107
Provey, Joe 34
Pullman, Philip 12

R

Regan, Dian Curtis 191
Reuther, David 91
Rey, H.A. and Margaret 12
Reynolds, Jean 7, 8, 11, 14, 23
Reynolds, Phyllis Naylor 12
Richer, Julie 61, 62
Robinson, Marileta 223, 224
Robinson, Richard 8
Rochman, Hazel 120
Rogers, Fred 88
Rogers, Tom 44
Romanos, Jack 9
Rood, Justin 22, 26, 27, 28
Roome, Hugh 8, 34
Rowland, Pleasant 95
Rowling, J.K. 7, 14, 86
Rylant, Cynthia 81

S

Sachar, Louis 114, 119
Saint-Exupéry, Antoine de 87
San Souci, Robert 217, 219, 221, 223, 225, 226, 227
Schneeman, Andrea 95
Schulz, Charles 95
Schwartz, Cheryl 42
Selfridge, John 13
Service, Pamela 102, 103, 105
Severe, Sal 22
Sewall, Marcia 88
Shepard, Aaron 218, 220, 221, 225, 227

Sherry, Toby 78, 80, 82, 86
Shore, Susan 107
Shoup, Barbara 99, 105, 108-110
Siegel, Alice 13
Silberg, Jackie 26
Silbey, Caroline 22
Simmons, Cyndi 71
Singleton, Linda Joy 260, 262
Sloan, Frank 13, 14, 29, 30, 31
Snyder, Bethany 80
Somers, Beth 107
Spencer, Richard 95
Spinelli, Jerry 12, 14, 93
Stafford, Susan 102, 103, 104, 105
Stanley, Diane 13
Stanley, Jerry, 11, 121
Stewart, Martha 44
Stine, R.L. 94
Strasser, Todd 12, 14
Stutzman, Rose Mary 262
Sutton, Roger 126
Swartz, Steve 44

T

Taback, Simms 10, 11, 88, 111, 112, 134-136
Tasini, Jonathan 165-171
Tedesco, Anthony 62
Tedesco, Paul 62
Temko, Florence 218, 220, 222, 227
Thomas, Garen 95

U

Underdown, Harold 153, 157, 217, 223, 224, 226
Urmston, Craig 82, 83

V

Van Leeuwen, Jean 78
Verdick, Dan 27
Verney, Sarah 215
Vestal, Joan 29

W

Wachsberger, Ken 169
Walker, Craig 9, 23
Wardlaw, Lee 187, 189, 190, 192, 195, 196
Waryncia, Lou 35
Weinstock, Dawn 152, 154, 155
Weisgard, Leonard 95
Wells, Rosemary 12
Wentzel, Katrina 151, 152, 156, 157, 158
Whelan, Gloria, 10, 121
Wilson, Judy 29

Title Index

This index includes books, magazines, articles, stories, and series. For topics, publishers, and companies, see the Subject Index, page 369. For editors, authors, and other individuals, see the Name Index, page 384.

A

Acorn 36
Aim 178
The ALAN Review 36
Amanda and Oliver tales 77
Amanda Pig and Her Big Brother Oliver 78
Amazing Adventure Series: Stories of Imagination 57
The Amber Spyglass 12
American Baby 44
American Diaries in Manuscript, 1580-1954, A Descriptive Bibliography 214
American Diaries series 190
American Girl 10
  See Pleasant Company.
American School Board Journal 36
American String Teacher 36
The Ancient Egyptians 227
Ancient Greeks 227
Ancient Romans 227
Angelina Ballerina 10, 90
Angels of Mercy: The Army Nurses of World War II 13
Animal Dads 118, 161
Animorphs series 118

An Ant's Day Off 191
AppleSeeds 49, 92, 224
  See Cobblestone Publishing.
Arabian Nights 227
Archaeology's dig! 224
Armadillo Tattletale 188
Arsenic and Old Lace 108-110
Art Attack: A Short Cultural History of the Avant-Garde 15
Arthur books 87
Arthur's Nose 87
Arts & Activities 36

B

Babar and the Succotash Bird 12
Babybug 50, 58
Baby-sitter's Club 23, 215
The Baker's Dozen: A Saint Nicholas Tale 227
A Band of Angels 88
Bat 6 88
A Bear for Miguel 190, 214
The Beet Fields: A Sixteenth Summer 12
Between the Lions 93
The Big Picture 51, 52, 92.
  See also Time, Inc.

The Bigger Picture 52
Black Belt for Kids 96
Black Cat 117
The Blackbirch Kid's Almanac of
  Geography 13
Blue's Clues 33
Book Links 15, 36, 92
Booklist 15, 111, 116, 122
The Book of the Lion, 11, 121
Book Publishing Reports 163
The Book Report 36
Books in Print 157, 163
BookWire 163
Boston 65
Boston Globe-Horn Book Award 131
The Boy and His Ghost 227
The Boyfriend Clinic 43
Boys Illustrated 40, 92
Boys' Life 58
Brave Margaret: An Irish Adventure 227
Bucking the Sarge 129
Bud, Not Buddy 10, 11, 88, 113, 117,
  119, 128, 129
The Business Traveling Parent 27

C

California Chronicles 95
Calliope 47, 48, 49, 92, 220, 224
  See Cobblestone Publishing.
Cam Jansen 87
Can of Worms 260, 262
Canadian Children's Literature 36
Career World 36
Catcher in the Rye 118
The Cat in the Hat 80, 94
Cendrillon: A Caribbean Cinderella 227
Challenge 36
Charlotte's Web 7

Chatelaine 71
chickaDEE Net 59
The Child and the Machine 27
Childbirth 44
Child Life 58
Children's Digest 58
Children's Playmate 58
Children's Writer 176
A Child's Calendar 118
The Chocolate War 95
Christian Science Monitor 33, 48
The Christmas Crocodile 191
The Chronicles of Narnia 7, 87
Cicada 50, 95, 98, 100, 101, 262, 263
Class Act 37
Classical Calliope 47, 49
Classical Companion 227
Classical Ingenuity 227
Classically Human and All That Jazz
  155
Click 15, 58, 224
Clifford the Big Red Dog 93
The Cliffs of Cairo 227
Climax 105
Club Girl Tech 60, 61, 62
Clubhouse Jr. Magazine 173
Clubhouse Magazine 173
Coach 34
Coal Country 119
Cobblestone 49, 92, 218, 224
College Bound 36
College Outlook 37
College PreVue 37
Colorado Parent 69
Connect 37
Consumer Reports 44, 92
Consumer Reports Online 44
Counterfeit Son 109, 190
Crayola Kids 33, 34, 96
Creative Classroom 37

Cricket 50, 58, 114, 218, 224, 227, 262
The Crystal Heart: A Vietnamese Legend 227
Curiocity for Kids 60
Curious George books 12, 93
Current Health 1 36
Current Health 2 36
Cut 14
Cyberkids 61, 62, 63
Cyberteens 61, 63
Cynthia and the Runaway Gazebo 108-110

D

dads 43, 92
Daily Genealogy Column 204
Dancing in Cadillac Light 133
Dancing on the Edge 121
Danny and the Dinosaur 77
Darke County Profile 71, 72
David v. God 259
A Day in the Life of a Teacher 192
Dear Myrtle 204
Dial's Easy To Read series 77
Did You See What I Saw? Poems About School 187
Dimensions of Early Childhood 37
Discovery Trails 101
"A Dozen Answers to the Multicultural Heckler" 227
The Dragon's Robe 227
Dream Soul 12
The Drinking Gourd 96

E

Early Childhood Education Journal 37
Early Childhood News 37
Early Childhood Today 37
Educational Leadership 37
Educational Oasis 37
Education Forum 37
Education Week 37
The Emperor and the Kite 227
Encounter 95
English Journal 37
Entertainmenteen 42

F

Faces 49, 92, 224, 227
  See Cobblestone Publishing.
The Faithful Friend 227
Family Heritage series 91
Faraway Home 189, 259
Fathering Magazine 57
Favorite Folktales of the World 227
FF 40, 92
Fiddler on the Roof 101, 109
The Flame of Peace 227
Folio 42, 43
The Folk Keeper 187
Footsteps 47, 49, 50, 92, 220, 224
  See Cobblestone Publishing.
Forged by Fire 117
Forgotten Fire 10, 121
Forty Fortunes: A Tale of Iran 227
Free as the Desert Wind 227
FreeZone 60, 63
Frenchtown Summer 88, 95
FreshLimeSoda 61
The Friendship of Milly and Tug 191
Frog and Toad 77, 83, 86
Frontier Children 227
Funny Money series 227
FutureScan 57

G

G Is for Googol: A Math Alphabet Book 162
Games Girls Play: Understanding and Guiding Young Female Athletes 22
Games to Play with Babies 26
Getting to Know the World's Greatest Artists series 13
The Gift of Sarah Barker 110
Gifted Education Press 37
Giotto 13
Girl 43
Girl Power! 57
Girl Scout Leader 174
Girls' Life 40, 92
A Girl's World 61
Give a Boy a Gun 12
The Goldfinch 96
Good Apple Newspaper 37
Goodnight Moon 7
gp4k.com 35
Gratefully Yours 215
Gray Heroes 227
Green Eggs and Ham 80
Green Teacher 37
Guideposts 35
Guideposts for Kids 35, 96, 118, 262
Guideposts for Teens 35, 262

H

Hamlet 110
Hard Love 116
Harlem 111, 117
Harry Potter and the Goblet of Fire 7, 93
Harry Potter series 9, 14, 31, 86
Harry the Dirty Dog 77
The Head Bone's Connected to the Neck Bone: The Weird, Wacky, and Wonderful X-Ray 161
Healthy Kids 44
Hearing Health 118
The Heart Is a Lonely Hunter 131
Hector's Hiccups 187
Hello Reader! 77, 80, 82, 86
Help! A Girl's Guide to Divorce and Stepfamilies 162
Henry V 110
Hernando de Soto and the Explorers of the American South 227
Heroes 95
The High School Journal 37
The High School Magazine 37
Highlights for Children 45, 100, 118, 124, 174, 223, 224
History Mysteries 10
Holes 114, 119
Holidays & Seasonal Celebrations 37
Home Child 189
Home Education Magazine 37
Homeless Bird, 11, 121
Home Schooling Today 37
Horn Book 37, 126, 227
Horsepower 102, 103, 104, 105
Hot! 40, 92
Houston Homeschooler 71
How the Grinch Stole Christmas 94
How to be Gorgeous 43
How to Behave So Your Children Will, Too! 22
Humpty Dumpty 58
Hurry Freedom! 11, 121

I

I Am the Cheese 95
I Can Read Chapter Books 80

I Can Read series 77, 80
I Hate to Go to Bed 260
If You Give a Mouse a Cookie 12
If You Take a Mouse to the Movies 12
I'm Sorry, Almira Ann 189
Instructor 37
In the Time of the Drums 88
"Ireland" 227
It's My Life! A Power Journal for Teens: A Workout for Your Mind 16

J

Jack And Jill 58
Joseph Had A Little Overcoat 10, 11, 88, 111, 112, 134
Journal of Adolescent & Adult Literacy 37
Journal of Children's Literature 37
Journal of Health Education 37
Journal of School Health 38
Junie B. Jones series 86
Just 4 Girls 61

K

Kansas School Naturalist 38
Keynoter 36
Kid Crosswords 60, 62, 63
Kids 92
Kids' Castle 57
The Kids' Clay Ceramic Book 162
A Kid's Life 57
KIDS Report 61
Kidtalk News Family Magazine 57
KidzMagazine 61
King Solomon and His Magic Ring 88
Kirkus Reviews 93

L

Ladybug 50, 58, 91
Lady White Snake: A Tale from Chinese Opera 227
Lady with the Ship on Her Head 227
Language Arts 38
L.A. Parent 69
"Last Testament" 174, 179
Leadership for Student Activities 36
Learning and Leading with Technology 38
The Learning Edge 38
Learning Outside the Lines 22
Lebanon: New Light in an Ancient Land 227
The Legend of Scarface: A Blackfeet Tale 227
The Legend of Slappy Hooper: An American Tall Tale 227
Leonardo da Vinci 13
"Liam McLafferty's Choice" 227
Libraries: Your Passport to the World 227
Library Talk 38
Lincoln: A Photobiography 113
Listen 95
Literary Market Place 163
Little Bear 77, 83
Little House on the Prairie books 131
The Little Prince 87
Little Women 131
Lollipops 38
A Long Way from Chicago: A Novel of Stories 114
Los Angeles Times 88
Loud Emily 227
Love-Lies-Bleeding 189

M

Mad Magazine 129
Magazines for Libraries 56
Magic Tree House series 86
The Maiden of Northland: A Hero Tale of Finland 227
THE MAILBOX 38
Making Animal Babies 118
Malcolm in the Middle 9
Mama's Little Helper 72
Mama's Way 188
Maniac McGee 93
Mapping the World 13
Marc Chagall 13
Marion Zimmer Bradley's Fantasy Magazine 96
Martha Stewart Baby 44
Martindale-Hubbell Law Directory 179
Mary-Kate and Ashley 42
Master Maid: A Tale of Norway 227
Master Man: A Tall Tale of Nigeria 227
Matchbox Books 11, 90.
  See Pleasant Company.
Matilda Bone 12
Max Cleans Up 12
Maxim 40
Medusa 227
Men's Health 92.
  See also Rodale Press.
Merlin, Wizard Boy 105
MH-18 40, 43
Michelangelo 13
Middle School Journal 38
MidLink Magazine 55, 63
A Midsummer's Night Dream 102
Midwest Living 211
Milk & Honey 227
Minnesota Parent 69

Mirror/Mirror 227
Mode 43
Momentum 38
Money: Save It, Manage It, Spend It 192
Monster 88, 115
Monster of the Month Club series 191
Montessori LIFE 38
The Mozart Effect for Children: Awakening Your Child's Mind, Health, and Creativity with Music 22
Muhammad of Mecca, Prophet of Islam 227
MultiCultural Review 38
Muse 15, 50, 58, 224
My America: A Poetry Atlas of the United States 13
My Brother and I 80
"My Brothers Ate My Homework" 263
My First Day of School 80
My First Hello Readers 80
My First I Can Read 80
"My Grandma Can Fly" 262
My Louisiana Sky 132
My Mother and I 80
Myths and Legends of Mount Olympus 227

N

"N" Is for New York 192
Nancy Drew books 131
NASSP Bulletin 38
National Geographic 44
National Geographic World 44, 58
The New Advocate 38
New Moon 224

New York Family 69
New York Times 7, 14, 23, 42, 48, 53, 91, 95, 165-171
Newfangled Fairy Tales 118
News Scoop 51
Newsweek 53
Nickelodeon 93
Nick Jr. 33
The Nightmare Room 94
Nory Ryan's Song 12
Not One Damsel in Distress 227
"Notes from a Different Caroler" 227

O

Odyssey 49, 92
  See also Cobblestone Publishing.
Offspring 43
"The Olive Tree" 100
101 Ways to Bug Your Parents, 187
1,000 Years Ago on Planet Earth 118
Online Markets for Writers: How to Make Money by Selling Your Writing on the Internet 62
Origami Favorites series, 227
Our Children 38
Our Gifted Children 38
Our Town 110
Our Wet World 161
Outer-Net Links for Kids: Ezines and Magazines 56
Owl Kids Online 59

P

Painted Words/Spoken Memories: Marianthe's Story 88
Paper Clip Jewelry 162
Parade 35

Parents and Children Together Online 55, 60
Peanuts 95
"Penny Stables" 104
The Phoenicians 227
The Plant 23, 171
Plays, The Drama Magazine for Young People 107
Portland Parent 69
Power and Light 174
Prevention 92
Prince and the Golden Ax 227
"The Problem with Linnie" 104
Publishers Weekly 163
Punga, the Goddess of Ugly 227

Q

Quantum 36

R

Raggedy Ann 87
Ranger Rick 45, 59
react 35, 96
Read 36
Read, America! 38
Reading Alone series 80
The Reading Teacher 38
Reading Today 38
Reading Together series 80
Ready for Chapters series 81, 83
Ready to Read series 77, 80, 81
The Recess Queen 227
Recognizing Words Easy Readers 80
Regeneration series 260
Remix: Conversations with Immigrant Teenagers 164
Restless Spirit: The Life and Works of

Dorothea Lange 161
"Riding the Bullet" 23, 171
River Friendly, River Wild 189, 259
The Rose and the Beast 12
r*w*t 38

S

The Sailor Who Captured the Sea 227
St. Joseph's Magazine 174
The Samurai's Daughter 227
San Diego 65-71
San Diego Parent 69
Saturday Evening Post 174
Savitri: A Tale of Ancient India 227
Scared Stiff 189
Scholastic Atlas of the United States 13
Scholastic Choices 36
Scholastic DynaMath 36
Scholastic Scope 36
SchoolArts 38
Schooldays 38
The School Librarian's Workshop 38
School Library Journal 38
School Library Media Activities Monthly 38
School Smarts 162
Science Activities 38
Science and Children 39
The Science Teacher 39
Science Weekly 36
Science World 36
Scribbler of Dreams 261
The Sea King's Daughter: A Russian Legend 227
"Seamus Kenny's Well" 227
Seattle Child 69, 72
The Secret of Platform 13 14
The Secret of the Stones 227

Sell and Resell Your Magazine Articles 166
Seventeen 16, 40, 43, 59, 90, 95
The Seventh Mandarin 227
The Shakespeare Stealer 100
"Shlemiel Crooks" 118
Shoeshine Whittaker 188
Short & Shivery: Thirty Chilling Tales 227
Shy Mama's Halloween 158
Silver Blades 215
Silver Dollar 12
Single Parents 44, 92
Sir Walter Ralegh and the Quest for El Dorado 15
The Sistine Chapel: Its History and Masterpieces 13
The Sixth Sense 9
Skateboard Renegade 12
Skellig 116
Small Farmer's Journal 174
SmartMoney 43
Snappy Pop-up books 11
  See also The Millbrook Press.
Soccer for Parents 89
Soccer Jr. 34, 89
Social Studies and the Young Learner 39
Something's Happening on Calabash Street 218, 220, 227
Southern Living 65-71, 211
Space Station Science: Life in Free Fall 88
Speak 88, 116, 119, 121, 123-125
Spider 50, 58, 118, 224
Sports Illustrated For Kids 59, 87
Spot books 87
A Spy Among the Girls 12
Stance 40
Standard Periodical Directory 73

Stargirl 12
Star Trek 23
Star Wars 9
Starting to Read series 80
Step into Reading 77
Stepping Stone Books 77
Story Friends 262
StoryPlace: The Children's Digital Library 57
Straight from the Horse's Mouth 260
Strega Nona 87
Strega Nona Takes a Vacation 87
Stuart Little 7
Subject Index to the Children's Books in Print 283
Subtext 163
Sukey and the Mermaid 227
Suki, the Siamese Puppy 95
Summer Begins 110
Sunset 65, 211
SuperScience 36
Sweet16.com 42
Sweet Valley series 215

T

The Talking Eggs 227
Teacher Librarian 39
Teacher Magazine 39
Teachers & Writers 39
Teachers in Focus 39
Teaching Elementary Physical Education 39
TEACHING Exceptional Children 39
Teaching PreK-8 39
Teaching Theatre 39
Tears of a Tiger 117
Tech Directions 39
Technology & Learning 39

Teen 42, 91
Teen Movieline 42
Teen Newsweek 53
Teen People 16, 40, 42
TeenStyle 40, 92
Teen Vogue 42, 92
Teenvoice.com 61
The Teeny Tiny Ghost 187
Telephones 190
Terrific Connections with Authors, Illustrators, and Storytellers: Real Space and Virtual Links 188, 194
There Was an Old Lady Who Swallowed a Fly 111, 134
This Is the House that Jack Built 134
Tickly Prickly 191
Tiger Trail 187
Time For Kids 51, 59, 92
  See also Time, Inc.
Time For Kids World Report 34
Timeline 23
Today's Catholic Teacher 39
Today's Child 44
Total Astrology 43
Tradition and Change 227
Traditional Craft Series 227
TransWorld Skateboarding 40
TransWorld Snowboarding 40
Trickster and the Fainting Birds 88
Tuck Everlasting 87
Tunisia: Arranging for Marriage 227
Turtle 58
Twist 95
Two Bear Cubs: A Miwok Story from California's Yosemite Valley 223, 227
The Two Brothers 91